CYBERSECURITY IN THE DIGITAL AGE

Tools, Techniques, and Best Practices

Gregory A. Garrett

Copyright Notice

Notice of Trademarks

Media Issue No.: 10070558-0001
ISBN: 978-1-5438-0880-3

SUSTAINABLE FORESTRY INITIATIVE Certified Sourcing www.sfiprogram.org SFI-00756

Contents

Preface

By: Michael Abboud, CEO TetherView

You will find unique perspectives about cybersecurity in this insightful and thought provoking book! 14 seasoned professionals from diverse industries in five countries provide concrete understanding and direction to managing and thwarting cyber threats.

The book provides the reader a great understanding of the complex cybersecurity regulatory landscape and the various cybersecurity risk management frameworks which are used to determine the appropriate cybersecurity measures. Because the cyber threat landscape is constantly evolving, satisfying a cyber risk management framework and achieving compliance does not mean a business is secure. Organizations must be vigilant and arm themselves with the tools and professionals capable of identifying a threat before it has an impact.

The chapter on threat intelligence explains that cyber threats come in all shapes and sizes, insiders, competitors, nation states, for profit criminal cyber attackers, and dare we say it, litigants. Throughout this book you will learn about tools, techniques, and best practices utilized by experts. One prevailing message you will notice is the importance of visibility into your network, users, data, and cyber attack threats. Achieving visibility into your entire information system and the potential cyber threats is paramount and foundational. Without visibility into the network you will not know if you have been compromised and most certainly will not be able to prevent or mitigate a cyber attack.

The author(s) demonstrate that monitoring or line-of-site on user activity, data, and network activity allows professionals to predict, detect, and respond to cyber intrusions before they are able to evolve into a data breach. Visibility also means that organizations must have a constant pulse on the cyber threats around them. Complacency about cybersecurity, while self-inflicted, is another major threat and occurs when a team does not look outwards or forward. This is very common for in house teams who don't have the perspective from other industries and business sizes. With the proper cybersecurity monitoring, detection, and response and data collection we can achieve resilience, allowing the organization to evolve as cyber threats evolve.

As explained in chapter six routine vulnerability testing provides businesses with a perspective of how to design new requirements. Although painful, performing a proper incident response analysis or cyber investigation after a breach is critical and even more vital is communication of the gaps within the entire organization.

This book clearly communicates that we have entered into a global cyber war. Further, the book informs the reader that it is imperative to find the right balance between security and convenience, which is one of the largest challenges facing companies today. A proper cybersecurity balance can only be achieved by visibility into the user(s) needs, cyber threats, and providing the tools for people to work securely and effectively.

As the book communicates, cybersecurity education, training, and professional certifications are a critical step in generating awareness and help prevent users from harming themselves. Cybersecurity risk assessments, email and network threat assessments, penetration testing, education, and training should almost always be provided by an independent party to help avoid complacency, limit risk, and provide a fresh set of eyes on your user's habits.

Cybersecurity in the Digital Age is about the realization as every business transforms into a digital platform, leaders must learn how to build IT and cybersecurity strategies that cost-effectively solve for protection, governance, and performance. Leadership of every organization should provide the imperative to regularly assess their cybersecurity requirements, prepare the team (internal and external) for potential cyber incidents, and develop the resilience necessary to survive the cyber-challenges that lay ahead.

Dedication

To my wonderful wife of over 30 years Carolyn and my three greatest gifts: Christopher, Scott, and Jennifer

In addition, we would like to dedicate this book to all of the hard-working and ethical cybersecurity professionals worldwide. Together, we defend our nations, communities, industries, and families against the nation-state cyber warfare groups, cybercriminal groups, and hackers who use their cyber attacks, illegal data breaches, and theft to steal our money and destroy our way of life.

Introduction

Make no mistake, we are all under attack in a dangerous and on-going cyber war. The number of cyber attacks are growing both in number and sophistication worldwide. According to Risk IQ, as of May 2018 about 1,861 people worldwide fall victim to cyber attacks every minute of every day. In the past year, the number of cyber ransomware attacks has increased by over 350% according to CISCO, 2018. Cybersecurity Ventures estimates that global ransomware damage cost will rise to $11.5 Billion in 2019.

As the world transforms into a truly digital society the need for security of our personal identifiable information, protected health information, payment card information, intellectual property, and vast amounts of digital assets increases daily. Likewise, the rapid global expansion of data and the connection of devices to the internet to have led to a 600% increase in the number of cyber attacks on the Internet of Things according to Symatec, 2018.

Further, Webroot and Health Information Privacy/Security Alert estimate that about 46,000 new email phishing sites are created every day, with an average of 1.3 million new unique email phishing sites are created globally every month. Nation-State cyberwarfare groups, cybercriminal groups, and organized hackers groups are attacking nearly every organization and everyone. The cyber attackers are looking to disrupt, steal, and destroy – our institutions, our money and our lives!

This book is focused on enhancing the understanding of cybersecurity strategies, tools, techniques, and best practices in the digital age. We have assembled a team of 14 leading cybersecurity experts from five nations: USA, Israel, Netherlands, South Africa, and the United Kingdom to share their collective cybersecurity insights in the human aspects, hardware and software aspects, technological aspects, and key target market segments to help you better defend your organizations from cyber attacks and to enable you to reduce the damages from a cyber data breach.

The key question is not: Will you and your organization be the victim of a cyber attack? Rather, the key questions are: (1) How well prepared are you and your organization to mitigate the damages of a cyber data breach? (2) How resilient is your information system and most valuable data assets? (3) How well-educated and trained in cybersecurity are the people within your organization, from the top-down?

Acknowledgements

First, I would like to thank my long-time friend and book editor Aaron Broaddus for his outstanding support!

Second, I want to express my sincere appreciation to the senior executive leadership of BDO USA, LLP and BDO International for their professional support to improve global cybersecurity advisory services and managed security services worldwide.

Third, I would like to thank the members of our BDO Global Cybersecurity Leadership Team, BDO USA Cybersecurity Leadership Team, and BDO Israel Cybersecurity Team listed below, who contributed to the writing of this book!

Contributing Authors - Members of BDO Global Cybersecurity Leadership Team
- Ophir Zilbiger (Israel)
- Jason Gottschalk (United Kingdom)
- Graham Croock (South Africa)
- Sandra Konings (Netherlands)
- Bart Jenniskens (Netherlands)

Contributing Authors - Members of BDO USA Cybersecurity Leadership Team
- Greg Schu
- Fred Brantner
- Andrew Silberstein
- Mike Stiglianese
- Eric Chuang
- Laura Hars

Contributing Authors - Members of BDO Israel Cybersecurity Team
- Danny Solomon
- Dori Fisher

About the Principal Author

GREGORY A. GARRETT, CISSP, PMP, CPCM

Gregory A. Garrett is the Head of U.S. and International Cybersecurity for BDO supporting over 2,500 Information Technology (IT) and cybersecurity professionals currently in 18 countries on six continents worldwide. With more than 30 years of experience, Gregg is a recognized IT and cybersecurity expert, having managed more than $40 billion of complex, high-tech programs, contracts, and related consulting and professional services for government agencies and Fortune 500 companies across the globe. He is a respected international IT business consultant, acclaimed expert witness, best-selling author of 23 published books and over 125 published articles, and a highly decorated former U.S. Air Force Military Officer. Gregg is the recipient of numerous national and international business awards for his writing, teaching, consulting, and leadership.

An expert in strategic business planning, Gregg has significant experience developing and implementing cyber risk management programs designed to enhance information security and manage cost, risk, and compliance. He has significant experience with cloud migration, data analytics, supply chain management, program management, and systems engineering. Gregg is also highly skilled with respect to government contract compliance and management.

Prior to joining BDO, Gregg served as Corporate Vice President of Information Technology and President and General Manager of Cybersecurity for the UIC Corporation. Previously, he served as a Partner and Head of Cybersecurity for Blue Canopy Group LLC. In addition, Gregg has also held senior executive positions with Artel LLC, Navigant Consulting, Lucent Technologies, and ESI International.

Chapter 1

CYBERSECURITY IN THE DIGITAL AGE

By: Gregory A. Garrett, CISSP, CPCM, PMP

INTRODUCTION

Cyber attacks, network breaches, and information security incidents are negatively impacting government agencies and corporations worldwide regardless of size or industry. Nation-state cyber groups, cyber criminal groups, and hackers, are becoming much more sophisticated in their methods, and the frequency of breaches is increasing across all industries and government sectors for a variety of reasons. According to the U.S. Security Exchange Commission (SEC) guidance in February 2018 the average cost of a data breach is now $7.5 Million, not including the financial impact upon the reputation of the organization, lost revenue, and reduction in market valuation.

With the growth of the Internet of Things (IoT), millions of devices are being connected to the Internet every day worldwide. The IoT implied promise is easy, secure, and rapid access to vast amounts of digital assets, which reduce costs of operations and drive productivity. Thus, the IoT is a true system of systems digital environment. Unfortunately, the IoT creates enormous potential cyber vulnerabilities via the connection of the systems, internal software within each information system, and all related network endpoints. Some people naively believe that cybersecurity is an obstacle to the global digital transformation. They could not be more wrong. Cybersecurity is the essential element of digital transformation, because without data integrity and true information security then digitization of data just becomes an unsecure pathway for criminal actions globally.

The Trump Administration mandated by Executive Order 13800, dated May 11, 2017, that all U.S. federal government agencies plan, develop, and submit formal cybersecurity risk management plans to help mitigate the growing adverse effects upon the classified information, sensitive information, and controlled unclassified information (CUI) in their possession. The Cybersecurity EO requires U.S. federal agencies to manage risk across the government, holds agency heads personally responsible for network protection, and pushes information technology (IT) modernization into overdrive. Pursuant to the Cybersecurity EO, each agency is required to utilize the National Institute of Standards and Technology (NIST) cybersecurity Risk Management Framework (RMF). Yet, applying the NIST cybersecurity RMF to each unique federal agency is a challenge, especially due to the scope of knowledge required; the cost of implementation; and the speed at which the EO requires risk management plans to be developed, submitted, and implemented.

Further, the U.S. federal government and many foreign governments are now requiring that all companies, including predominately commercial companies, develop and implement proactive cybersecurity risk management plans to protect valuable information assets, which may impact national security, economic matters, healthcare, energy, transportation, and other vital industries. Thus, cybersecurity is now an organizational risk management imperative for nearly all government agencies and companies worldwide. So, the real question is: how can an organization efficiently and cost-effectively plan and implement a holistic cybersecurity risk management program both proactively (identify risks, analyze risks, and mitigate risks) and reactively (detect incidents, respond to incidents, and recover from incidents) in turbulent times?

KEY CYBERSECURITY QUESTIONS

The need for cybersecurity for any organization quickly prompts the following key questions, the answers to which are essential for any organization to understand and determine appropriate responses in order to create and implement an efficient and cost-effective cybersecurity risk management program.

1. What are the potential cybersecurity legal risks and liabilities?

There are numerous potential legal risks and significant potential adverse financial liabilities if a company does not take an appropriate holistic approach to cybersecurity risk management – both proactively and reactively. For example, some commercial companies have faced significant litigation for their failure to develop and maintain proper business internal controls related to information security, including:

- **Target shareholder derivative lawsuit (U.S. Dist. Ct. Minn., No. 14-cv-203 (PAM/JJK))**
  Alleged Target's board breached their fiduciary duties to the company by failing "to maintain proper internal controls related to data security and misleading affected consumers."
- **Wyndham Worldwide Corporation and Certain of its Officers and Directors, cybersecurity-related derivative lawsuit (U.S. Dist. Ct. NJ, No. 2:14-cv-01234 (SRC))**
  Alleging, "In violation of their express promise to do so, and contrary to reasonable customer expectations" the company and its subsidiaries "failed to take reasonable steps to maintain their customers' personal data."
- **Wyndham Worldwide Corporation is also facing scrutiny in a Federal Trade Commission (FTC) enforcement action (U.S. Dist. Ct. NJ, No. 2:13-cv-01887-ES-JAD)**
  Alleges, Wyndham violated Section 5(a) of the FTC Act, which prohibits "acts or practices in or affecting commerce" that are unfair or "deceptive." According to the FTC, Wyndham and certain subsidiaries failed "to maintain reasonable and appropriate data security for consumers' sensitive personal information."
- **Kaspersky files antitrust complaints against Microsoft**
  Russian antivirus vendor Kaspersky Lab has filed two antitrust complaints against Microsoft in Europe, contending that the company has engineered Windows 10 to favor its preinstalled malware-fighting program.
- **McDowell v. CGI Federal, Inc. (U.S. Dist. Ct. D.C., No. 15-1157 (GK))**
  A recent decision from the United States District Court for the District of Columbia highlights a new potential basis for liability that any contractor handling personally identifiable information (PII) or other sensitive information for the government should keep in mind. A data breach resulting in the disclosure of such information may result in not just a breach of contract claim by the government, but by the individual whom the information concerns where the contract demonstrates "that the contracting parties' clearly intended that the contract would benefit the plaintiff, or an identifiable class to which the plaintiff belongs." In McDowell, the court denied a U.S. State Department contractor's motion to dismiss a class action lawsuit filed by the plaintiff for a breach of contract that allegedly resulted in the theft of the plaintiff's PII by employees of the Defendant contractor. The lawsuit argues that the contractor, CGI Federal, Inc., failed to secure the personal information of members of the public that it

received as part of its contract to process passport applications for the State Department.

These legal developments foreshadow the impending regulatory enforcement actions against companies that maintain inadequate cybersecurity measures, along with the highly competitive aspects of the related software industry.

Further, the 2017 BDO Board Survey, an annual survey created to measure the attitudes of public company directors, examined the opinions of 160 corporate directors of public company boards and uncovered the following key trends:

- About one-fifth (18%) of board members indicated their company experienced a cyber-breach during the two previous years, a slightly lower percentage than 2016 (22%) and much higher than 2013 (11%).
- Nearly three-quarters (79%) of companies reported an increased level of board involvement in cybersecurity issues, up 5% year-over-year.
- Nearly Four-fifths (78%) of board members reported that their company had increased investments in cybersecurity since the prior year, with an average budget expansion of 22 percent.
- Less than half of board members reported they had both identified and developed solutions to protect their critical digital assets, and an even smaller proportion indicated they had put cyber-risk requirements in place for third-party vendors, a major source of cyber attacks.
- Most companies are addressing the cybersecurity liabilities by increasing their related insurance coverage, driving-up their insurance-related expenses.

Additionally, RedSeal conducted a 72 Point study of 200 CEOs inquiring about their perceptions of cybersecurity. The study discovered that many executives are dangerously unrealistic about how vulnerable their companies are to cyber breaches. In fact, according to the study, more than 80 percent displayed "cyber naiveté," allowing their organizations to be exposed to cyber attack. This study reveals the disconnection between confidence in cyber strategies and actual results, and points to a need for more real-time measurement of network security.

2. What is the cybersecurity regulatory, risk, and compliance landscape?

The cybersecurity regulatory and compliance landscape is both complex and continually evolving. Commercial industry, both in the U.S. and internationally, has taken steps to improve cybersecurity risk management for companies. For example, the American Institute of Certified Public Accountants (AICPA) has developed the System of Organizational Controls (SOC) for

Cybersecurity, a cybersecurity risk management reporting framework that provides a standard method for organizations to report enterprise-wide cybersecurity risk management. In New York, the state's Department of Financial Services (NYDFS) issued a first-of-its-kind cyber regulation impacting all New York-regulated financial institutions, including New York branches of foreign banks. The NYDFS regulation mandates the implementation of a cyber risk management program, the appointment of an individual to oversee the program, and, in an unprecedented step, the groundbreaking regulation holds company board members and senior officers personally liable for annual compliance certification.

Abroad, the EU General Data Protection Regulation (GDPR) came into force in May 2018 and significantly expanded the scope and enforceability of the European Union's data privacy regime. Companies are required to inventory all personal data, incorporate risk-based cybersecurity measures, and report any data breach to the supervisory authority within 72 hours. Non-compliant organizations may be fined up to four percent of annual global turnover or €20 Million (whichever is greater).

Additionally, in the U.S., key federal regulations surrounding cybersecurity risk management are already in place and include thousands of pages of detailed requirements for cybersecurity compliance for both U.S. federal agencies and government contractors. The U.S. Department of Defense (DOD) has created defense-specific cybersecurity risk management regulations to ensure that covered defense information (CDI) is properly protected by government contractors. DOD contractors and subcontractors storing CDI are subject to regulations which require all contractors to notify the DOD chief information officer (CIO) within 30 days of any security requirements not met or where an incident may have occurred. The Federal Information Systems Management Act (FISMA), a U.S. public law, also requires significant cybersecurity reporting requirements for U.S. federal agencies and for government contractors who provide IT products and support services.

Clearly, the cybersecurity regulatory and compliance landscape is very complex (see chart below). New laws, regulations, industry standards, and guidelines continue to evolve to address new cyber threats, and both government agencies and companies try to make sense of and implement cyber risk management programs in a timely, cost-effective manner to avoid the exponentially increasing potential liability for non-compliance and damages. Thus, the need for a robust information governance, risk management, and compliance capability is vital for all organizations in both the public and private sectors.

USA
Cybersecurity Complex Regulatory Landscape

Industry	Cybersecurity Risk Management Framework	Mandatory or Voluntary
Financial Services	• New York Department of Financial Services (NYDFS) • Security Exchange Commission (SEC)	• Mandatory or • Voluntary
Healthcare Services	• Health Insurance Portability and Affordability Act (HIPAA) • HITRUST – Common Security Framework (CSF)	• Mandatory • Voluntary
Federal Government	• National Institute of Standards and Technology (NIST) • NIST SP 800-Series	• Mandatory
Government Contractors	• NIST 800-37 Risk Management Framework (RMF) • NIST 800-171 Controlled Unclassified Information (CUI)	• Varies
Defense Contractors	• DFARS 252.204-7012 • NIST 800-171 CUI and Covered Defense Information (CDI)	• Mandatory
Accounting Services	• American Institute of Certified Public Accountants (AICPA) System for Organizational Controls (SOC)	• Voluntary
Retail Industry	• Payment Card Industry (PCI) • Qualified Security Accessors (QSAs)	• Mandatory
Multi-National Companies	• International Standards Organization (ISO) • ISO 27001	• Varies
EU Citizens	• European Union (EU) • General Data Privacy Regulation (GDPR)	• Mandatory

3. How can an organization leverage new technologies and tools to cost effectively improve cybersecurity risk management?

The good news is that new information security technologies, new security tools (hardware and software), and expanded cybersecurity professional services are being developed and implemented nearly every day in an attempt to stay abreast of the increasing cyber threats and attacks. Today, most information security practices and controls are focused on protecting vital information assets from future cyber attacks. The new technology trend in information assurance is a fundamental shift in strategy that assumes IT systems have already been breached and then implements:

- Machine learning with mathematical concepts of probability to discover breaches and rapidly respond by developing software remedies.
- Artificial intelligence enabling the system to self-diagnose and implement fixes as needed in real-time.
- Data and threat visualization tools (i.e. Splunk data analytics tools, RSA's Cybersecurity Dashboards, etc.).
- Real-time total network immersion technology.
- User, mobile devices, and network correlation to use predictive analytics to identify abnormal activities, unusual connections, and significant changes in volumes of data being moved between machines.

Hewlett Packard Enterprise's (HPE) new Gen10 servers, which offer new firmware built directly into the server aimed at protecting the server from breaches of malicious attacks, are a breakthrough in IT hardware designed for enhanced cybersecurity. In the case of malware, or increasingly, a direct cyber attack on the firmware code, the new servers detect the problem and then securely restart to recover firmware back to its authenticated state. The new servers also add encryption and authenticated signatures into the supply chain to protect the services.

Additionally, artificial intelligence, often used by financial services firms to better understand customers, is increasingly being used for data security. Another excellent example of new technology helping an organization to cost effectively improve cybersecurity is the successful implementation of the Safety Net System, a new machine learning technology deployed by MASTERCARD Inc. to help them control and limit the financial damage caused by three separate cyber attacks targeting automated bank teller machines (ATMs). The transaction-monitoring system employs data visualization tools and analyzes over $1 billion in transactions daily using algorithms to assess customer behavior in real-time.

Above all else, the right place to start to improve cybersecurity for each organization is with a holistic assessment of the people within the organization and their level of cybersecurity awareness and education, information governance processes, systems/hardware and software vulnerability, records management, and control procedures for information assurance. Currently, there are numerous generic and industry-specific cyber risk assessment methodologies and tools, some partially automated and others highly automated. Some risk assessment tools align specifically to ISO or NIST standards while other cyber risk assessment tools focus on certain areas within an organization such as vulnerability assessments, penetration testing, and user training.

4. What are the latest evolution of cyber attacks?

Global spending on security-related hardware, software and services is projected to grow from $81.7 billion in 2017 to $105 billion by 2020, according to International Data Corporation (IDC) research. The banking industry is among the top three biggest spenders and for good reason: With most cyber criminals motivated by money, banks are natural targets. Add to that the increase in cyberattacks against banks in recent years, and cybersecurity protection against increasingly powerful forces is warranted: Symantec reports that some of the biggest bank heists in the past two years included the work of organized criminal gangs and nation states, with North Korea extracting approximately $94 million from banks in Bangladesh, Vietnam, Ecuador and Poland.

2017 ushered in a new era of massive cyber attacks. In April 2017, an elusive cyber group called the "Shadow Brokers" leaked National Security Agency (NSA) hacking tools, including highly sophisticated software exploits. Trouble soon followed. The "WannaCry" ransomware program was the first to hit in May 2017, infecting 153 countries with more than 75,000 ransomware attacks; 3,300 infections were reported in the U.S. The attack affected several major institutions including FedEx, Nissan and the Russian Interior Ministry. The program held data files for ransom and demanded the equivalent of $300 in Bitcoin to restore user access. One infected computer on a network possessing administrative credentials could quickly spread the program to all other network computers. WannaCry targeted a vulnerability in Microsoft Windows, and users who hadn't updated their systems with a security update that Microsoft had issued in March were put at risk.

A little over a month later, the Petya virus made its presence known around the globe, infecting more than 12,500 machines across 64 countries. Similar to WannaCry, the attack used malicious software to prevent users from accessing their data until a $300 Bitcoin payment was made. The program targeted several attack vectors, including vulnerabilities in Microsoft's Server Message Block (SMB), known as MS17-010 SMB. However, it quickly distinguished itself as a more dangerous "wiper" virus, not only locking files but potentially destroying them; the program crippled devices by overwriting and encrypting the machine's master boot record, according to Symantec.

2018 SIGNIFICANT CYBER ATTACKS

Ransomware attacks

There is little concrete data regarding the overarching scale of ransomware payment, however, since the beginning of 2018 it has already surpassed US

$1 billion dollars. One of the most confounding problems in this regard is that ransomware attacks remain grossly under-reported. As many companies and organizations fear loss of clients' and/or investors' trust, victims often opt to pay the ransom as a means to promptly resolve the situation, or otherwise prefer to absorb the financial loss while trying to restore their systems from backups. Due to the potential loss of life from an attack, a quick resolution is especially pertinent to critical infrastructure and healthcare providers. Accordingly these sectors have become two of the most notable targets for such attacks.

Cryptocoin heists and Cryptojacking attacks

In 2018 there has been an increase in attacks involving the theft of millions in various cryptocoins. As cryptocurrencies are gaining mainstream momentum, individuals and companies recognizing their potential have amassed considerable amounts of money. This has also attracted the attention of criminal actors, resulting in ever more daring cryptocurrency attacks. For example, in February 2018, a cryptocurrency miner was reportedly detected for the first time on an Industrial Control System (ICS). In addition, there have been numerous attempts to conduct cryptocoin heists this year, some of them successful.

ATM jackpotting

In January 2018, a sophisticated attack dubbed "jackpotting", which causes Automated Teller Machines (ATM) machines to dispense all of their cash, hit the US. Jackpotting originated in Russia, spread to other countries in Europe and Asia, and has recently come to the US, targeting machines from various ATM manufacturers such as NCR Corporation and Diebold Nixdorf.

Cybercriminals targeting SWIFT banking systems

Cybercrime targeting financial institutions has significantly increased in recent years, namely on the SWIFT system, used by banks worldwide to send and receive transactional data in a standardized manner. This has become a profitable target of various threat actors. On January 10, 2018, the year's first attack on the SWIFT system was reported by Mexican state-owned bank "Bancomext." One hundred million dollars were reportedly stolen in this incident, and the bank's payment system was damaged. After analyzing various characteristics of the attack, we assessed that a Russian criminal group might be behind the attack against the Mexican bank, as well as a campaign against financial institutions in Latin American countries.

Amplified DDoS attacks

In late February and early March, two massive Distributed Denial of Service (DDoS) attacks of 1.3Tbps and 1.7Tbps, were executed against the code-sharing platform GitHub and an unnamed U.S. based internet service provider (ISP), respectively. These attacks are noteworthy for their attack vector; rather than the more commonplace tactic of using botnets, the attackers exploited vulnerable Memcached servers. Moreover, this method amplified the magnitude of DDoS attacks by a factor of 51,000. While unprecedented in scale, both attacks were mitigated swiftly with little to no damage. This is a result of implementation of robust DDoS protection measures and the prompt response of cyber protection service providers such as Akamai, as in the case of GitHub. In these incidents the attacks were successfully mitigated; however it should be noted that other companies and organizations might not leave DDoS attacks unscathed, and could lose a significant amount of money as a result.

APT attack hits German government networks

On March 28, 2018, the German government confirmed it had been the target of a large-scale cyber attack which compromised the computer networks of Germany's Foreign and Defense Ministries. The attack was treated as an ongoing threat against the government's systems, and was reportedly detected in December 2017. There has been no official confirmation of the attacker's identity, however it is believed that the attack was carried out by a Russian threat agent, namely APT28 group (Fancy Bear) or Snake (Turla).

Attacks Leveraging Adobe Zero-Day Vulnerability

On January 31, 2018, South Korea's Computer Emergency Response Team (CERT) issued an alert about a newly discovered Adobe Flash Player Zero-Day vulnerability. South Korean security firm HAURI reported that since mid-November 2017, North Korea had been using this vulnerability against various South Korean researchers. In this campaign, attackers used malicious documents or spreadsheets embedded with an SWF file. Upon being opened by the target, a payload would be downloaded from compromised third-party websites hosted in South Korea. This attack was likely executed by a North Korean threat agent dubbed TEMP.Reaper (Group 123), which primarily targets South Korean entities across various sectors such as government, military, and industrial-defense. During 2018, this actor has expanded its activities to other international targets.

Olympic Destroyer

On the eve of the opening ceremony, a series of destructive cyber attacks led to disruptions in the computer infrastructure of the Pyeongchang Olympic Games, which took place in South Korea between February 9 and February 25, 2018. The attack compromised and temporarily paralyzed various systems (several of which were not reported), such as the stadiums' WiFi networks and broadcasting. A malware dubbed "Olympic Destroyer" by Talos researchers was likely used in the attack. The attack and infection vectors were most likely via the supply chain-penetrating Atos, the key IT vendor of the Olympics. The identity of the attacker remains unknown. Various security experts have attributed the attack to Russia, North Korea, and/or China.

Spectre and Meltdown – vulnerabilities in systems with microchips from major manufacturers

An underlying Central Processing Unit (CPU) architecture design vulnerability has left systems with AMD, Intel and Arm microchips exposed to potential cyber attacks. We have not seen any indications of this vulnerability being exploited to date. However, it is still possible that, in the future, we could see attacks taking advantage of this. As this is a hardware vulnerability, the solution requires massive organization-wide computer system updates.

5. What recommendations for mitigating cyber vulnerabilities should organizations adopt to reduce the cost of a data breach?

Recommendations for mitigating vulnerabilities

a. Reallocate additional resources for inter-organizational security systems. With recent developments in hybrid attack vectors, the outer security shell can no longer be prioritized over the internal security framework. Accordingly, organizations and companies must transition to a more holistic security model that can effectively cope with the accelerated evolution of attack methods that we have witnessed over the last couple of years.
b. Segment networks and take core systems offline
c. Create an emergency backup system that could allow a company to operate up to three months after being hit by a destructive cyber attack.
d. Minimize the amount of time between when the security patches are released, and when they are installed. Determine how to rapidly implement a policy to install security patches, despite the potential risk of disruption to an organization's normal operations. It is advisable to define

a timeframe which is both realistic and agreed upon by the relevant parties within the organization.

e. Raise employees' awareness of new attack vectors – most notably about
   social engineering techniques and significant campaigns.
f. Perform periodic security testing of cloud-based systems
g. Implement scanning services on cloud-based applications to alert of any
   security breaches.
h. Save backups and sensitive information (passwords, etc.) in an encrypted
   manner.

6. What does it take to efficiently develop and implement a holistic cybersecurity risk management program?

Successful development and implementation of a holistic cybersecurity risk
management program for an organization, whether large or small, requires
the following actions:

- Begin with a series of diagnostic testing of the organization's information
  system, including:
  - Email Threat Assessment
  - Network Threat Assessment
  - Vulnerability Assessment
  - Penetration Testing
  - Email Spear-phishing campaign (based upon social media analysis)
- Create and communicate a proactive and reactive information security
  policy, information governance, records management processes, infor-
  mation security assessment tools, information security training, and
  information security internal controls throughout the organization and
  the supply chain.
- Hire experienced, qualified, and certified IT and cybersecurity profes-
  sionals.
- Provide effective information security awareness and training programs
  for all members of the organization, including simulation training and
  table-top exercises for the cybersecurity professionals.
- Conduct periodic cybersecurity assessments both internally and via
  independent consultants.
- Develop an incident/breach response process.
- Create and implement an information assurance business continuity plan.
- Select and implement appropriate and affordable information security
  tools (hardware and software) and technologies (i.e., machine learning,
  AI, continuous diagnostics and monitoring, predictive data analytics).
- Decide which cybersecurity services to perform in-house and which
  services to outsource or purchase:

o   Chief information security officer (CISO) advisory services

o   Security design/planning, risk management framework services

o   Risk management assessments

o   Security operations center (SOC) managed services

o   Cyber incident response (IR) services

o   Cyber threat intelligence services

o   Cyber education, training, and simulation services

Cybersecurity is not an option, but rather an organizational risk management imperative for all government agencies and companies worldwide. Cyber attacks are on the rise and the potential damages and liabilities are increasing exponentially. Thus, it is vital that all organizations operating in this new digital age assess their information security programs and wisely invest in the necessary resources to protect, detect, and recover from imminent cyber data breaches.

The next chapter will focus on the importance of the C-suite and board of directors understanding the nature of the cyber threats upon their respective organization and recognizing what they need to know and do about cybersecurity to protect their valuable data assets.

Chapter 2

CYBERSECURITY FOR THE C-SUITE AND BOARD

By: Gregory A. Garrett, CISSP, CPCM, PMP

INTRODUCTION

The tone at the top of every organization is critical to success. Thus, in the digital age where more and more electronic devices are linked to the Internet, forming the Internet of Things (IoT), cybersecurity awareness is vital for everyone in the organization. Since senior executives have the greatest access to the most valuable information it is essential that they receive appropriate cybersecurity education and training. Unfortunately, most chief executive officers (CEOs), other members of the typical C-suite listed below, plus members of the board of directors of many organizations are not as knowledgeable of cybersecurity as they should be and that is an item of significant concern.

Typical C-suite executives, include:
- CEO
- Chief financial officer (CFO)
- Chief legal officer (CLO) or General Counsel (GC)
- Chief operating officer (COO)
- Chief information officer (CIO)
- Chief information security officer (CISO)

So, it is important to understand just what the C-suite and board of directors should know and do about cybersecurity.

WHAT CEOS SHOULD KNOW AND DO ABOUT CYBERSECURITY

Based upon discussions conducted in 2018 with hundreds of companies CEOs from numerous U.S. and global industries, including financial services, healthcare, government contracting, automotive, manufacturing, private equity, and law firms, it appears there exists a real gap in both knowledge and proactive actions to enhance cyber defense. From these conversations, the three most frequently asked questions by CEOs were:

1. What should the CEO know about cybersecurity?
2. What should the CEO do about cybersecurity?
3. How should the CEO assess the quality of the organization's cybersecurity program?

It is vital that CEOs establish the appropriate cybersecurity "tone at the top" for their respective organization, regarding the importance of information security and how cybersecurity is everyone's shared responsibility in a truly digital world. Establishing an organizational "culture of cybersecurity" has proven to be one of the best defenses against cyber adversaries. It is the people, not the technology, which can either be an organization's greatest defense, or its weakest link against a cyber attack. Further, it is incumbent upon CEOs to learn more about cybersecurity to ensure their company is taking appropriate actions to secure their most valuable information assets. This does not mean that every CEO needs to become a certified information system security professional (CISSP). Rather, CEOs should increase their knowledge of core cybersecurity concepts and leverage their own leadership skills to conceptualize and manage risk in strategic terms and how best to invest their time and resources to improve cyber defense.

Top Five Things CEOs Should Know About Cybersecurity

1. Cyber attacks and security breaches will occur and will negatively impact the business. Today, the average cost of the impact of a cyber breach is $7.5 million.
2. According to most cybersecurity surveys, over 60% of all data breaches originate from unauthorized access from one of the organization's current or former employees, or third-party suppliers.
3. Achieving information security compliance with one or more government regulatory standards for information security (i.e. ISO 27001, NIST

800-171, HIPAA, NYDFS, etc.) is good, but not sufficient to ensure real cybersecurity.
4. Cyber liability insurance premiums are significantly increasing in cost and often do not cover all of the damages caused by a cyber breach.
5. To achieve real information security and data resilience it is vital to combine managed monitoring, detection, and response (MDR) managed security services (MSS) with comprehensive disaster recovery (DR) and business continuity plans (BCP).

Top Ten Things CEOs Should Do About Cybersecurity

1. Ensure everyone in the organization from the top-down receives appropriate cybersecurity education and awareness training.
2. Hire an independent company to conduct a cyber risk assessment against government regulatory compliance requirements and industry standards to identify potential gaps in the organization's information security policies, processes, plans, and procedures.
3. Verify that periodic penetration testing by certified Ethical Hackers is being conducted to identify potential cybersecurity vulnerabilities in the organization's information systems.
4. Require a timely and effective software patch management program be implemented by the organization's Information Technology team to mitigate known security vulnerabilities as quickly as possible.
5. Ensure the organization has 24x7x365 monitoring, detection, and response capabilities for its information systems.
6. Verify the organization has an appropriate cyber breach incident response plan, including policies and procedures related to ransomware attacks.
7. Hire an independent firm to conduct a cyber liability insurance coverage adequacy evaluation.
8. Establish information security key performance indicators (i.e. number of cyber attacks, number of data breaches, network uptime, network downtime, cost of cyber breaches, cost of cyber insurance, cost of information security as a percentage of total company information technology (IT) cost, etc.).
9. Ensure the organization has well-documented and periodically tested disaster recovery and business continuity plans to quickly recover lost or stolen data to mitigate potential damages of cyber breaches.
10. Mandate additional layers of information security via encryption, multi-factor authentication, and highly restricted access to the organization's most valuable information assets.

Seven Strategic Questions a CEO Should Ask to Assess the Quality of the Cybersecurity Program

1. What is the threat profile of our organization based on our business model and the type of data our organization holds?
2. Who may be after the organization's data assets - nation states, sophisticated international criminal organizations, ideologically motivated hacktivists, competitors in the market, disgruntled former employees?
3. Does the organization's cybersecurity strategy align with organization's threat profile?
4. Is cybersecurity risk viewed as an enterprise-wide risk issue and incorporated into the overall risk identification, management and mitigation process?
5. What percentage of our IT budget is dedicated to cybersecurity? Does it conform to industry standards? Is it adequate based on the organization's threat profile?
6. Is there someone in the organization dedicated full-time to our cybersecurity mission and function, such as a chief information security officer?
7. Is the cybersecurity function properly aligned within the organization? Aligning the CISO under the CIO may not always be the best model as it may present a conflict. Many organizations align this function under the risk, compliance, audit or legal functions - some with direct or "dotted line" reporting to the CEO.

What CFOs Should Know About Cybersecurity

Clearly, the role and responsibilities of CFOs vary by organization. Some CFOs are responsible for not only all accounting and financial matters but also:
- information technology
- procurement
- risk management
- tax and audit

Top Ten Questions the CFO Should Ask and Know About Cybersecurity

1. What is the organization's overall risk of a data breach in terms of both probability of occurrence and financial impact?
2. How much cyber liability insurance coverage does the organization need to protect the organization's financial interest?
3. What is the average cost of a cyber data breach?

4. What are the financial penalties for failure to fully comply with cyber-security industry specific requirements?
5. What is the cost of compliance as it relates to the cybersecurity industry requirements and/or specific contract/subcontract requirements?
6. Is it better financially to insource or outsource necessary cybersecurity hardware, software, and professional services?
7. Whom can we trust to advise the organization if a significant cyber attack and data breach occurs?
8. What information regarding cybersecurity risks and mitigation actions should be reported to the board of directors?
9. Does the organization have the right people to make informed business decisions about cybersecurity?
10. Does the organization need to engage outside consultants with more experience in cyber incident response and cyber claim preparation and processing?

Top Ten Questions General Counsels Should Ask and Know About Cybersecurity?

1. What is the risk of a law suit by Federal, State, or local government(s) for information security negligence and/or penalties for non-compliance?
2. What is the potential risk of a law suit from shareholders for a negative impact to company market value as a result of a major cyber data breach?
3. Does the organization have an adequate cybersecurity awareness, education, and training program?
4. Does the organization have a sufficient cybersecurity risk management program in place?
5. Has the organization hired an independent firm to conduct a Cyber Risk Assessment, pursuant to the appropriate cyber security risk management framework/requirements?
6. Are the findings provided via in-house or out-side counsel under attorney-client privilege?
7. When did the organization conduct the last independent vulnerability assessment and penetration testing?
8. How much cyber liability insurance coverage is sufficient?
9. Does the organization need to have a cyber incident response team via a managed security services provider on retainer? If so, then who should we engage?
10. After a breach should the organization contact the FBI? If so, whom should be contacted at the FBI?

Top Ten Questions COOs Should Ask and Know About Cybersecurity

1. Is the organization hiring ethical people?
2. Does the organization provide appropriate cybersecurity awareness, education, and training?
3. What action(s) does the organization take to motivate everyone to be more aware and diligent about cybersecurity actions?
4. Does the organization have appropriate and compliant information security policies and procedures in place?
5. Do the subcontractors the organization hires comply with the cybersecurity risk management framework required for the industry?
6. Does the organization have well educated, trained, and experienced information technology and cybersecurity professionals?
7. Does the organization have a timely and reliable information back-up plan and business continuity plan?
8. Does the organization have a proven effective cyber incident response plan?
9. Has the organization independently verified the cyber threats they're facing and developed an appropriate cyber defense program?
10. Does the organization properly control information access?

Top Ten Things CIOs Should Do About Cybersecurity

1. Work with the CEO and/or board of directors to hire a dedicated, well educated, experienced, certified information technology and cybersecurity professional to serve as the chief information security officer, if possible.
2. Ensure the CISO reports to either the CEO, chief risk officer (CRO), chief compliance officer, or general counsel.
3. Work with the C-suite to assess cyber risks from every functional area of the organization?
4. Create an appropriate budgetary balance between information technology, information governance, risk, security, and compliance.
5. Ensure an appropriate data privacy program.
6. Verify a timely and effective software patch management program.
7. Ensure appropriate information access, storage, dissemination, and business continuity.
8. Work to create an organization–wide cybersecurity culture.
9. Outsource the 24x7x365 monitoring, detection, and response (MDR) services to a qualified and experienced managed security services provider (MSSP)
10. Ensure timely reporting of all data breaches.

What is the Right Reporting Structure for the CISO?

As cybersecurity risk management has emerged as a top strategic priority for organizations in the public and private sectors worldwide, the question of whom the chief information security officer should report to has likewise risen in importance. In fact, many industry cybersecurity risk management frameworks require the selection and staffing of a CISO to lead all information security planning and implementation matters. Historically, the CISO reported to the CIO, but companies are increasingly considering a number of alternatives-from placing the CISO in the risk, financial, compliance, or legal groups, to having them report directly to the CEO or board of directors. Although there is no one-size-fits-all answer, here is some guidance about the pros and cons of the various CISO organizational reporting options.

Option #1: Reporting to the CIO

Most CISOs have reported to the chief information officer since the cybersecurity position was first created.

Pros: The CIO is the member of the C-suite who best understands cybersecurity issues and, in many cases, is reporting to the board on the topic. Much of a CISO's spending is directly related to IT, which the CIO manages. Some CIOs have formerly served as CISOs, so they know the CISO role, responsibilities, and challenges quite well.

Cons: Although the CISO role was created to secure IT systems and data, a big part of the role is outside of IT. CISOs have to consider employee awareness and education, develop security policy and procedures, and cultural change. When the CISO is reporting to the CIO, it may not be easy to influence IT. CISOs reporting to CIOs may also be pressured to focus on technological solutions at the expense of more holistic solutions. The most significant cybersecurity vulnerabilities are the humans in an organization, not in the technology hardware and software. Falling under the CIO reinforces the notion that cybersecurity is simply an IT issue, rather than an enterprise issue. There can be a conflict of interest when the CIO must weight security against other priorities such as networking capacity, application development, infrastructure support, customer/user support, and outsourcing.

Option #2: Reporting to the CRO

Over the last few years, some organizations such as financial services firms and large multi-national companies, have opted to place the CISO under the chief risk officer.

Pros: The role of the risk management function is to give the organization's senior executives and the board of directors a greater insight into the enterprise risk of the company, not just financial risk. It is an oversight function and that can help to ensure that everyone does what is needed to put the right solutions in place.

Cons: In many companies, the CRO does not exist or does not report to the CEO, so this reporting structure can further distance CISOs from top executives and company strategy.

Option #3: Reporting to the CFO

Pros: The CFO is focused on understanding the financial impacts of all business risk, reports to the board, and may make critical decisions about cybersecurity spending. Although some other C-level leaders have bemoaned the cost-centric focus of a CFO strong leader, increasing number of CFOs are evolving in their management approach in the hopes of taking over CEO roles in the future.

Cons: The downside, is that many CFOs want to see returns quickly, particularly if they are incentivized on year-over-year earnings growth. That can be a tough discussion for CISOs to have, because it can be difficult to show the benefits of cybersecurity investment on a quarterly or annual basis.

Option #4: Reporting to GC

Some organizations have opted to move the CISO out from under IT and into the office of the general counsel or chief legal officer. This happens in cases where CEOs recognize the critical nature of cybersecurity, the potential for law suits related to cyber attacks, and deems that GC as someone to trust.

Pros: GCs handle significant issues related to information governance and compliance and understand about corporate direction, since they often serve as board of director secretaries. GCs typically get involved when there is a cybersecurity incident.

Cons: Because GCs do not typically have many non-legal direct reports and may not be the best technical and operational managers. GCs are also more engaged in episodic security activities, like breaches, than operational issues.

Option #5: Reporting to the CEO

Three years ago, IDC predicted that 75% of CISOs would report to the CEO, but it is still the exception rather than the rule. CISOs reporting to CEOs typically occurs in tech-centric organizations or those that have suffered high-profile cyber data breaches.

Pros: Reporting to the CEO maintains the independence of the CISO role and can enable direct, honest, and candid discussion with respect to risk, resources, and priorities.

Cons: Cybersecurity, is not central to CEO responsibilities in many organizations. The greater number of principles who directly report to the CEO reduces the executive's ability to focus on strategy and organizational leadership.

Option #6: Reporting to the Board of Directors

Few organizations have implemented an approach where the CISO reports directly to the board of directors or one of its committees such as the audit committee.

Pros: The board is responsible for supervising management. The board needs unvarnished information about the organization's cyber performance. Direct reporting to the board enables directors to ask probing questions of management without the information being sanitized. This approach enables the board to get discrete cyber information outside of board meetings.

Cons: The organization's board must have members with specific knowledge of cybersecurity issues and a willingness to oversee the CISO role and function.

The reality is there is no single best approach for the CISO reporting structure. Each organization should conduct an internal informed discussion of the pros and cons and make the decision, which they think is best for their operation.

BDO Public Company Board of Directors Survey on Cybersecurity

According to a 2017 survey by BDO USA, LLP, one of the nation's leading accounting and advisory organizations: (1) more than three-quarters (79%) of public company directors report that their board is more involved with cybersecurity than it was 12 months ago, (2) a similar percentage (78%) say they have increased company investments during the past year to defend against cyber attacks, with an average budget expansion of 19 percent.

This is the fourth consecutive year that board members have reported increases in time and dollars invested in cybersecurity. Despite this positive progress, the BDO survey also found that businesses continue to resist sharing information on cyber attacks with entities outside of their company. Just one-quarter (25%) are sharing information gleaned from cyber attacks with external entities – a practice that needs to become more prevalent for the safety of critical infrastructure and national security.

Risk of a Cyber-Breach

Almost one in five (18%) board members indicate that their company experienced a cyber-breach during the past two years, a percentage very similar to the previous two years (22%). A majority (61%) of corporate directors say their company has a cyber-breach/incident response (IR) plan in place, compared to less than one-fifth (16%) who do not have a plan and close to one-quarter (23%) who are not sure whether they have such a plan. The percentage with IR plans is approximately the same as a year ago (63%), but a major improvement from 2015 when less than half (45%) of directors reported having them.

Public Company Board Members Maintain Positive Trends on Cybersecurity

	2014	2015	2016	2017
Increased Board Involvement	59%	69%	74%	79%
Increased Cybersecurity Investments	55%	70%	80%	78%
Breach Response Plan in Place	NA	45%	63%	61%
Experienced a Cyber-Breach in Past 2 Years	NA	22%	22%	18%

Close to four-fifths (79%) of public company board members report that their board is more involved with cybersecurity than it was 12 months ago. The vast majority of directors (91%) are briefed on cybersecurity at least once a year - this includes more than a quarter (28%) that are briefed quarterly and better than one-fifth that are briefed twice a year (21%). The balance are briefed annually (36%) or more often than quarterly (6%). Surprisingly, nine percent of board members say they are still not briefed at all on cybersecurity. However, during the four years of the survey, the percentage of directors reporting no cybersecurity briefings has dropped consistently (see chart below).

Frequency of Cybersecurity Briefings for Public Company Boards

	2014	2015	2016	2017
Once a Year	30%	37%	37%	36%
Twice a Year	16%	17%	9%	21%
Quarterly or More Often	25%	33%	42%	34%
Not at All	29%	13%	12%	9%

Lack of Sharing on Cyber Attacks

Sharing information gleaned from cyber attacks is key to defeating hackers and the U.S. government has consistently communicated how businesses can contact relevant federal agencies about cyber incidents they experience. Unfortunately, when asked whether they share information they gather from cyber attacks, only one-quarter (25%) of directors - virtually unchanged from 2016 (27%) - say they share the information externally. A similar proportion (24%) say they do not share the information with anyone and approximately half (51 %) aren't sure whether they do or not. Of those sharing information on their cyber attacks, the vast majority (86%) share with government agencies (FBI, Dept. of Homeland Security) and close to half (47%) share with ISAC (Information Sharing and Analysis Centers). Very few (8%) share with competitors.

Ransomware

In 2017, the "Wanna Cry" cyber attack, which impacted businesses in more than 150 countries, greatly raised awareness of the threat posed by ransomware. When asked whether their company had taken steps to minimize its vulnerability to ransomware, a majority (60%) indicate they are addressing this threat. Of those targeting ransomware vulnerabilities, a majority (58%) are placing an increased emphasis on patch management and increasing the frequency of data back-ups (58%). Close to half (46%) say they have increased their ability to restore data faster.

SOC for Cybersecurity

In 2017, the American Institute of Certified Public Accountants (AICPA) introduced a voluntary cybersecurity risk management framework for the U.S. accounting industry - known as the System of Organizational Controls (SOC) now called "SOC for Cybersecurity" – that provides companies with a proactive approach for designing a risk management program and communicating about its effectiveness. When asked about this initiative, just 40 percent of directors are familiar with it. Of those aware of the voluntary framework, more than a third (35%) indicate that they are likely to utilize both readiness testing and formal audit/attestation for their program. A little more than one-quarter (27%) indicate they will just utilize the readiness testing for their programs, while a much smaller minority (6%) plan to use the formal audit/attestation exclusively. Almost one-third (32%) indicate they either do not plan to utilize the framework (14%) or were unsure (18%) if they would.

These are just a few of the findings of the 2017 BDO Survey on Cyber Governance, conducted by the Corporate Governance Practice of BOO USA in August 2017.

Conclusion

It is abundantly clear that some CEOs simply do not know enough about cybersecurity and that their C-suite executives, including the chief financial officer, general counsel or chief legal officer, chief operating officer, chief information officer, and chief information security officers do not always provide them with an accurate portrait of the cyber risks which their company is facing every day. Other CEOs appear to be suffering from a 'knowing" versus "doing" gap. It is clear that many CEOs are well aware of the cyber risks, but for one or more reasons, often short-term financially motivated, they choose not to do what needs to be done in order to reduce the probability and/or impact of a cyber breach in their organizations. In the world of cybersecurity the old adage is quite true "You can pay now, or you can pay much more later!"

The next chapter provides a historical perspective of the evolution of cybersecurity from the creation and early adoption of the Internet and initial network security, to basic information assurance, to information governance, risk, and compliance (GRC), to true cybersecurity and data resilience.

Chapter 3

INFORMATION SECURITY TO CYBER DEFENSE

By: Ophir Zilbiger, CISSP, CRISC

INTRODUCTION

The term cybersecurity in its various forms started showing up on the IT security and information security experts' radar in 2012, approximately 18 years after the Internet started its commercialization in late 1994. Many experts and industry analysts thought that mentions of cybersecurity, especially as it grew into a trend, represented nothing more than marketing hype. There are a few published quotes stating just that, including a leading industry analyst firm's senior vice president quoted in November of 2014 saying: "I am not fond of the term cybersecurity, as it is mostly used for marketing purposes. It is all one form or another of information security." This discussion about whether cybersecurity is just another marketing term or actually represents a significant shift might have easily been overlooked by the author of these lines, but for an opinion letter requested by a client's management team in late 2012, asking to understand what cybersecurity represents. It was already clear that the reality information security experts were facing in 2012 was dramatically different than the one faced in the early years of the twenty-first century when worms like Melissa and SQL Slammer attacked computers across the Internet. The key differences in the threat landscape between the early Internet period and the mature and wide Internet adoption period is described in Table 1 below:

Table 1: Threat landscape comparison		
	Early Internet Days	Mature and Wide Internet Adoption
Risk Impact Potential	Limited Internet adoption, initial e-commerce, organizational and government use of the Internet. Low breach potential impact.	High Internet adoption, advanced implementation of business and commerce, initial discussion of Internet of Things. Medium to high breach potential impact for businesses, governments and countries.
Threat	Mainly script kiddies, underground hacktivists.	Cyber-criminal organization and government funded operations.
Motivation	Mainly fame and fun.	Mainly making money and stealing information and intellectual property.
Capability	Basic capability is widespread. Advanced capability requires high level of knowledge.	Advanced capability is increasingly more common. Available advanced hacking tools published by the hacker community allow for high impact breaches using low levels of knowledge.

This chapter explains the evolution of the information security profession to its current state – referred to as cybersecurity and provides an explanation to why cybersecurity is not just a term but a transformed approach to secure organizations and countries alike.

BACKGROUND

It has not always been about defending cyberspace. It has not always been cybersecurity. The cybersecurity industry has gone through various twists and turns that have influenced it in various ways but has also gone through a few groundbreaking shifts that dramatically changed it into what it is today. In fact, it's possible to refer to this series of shifts that occurred over more than two decades as an evolution. This is a story of an industry which roots go all the way back to the history of human kind. The past of cybersecurity was heavily influenced by military, government and intelligence agencies, but has only started to mature in an accelerated rate and form into its latest state when the Internet became a domain owned, used and dependent by all - people, businesses and countries alike. The rate of adoption of the Internet and its wide use over the past almost 25 years, since late 1994, require tremendous efforts to ensure that the digital culture and civilization stays safe. These efforts and the developments in approach and technology are the heart of this discussion.

The cybersecurity evolution is not just influenced by Internet adoption for social or e-commerce use, but is also influenced by how the Internet is serving as the foundation for the fourth industrial revolution and its association with the Internet of Things (IoT). Major trends in society, business and government, have truly transformed information security into cybersecurity. Thus, it is important to discuss how information evolved over time. As mankind progressed, information and its storage took different forms, starting with knowledge in spoken form and in people's minds, hand-written information, printed information, photographed information, and audio recorded information. Plus, the digital transformation of information that digitized text, photo, video and audio into digital data stored on various forms of media: magnetic, optical, electronic, and even biologic, increasing in size year by year. Today, historic information has mostly been digitized and new information is stored digitally at the source with massive network storage resources, the Internet and the cloud serving as information repositories.

TIMELINE

The journey from information security to cybersecurity does not begin when the Internet started to be commercialized and organizations began to connect to it, although this is the point in time in which significant development started to accelerate. Computer security before the Internet and personal computing period was mostly physical security and authorization to access functions and data within central computing facilities (e.g., mainframes). Therefore, the first significant point on this timeline describing the transition from information security to cybersecurity is placed at around the period the Internet started to play a significant role for business and organizations. The most significant shifts in the information security profession that brought us to where we are today, and that are described in this chapter, are mapped into four periods of time as shown in the chart below. The suggested points in time where these four periods begin, and end, are not set in stone. The adoption rate of Internet, e-business, IT technology and management practices as well as the way regulators address these shifts vary from geography to geography, country to country and industry to industry. The timeline in chart 1 is suggested as a timeline that information security practitioners would have experienced if they were part of the financial sector, which is traditionally the most advanced adopter of information security practices and technology and is a fairly advanced adopter of Internet technologies and online business.

This timeline is applicable to countries which are early adopters of technology and Internet. The following chart describes the timeline that represents the major shifts in the information security profession that transformed it, and the periods of time that are described further in this chapter:

Chart 1 – Timeline

INFORMATION SECURITY PRIOR TO THE INTERNET ERA (PHYSICAL SECURITY)

The journey of the cybersecurity profession started long before the Internet was invented. Human kind has always struggled with keeping secrets. People were involved in activities to gather information and intelligence dating all the way back to the bible. As means of communications and information storage were developed, countries and organizations (e.g., criminal organizations) were busy developing means to listen to communications and to gather information stored in different forms. Prior to the Internet, the only ways to steal information were to:

- Physically steal the information (e.g., make a copy of papers or just steal the files);
- Get the information from a person using a variety of techniques; or
- Listen to communications (e.g., radio communications or telephone lines).

To protect information, it was necessary to first classify the information in order to tell which was "secret" or "top-secret" and which was "non-classified" or for public use. As a result, responsibility for information security was mostly in the hands of security people. These professionals, usually with security forces or intelligence background, were mostly dealing with physical security, people security, and in extreme circumstances, old style information encryption. The basis was physical security, ensuring physical access was allowed for those with proper authorization and prevented to non-authorized people. This included guards, surveillance systems and security monitoring to ensure that physical security measures are not tampered with or circumvented. A major component of information security was focused on people security by means of vetting people, performing background checks, ensuring allegiance and checking their actions using methods like questioning, tailing and polygraph checks. These methods were used, depending on the level of secrets and the impact of losing them, mostly by governments, armies and other intelligence agencies. Very rarely were such methods used in businesses. Only businesses with high breach impact potential were focused on physical security. Among those were banks and other financial institutions alongside civilian defense contractors.

The officer in charge of all the above activities was given the role of the chief security officer (CSO). We can call this period, the "Physical Security" period. Computer security already existed, but it was very simple, mostly physical security and with no network connecting computers outside of the local area network in the office, it mostly dealt with central computer authorization and user management and antivirus on the PC in the office or at home.

Chart 2 – Physical Security Period

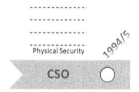

INTERNET SECURITY INFANCY (TECHNICAL SECURITY)

Early day Internet adoption in organizations started with more questions than answers. Organizations did not understand why they needed Internet connectivity and what it could be used for. For most organizations, the first major Internet uses were:

- email and www for users in the organization,
- basic brochure style client facing web site,
- very initial e-commerce applications (online store), and
- client file download using FTP (e.g., updates for software).

These basic use cases usually required setting up an Internet line and Internet compatible communications including a router and TCP/IP connectivity and installing an Internet server to enable organizational email and host the other services. A famous story is told about an Internet technician, sent to set-up Internet connectivity and an email server in a bank. While he sat in the computer room, someone taps on his shoulder saying he is the chief security officer of the bank and he needs to understand and approve what he does since the CSO oversees anything that is security. They spend the next few hours discussing Internet, servers, email and TCP/IP until the CSO gives up and unwillingly approves the work. Back in those days, CSOs did not have the knowledge or training to understand Internet technology and its associated risks or how to address them. Very soon thereafter the responsibility for Internet security was given to the only people capable of addressing it at the time – the IT techies.

Back in those days, the term chief information security officer (CISO) was not even coined, and frameworks for information security were very young (e.g., British Standard 7799, which was the basis to today's ISO 27001, the most acceptable information security framework globally, was only published in 1995). So, the IT security role emerged equipped with technical knowhow that no one else had, but, no plan and no real understanding of business strategy or even Information systems strategy and with no clear plan on what needs protection (not even what is sensitive data and where it is stored). Further, the IT security team typically had no risk management methodology to enable their focusing on what was most important. During the technical security period, there were a few events worth noting as they influenced IT and Internet security by creating concert with top management, accelerated the development of security products and increased the IT security spend that organizations budgeted for. These were the happy days of the Internet bubble and funds were, for the most part, in abundance. During those years, more and more security incidents made the news. In the late 1990's, newspapers looked a bit like today, a major security breach was published month after month side by side with businesses relying on Internet and email more and more. This made management aware of the importance of Internet supporting IT, and had them approve almost any budget requested by IT, including IT security budget requests. During those days the knowledge gap between management and IT was so deep, no one above IT was able to fully understand what those IT security techies were doing. IT security did not require a lot of invested effort in planning and justifying budgets. The only objective was to provide peace and quiet to the business folks, and that was fairly easy to achieve as security was relatively simple and threat levels were relatively low.

In the early part of this period, technical security was mostly about network security - implementation of firewalls to protect organizations' networks from attacks originating on the Internet. Additionally, organizations implemented antiviruses for email and personal computers (PCs) and additional tools like virtual private networks (VPNs) to enable secure connectivity over the Internet. Over time, security tools became more advanced and vendors started offering different flavors of network security including, intrusion detection systems (IDS) allowing organizations to get alerts if a certain vulnerability is exploited, network scanners to enable organizations to understand where they are vulnerable, URL filters to prevent users from accessing malicious or bad reputation sites and more. This was still a very technical profession with no real connection to what the organization was busy doing in its business delivery layers and how it operated. Towards the end of the period, vendors started offering more comprehensive and complex security products and management tools, such as: software patch management tools allowing automation of the patching process, risk management tools to allowing organizations to prioritize endless security tasks based on impact, and probability and governance supporting tools like IdM (identity management) which enable user lifecycle management and automation. Those were also the very early days of policy management tools enabling policies to be published electronically to users within an enterprise and maintainance of those policies over time. This period was clearly led by technical experts with very little interest or need to communicate with management, or with the physical security functions, making IT security and physical security two separated entities with different mission statements. It would be quite a shock for these very happy individuals to have to go through the transformation into the next evolutionary phase of information security.

Chart 3 – Technical Security Period

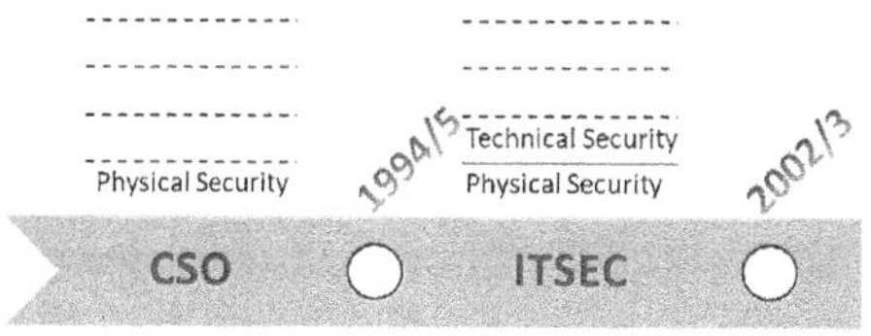

SECURITY POST THE DOT.COM BUBBLE BURST AND THE COLLAPSE OF ENRON (GRC SECURITY)

In the first years of commercial Internet, adoption and growth, particularly in certain parts of the world, was phenomenal. Businesses and entrepreneurs of various industries, fearing the risk of lost opportunity, rushed into developing various kinds of offerings online. The public and other investors, interested in a piece of the huge golden opportunity, invested in new companies springing up online like mushrooms after the rain, and the stock market reached an all time high. These were the incredible days of the dot.com bubble which saw Internet companies and technology shares peak in value, maxing out on March 10, 2000, before starting to crash the next day and over the next couple of years until October 9, 2002. The stock market would take until 2015 to fully recover. The dot.com bubble burst had significant economic impact that influenced business and society in a variety of different aspects.

Focusing on IT spending within organizations, the technology bubble burst and additionally, the effects of the 2008 economic crisis had caused a recession in IT spending that lasted for almost a decade, according to a Gartner IT Spending 2010 report by Barbara Gomolski. This significant decrease in IT spending also influenced IT security budgets and spending, which have traditionally been tied closely to IT spending. Traditionally, one of the indicators for organizational information security maturity has been the percentage of IT security spending out of total IT spending. In fact, this indicator is still used today. And so, after a period of uncontrolled, large IT security investments and buildup of the initial IT security capability, came an even longer period of time in which investment markedly declined.

Governance

In this period of time, most technical IT security spending was dedicated to ongoing maintenance of existing tools that were acquired earlier, and just like in other areas of IT, weren't fully implemented or used. Some of the ongoing technical activities such as Firewall management and antivirus maintenance became "a commodity" and were left in the hands of IT, keeping IT security functions technical and tactical while establishing the new required layers of security management that were missing, these could also be referred to as information security governance. After almost a decade of uncontrolled IT security spending, IT security managers, people of technical background mostly, and little if any management background, needed to start building proper budgetary plans that aligned with business strategy and prioritized based on risk. These requirements for change in management methods came from top management, who for the first time, understood they had to be more involved and better control IT security spending. Top management were looking for a common language to enable them to connect business strategy and initiatives to security projects and budget and to enable them to have more transparency to what information security was doing. In other words, what management was required was, again, governance. In 2005 the term Information Security Governance was hardly used, and only advanced consulting practices and mature organizations were looking for ways to formalize this concept.

Risk

In addition to seeking transparency and alignment, management were also looking for a common language to enable them to understand prioritization and make sense of annual work plans and budget allocation. Security organizations also started implementing risk methods, because of the dramatic decrease in budget and in parallel the rapidly growing challenge of securing an organization. IT was continually growing more and more complex, and system vulnerabilities were growing at an exponential rate. The use of risk management allowed security managers to prioritize the ever growing, endless list of to-do tasks and prioritize IT based on criticality to the business. At the time security organizations started implementing risk management methods, they were the first to do so out of the list of risk types under the operational risk management umbrella (e.g., IT, business continuity, fraud, process failure). Those were still the days before June 2004, when the Basel committee signed the Basel II accord which addressed the amount of capital banks were required to hold to guard against financial and operational risks. This accord and the one following it - Solvency II, targeting the insurance industry - were the most significant accelerators of operational risk management implementation in the global markets. Being the first to implement risk management did not come easy as information security managers faced many challenges:

- Business was not ready - The business side of the organization was not ready to perform their side of the security risk assessment, or any operational risk assessment. The business should be in charge of determining the impact of a risk under the assumption that it materializes. There was no risk management language nor process implementation at the time and so information security did not have anyone to complete this business task with and had to make their own assumptions.

- No central risk control – The chief risk officer (CRO) function had not been established at the time, and so there was no central controller of risk to prioritize between information security risks and other risks that the organization was assessing such as financial risk and credit risk in banks. The CRO would have also overseen risk management framework consistency and compatibility across the organization.

- Lack of methodology, tools and experience – Security staff, which until that time were mostly technical, did not possess any knowledge or experience in risk management and performing risk assessment. Risk management methodologies were generic and initial, and if they addressed operational risk assessment at all, they did not provide guidance as to how security and technical risk assessments need to be performed. On top of all of these, risk assessment and management tools did not exist to enable consistent management of the data that was collected. These were initially collected in large excel files making it hard to maintain and use.

- Too theoretical – Information security has a lot to do with technology, certainly in those early days, where Internet security was mostly technical. At that early stage, there were no real means to gather technical information and turn it into management information that could be used as part of the risk assessment process. This made the risk assessment process rely mostly on either non-technical data (e.g., policies review, user interview) or data collected manually which was not enough to get a proper deep understanding of what was going on.

- No statistical foundation – In order to properly perform a risk assessment, the assessor needs to calculate the probability for exploiting a weakness or for an incident to occur. At the time when security professionals started performing risk assessments, there was no statistical information available and so the assessment was mostly reliant on common sense of the assessor.

The above stated factors were the main reasons why risk management became compliance orientated and not effectiveness driven. It would take an additional 10 years before risk management would truly become a language that would drive cybersecurity.

Compliance

The bubble burst brought investor confidence in the stock market to a dramatic low. Additional highly visible bankruptcies eroded investor confidence even further. The Enron collapse in October of 2001 and the Worldcom collapse in June 2002 were among the most visible and publicized of the giant collapses. Although mostly not related to the bubble burst, the Enron collapse, which was mainly a form of corporate fraud, also cast a shadow on accounting practices, triggered the creation of the most significant regulation influencing information security and many other corporate management aspects of that time (2002). This was a U.S. federal law named after Congressman Michael Oxley and Senator Paul Sarbanes, the Sarbanes-Oxley Act, or SOX.

The overall objective of SOX was to increase shareholder confidence in public companies. The law details the responsibilities of the board of directors of publicly traded companies, adds criminal penalties for certain actions of top officers within the organization and requires the Securities and Exchange Commission (SEC) to detail to public companies how to comply with the law.

SOX does not address information security specifically, and hardly even addresses IT. In fact, the whole section that covers IT and security, section 404 of the bill, is 180 words including the title. The way SOX has influenced information security was detailed by the Public Company Accounting Oversight Board (PCAOB), which was established by SOX and governed by the SEC. The PCAOB provided a detailed standard on how to perform SOX audits as they related to IT and information security controls. In preparing for an audit, IT has to define proper controls, ensure they have clear policies and procedures documenting the controls and the control objectives, and go through an annual audit ensuring controls existence and sample-based testing of the actions users and managers perform based on documented procedures. SOX compliance created a new IT and IT security spending line item which, over the next few years, became the heaviest of investments for public US companies. Over the years, SOX has become a globally accepted standard for public companies, even if they are not traded in the US. Furthermore, SOX influenced the way companies manage their IT and IT security even in non-public companies. Additionally, several other significant regulations were published in different countries in the early 2000s, targeting different industries and covering IT and information security governance and management.

GRC (Governance Risk and Compliance)

The overall effect of the reduction of budget and increase in governance need, side by side with the introduction of SOX and additional regulations that had significant compliance cost and governance requirements of their own, made the next period of information security management, the governance risk and compliance security period (GRC security period). The GRC period is the second major shift in information security management and represent the third significant period of the profession, as described in chart 4 below.

Chart 4 – GRC Security Period

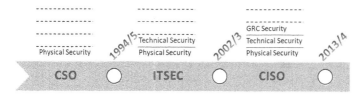

The term GRC was introduced a couple of years into the GRC period. It made a lot of sense as Governance, Risk and Compliance are indeed very much inter-connected, as shown in chart 5 below, which details the main objectives of each and the way they influence each other. Taking care of one would affect the other two. All lines are bi-directional, meaning any change in the level of any objective would influence the other and visa-versa.

Chart 5 – GRC Objectives Interconnected

The GRC security period is significantly different than the technical security period. Each of the GRC components introduces new challenges and requirements to implement in the organizational management framework. This transition dramatically influenced the role of the information security manager, transforming it from a technical role to a management role, requiring a completely different skill set.

The main differences between the technical security period and the GRC security period are detailed in table 2, below.

Period/ Characteristic	Technical Security	GRC Security
Budget	In abundance	Reduced and limited
Regulation	Initial if any	SOX and other significant regulations with applicable costs
Compliance	No compliance drivers	Significant complaisance drivers
Risk	No risk basis	Initial risk implementation
Governance	No requirement	Required and implemented enabling business aligned information security
Manager	Technical	Seasoned manager; GRC specialist

Table 2: Technical and GRC security period differences

This period marks the first time the term chief information security officer would be used and become the standard as organizations of large scale started recruiting CISOs to perform the role as described above. The technical knowledge would continue to be important for the CISO role, but as a supporting function, rather than a main driver. As stated above, many of the technical activities remained in the hands of IT security and were performed under the supervision of the CISO, who was much more engaged with strategy, business, risk, governance establishment, but first and foremost, compliance. The years after the introduction of SOX became the years that everything revolved around the new law, with the main focus being to make certain any action or investment supported SOX compliance.

This was a critical time in information security evolution, one that determined the path that information security would take for the next 10 years. A path leading to a situation in which compliance was king and information security was a compliance-driven profession. The role of the CISO in the GRC period was the ensure compliance. This was the way that all layers of the organization considered security, from the board and top management including the CEO, CFO, and CIO, through internal audit, the compliance and legal officers, regulators and even clients. The main measurement for security maturity in the GRC period, and, in certain geographies and industries, still is, even today.

COMPLIANCE DRIVEN SECURITY

The process of ensuring compliance starts with understanding what regulations and standards and other requirements an organization needs to comply with. From 2003 and onwards, organizations' compliance programs have dealt with a growing list that includes (in the US, depending on industry): Health Insurance Portability and Accountability Act (HIPAA), Gramm–Leach–Bliley Act (GLBA), Sarbanes-Oxley (SOX), ISO 17799 / ISO 27001, Payment Card Industry – Data Security Standard (PCI-DSS) and many more.

Once the regulations and standards are identified, organizations perform a gap analysis to determine the level of compliance it has and then develop a remediation plan that will enable the organization to perform all required tasks to become compliant. The first step of the gap analysis phase is to map the controls. Many of the security regulations and standards have similar or overlapping controls and controls objectives. This means organizations have to maintain different compliance programs to meet similar objectives. The cost of compliance has increased over time and has became a major component of the CISO budget. Budgets are always tight and were especially so in the GRC period, as described above, which made CISO's drive compliance costs down as much as they could by introducing efficiency and cost reduction to the compliance process. One way to reduce cost is to push external vendors costs down. An example is penetration testing costs, which for compliance purposes were often driven down to as low as 50% below market standards. Driving vendors to use less experienced personnel who carry less costs in order to remain profitable. As long as compliance was met, and penetration testing was performed based on the regulation requirements, the CISO was happy with the result. The problem was that penetration testing, as an example, could be much more effective, and test many different points of view of a system. Utilizing highly experienced resources, can reveal many more vulnerabilities and system weaknesses, which need to be fixed. Using a compliance only mindset, an organization cannot afford the higher quality penetration testing work, the compliant focused CISO is in fact not interested in receiving a more detailed report revealing so many more security weaknesses. This example sets the scene for compliance driven security.

Another aspect of compliance driven security is that it is completely focused on what the regulation requires and nothing more. It's like having blindfolds on a horse's eyes, not allowing it to get distracted by anything except for what's in front of it. Capable and experienced CISOs in large enterprise organizations surely know there is so much more to do in order to effectively secure the organization, above and beyond what the government or industry regulators require. In fact, many CISOs manage security budgets that allow nothing more than meeting compliance requirements, leaving many aspects of information security unattended. It has become quite apparent that some organizations have decided to hire CISOs who are less proactive and are docile enough to focus only on compliance programs required by management and regulators, and nothing more.

During the GRC period, the compliance driven security period, as stated above, were pivotal in the way they influenced the corporate information security. Chart 6 below shows the effect of compliance driven security. It describes how in the technical security period, effective security increased from non-existent to a fairly effective level. During the GRC security period, compliance levels increased dramatically, enabling organizations to meet regulators' requirements. The result was that effective security has actually decreased compared to the level it should have had during the GRC period. As threat levels continued to increase, business became more digital, organizations had more to loose and hackers and criminal organizations' motivation continued to rise, while hackers continued to increase their technical and other capabilities to break into organizations.

Chart 6 – Compliance driven security effect

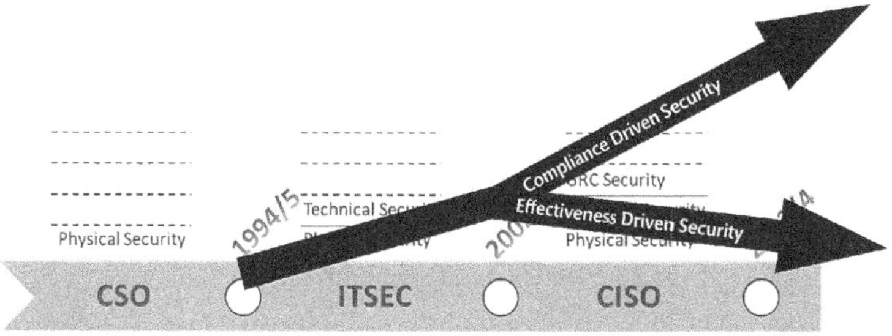

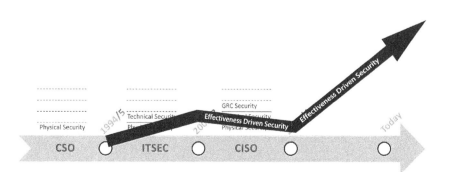

EFFECTIVE (THREAT-BASED) CYBERSECURITY

As shown in the chart, the effectiveness driven security vector and the compliance driven security vector move to two separate directions, creating a gap. This gap in effective security has maxed towards the end of the GRC period and has become the reason why in the early days of the cybersecurity period and until today we see so many breaches happening at an accelerating rate. It is as if reality exceeds our wildest dreams when it comes to major security breaches. Almost as if we are just not secure and hackers do almost whatever they want. This gap in readiness is what cybersecurity is all about. The mission is to address the gap, increase the level of effective security, not neglecting compliance but allowing compliance and compliance budgets to run on their own while building effectiveness driven security budgets that address what needs addressing, stepping away from the compliance mindset described above. Chart 7 below describes the change of direction and effective cyber defense vector.

Chart 7 – The Mission: Effective (Threat-Based) Cybersecurity

DEFENSE FORCES CYBER (OFFENSE AND) DEFENSE CAPABILITY

Going back to the bank's CSO in the story above, tapping that guy's shoulder. The background of these CSOs has traditionally been defense forces and agencies, specializing in physical security. As stated above, at that time, right after the Internet became commercialized, these CSOs did not have any technical understanding or IT security capability. Twenty years have passed and with them, many things have changed. Defense forces and agencies have been very busy during the past 20 years developing advanced technical capabilities. In fact, these capabilities were there even before the Internet, supporting operations and of different sorts, going all the way back to the early days of the 20th century. Defense forces and agencies have been busy developing technology capabilities applicable for the period they have been developed. Technologies such as the ability to listen to radio broadcast, decryption of messages sent by simple means (e.g., the Enigma in World War II) and as time and technology progressed, these defense agencies needed to develop advanced means that apply the age of digital transformation that started with the introduction of centralized computers, personal computers, all the way to advanced weapon systems that are computer based and Internet connected.

Defense agencies around the world have been extremely busy in the past two decades developing weapons that allow them access to data and systems as they needed and required. One of the accelerants of this military development was the need to gain access to data and collect intelligence. Intelligence is an incredible motivator for defense agencies. It has always been a major effort in any army, country or police force. It is always important to know what the adversary is planning.

Ever since the days of the Internet and cellular communications, and certainly after they converged, it has been infinitely easier for these agencies to collect intelligence from Internet connected devices such as personal computers and mobile phones, remotely listening to conversations, either written or spoken, and other ways to collect information and perform military operations remotely. There are numerous advantages to engaging adversaries with software-based resources vs. real humans. In fact, it's possible to say that defense agencies developed real cyber-offensive capabilities that have been also documented and reported in cases such as Stuxnet which demonstrated very advanced offensive capability as early as 2005.

Cyber offensive capability can also be referred to simply as hacking capability. For example, defense agencies' offensive tools include very high technical capability, in terms of research to find vulnerabilities and exploit development (i.e., hacking), physical breach capability, human manipulation capability as well as weapons capability and delivery capability (the ability to introduce people or technology physically at the location of the adversary). These skills together comprise the perfect cyber warrior, and in fact, also the perfect cybercriminal or hacker.

If the world is divided into black and white hats, referring to the color of hackers' hats, then it is safe to say that out of the white hats community globally, the only white hat community today that understands hackers, how they operate, their mindset, the methods to gain access to their targets, is the defense community. They have fulfilled a famous quote from Sun Tzu, the author of the book, the *Art of War*: "To know your Enemy, you must become your Enemy." They became the enemy and thus they know the enemy. This sentence cannot be said about information security experts of the previous 20 years. Information security experts have not developed similar skills to the ones described above. They were busy with IT security and then heavily busy with compliance. They did not specialize in hacking and gaining access to systems using whatever means available, as hackers do.

This represents the last (and possibly not the final) pivotal shift in the journey from information security to cybersecurity, which some prefer to call cyber defense to sharpen even further, the difference between information security of the past and cybersecurity of the present. The people who started the discussion about cybersecurity in the early days of the period were people with defense agency background that started taking leadership positions with vendors, analysts, consultants and of course within organizations.

Equipped with their unique knowledge and experience, which was very different than what civilian industry experts had, they started influencing the market and introduced fresh thinking that was needed in order to shift CISOs and organizations from the GRC security thinking to cybersecurity thinking, enabling the implementation of effective cyber defense. This also turned the CISO role into a cybersecurity management role. As a example of this change, the Bank of Israel adopted the world's first cyber defense management regulation, whcih applies to all Isreali banks, in 2015. The regulation even includes the new role and title of chief cyber defense officer (CCDO).

This takes us into the last phase of the evolution from information security to cybersecurity as described in Chart 8:

Chart 8 –The Cybersecurity Period

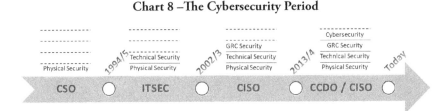

EFFECTIVE (THREAT-BASED) CYBERSECURITY

Effective cyber defense is first and foremost about threat-based cybersecurity. Stepping away from compliance driven security. Compliance driven security was about cost reduction, focusing only on regulatory requirements, and leaving other considerations aside. Effectiveness driven security is about identifying where the threats and risks are, based on an effective cyber risk assessment, investing in effective measures of security to ensure that the highest sensitivity areas in the organization are secure. While not investing in security measures in areas which are not important to the organization, based on the results of the risk assessment. It is like compliance driven security requires the organization to cover itself with a blanket of security measures, consistently, across the whole organization. While effectiveness driven security identifies where the information crown jewels are and requires building extremely well protected fortresses to defend them.

Effective cybersecurity can be divided into three parts. The diagram below describes the three parts of effectiveness driven cybersecurity and what they include.

Chart 9 – Effectiveness Driven Cybersecurity

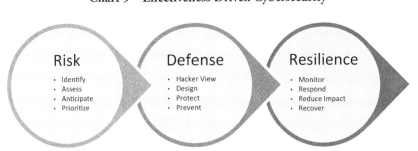

Risk

In addition to the above section about information security risk, effectiveness driven cyber risk assessment has to be quite different than traditional operational risk assessment methods suggest. Cyber risk should be clearly defined with the chief risk officer (CRO) and within the organization's risk management policies. Cyber risk is not a new kind of operational risk, but rather a risk attribute of every existing operational risk type that has already been identified. For example, business continuity risk can be a cyber risk or a non-cyber risk depending on the scenario creating the disruption for the business. Same goes for fraud, which can be a cyber risk if the fraudster uses the cyber domain in their fraud attempts. Furthermore, cyber risks should be assessed using a hacker's perspective. Hackers think differently from management about the organizational assets, and assets that management feels have significant value may not seem valuable to hackers if they aren't able to monetize them, which is the top motivator for cybercriminals. Motivation can be derived out of intelligence. Cyber risk assessments should use cyber intelligence that provides a lookout at threat actors, their motivation, availability, tools and capability and others factors. This valuable information should be fused into the risk assessment model to influence the probability of the attacker's interest in the organization and then add the probability for attack success based on the existence and effectiveness of controls.

An additional aspect of risk management is the defense objective. In traditional information security, the assets that were defended were mostly information. As a matter of fact, any information security risk assessment starts with the first question being "what are your information assets?" The whole purpose of the information security risk assessment is to identify information assets and to assess how well they are protected. In the cybersecurity, cyber assets are broader and include systems, manufacturing processes, money, reputation and even human lives.

Defense

The defense part includes any preventative means that needs to be implemented in order to reduce the probability of an attacker actually getting in. The use of a hacker's perspective on designing and implementing controls is critical as hackers think differently than information security professionals about what would work and what would not work when it comes to a security mechanism. The effectiveness approach is also key to ensure that the controls implemented provide the required defenses.

Resilience

Just like in physical world, no matter how many defenses are implemented, someone has to be on the lookout for those trying to break in. Perpetrators will always be able to gain access, even to very secure locations, given enough time. And so, it is a time-based equation; designing defenses that will prevent the perpetrator from gaining unauthorized access for enough time until someone can come and intervene. Cybersecurity is very similar, and resilience deals with all the controls required to detect a breach and respond to it in a timely manner and either block the attempt or in the very least, reduce the amount of time a hacker can be on a system from weeks and months to hours or days. Areas that are dealt with are detection and incident response up to the corporate business continuity plans that should have cyber incidents readiness built into them and management training facilitated so that nothing is done without prior analysis and training.

A NEW PARADIGM

The effectiveness (threat-based) driven security is just one aspect of a larger shift represented by the term cybersecurity, or moreover, cyber defense. Having discussed security agencies' understanding of offensive cyber and hacking, it is important to also note the shift their internal knowledge created in their own security programs. Defense agencies injecting their knowledge of how an attacker works and thinks, have built a defense model that represents a shift in paradigm, from IT-driven security to a military warfare-based paradigm. A great example of the difference between information security of the past and the military-based security paradigm of today lies in cyber intelligence. Cyber intelligence started to appear in conversations in the civilian market in 2012-3, maturing to commercial offerings a few years later. Information security has been around in its modern state since 1995, and ISO 27001 and its derivatives have been the standard controls framework for information security through this long period of time. However, intelligence was never an objective for information security professionals.

Intelligence is a key military activity, but information security professionals were walking around doing what they were doing with not even one piece of intelligence. They were walking blindfolded with no knowledge of their adversaries, their capability or intent, and not understanding their motivation or operational readiness. This has been the case for almost 20 years. But the situation is changing today, with more and more military and defense agency resources filling in positions in the cybersecurity industry and converging military disciplines and paradigms into the traditional information security management models. The lingo now includes not only intelligence, but also: threat landscaping, weaponizing cyberspace, and offensive cyber attacks or retaliation attacks.

FINAL NOTE

The evolution of the profession has not necessarily ended. We are facing an unknown future with threats evolving rapidly and even relying on artificial intelligence (AI) and machine learning applications. The defense concepts of the future still have yet to be developed and most likely will require additional shifts in education and technology. There is still a final discussion point about why a different name – why cybersecurity and not just leave it information security? With the paradigm shift, transition to security effectiveness, and most importantly, the extended asset coverage which includes more than just information, it makes sense to call the latest shift in evolution by a new name – cybersecurity.

The next chapter will focus on the nature and value of cyber intelligence and the difference between information and actionable intelligence. True cybersecurity is based upon a solid understanding of the real cyber threats an organization encounters or may face in the future, not simply compliance to a preexisting cyber risk management framework.

Chapter 4

CYBER THREAT INTELLIGENCE

By: Dr. Eric Chuang

INTRODUCTION

One of the most surprising impressions this writer gathered from public cybersecurity events is whenever the subject of cyber threat intelligence comes up during conferences or discussions, the customers, who are often senior executives, do not know what the words "threat intelligence" really mean. Everybody has their own idea of what it is, many think Threat Intelligence is a synonym for Dark Web intelligence. While others believe every cybersecurity subscription they receive is considered Threat Intelligence. The one universally shared belief is that nearly everyone feels overwhelmed by either the sheer volume of threat intelligence, or the actual usefulness of threat intelligence to their specific organization. Almost everyone nods in agreement that threat intelligence of some sort is important. Most receive and review some type of threat intelligence, but the agreement quickly breaks down regarding which specific type of threat intelligence is actually useful, and what executives should do with the intelligence they receive. The conversation often become even livelier, if the topic turns into how much each organization should pay for such intelligence and if the intelligence is worth the price.

The same trends in the proffering of traditional human intelligence (HUMINT) and signal intelligence (SIGINT) are being adopted in the emerging field of cyber intelligence. Corporate consumers are falling for the same salesmanship and fallacies that plagued the government intelligence services. Clearly, the intelligence purveyors are generating information for the sake of volume, to the point where consumers simply cannot effectively absorb or make use of it. Every incoming piece of intelligence is buried by the next wave of intelligence and relegated to the huge pile of unprocessed data, or worse yet, only discovered after an incident has occurred. Unfortunately, this practice then restarts the cycle of finding new intelligence sources and vendors, never realizing the issue was not the lack of intelligence, but rather the intelligence they have is not in the hands of the right people. A trend that is sadly happening everywhere in the corporate world as well.

Whenever there is a cyber incident, the easy answer is always to blame the person responsible for "reading" the intelligence and failing to do something about it. We have all seen companies after a major cyber breach blame the information technology (IT) person for not implementing a particular software security patch that was circulated by various intelligence reporting for months. Although there is always plenty of blame to go around in a cyber breach, firing the IT person generally will not improve the company's ability to use the intelligence properly. Unless the company changes how intelligence is purchased, processed, and applied, the same problem will remain, and the true responsibility lies not with the entry level IT staff, but with the higher level decision makers.

To understand how to make use of cyber intelligence effectively, or at least the ability to evaluate the applicability of an intelligence product for the company, the decision makers themselves need to know how cyber attacks are actually conducted. Once the decision makers understand the components of the attack, they will have enough knowledge to challenge the vendors and know what components of the cyber attack the cyber intelligence product actually focus on. Then senior leadership can make truly informed decisions regarding which intelligence product they should purchase in order to fulfill their company's specific needs. More importantly, senior leadership can then decide which department and which individual will be responsible for what type of intelligence. Rather than assuming the CISO, CIO, or the IT department head will be responsible for processing all the intelligence, becoming a victim of the fallacy that any individual is naturally an intelligence expert just because the title of their position.

Cybersecurity intelligence consumers, especially the senior executives and decision makers, need to know at least how to differentiate actionable versus information intelligence. Unlike the government who send intelligence analysts to months and years of training to be able to learn and practice the art of finding the thread of usable intelligence among an ocean of bulk data, this chapter is not meant to make the senior executives into intelligence analysts. Rather, it is meant to educate executives about the fundamentals in the day-to-day applications of cyber intelligence, thus enabling them to be better business decision makers.

Cyber Attack and Mythology

The fundamental principle of cybersecurity is that it is a defensive activity. One must first understand how our adversaries conduct their offensive activities. Cyber attacks, or hacking, can be a subject of discussion that can last for days, if not weeks, or months by enthusiast and subject matter experts. When explaining hacking to senior executives, law makers, counsel, judges and finance managers, this writer has learned that the best way to understand hacking is by breaking it down into components that can be explained in simple every day and relatable concepts. Once the audience can grasp the concept of the components, hacking is no longer a dark art or black magic. Rather just a combination of everyday parts that the audience is already familiar with, then all of the technical details become much easier to absorb. Even if the senior executives do not fully understand all of the details, they can at least appreciate the overall concept.

Many people believe cyber criminals are computer geniuses who are 10 feet tall and can hack into your computer as if they are using black magic. People do not typically understand how an attack actually works. I was fortunate to have the opportunity to lead the FBI's cyber operations group for the latter part of my Bureau career, which required the end-to-end life cycle of conducting cyber operations, including the development of components needed to perform such cyber operations. After many years in practicing both the offensive and the defensive art of cyber operations, I can categorically dispel the notion that cyber criminals are smarter than any of us. The fact is that almost all cybercriminals are simply users of hacking tools developed by others, and yes, that included those tools developed by our government that were leaked out to the world by the traitors amongst us. There is no real mystique in that the criminals use those tools just like we use Microsoft Office, but instead of building a spreadsheet or presentation, these criminal hackers use their tools to steal information. In fact, most of the so called cyber criminals are just plain old con-artists. Instead of using the telephones or snail mail, they now use computers and email. There are very few individuals who actually develop the software or discover the vulnerabilities themselves and use them for evil. Most criminals are simply re-purposing existing commercially available software tools and using them for a malicious purpose.

Many cybersecurity professionals often feed into the myth by over exaggerating the theoretical versus the practical reality. Some purposely over complicate the concepts and terminologies, when there are much easier to understand ways of explaining a cyber attack. Drawing on my years of experience in explaining cyber concepts to a wide range of people who do not have a technical background, I will outline the process of cyber attack in the next six sections: Attacker, Victim, Payload, Exploits, Delivery Vectors, and Command and Control in very easy to understand language with simple analogies and dispel all the myth associated with hacking and cybercrimes in general.

COMPONENTS OF CYBER ATTACKS AND THE RELEVANT THREAT INTELLIGENCE

There are six components involved in every cyber attack and every hacking. It doesn't matter whether the perpetrator uses low sophistication techniques to deliver a virus via a thumb drive, or a highly sophisticated nation-state level actor using zero-day exploits to remotely deliver seemingly undetectable payloads that are also known as an advanced prsistent threat (APT). There are always six components involved in any attack. Of course the complexity of each component can vary greatly from one attack to another, and have vastly different outcomes, but once the audience understands how the components work, they will appreciate the differences without being confused by the lingos and technical jargon that are so prevalent in this industry.

Below are the 6 components needed for every cyber attack. Each component will be explained in detail. A discussion of the availability and the utility of cyber intelligence for each component is included. The components are:

1. Attacker
2. Victim
3. Payload
4. Exploit
5. Delivery Vector
6. Command and Control

1. Attacker

Who the attacker is can be either completely irrelevant or can heavily influence the decision making process during a cyber attack. It is all highly dependent upon the specific nature of the attack. For example, in situations such as common business email compromise (BEC) phishing emails or brute force password guessing attacks that are launched by seemingly tens of thousands of anonymous attackers from far-away foreign lands. It makes very little sense to attempt to ascertain who the attackers really are, or to spend time reading up about the latest research on such global criminal enterprise out of Nigeria, Russia, India, China, or the like. In these situations, a defense strategy is best formed based on the techniques and attack vectors, rather than to spend resources on identifying the actual attackers. Identification and prosecution of actual attackers is squarely the responsibility of our federal government. This perspective will certainly trigger the ire of many threat intelligence firms that pride themselves on their ability to penetrate the forums and discussion boards on the dark web and publish their findings on a subscription basis. This writer by no means categorically dismisses such research and reporting as unnecessary, but simply points out that these findings are only useful if the consumer has a specific reason to know the identity of the attacker, or is in a particular situation where such attacker-based threat intelligence can be the most effective use of time and resources.

One situation where knowing who your attackers are can greatly benefit the decision making process is when a company is the victim of a ransomware attack. In these situations, once the victim organization realizes that their business continuity or disaster recovery was ineffective in restoring their now-encrypted systems, the decision makers will need two questions answered immediately in order to determine what the next steps are. Only a competent attacker-based threat intelligence firms can provide the answers. The two questions are:

1) Has the same ransomware "variant" been discovered elsewhere before, has it been analyzed and is a decryption technique available? If Lady Luck favors the organization, professional research companies can quickly provide all the postings by both security firms as well as hacker forums on the methods to decrypt that particular ransomware variant, as most attackers are not capable of developing their own ransomware and are simply downloading the same ones published by others, and only make simple changes as to the ransom payment information and a few logo and file extension changes here and there. All the major components of the ransomware remain the same as the other variants, which has already been fully identified and analyzed by security research and antivirus firms. Although the ransomware and its components may be well researched and analyzed, the simple fact exists that without a decryption key, understanding how it works will do little to help the victim restore the encrypted systems. Even Lady Luck may not be able to overcome the free encryption technology that is widely available today, and there are only limited ways to obtain the decryption key short of getting it from the attackers themselves.

   a. One way is trying to brute-force cracking the encryption algorithm. Unlike what we have seen from Hollywood movies, where this is accomplished in seconds, decrypting modern encryption by brute force is measured in months, years, and decades, and requires supercomputers and technologies that belong only to the Nation States and are highly classified and not available to the public.

b. A second way is to recover the key from the machines that the attacker used to generate the encryption key. We've all seen movies and TV shows where a team of FBI agents in the ever fashionable blue wind breakers walks out of a perpetrator's home with computers in their hands. One of the reasons that this is a standard procedure in all evidence collection is to be able to retrieve the encryption key for the various files and passwords that may be needed later for prosecution. Although this method may appear to be non-relevant in the middle of a ransomware attack crisis, it is actually where properly researched threat intelligence may be of some help, albeit a long shot. As mentioned earlier, most attackers that we face today are not software developers themselves, but rather are common criminals who simply download a ransomware "tool kit" developed by others. If any of the attackers are arrested and have their computers with the decryption key seized, these can be of significant value in the hands of competent security firms who are researching the ransomware and the decryption methods. Again, this is a very long shot, but it has been successful in the past when the seizing agency and security firms disclose and publish their findings, which will then be revealed in the threat intelligence.

2) The second question that the victim often asks in a ransomware situation is whether the victim should pay the ransom. Although many do not advise or support the payment of ransoms for larger societal impact considerations. Companies clearly have an obligation to protect their clients and shareholders' interest as a priority, which makes the immediate resolution of a crisis by paying the ransom a viable option that has to be considered. Especially when the attackers often make the ransom demand fairly inexpensive when compared to the cost of rebuilding an information system or hiring outside consultants, security firms, and counsel.

So the question is not whether the victim should pay the ransom, but whether paying the ransom will actually get the files restored, and in some instances, protect these same files from being released to the public or sold in the underground. This is where proper Threat Intelligence can assist in this critical decision making process, if done in a timely and competent manner.

A proven effective approach has always been to ignore everything said or written by the individual, and focus only on the behavior. There is no better rule to follow than "the best predictor of future behavior is past behavior". Applying this philosophy to buying products online is the equivalent of reading other people's reviews. In the case of ransomware, the same philosophy applies because the likelihood is high that there are others before you who have fallen victim to the same attacker. Researching the attacker's history may reveal the track record of whether paying the ransom will actually lead to successful restoration of the files that were encrypted by the ransomware. At the time of this writing, there is a 50 percent chance of the ransomware attackers actually restoring the encrypted files. So, a one-time purchase of threat intelligence from a company that focuses on ransomware attackers might be worth the investment to assist with the decision-making process during a very difficult time. A longer term managed threat intelligence service may also be useful if your organization has reason to believe that the attacker not only encrypted your files, but also has taken your files, and your organization is weary that such information may be publically posted or put up for sale to other attackers on the dark web.

2. Victim

Every cyber attack has a victim. Not all threat intelligence is necessarily useful or of the same value for everyone. The two most popular types of victim-specific threat intelligence that are available but are generally misunderstood are: a) intelligence about other organizations, and b) intelligence specifically about your organization.

A. Intelligence about other organizations:

Organizations who possess sensitive third-party data, whether they are PCI, PII, PHI, or government data, are usually already heavily regulated for very good reasons, as they are the priority targets for cyber criminals everywhere. Much of the threat intelligence market is catered to feed this group of organizations, as they are the largest consumer of threat intelligence due to their high likelihood to be the victims of cyber attacks. For this group of critical infrastructure and regulated industries, the concern is not the lack of threat intelligence, but rather the over saturation of intelligence that leads to apathy and desensitization, which results in inaction and complacency.

For such organization, the decision makers should make a clear distinction between informational threat intelligence and actionable threat intelligence. Because threat intelligence can be a very profitable business, and as with all marketable products, quantity often supersedes quality. Unless an organization has an over-abundance of in-house intelligence analysts, priority should be given to that threat intelligence that contain specific actionable items such as what hardware or software needs to be patched, updated, blocked, etc., rather than devoting time to intelligence sources.

There are also organizations that are not necessarily in the critical infrastructure or regulated industries, but are in industries that provide high profile or politically contentious products or services, or are undergoing certain business processes such as mergers and acquisition, or may have a foreign presence in countries that causes negative sentiments domestically or abroad. In these cases, organizations may need to pay for threat intelligence specifically addressing the issues or countries they operate in. As many ideology driven cyber attacks are widely discussed in social media and the dark web prior to the actual attack, such threat intelligence may be of great value to companies that are the focus of such groups, and a subscription based threat intelligence may be a wise investment for these companies.

B. Intelligence specifically about your organization:

Every organization should invest in their social media and internet presence. This is an area that is often discussed, but rarely acted upon by organizations. Most decision makers do not realize the extent of research that attackers will perform prior to their target selection and attack formulation. Nor do most decision makers understand how much information is available on the internet as a result of years of cumulative publication by and about their employees, vendors, clients, press, regulatory agencies, equipment manufactures, and countless other sources.

Using social engineering attacks as an example. In order for attackers to compose a realistic communication to you, they need real names, job titles, relationships, interests, personal activities, and any other information of a personal nature so you will move toward the next step. One of the most commonly held misconceptions is that the attackers have to start from scratch and research everything about an individual. Although that may be true in some cases, most social engineering attacks don't require that much effort. So much information is available from previously compromised accounts of someone in your organization or a business partner. Imagine how easy it is to craft an extremely believable email to your Account Payable personnel if you have full access to your CFO's email account and can read everything. This is precisely how social engineering attacks become so prevalent and successful, because all it takes is one email account to be compromised. Everyone that person ever dealt with both within the same organization and everyone outside the organization that individual had ever had contact with is now a target of the next wave of attack.

Another commonly held misconception is that emails are the only source where social engineering attacks occur. That may be true in terms of volume, as it is the most cost effective method for less sophisticated attackers who do not have the time and resources to conduct social engineering attacks via other platforms, but for targeted spear-phishing or whale-phishing by more sophisticated attackers, email is just one of the many tools used. Much of their time and effort is expended on researching and interacting with the victim or people who are a degree or two removed from the victim. The sophisticated social engineering attacks will craft the attack from a combination of emails, websites, social media platforms, and even old fashioned telephone calls to lure their victim to provide that highly sought after user credentials. The more sophisticated attacker will take a multi-stage approach. Stage 1 may be as simple as an attacker finding out the target's social and professional affiliations, and sending an email to introduce themselves as an individual or an organization that the target is a member of, such as golf club member, or an organizer of an event that you have attended in the past. Only after you reply will they send additional emails likely containing links to other websites. How many of you would decline to click on a link to register for upcoming events that you are invited to attend, when you have attended similar events in the past?

In addition to social engineering, there are also attackers who choose to perform technical attacks without any human interaction. This type of attack relies mostly on using stolen and published user credentials and performing technical scans for vulnerabilities and brute force password guessing, which will be discussed more in the "Command and Control" section below. Because this type of attack often also involves open source research to collect as much information about your network and systems as possible, just as the social engineering type of attacks, these victim-specific vulnerabilities can be discovered with the appropriate threat intelligence.

There are two relatively effective methods of obtaining this type of organization-specific threat intelligence: a) open source intelligence subscription and b) social engineering attack exercise.

Open source intelligence analysis is a threat intelligence service that monitors the social media, dark web, internet, and other publically available sources of information for any posting of information that may be used to mount an attack based on all the information that is available. Since most organizations do not fully appreciate the sheer volume of years of cumulative publications out there by hundreds if not thousands of their employees, vendors, customers, regulatory agencies, marketing, press coverage, conferences and presentations, and not to mention information released as the result of a breach by their third party vendors, we strongly recommend every organization invests into at least a one-time open-source threat analysis to determine how much information that is publicly available that shouldn't be. This recommendation is even more acute for organizations that are part of the critical infrastructure and regulated industries, as well as those engaging in high value or high risk businesses practices such as mergers and acquisitions or politically sensitive activities.

Social engineering attack exercises are another method of finding what attackers can gather from open source research to formulate an attack against an organization. Unlike the aforementioned open source intelligence analysis, which focuses on "potential" vulnerabilities and attack vectors, a full scale social engineering attack exercise takes it one step closer and will involve an actual attack using all available open source information against all systems on the organization's network.

This type of attack exercise should not be confused with a red team or blue team-type exercise, where the scope and participants are generally fully identified and are often focused on specific systems using traditional, technical exploitation techniques. Although any exercise is better than none at all, such red team/blue team-type exercises are generally designed to test the functionalities of the defense of the organizations' hardware and software. They are not meant, or able, to provide intelligence on the comprehensive state of the organization's vulnerabilities from an attacker's perspective.

The same is true for the ever popular phishing campaign exercises, where an organization generates phishing emails to its own employees in an effort to identify those who will click on the messages. Although this is a very effective training and awareness exercise that keeps employees vigilant on the topic of email threats, it does not identify the true extent of what an attacker would do in a more sophisticated multi-phased social engineering attack that can include any and all methods of communication that are far above and beyond just emails. Even when some vendors provide more sophisticated social engineering exercises, phishing campaign exercises generally do not follow up with using the information gathered to mount an attack on the organization's systems. These types of phishing exercises are good for companies to use as a first time test for baseline purpose, but they lose effectiveness quickly and do not test the overall organizational vulnerability to social engineering.

A true social engineering attack exercise is conducted less frequently because it is often much more expensive and the campaign can last six months or longer to be effective. It is significantly more complex, sophisticated, and effective when compared to traditional red team/blue team and phishing exercises because it is not limited by artificial scopes and boundaries, and is designed to overcome the more experienced and security aware employees, just as a real attacker would.

Most companies perform the low cost phishing test that is a one-dimensional pre-built software-based distribution, meaning that emails will be sent across the organization, and whether people fall for the email or not are based solely on the content of the email. Some tests are better crafted than others, but most still rely on software-generated emails. Many such "tests" also require internal IT assistance to avoid being identified and quarantined as junk mail before ever reaching the employees. This is because in order for a truly convincing phishing email capable of bypassing the email filters would require a delivery infrastructure (discussed below) that would quickly add to the cost.

A true social engineering attack exercise, on the other hand, is multi-dimensional and custom crafted against specific individuals. Such an exercise does not need IT assistance, in fact, the IT team's reaction should be part of the test so the second wave and third waves of attacks will adapt to the IT team's defense, just as real attackers would do. Furthermore, the emails are custom built to each targeted individual. What is sent to the CFO will be different than what is sent to the IT system adminstator or to accounts payable, just as real attackers would do in real life. For this reason, a full-scope social engineering attack exercise devotes the first month to researching the internet, social media, any public source information, and starting to build profiles against the employees, the infrastructure and the organization's defense, and then devotes another month or so to purchasing and building email domains that match the attack vector, just as real attackers would when they send those convincingly realistic emails with an address that's visually indistinguishable from the real email address. The social engineering attack exercise would then build relationships with the employees first, via social media such as LinkedIn or Facebook, or maybe a non-email based charity drive, a conference invitation, industry meeting websites, etc., using all the approaches that a real sophisticated attacker would use to lead the employee from one stage to the next, and eventually obtain the credentials from the employee. The final stage of the exercise is then to use all the captured employees' credentials to attempt to access all the systems on the organization's network to see how far and how much those credential would get.

The results yielded in the aforementioned social engineering attack exercise are among the most valuable threat intelligence any organization can obtain, as they provide a picture of how one system in the organization can affect the other and to what degree. To believe that red team/blue team and phishing campaign exercises alone will generate the same intelligence on the organization's overall vulnerability is a misconception that is held all too often by the decision makers, and fosters a false sense of security. If an organization can only afford to pay for two sources of threat intelligence, the social engineering attack exercise should be one of them. The second will be discussed in the command and control section.

3. Payload

Payload is a general umbrella term that covers all software, also known as codes, which instruct the computer to perform specific functions after it is delivered onto the system. The word "payload" sounds more ominous than it really is. Our computers receive payloads on a daily basis, if not every minute when surfing the internet. A payload can be something as innocuous as a cookie, or an attachment to an email, an app that you just download for a specific function such as weather, or a full-blown software program you just purchased that contain multiple payloads due to the complexity of the software program, such as Microsoft Office.

A common example would be when you visit a website, the website leaves a "cookie" behind. The cookie is a payload to collect your basic machine information and send that information back to the company that makes money by tracking and profiting from that information. It is a way of life and nobody thinks anything of it. Some cookies even offer to save your userid and password by capturing the keystrokes as you are logging into your account at those web sites, and many users gladly agree to it because users enjoy the convenience and entrust the website's security to protect their information. All of this occurs every second on the internet where payloads in the form of cookies and apps and software programs are dropped on computers everywhere in the world. Now, let's change just the player in the same scenario. Instead of a legitimate website that is dropping the cookie, imagine it is now the attacker who is using the same technology, but with a malicious intent and motivation. You somehow went to a website that was operated or infected by the attacker, and entered your userid and password just as you would in your other websites, but now that very same cookie "payload" using the same keystroke capturing function, is now a "malware" and a "key logger."

In the world of cybersecurity, two different terminologies are developed to describe the exact same function, but which terminology to be assigned is based on the intent behind that function. When a payload is used for the intended purpose of good, it's called "software" or "app" or "cookie" or "extension," and the like. But when it is used for bad things by criminals, it is then called "virus," "malware," "ransomware," or "key logger," which strikes fear and trepidation among the readers. But as you well know, there is no black magic, no superhuman intellect, but rather a simple re-purposing of an existing everyday technology used by every website, and the criminals and con-artists are just using them for criminal purpose.

The astute reader will quickly ask "why don't you just avoid going to those websites so no bad payload can be delivered onto your computer and capture your credentials?" This is a valid question indeed, as most malicious payloads only work if the victim make multiple mistakes that bypass layers of security controls in order for the attack to succeed, which is exactly why the attackers and con artists spend most of their effort trying to lure victims into those websites with phishing emails and social engineering scams, and why having the right threat intelligence on those efforts might be more important than the threat intelligence on the payloads themselves, which will be covered in the command and control section below.

The idea of paying less attention to threat intelligence on payloads may not be welcomed by many in the cybersecurity profession on first glance, as payload threat intelligence is the mainstay of antivirus and antimalware companies, whose primary duty is to detect payloads that are suspicious or malicious. This is generally done by performing code signing certificate checks, signature analysis and heuristics analysis. Payloads with the appropriate code signing certificates from known and vetted certificate authority will be allowed onto a user's systems by the antivirus program without any additional pop-up warnings. However, those without the proper certificates will be flagged by the antivirus program, which will then go through a series of signature and heuristics analyses to determine if the payload may be dangerous.

Decision makers should not spend additional resources on payload threat intelligence, because it is not important. Rather, this component of attack is so important, the antivirus industry is already dedicating tremendous expertise in such matters and are continuously updating the antivirus service in order to detect and stop the malicious payload from executing on computers. There simply is not much an organization can do or needs to do with threat intelligence on all the new payloads and variants that have spawned in the wild. By the time the organizations receive such intelligence, the antivirus software will most likely have already incorporated the same finding into their definition base. Thus, the simple act of running a full antivirus scan with the latest definitions is the best method of utilizing this type of threat intelligence. As opposed to having the already over-burdened IT staff manually perform such tasks.

Another reason why the philosophy that payload threat intelligence should not be a priority for organizations to receive or subscribe to is because payload threat intelligence is different than threat intelligence on other components of cyber attacks. In the payload threat intelligence, the provider-consumer relationship is inversed. Organizations and end-users are actually providing payload threat intelligence to the antivirus companies and not the other way around. Antivirus software build their library of codes and definitions by uploading a variety of data from all of their customers' computers. Every "payload" that is attempting to execute on an organization's computers is uploaded to your antivirus provider's analytic engine in the cloud. The antivirus provider is also collecting the same information from the rest of their customer base, and may be even share their findings and libraries among their partnerships with other antivirus and security companies.

This ability to bulk-collect data from machines is what makes antivirus effective, as it can detect an anomaly on one machine based on data analysis collected from other machines throughout the world. But this ability to continuously obtain data from behind-the-scene on so many organizations at the same time is also very alarming and potentially dangerous. Many readers may recall recent warnings from the U.S. government to advise companies not to use Kaspersky antivirus software, which is a Russian-owned company, as the government suspected that all the "threat intelligence" taken from the users' computers may be for Russian intelligence gathering rather than just to examine malicious codes.

In today's geo-political atmosphere, one can never be certain what are facts and what is hyperbole and rhetoric. The selection of the organization's antivirus service is one of the most critical choices that a company has to make, as the is basically the "ultimate payload" on all computers at the same time. It has full access to extract and install anything and everything it wants to on machines without any checks or balances. In the world of cyber attacks, payload is a forever game of cat and mouse between the attacker and the security industry, with the interesting twist that not all vendors in the security industry can be trusted.

It is a complex technical, political, and financial equation for the decision maker to choose the right antivirus software, as this antivirus is the absolute last line of defense on your systems. Once the codes get past the antivirus, the attackers have succeeded in establishing a connection between them and your computer. Due to the gravity and importance of this line of defense, organizations should procure redundant antivirus/antimalware services if they can afford it, and add additional lines of defense before the payload can even be delivered. For those organizations who are limited in their resources, we recommend supplementing antivirus software with threat intelligence on command and control component to be discussed below.

4. Exploit

Exploits is a word that strikes fear into many IT professionals and decision makers, and is a term filled with mythology and intrigue, while at the same time being used freely by cybersecurity vendors and researchers as the main tool to proffer their wares. In reality, an exploit is simply a method or technique that can bypass security features so a computer will allow you to do the things you want it to do, but not what it was originally instructed to do. The security gap that allows software, or to a lesser degree, firmware and hardware to be exploited is referred to as a "vulnerability," whereas the technique to take advantage of such vulnerability is called an "exploit." The term "zero-day exploit," despite its ominous sounding name, simply refers to the fact that the vulnerability has not been patched by the software vendor, thus the vendor knew about the vulnerability for zero number of days. The sad reality is that in recent history, most cyber attacks were successful because they exploited vulnerabilities that had been previously discovered, and patches that had been made available for months if not years were not applied. The organizations fell victim not to super villains or advanced technology, but simply to poor update and patch management that can be quickly mitigated by adopting industry standard patch management policies and procedures.

Many people wonder why there are so many vulnerabilities out there, to the point that "patch Tuesday," once a common joke among IT professionals in the 2000's has now escalated to "patch everyday." For example, a Windows operating system has approximately 50 million or more of lines of instruction/code just by itself. Now picture that every single line of code has to work seamlessly with the Office suite's additional 60 million lines of code, and then still work with Google's astounding 2 billion lines of code, not to mention all the other software and applications. The chances of a vulnerability that exists somewhere in any of the software, or in the interaction among the software, is much more likely than one might imagine, not to mention every update and new release by any one of the numerous software vendors will produce new vulnerabilities and start the whole cycle all over again. It is not surprising that there are vulnerabilities, after all, those billions of lines of codes are written by tens of thousands of human beings who are working independently of each other across a long period of time. The wonder is not whether there are vulnerabilities, but rather that any of the software worked at all, which is evident in that it took almost two decades for the Windows operating system to shed the "blue screen of death" reputation.

Because vulnerabilities are accepted as an unavoidable inherent risk by all software developers, major companies such as Microsoft, Google, and Apple hire multitudes of researchers and testers who do absolutely nothing except to find vulnerabilities in their own products as well as interaction with other products, so they can be the first to discover them and prevent exploitation. However, there are as many, if not more, hackers out there, who are doing exactly the opposite, which is to find that vulnerability before the vendors can patch them. This is yet another cat and mouse game that goes on forever which also explains why every software and application are constantly updating, in a race against time between the good guys and the bad guys.

However, the good guy versus bad guy distinction is often blurred in the world of exploit research. The term "zero day exploit" is often used in many conferences and threat intelligence forums, because the term brings attention, publicity and accolades if one is the first to discover or announce the discovery of a new vulnerability. It is almost a competitive sport, with monetary rewards and financial gains rival that of professional sports. Major companies have been known to offer bounty and rewards for zero days that are in the millions of dollars, as that is a small price to pay for closing the vulnerability that can cost them much more in the long run if those vulnerabilities fall into the hands of criminals. This approach only drives the exploit research into a feverish frenzy that on any given day, anyone can download a full catalog of vulnerabilities and even the exploits themselves on the internet, as researchers are only too eager to publish everything they discover, and the cybercriminals quietly sit back and enjoy the loot. So again, it is not the cyber criminals who have the superior intellect or resources to discover the exploits, but the security industry's indiscretion in publicizing everything for the sake of publicity and market share.

What's more, in the world of exploitation, a cottage industry has emerged: blackmailers disguised as security researchers. These alleged "security researchers" basically discovered that it is too difficult to discover true zero day exploits and earn the reward money, but it is much easier to use known, existing exploits against organizations that have not patched their systems yet. Further, if they successfully exploit an organization's vulnerability, they can then demand the organization to pay for their "research" or otherwise the organization's vulnerability and content of the lost data will be published on the internet. The difference between this type of "research-extortion" and a traditional cybercriminal is really only semantics, and we can confidently predict that this issue will be more commonplace in a few more years. Perhaps legislation will follow to curb these type of research-extortionist as long as the victim organizations are willing to inform law enforcement and their legislature.

Just as with payload threat intelligence, we do not see a tremendous benefit or value proposition for organizations and decision makers to spend valuable resources on subscribing to or processing exploit-based threat intelligence. This is well within the responsibility and expertise of the manufactures and vendors of the hardware and software, and it is already part of their service and use agreement. There is very little that end users can or need to do in combating this particular component of a cyber attack, other than unfailingly adhering to the update and patch release by their hardware and software vendors. The old school of thought from the early 2000's of waiting for 3-6 months for every update and patch before deployment is no longer applicable in today's cyber threat environment. The rationale for waiting is because the new patches and releases are unstable and untested, and can cause crashes until thoroughly tested by the organization prior to full enterprise roll out. However, the threat landscape has changed significantly in the past few years, and criminals are exploiting not just the vulnerabilities themselves, but the fact that organizations are not patching or shutting down the vulnerabilities that are already well known. This was made abundantly evident in the Petya ransomware attack that took down many major organizations even with their significant IT and cybersecurity resources, as well as smaller organizations that continue to fall victim to ransomware payloads dropped via exploiting the long publicized remote desktop protocol (RDP) vulnerability.

After the rather lengthy explanation of the dangers of vulnerabilities described above, we will conclude this section by advising the readers and decision makers not to fall victim to the all-too-common "sky is falling" rhetoric in the cybersecurity industry, which is that there are vulnerabilities everywhere and that we are all doomed to be exploited at any given moment. Although it may be true that vulnerabilities are relatively pervasive and readily discoverable, there is a very lengthy, difficult and expensive research and development cycle in between before a vulnerability can be turned into a truly usable exploit. To put it simply, there may be hundreds or thousands of vulnerabilities, but only a few are exploitable, and even less can be exploited to the point that a payload can be successfully deployed remotely onto a system without triggering at least one or more security controls. In fact, we can confidently say that given the current state of software security and other security controls, there is not one exploit in existence that can complete the full end-to-end remote delivery of a payload without being detected or stopped, and that this can only be done by chaining together a combination of exploits, which requires the intended target system to possess all the vulnerabilities that each one of the exploit chain is designed to take advantage of simultaneously. It is because of this extremely technically challenging feat, true remote cyber attacks without any social engineering are still a rare phenomenon and generally reserved for the nation state or the very dedicated and well-resourced adversary, while phishing and other social engineering efforts are still the most prevalent attack vector, as humans are clearly still the most vulnerable and the weakest link in the chain to exploit without the need for technical sophistication. With this knowledge, shouldn't organizations and decision makers allocate their threat intelligence resources accordingly?

5. Delivery Vector

The delivery vector is the simplest, yet most confusing component of a cyber attack to explain. The old proverb that "there's more than one way to skin a cat" may be the root of the confusion, as there are multiple ways to get the exploit or payload onto a system, but the final selection would depend greatly on the other components of the attack described previously, which are the attacker-victim relationship, the nature of the payload and the availability of the exploits. In its simplest form, a delivery vector is how the attacker chooses to send the exploit and/or payload onto the victim's system. In this section, we will explain the various delivery vectors, which sometimes are referred to as attack vectors, with the hope that the readers can then see why certain vectors are more widely used while others remain the topic of debate at various security conferences. Since we have already covered the topic of attacker, victim, payload and exploit, it is important to remind our readers that as we are discussing the delivery vector, it is just another one of the six components needed in the equation. Any vulnerability in the delivery vector by itself does not necessarily mean that an exploit or payload can be successfully executed.

Generally, the difference in types of delivery vectors is based on the distance between the attacker and the victim, because the distance equates to the technology involved, the underlying attacker-victim relationship, as well as the risk-benefit ratio posed to the attacker. In most instances, the closer the distance the attacker is to the victim when delivering a payload, the closer their relationship is in some way, shape or form, resulting in a higher risk of exposure and capture of the attacker. Hence, it is unlikely that a close prox-imity delivery vector will be used against most organizations, except those specifically targeted by an attacker who is focused strictly on that particular organization or its key employees. The farther away the attacker is, the more the attacker can be anonymous and indiscriminant about the targets, while using techniques that can encompass a much larger victim base, and poses almost no risk of being caught, especially if they reside outside of the US. Below are the most commonly discussed delivery vectors, although not all are commonly used:

A. No Distance: Physical Access
B. Short Distance: Radio-Based - Wifi/Cellular/Bluetooth
C. Long Distance: Internet-based - Websites, RDP, etc.

A. No Distance: Physical Access

Let's start with the simplest delivery vector which is the hands-on physical access. This is still the most effective delivery vector if the attacker has access either to the victim's physical location, or can somehow use social engineering to lure the victim to install the software for them via a CD or thumb drive. This delivery vector, although infrequently encountered in the commercial world, still requires close protection by organizations because this delivery vector can often eliminate the need for exploits, or at least reduce the number of exploits needed for the payload to be installed, because most security controls presume that the person having physical access to the computer has more privilege than those who are trying to do it remotely, and therefore allows the individual with physical access to perform more functions and tasks.

This attack vector is usually seen when an organization or individuals within the organization are specifically targeted for the attack, and the attacker is often the employees from within, as they tend to rely on their physical access to deliver harm to the organization. However, this delivery vector can also be used by attackers from outside of the organization via social engineering efforts, such as providing an infected CD or thumb drive to be viewed on the organization's computer. For organizations and employees who are in the critical infrastructure or highly regulated industries, or have access to intellectual property or knowledge of financially sensitive or politically charged business operations, this attack vector should be of higher concern than those organizations who do not engage in such businesses. Foreign travel increases the risks even more as travelers often leave their computers and/or their removable media unattended, and therefore, open for physical access opportunities.

The reader needs to keep in mind that this is not a frequently used attack vector because of the trail it leaves behind places the attacker in a much greater risk of discovery, a risk that generally only the attacker who is dedicated to targeting the specific organization is willing to take. The threat intelligence obtained on the previously discussed "attacker" and "victim" components should be a good indication of whether the organization should take additional steps to further protect against this type of delivery vector. But as a general rule, time-triggered password lock, removal of administrative privilege, and the disabling of external ports can quickly remediate all but the most sophisticated physical access attack attempts.

B. Short Distance: Radio-Based - WiFi/Bluetooth/Cellular

WiFi vulnerability has long been a topic of vigorous discussions. It is certainly true that if an attacker is on the organization's wireless network, the attacker can open up the threat of capturing the user credentials stored on the systems, thus creating opportunity for the delivery of payloads onto devices connected to the network. However, if the concern is an attack against your organization or your home WiFi network, this risk is more an exaggeration than reality. The reason is that just as with aforementioned Physical Access delivery vector, using WiFi as a delivery vector requires the attacker to be within a few hundred feet of distance from their targets, which is not an attractive or viable option to most cyber criminals because it requires them to be in the same location as their targets, thus taking a significant risk of being in the public with very incriminating WiFi hacking equipment in their hands. In the end, this delivery vector is generally not worth the risk and effort that is required for an attacker.

However, if the victim or the organization falls into the aforementioned special status where the payoff is deemed to be worth the risk and effort for the attacker to come into within a few hundred of the organization or the key employees of the organization, then the risk extends to the key employees' home WiFi as much as their work WiFi. If the organization has reason to believe that their communication is at risk, they should procure the services of specialists to monitor all the WiFi and network traffic for signs of attack, which will be discussed in the command and control section. At a minimum, those high risk organizations and employees should exercise an elevated security posture by changing their passwords, updating the firmware of their Wifi access point and patch their computer hardware and software unfailingly, just as described in the Exploit section previously.

There is another more concerning type of WiFi danger, which is characterized by an attacker remotely hacking into a WiFi access point from an unsuspecting business such as a hotel or a restaurant, and the attacker is then remotely controlling the access point. This is a legitimate concern but still a very low probability event in the US, because the effort involved in hacking into a wireless access point does not quite justify the limited number of potential targets it yields, as not all users who are connected to the infected access point are exploitable, because some will have fully updated hardware and software, while others have just enough security control to prevent a successful payload execution (see previous sections on this topic), which leaves only a fraction of vulnerable targets that may or may not even connect to the access point long enough for a successful exploitation and payload delivery. Therefore, it makes very unconvincing financial motivation for cyber criminals to use this delivery vector to conduct their attacks. However, the risk-benefit analysis changes if the victim falls into the aforementioned special status, and the risk became significantly higher if foreign travel is involved, since many foreign WiFi access points have questionable security controls and may be operated by people who harbor ulterior motives.

Bluetooth as a delivery vector is fraught with even more complications and risks for the attacker than WiFi, as Bluetooth suffers several additional burdens to make this a non-viable delivery vector. First, Bluetooth has a much shorter range than WiFi, which necessitates the attacker to be within visual distance of the victim, making this a very unattractive delivery option for most criminals. Second, Bluetooth is a personal communication protocol that is connected to multiple devices but generally accessed by only one individual, which make the potential pool of victims very small for the effort. Third, since this is not a readily viable delivery method, very little vulnerability research is conducted versus other delivery vectors, thus making exploits very difficult for the attackers to obtain, if any is available at all. Lastly, most of the information Bluetooth communication transmits is not readily profitable for the attacker, as Bluetooth is generally used for entertainment and voice conversations, with only a relatively few devices are used for data transmission such as keyboards and mice. Although there is no question a keylogger payload successfully deployed by the attacker would yield a significant bounty, the likelihood of success is so low that outside of research, there are no known compromises as the result of payload delivery via Bluetooth.

Using Bluetooth as a delivery vector to drop a payload onto smart phones is the Holy Grail, as having command and control over the target's phone is the ultimate prize to many hackers. Some went as far as attempting to exploit an automobile's Bluetooth system first as a gateway onto the phone, which complicates the exploitation effort exponentially as the attacker must now defeat the vehicle's security system first. As interesting and ominous this may sound, not only the complexity in itself makes this an unlikely attack vector by cybercriminals, most readers probably do not fully appreciate the fact that cell phones are one of the most difficult devices to exploit. So much so, that the FBI had to sue Apple so that it didn't have to exploit in order to unlock the iPhone used by the 2015 San Bernardino terrorist, Syed Farook. Although the FBI eventually found an exploit and succeed in unlocking the phone, it stands testament to the fact that smartphone are extremely secure against exploitation, and the ability to deliver a payload onto a cell phone via

Bluetooth or any aforementioned delivery vector, is well beyond the reach and capability of all but the most well resources nation states.

The same is true but to an even greater degree of difficulty for other radio-based delivery vectors such as near-field communication (NFC), where the distance is shrunk to inches, thus render it non-viable as a delivery vector to all but the most unusual circumstances.

Cellular hacking is also a hot topic in security conferences, and there are often demonstrations of security experts sending a SMS messaging to deliver a payload. Although theoretically accurate and technologically feasible, this delivery vector is very difficult if not impossible to carry out, especially in the US where different cellular technology are used, and access into the baseband radio is tightly controlled by manufactures and carriers so that only a few vendors can actually access that layer of technology. Additionally, the baseband operating system source codes are highly guarded intellectual properties that are off limits and non-accessible to anyone but the manufacturer and select few vendors, thus making vulnerability research and exploitation practically non-existent except in the government or government sponsored research. Without exploits to the baseband radio, true remote delivery via the cellular network is a thing that only exist in a hacker's wish list or in the deepest vaults within the most secretive of agencies.

Some readers might ask "what about the demo where a payload was delivered remotely to a phone?" In those demos, what the readers saw was not remote delivery using the real cellular network, but rather remote delivery using a decoy network by means of a cell site simulators. A cell site simulator tricks one's cell phone into disconnecting from the legitimate cell towers of Verizon and AT&T and connect to the fake one by emitting signals that are stronger than the cell tower, thus exploiting the default setting of most phones to automatically connect to the strongest signal. However, there are significant issues with using this technology as a viable delivery vector for cyber criminals. First, just as with all other radio-based delivery vector described previously, a cell site simulator needs to be in a fairly close proximity to the intended target in order to generate a signal that is significantly stronger than those emitted by the cell towers. Second, it requires carrying around a fairly bulky and heavy transmitter that is clearly a piece of hacking equipment. The stronger the signal, the bigger and more costly the equipment needs to be, which is a proposition and investment that is generally not embraced by most cyber criminals. Third, as U.S. cellular technology moves toward 4G and even 5G, even if the cell site simulator can continue to trick phones into connecting to it, all the other vulnerabilities required to deliver malwares are closed to all but the most well-resources nation states. Taking all points into consideration, cellular as delivery vector is a fun show-and-tell at security conferences and corporate demonstrations, but it is hardly the delivery vector that organizations and decision makers need to be concerned about as a priority.

Just as with the physical access attack vector, radio based delivery vector via WiFi, cellular, Bluetooth and the like, although frequently talked about in conferences and presentations, is not a realistic delivery vector for most cyber criminals. However, for victims who fall into the special categories as discussed previously where they would attract specific attention by sophisticated and well-resourced attackers, especially during foreign travel, radio based delivery vector remains a legitimate concern to be guarded against, which a U.S. provisioned cellular-based MiFi or hotspot with a strong password should mitigate almost all concerns against this particular delivery vector.

C. Long Distance: Internet-based - Websites, RDP, etc.

There really is only one delivery vector that poses a real and imminent threat to modern organizations, and that is the internet based delivery vector. Internet based delivery vector affords the attackers the ability to maintain anonymity while targeting a large pool of potential targets, using an abundance of exploits and payloads developed over the years against the browsers, plug-ins, mail systems, remote connection protocols, plus a host of vulnerabilities discovered in various internet-facing hardware and software systems. Internet is the most cost effective delivery vector, hence the reason why they are the most widely used attacks that organizations face.

This should be of no surprise to any reader as most have already experienced attacks or attempted attacks using this delivery vector to drop an exploit or payload onto their system. To illustrate how pervasively this attack vector is being used, all one needs to do is check his or her antivirus software's logs to see how many codes were delivered and captured by the antivirus. This delivery vector is extremely versatile for an attacker. It can be used to send emails with a malicious attachments (payloads), or use website advertising (Iframe) to deliver a malware payload, or to exploit a browser or plugin vulnerability to conduct a DNS re-direct and harvest the victim's user credentials. This delivery vector can even be used to conduct brute force password guessing to enter your internet facing systems such as the web server, or exploit the remote desktop connection and deliver a malicious payload. The possibilities seem endless and are only limited by the attacker's imagination and resources.

Luckily for most organizations, the responsibility to protect against attacks via this delivery vector is generally picked up by the software and equipment vendors that allow the organization to connect to the internet. For example,

Google is responsible for patching all the vulnerabilities in their browser, Adobe is responsible for patching their Flash vulnerabilities, Microsoft is responsible for patching their remote desktop protocols, while email providers are responsible for filtering out malicious attachments before they reach your inbox, and antivirus companies are responsible for making sure no malicious payload or exploits can be executed on a machine. The only responsibility that is left to completely protect against this particular attack vector is for organizations to follow and adhere to the manufactures and vendors patch recommendations, and ensure that their employees do not negligently bypass all the security controls and allow the attackers into the organization via social engineering, which is something no manufacture can patch. To help organization to protect against their worst enemy – themselves, in the form of careless or negligent employees exploited by social engineering, there is help available via advanced analytics threat intelligence, which is discussed below in command and control.

6. Command and Control

As the old saying goes, the best is saved for last. The command and control component of any cyber attack is usually the most misunderstood and overlooked aspect in cybersecurity. The concept of command and control is quite straight forward: if someone wants to do something to your computer, there has to be a network connection from the attacker to the victim during all the aforementioned stages of exploitation, payload delivery, data exfiltration or any other payload objectives, where the attacker can perform all the functions that he or she sets out to accomplish, hence, commanding and controlling the various components and stages of the attack. The problem for the attacker is that all internet traffic can be logged and analyzed for such connections, and if the target knows where and what to look for, the attacker's trail can be detected long before the attack becomes successful.

After nearly a decade of conducting cyber operation on behalf of the FBI, the command and control component was the only thing that kept this writer up at night whenever a cyber operation was being conducted. This is the one component that is completely out of our control, and this connection to the target's network is the only thing that can be detected by our adversaries if they perform network monitoring and traffic analysis. Although there are ways to disguise, misattribute, or otherwise hide among an ocean of network traffic, there is simply no way for anyone to remotely connect to a computer without having an internet connection and leaving a trail behind.

We are confident in advising all organizations and decision makers that if they have to prioritize, or have only enough resources to focus on just one thread of threat intelligence, we absolutely recommend that they focus on collecting and analyzing the command and control intelligence of their own network.

Some might say that the command and control trail can be obfuscated so that so that the attacker's true IP address is non-traceable, or attributed to somewhere or someone else by using a VPN or TOR and the likes, when conducting their attacks. However, although the attacker's true identity may not be discovered through the obfuscation of the command and control connection, the fact that there is such command and control connection is the most valuable intelligence an organization can have, because the fact that such connection is there basically just announced to the organization's security that someone who is hiding their identity is trying to get on their network and actions need to be taken immediately to either verify or block the connection.

It is true that highly sophisticated and well-resourced adversary can mask their command and control connections by using real physical IP addresses, and for even more advanced attackers, the physical IP will be geographically consistent to their target's area of operation, so their connection would appear even more legitimate and cannot be blocked geographically. However, in order to pull off such feat, a huge amount of financial and personnel resources will be needed, as it would require physical access to real estate, circuits and equipment, all of which would require personal identification, credit history, and layers of security vetting by the vendors. Therefore, although not impossible, this level of sophistication has not been observed in the cyber criminals' realm, it is more of a tradecraft that can only be pulled off by attackers that possess nation-state level of resources and control, which makes it unlikely to be of a real concern to the majority of our non-critical infrastructure clientele.

Command and control behavior can be detected by experienced analysts with the proper software that can ingest large quantities of data, and perform multiple layers of cross correlational analysis. This analysis can be performed in both the email systems as well as all internet connected systems by analyzing the traffic pattern of all connection attempts to the organization. Below are some of the favorite tell-tale attacker command and control behaviors:
1. Login or attempts from machines inconsistent with home or work machines
2. Login or attempts from IPs inconsistent home or work networks
3. Simultaneous logins / impossible logins
4. Rotation of logins
5. Logins from VPN
6. Logins from high risk geo / IP / domain /provider

7. Logins made with scripting (automated access) to the account
8. Logins with invalid user-agent
9. Use of open source email platform on top of existing email platform
10. Login using machines with time zone / language pack inconsistent with valid user

Organizations should acquire threat intelligence on any and all command and control connections to the organization's domains, with particular attention to email and web-facing systems. The most common attack vectors are internet-based, with email being used the most, to re-direct victims to credential harvesting websites and payment redirect scams; while other network systems are most susceptible to brute-force password guess attacks. All of which can be detected by monitoring and analyzing traffic patterns.

If an organization receives payment redirect emails or links to visit malicious sites with real employee names and real company names that the organization has relationships with, but the email addresses are look-alikes, aka spoofed addresses, then this is a sign that the organization is actively being targeted and the attacker is researching and studying the organization, but likely has not yet successfully compromised any email accounts. However, if an organization receives payment redirect emails or links to visit malicious sites from authentic internal email addresses, this is a sure indicator that the sender's email account is already compromised by the attacker.

Both of the above command and control behavior examples can be detected by analyzing the organization's email traffic for the aforementioned tell-tale command and control behaviors. If the organization monitors for such internally generated threat intelligence, a compromised account will likely be detected while still in the attempt stage. Of course many email credentials are actually lost at credential harvesting websites, and other systems on the network are also constantly under attack attempts, all of which can also be detected and prevented if network and web traffic monitoring is in place and analyzed by competent individuals.

This type of threat intelligence is the most cost effective and relevant threat intelligence that any organization can acquire for the following reasons: First, this type of intelligence is specifically addressing the vulnerabilities of the organization's network in real time. It is only about the organization and not generalized intelligence that covers the industry or the entire world. Second, this intelligence already belongs to the organization, so no purchase is necessary other than to hire qualified service to analyze them. Third and most importantly, command and control threat intelligence is real time and real world, not theoretical or academic. It is the only component in all cyber attacks that no attacker can hide or overcome, so if command and control behavior is detected, there is an ongoing attack or attempt against the organization, which makes this threat intelligence the most valuable intelligence of them all. After all, isn't the whole point of threat intelligence is to help organizations identify threats they need to protect against? What could be more pertinent and effective than internally generated threat intelligence about specific attacks happening on the organization?

There is one caution with regard to the procurement of such command and control threat intelligence, which is that many security vendors claim their products "can" do such analysis, while other providers proclaim that their service "includes" such analysis. The reality is that almost none of them actually do what has been described above as a comprehensive attack detection service. There are those who sell analytical software but expect the organization to hire their own subject matter expert to use the product and perform the analysis. Others collect some, but not all traffic data, and have their entry level help desk personnel perform the analysis as a collateral duty. As one of the most critical lines of defense in the protection of the organization from ongoing and imminent attacks, this type of threat intelligence analysis must be performed by competent and well experienced analysts who have no other responsibilities than to dedicate their full attention to the monitoring and detecting any and all malicious traffic connecting to the organization. Therefore, as important as the threat intelligence itself may be, selecting the proper analytical service provider is equally important.

Closing Comments on Threat Intelligence

The world of intelligence is not really as cloak and dagger as the movies and media would like you to believe. It is very much a commodities business, and the business of intelligence, just as with all commodities that many competing parties are offering, is driven heavily by marketing, and the marketing hype is causing confusion among cybersecurity consumers. After reading this chapter, the reader should have a better understanding of how cyber attacks are perpetrated and how threat intelligence can or cannot help with any of it. Plus, appreciate the difference between actionable vs information intelligence, as well as how to actually make use of or ignore the intelligence that the organization receives.

In a business that thrives on myth and fear, the threat intelligence industry is driven to perpetuate panic among the masses. Some hype the mythical super villainous attackers with magical powers, then espouse gratuitous techno-babble to exaggerate the complexity unnecessarily. A lot of threat intelligence is generated simply for the sake of perpetuating this falsehood in order to drive business. This approach often confuses consumers.

Many organizations invest significant amount of resources to meet compliance requirements, but are reluctant to spend just a little money to procure threat intelligence. Often decision makers do not fully appreciate the fact that compliance satisfies only regulatory and commercial requirements, and does very little in advising the decision maker of the actual state of information security. When an organization finds itself in a situation of non-compliance, the repercussions are fines and perhaps some lost business. However, if an organization fails to acquire the proper threat intelligence and suffers a cyber attack, then the cost will be significantly higher than any regulatory agencies may levy. This chapter has focused on advising decision makers to become better informed about cyber threats and the value of obtaining solid and actionable threat intelligence. Cyber threat intelligence is a wise investment. It is critical to design a cybersecurity solution which is customized to the threats that an organization is currently encountering as well as threats it may face in the future. Organizational cybersecurity strategy should be threat-based cybersecurity tailored to the unique situation, not compliance-based cybersecurity solely aligned to generic government or industry information security standards.

The next chapter is focused on understanding the constantly evolving cybersecurity regulatory landscape and the numerous cybersecurity risk management frameworks implemented within the U.S. and internationally.

Chapter 5

CYBERSECURITY RISK MANAGEMENT FRAMEWORKS – COMPARISON

By: Greg Schu

FRAMEWORK OVERVIEW

Organizations, no matter how large or small or how long they have been in business have technology-related tasks that require some level of effort to be put forth. The efforts can vary depending on the services the organization provides, the data they have access to, or the intellectual property they maintain. The organization may also have to demonstrate how they are securing their environment, what business controls are in place, and if they are interacting with other companies, including healthcare organizations, financial institutions, or government organizations. There are multiple cybersecurity risk management frameworks that can help an organization evaluate the robustness of the security and controls they have implemented. The current cybersecurity risk management frameworks tend to have a combination of security and compliance requirements, in an effort to enhance the organization's technology environment. The numerous cybersecurity risk management frameworks are managed by multiple, independent groups. A snapshot of the representative groups includes:

Compliance-focused requirements tend to prioritize the protection of specific data. Common frameworks are:

- General Data Protection Regulation (GDPR)
- Gramm-Leach Bliley Act (GLBA)
- Health Insurance Portability and Accountability Act (HIPAA)
- The Health Information Trust Alliance (HITRUST)
- Sarbanes-Oxley Act (SOX)
- Payment Card Industry Data Security Standard (PCI DSS)
- Systems and Organization Controls (SOC)
- Federal Information Security Management Act (FISMA)

Security focused requirements mostly concern an organization's environment, such as:

- National Institute of Standards and Technology (NIST)
- International Standards Organization (ISO)

Another way to analyze the requirements is to drop them into the buckets they are commonly viewed as.

Regulatory	Contractually Enforced	Voluntary
• GDPR		• NIST
• GLBA	• PCI DSS	• ISO
• FISMA	• SSAE18 (SOC1)	
• HIPAA	• SOC 2	
• SOX		

How to Use the Guidance

When assessing the above stated cybersecurity risk management frameworks there are a few terms to take in to consideration. The following are some of the key definitions to apply to the organizational assessment structures.

- **Framework**: the basic structure of something; a supporting structure; a structural frame.

- **Oversight** - A structure through which an organization directs, manages and reports its security management activities. It defines roles and responsibilities, decision, risk governance, and reporting lines.
- **People** - A strong security culture helps to encourage strategic decisions that are in the long-term best interest of the organization, its shareholders and employees.
- **Processes** - The activities in place that allow an organization to identify, assess and quantify known and emerging security risks. It encompasses processes, tools and systems.
- **Technology** - It includes development tools, software, databases, technology architecture, and systems that support risk management.

To expand on terminology and definitions, further details about requirements and standards have been gathered to help evaluate which standard may be applicable to an organization.

National Institute of Standards and Technology (NIST)	NIST is responsible for developing standards, guidelines, and associated methods and techniques for providing adequate information security for all agency operations and assets, excluding national security systems. NIST works closely with federal agencies to improve their understanding and implementation of FISMA to protect their information and information systems and publishes standards and guidelines which provide the foundation for strong information security programs at agencies. NIST performs its statutory responsibilities through the Computer Security Division of the Information Technology Laboratory. NIST is a division of the U.S. Department of Commerce. *https://www.nist.gov/* NIST guidance selected by organizations include (but are not limited to). - 800-30 (Risk management) - 800-53 (Recommended security controls for Federal Information Systems and Organizations) - 800-57 (Cryptographic key changes) - 800-66 (Intro guide for implementing HIPAA security) - 800-115 (Penetration methodology) - 800-171 (Cybersecurity standard or formally - Protecting Controlled Unclassified Information (CUI) in Nonfederal Information Systems and Organization)

Standard/Framework	Description
Federal Information Security Management Act of 2002 (FISMA)	FISMA is a United States federal law passed in 2002 that requires federal agencies to develop, document, and implement an information security and protection program. NIST SP 800-53, Recommended Security Controls for Federal Information Systems, was developed in support of FISMA.
	NIST SP 800-53 is the primary source of recommended security controls for federal agencies. It describes several controls related to log management, including the generation, review, protection, and retention of audit records, as well as the actions to be taken due to audit failure.
ISO 2700x	ISO is an international standard, with worldwide recognition, which sets the requirements for the establishment of an information security management system. It applies to any type of organization, and their implementation and certification is optional, so it is not mandatory for a company. ISO/IEC27001 is the best-known standard in the family providing requirements for an information security management system (ISMS). ISO is governed by the International Organization for Standardization. *https://www.iso.org/isoiec-27001-information-security.html*
Health Insurance Portability and Accountability Act of 1996 (HIPAA)	HIPAA is U.S. federal law that provides data privacy and security provisions for safeguarding medical information. HIPAA required the Secretary of the U.S. Department of Health and Human Services (HHS) to develop regulations protecting the privacy and security of certain health information. To fulfill this requirement, HHS published what are commonly known as the HIPAA Privacy Rule and the HIPAA Security Rule. *https://www.hhs.gov/hipaa*
System and Organization Controls (SOC)	SOC 1 is a report on controls at a service organization relevant to a user entity's internal control over financial reporting. SOC 2 is a report on the Trust Services Principles. The SOC 2 report focuses on a business's non-financial reporting controls as they relate to security, availability, processing integrity, confidentiality, and privacy of a system. SOC assessments are governed by the American Institute of CPAs (AICPA). *https://www.aicpa.org*

Standard/Framework	Description
Payment Card Industry Data Security Standard (PCI DSS)	PCI-DSS is an information security standard for organizations that process, store transmit or could impact the security of the cardholder data environment. The PCI DSS pertains to branded credit and debit cards fo: Visa, MasterCard, Discover, American Express and JCB. The Payment Card Industry Security Standards Council (PCI SSC) manages and maintains the PCI DSS. *https://www. pcisecuritystandards.org*
Gramm-Leach-Bliley Act (GLB Act or GLBA)	GLBA is also known as the Financial Modernization Act of 1999. It is a United States federal law that requires financial institutions to explain how they share and protect their customers' private information. GLBA requires financial institutions that offer consumers financial products or services like loans, financial or investment advice, or insurance, to explain their information-sharing practices to their customers and to safeguard sensitive data. GLBA is enforced by the Federal Trade Commission (FTC). - *https://www.ftc.gov/*
Sarbanes-Oxley Act (SOX) of 2002	SOX is a U.S. federal law that set new or expanded requirements for all U.S. public company boards, management and public accounting firms. There are a number of provisions of the Act that also apply to privately held companies; for example, a prohibition on the willful destruction of evidence to impede a federal investigation. The bill, which contains eleven sections, was enacted as a reaction to a number of major corporate and accounting scandals, including Enron and WorldCom. As a result of SOX, top management must individually certify the accuracy of financial information. *https://www.aicpa.org/ advocacy/issues/section404bofsox.html*

Standard/Framework	Description
General Data Protection Regulation (GDPR)	GDPR is a regulation in European Union (EU) law on data protection and privacy for all individuals within the European Union. It addresses the export of personal data outside the EU. GDPR aims primarily to give control back to citizens and residents over their personal data and to simplify the regulatory environment for international business by unifying the regulation within the EU. When the GDPR takes effect, it will replace the 1995 Data Protection Directive (Directive 95/46/EC). *https://www.eugdpr.org/* GDPR was adopted on 27 April 2016 and became enforceable 25 May 2018; after a two-year transition period. Unlike a directive, GDPR does not require national governments to pass any enabling legislation and so it is directly binding and applicable.

Further Details Regarding Key Cybersecurity Risk Management Frameworks

The cybersecurity risk management frameworks described in this chapter have corresponding controls. There are similarities and differences between the control structure contained within each framework. To understand where there are overlaps and where differences may exist, it is necessary to have additional understanding of the structure of the guidelines. Another item to consider is that while each of the frameworks is outlined in this chapter, there are two key security and controls-oriented frameworks that are used across most guiding principles – NIST and ISO.

NIST

NIST – There are five focus areas within the NIST structure: Identify, Protect, Detect, Respond, and Recover.

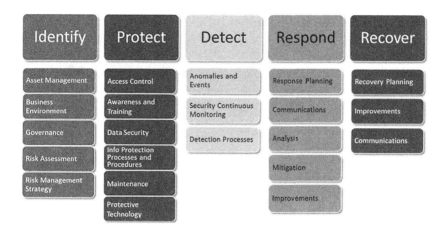

Two commonly used NIST standards are the 800-171 and 800-053. The NIST 800-171 is a framework an organization may use to demonstrate that security requirements have been implemented. Testing or validation against the NIST standards allows an organization to provide a level of assurance to its customers that a minimum security and compliance structure has been validated. The validation is performed by an independent third-party, which provides the reader with additional reliance on the output of the validation.

There are 14 areas or categories of control with a total count of over 110 controls. The categories are noted as:

TABLE 1: SECURITY REQUIREMENT FAMILIES

FAMILY	FAMILY
Access Control	Media Protection
Awareness and Training	Personnel Security
Audit and Accountability	Phyisical Protection
Configuration Management	Risk Assessment
Identification and Authentication	Security Assessment
Incident Response	System and Communications Protection
Maintenance	System and Information Integrity

The NIST 800-53 focuses on controls for federal information systems and organizations. It is mandatory for FISMA purposes, which requires the development and maintenance of minimum controls to protect federal information and information systems. The main focus is on organizations or information systems that process, store, or transmit information. The 800-53 is also the groundwork for HIPAA and HITRUST standards. There are 20 areas or categories of controls with a total count of over 173 controls. The categories are noted as:

TABLE 1: SECURITY AND PRIVACY CONTROL FAMILIES

ID	FAMILY	ID	FAMILY
AC	Access Control	MP	Media Protection
AT	Awareness and Training	PA	Privacy Authorization
AU	Audit and Accountability	PE	Physical and Environmental Protection
CA	Assessment, Authorization, and Monitoring	PL	Planning
CM	Configuration Management	PM	Program Management
CP	Contingency Planning	PS	Personnel Security
IA	Identification and Authentication	RA	Risk Assessment
IP	Individual Participation	SA	System and Services Acquisition
IR	Incident Response	SC	System and Communications Protection
MA	Maintenance	SI	System and Information Integrity

EXCERPT FROM NIST SP 800-53 REV 5 PUBLICATION

ISO

ISO – This is a framework for information security management. The ISO standard is often considered an international oriented standard and organizations with operations outside of the United States may receive inquires as to the controls standards recognized on an international basis. Testing or validation against the ISO standards allows an organization to provide a level of assurance to its customers that a minimum security and compliance structure has been validated. The validation is performed by an independent third-party, which provides the reader with additional reliance on the output of the validation.

One set of standards for ISO is referred to as the 2700x structure. Organizations usually select one of the following three ISO standards when evaluating their own environment:

- 27000 – An overview of information security management systems (ISMS).
- 27001 – Requirements for establishing, implementing, maintaining and continually improving an information security management. The requirements in ISO/IEC 27001:2013 are generic and are intended to be applicable to all organizations, regardless of type, size or nature.
- 27002 – Guidelines for information security standards and information security management practices including the selection, implementation

and management of controls taking into consideration the organization's information security risk environment(s).

- The ISO 27001 structure includes 14 different categories with 110 security control requirements and is represented as noted below.

Ref	Description	Ref	Description
A.5	Information security policies (2 controls)	A.12	Operations security (14 controls)
A.6	Organization of information security (7 controls)	A.13	Communications security (7 controls)
A.7	Human resource security - (6 controls)	A.14	System acquisition, development and maintenance (13 controls)
A.8	Asset management (10 controls)	A.15	Supplier relationships (5 controls)
A.9	Access control (14 controls)	A.16	Information security incident management (7 controls)
A.10	Cryptography (2 controls)	A.17	Information security aspects of business continuity management (4 controls)
A.11	Physical and environmental security (15 controls)	A.18	Compliance; with internal requirements, such as policies, and with external requirements, such as laws (8 controls)

AICPA SOC – System and Organization Controls

The American Institute of Certified Public Accountants (AICPA) System and Organizational Controls (SOC) structure is focused on testing controls for both business processes and information technology (IT) systems for the purpose of determining if an organization providing outsourced services (i.e. third-party service providers) has a structure implemented that allows customers to gain comfort that data, systems, devices and/or hardware are managed in a manner that reduces the risk of unauthorized access to systems or improper processing of transactions. While security components are integrated with the controls and testing of controls, this standard is oriented more on activities performed by a third-party service organization. The services are to be provided by a public accounting firm and the report or output is such that the firm performing the testing and validation will "opine" on the results of the assessment performed. The reader or user of the report will be able to gain a clear understanding of the in-scope environment, the controls, and when applicable, the test of controls. At an overview level, the SOC is defined as follows:

- A control framework for third-party companies providing services to other organizations.

- Guidance provided by the AICPA (American Institute of Certified Public Accountants).
- Reports are signed by a CPA/CPA firm.
- SOC 1 (financial reporting controls) that morphed from SAS 70 reports.
- SOC 2 (IT oriented controls) that was developed to focus on systems and IT processes and operations.

	SOC 1 REPORT	SOC 2 REPORT	SOC 3 REPORT
Type of controls addressed by the report	Controls relevant to user entities' internal controls over financial reporting	Controls relevant to Security, Availability, Processing Integrity, Confidentiality or Privacy	Controls relevant to Security, Availability, Processing Integrity, Confidentiality or Privacy
Standard under which the engagement is performed and other related guidance	SSAE No. 18, Reporting on Controls at a Service Organization AICPA Guide, Applying SSAE No. 16 (18), Reporting on Controls at a Service Organization	AT 101, Attestation Engagements AICPA Guide, Reporting on Controls at a Service Organization Relevant to Security, Availability, Processing Integrity, Confidentiality or Privacy	AT 101, Attestation Engagements TSP Section 100, AICPA Technical Practice Aid, Trust Services Principles, Criteria and Illustrations

SOC SUMMARY CHART (with Suggested Guidance)			
Intended users of this report	Auditors of the user entity's financial statements, management of the user entities and management of the Service Organization	Primary users generally are management of user entities. Other users may include parties that are knowledgeable about: • The nature of the service provided by the Service Organization • How the Service Organization's system interacts with user entities, subservice organizations and other parties • Internal control and its limitations • The applicable trust services criteria, risks that may threaten the achievement of the criteria and how controls address the risks	Any users who want assurance on controls at a Service Organization related to security, availability, processing integrity, confidentiality or privacy of a system, but do not have the need for the level of detail provided in a SOC 2 report. SOC 3 reports are general use reports and can be freely distributed or posted on a website as a seal.

The SOC 2 framework has evolved as a result of organizations having the need to show their customers that security and IT controls are important in today's digital world. The risk to loss of data or breaches of systems affects all organizations. Outsourcing tasks to a third-party does not eliminate a company's responsibility associated with protecting systems and information. Therefore, the controls associated with a SOC 2 are focused on protecting data and systems. The SOC 2 areas of focus include:

- SOC 2 – Trust Services Principles

- o Security (Common Criteria) – The system is protected, both logically and physically, against unauthorized access.
- o Availability – The system is available for operation and use as committed or agreed to.
- o Processing Integrity – The system processing is complete, accurate, timely and authorized.
- o Confidentiality – Information that is designated as "confidential" is protected as committed or agreed to.
- o Privacy – Personal information is collected, used, retained and disclosed in conformity with the commitments in the entity's privacy notice and with the privacy principles put forth by the AICPA and the Canadian Institute of Chartered Accountants (CICA).

PCI – Payment Card Industry

The Payment Card Industry Security Standards Council (PCI SSC) is a governing organization that develops and maintains security standards for the protection of cardholder data. The standards are a global framework that was introduced in 2006. They were derived from the individual data security compliance programs of five major payment brands; American Express, Discover Financial Services, JCB International, MasterCard, and Visa Inc.

At a high level, PCI includes:

- ■ Oversight by the Payment Card Industry Security Standards Council (PCI SSC).
- ■ The PCI SSC is a consortium of the card brands.
- ■ The intent is to protect payment information, specifically credit card data.
- ■ The card environments in-scope include systems and people involved with processing, transmitting, storing, or affecting the security of card data.

Please refer to the chapter describing the PCI Data Security Standard (PCI DSS) to obtain additional information regarding this standard.

HIPAA/HITRUST

The Health Insurance Portability and Accountability Act is intended to protect patient (protected) health information (PHI). HIPAA is defined as:

- Setting the standard for sensitive patient data protection. Organizations that come in contact with protected health information must have physical, network, and process security measures implemented.
- The framework originated with NIST 800-53/800-66.
- There are approximately 63 standards or controls.

Included with HIPAA is the security rule and privacy rule. Areas taken into consideration include:

- The privacy rule setting the standards for, among other things, those who may have access to PHI.
- The security rule setting the standards indicating that only those who should have access to EPHI will actually have access.
- Security being further categorized in to administrative, physical, and technical safeguards.

HITRUST - The Health Information Trust Alliance is a privately held company. In collaboration with the healthcare industry, healthcare providers, information and technology companies, and regulatory groups, have established a common security framework (CSF) for organizations that create, access, store or exchange sensitive and/or regulated data. Key components of HITRUST and CSF are:

- The controls are a combination of multiple frameworks – HIPAA, ISO, NIST, and COBIT
- The CSF has 135 controls
- There are 19 domains identified within the CSF (see table below)

A graphical representation of the HITRUST framework helps indicate the level of overlap and shared controls across the frameworks described in this section.

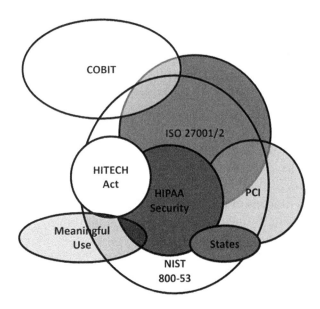

Similar to categories or domains for testing, the HITRUST domains (19 in total) or areas of focus were established for testing and assessing an organization across the agreed-to domains. The domains are categorized as follows:

Information Protection Program	Audit Logging and Monitoring
Endpoint Protection	Education, Training and Awareness
Portable Media Security	Third Party Security
Mobile Device Security	Incident Management
Wireless Protection	Business Continuity and Disaster Recovery
Configuration Management	Risk Management
Vulnerability Management	Physical and Environmental Security
Network Protection	Data Protection and Privacy
Transmission Protection	Password Management
Access Control	

Cybersecurity Risk Management Frameworks: Similarities and Differences

By analyzing the cybersecurity risk management frameworks in further detail, it is possible to identify similar intentions of the structure along with areas that differ across the frameworks below is an overview of both breakdowns for review.

	Oversight	People	Process	Technology
Similar controls and approaches	• Board and Exec Oversight • Litigation and Investigation • Risk Management	• Awareness Training • Roles and Responsibilities	• Application Development • Asset Identification • Physical Security • Vulnerability Management	• Configuration Management • End Point Security • IDS / IPS • Security Monitoring
Areas with differences	• Cyber Insurance • Public Relations • Regulatory Compliance • Strategic Planning	• Organizational Culture • Communications • Organizational Structure • Security Skills and Competency	• Business Continuity	• Data Loss Prevention

The key takeaway from the above view is that there is possible leverage if it becomes necessary to address multiple security frameworks. Organizations have implemented various versions of common control frameworks (CCFs) or unified compliance frameworks (UCFs).

The Unified Compliance Framework® (UCF®) is a large library database of interconnected compliance documents and is commercially available for an organization to license.

The Unified Compliance Framework contains:
- 1,000 mapped authority documents
- 100,000+ individual mandates
- 10,000+ common controls
- 250,000 interconnected words and phrases in dictionary

The UCF is another source for consideration when assessing potential methods of designing and implementing a security and compliance framework.

Similar to the UCF, the Common Control Framework (CCF) is a set of controls or requirements designed to eliminate or mitigate the duplication of multiple frameworks. In general, the organization has the flexibility to assess the requirements and controls that apply to their own environment and establish a common control framework. The goal of designing a custom structure may help eliminate the duplication of requirements within frameworks and simplify the process of scoping, defining, and maintaining compliance. This has the added benefit of potentially saving an organization time and resources, since they are not forced to recreate the GRC compliance and security structure each time a new compliance mandate is published. It gives organizations the power to test once and comply with many regulations and leverage data gathered and tested, interviews performed, and observations documented by the tester. To create a common control framework, organizations should determine which regulations they are subject to and the cost of non-compliance. There may be multiple factors associated with non-compliance, so the organization has to evaluate and calculate the risk and cost for each framework.

Cybersecurity Risk Management Frameworks - Comparison

To expand on the information provided above regarding UCF and CCF, a comparison has been mapped out to indicate possible areas of overlap to the five NIST cybersecurity: identity, protect, detect, respond, and recovery. When reading through the cybersecurity focus areas, the cross-over of categories, sub-categories and corresponding reference information clarify the controls and requirements that are common across multiple risk management frameworks.

Identity

Function	Category	Subcategory	Informative References
IDENTIFY (ID)	Asset Management (ID.AM): The data, personnel, devices, systems, and facilities that enable the organization to achieve business purposes are identified and managed consistent with their relative importance to business objectives and the organization's risk strategy.	ID.AM-1: Physical devices and systems within the organization are inventoried	• ISO/IEC 27001:2013 A.8.1.1, A.8.1.2 • NIST SP 800-53 Rev. 4 CM-8 • PCI DSS v3.2 2.4, 9.9, 1.1.1
		ID.AM-2: Software platforms and applications within the organization are inventoried	• ISO/IEC 27001:2013 A.8.1.1, A.8.1.2 • NIST SP 800-53 Rev. 4 CM-8 • PCI DSS v3.2 2.4
		ID.AM-3: Organizational communication and data flows are mapped	• ISO/IEC 27001:2013 A.13.2.1 • NIST SP 800-53 Rev. 4 AC-4, CA-3, CA-9, PL-8 • PCI DSS v3.2 1.1.2, 1.1.3
		ID.AM-1: Physical devices and systems within the organization are inventoried	• ISO/IEC 27001:2013 A.11.2.6 • NIST SP 800-53 Rev. 4 AC-20, SA-9 • PCI DSS v3.2 8.1.5

Protect

Function	Category	Subcategory	Informative References
PROTECT (PR)	Identity Management and Access Control (PR.AC): Access to physical and logical assets and associated facilities is limited to authorized users, processes, and devices, and is managed consistent with the assessed risk of unauthorized access.	PR.AC-1: Identities and credentials are issued, managed, revoked, and audited for authorized devices, users, and processes	• ISO/IEC 27001:2013 A.9.2.1, A.9.2.2, A.9.2.4, A.9.3.1, A.9.4.2, A.9.4.3 • NIST SP 800-53 Rev. 4 AC-2, IA Family • PCI DSS v3.2 8.1, 8.2, 12.3
		PR.AC-2: Physical access to assets is managed and protected	• ISO/IEC 27001:2013 A.11.1.1, A.11.1.2, A.11.1.4, • A.11.1.6, A.11.2.3 • NIST SP 800-53 Rev. 4 PE-2, PE-3, PE-4, PE-5, PE-6, • PE-9 • PCI DSS v3.2 9.1, 9.2, 9.3, 9.4, 9.5, 9.9, 9.10
		PR.AC-3: Remote access is managed	• ISO/IEC 27001:2013 A.6.2.2, A.13.1.1, A.13.2.1 • NIST SP 800-53 Rev. 4 AC-17, AC-19, AC-20 • PCI DSS v3.2 8.1.5, 8.3, 8.5.1, 12.3.8, 12.3.9, 12.3.10

Detect

Function	Category	Subcategory	Informative References
DETECT (DE)	Anomalies and Events (DE.AE): Anomalous activity is detected in a timely manner and the potential impact of events is understood.	DE.AE-1: A baseline of network operations and expected data flows for users and systems is established and managed	• NIST SP 800-53 Rev. 4 AC-4, CA-3, CM-2, SI-4
		DE.AE-2: Detected events are analyzed to understand attack targets and methods	• ISO/IEC 27001:2013 A.16.1.1, A.16.1.4 • NIST SP 800-53 Rev. 4 AU-6, CA-7, IR-4, SI-4 • PCI DSS v3.2 10.6.1, 11.4, 12.5.2
		DE.AE-3: Event data are aggregated and correlated from multiple sources and sensors	• NIST SP 800-53 Rev. 4 AU-6, CA-7, IR-4, IR-5, IR-8, • SI-4 • PCI DSS v3.2 10.1, 12.10.5

Respond

Function	Category	Subcategory	Informative References
RESPOND (RS)	Communications (RS.CO): Response activities are coordinated with internal and external stakeholders, as appropriate, to include external support from law enforcement agencies.	RS.CO-1: Personnel know their roles and order of operations when a response is needed	• ISO/IEC 27001:2013 A.6.1.1, A.16.1.1 • NIST SP 800-53 Rev. 4 CP-2, CP-3, IR-3, IR-8 • PCI DSS v3.2 12.10
		RS.CO-2: Events are reported consistent with established criteria	• ISO/IEC 27001:2013 A.6.1.3, A.16.1.2 • NIST SP 800-53 Rev. 4 AU-6, IR-6, IR-8 • PCI DSS v3.2 12.10
		RS.CO-3: Information is shared consistent with response plans	• ISO/IEC 27001:2013 A.16.1.2 • NIST SP 800-53 Rev. 4 CA-2, CA-7, CP-2, IR-4, IR-8, • PE-6, RA-5, SI-4 • PCI DSS v3.2 12.10

Recovery

Function	Category	Subcategory	Informative References
RECOVERY (RC)	Recovery Planning (RC.RP): Recovery processes and procedures are executed and maintained to ensure timely restoration of systems or assets affected by cybersecurity events.	RC.RP-1: Recovery plan is executed during or after an event	• ISO/IEC 27001:2013 A.16.1.5 • NIST SP 800-53 Rev. 4 CP-10, IR-4, IR-8 • PCI DSS v3.2 12.10.6
	Improvements (RC. IM): Recovery planning and processes are improved by incorporating lessons learned into future activities.	RC.IM-1: Recovery plans incorporate lessons learned	• NIST SP 800-53 Rev. 4 CP-2, IR-4, IR-8 • PCI DSS v3.2 12.10.6

This concludes the overview of cybersecurity risk management frameworks that are used by organizations to comply with regulatory requirements and/or to enhance the day-to-day control and security framework applicable to the technology platforms implemented.

Resources and Guidance

https://www.iso.org/isoiec-27001-information-security.html

https://www.hhs.gov/hipaa

https://www.aicpa.org

https://www.aicpa.org/advocacy/issues/section404bofsox.html

https://www.pcisecuritystandards.org/

https://www.ftc.gov

https://www.eugdpr.org/

NIST SP 800-171 publication

NIST SP 800-53 rev 5 publication

HITRUST guidance

Chapter 6

CYBER VULNERABILITY ASSESSMENTS AND PENETRATION TESTING –TOOLS, TECHNIQUES, AND BEST PRACTICES

By: Andrew Silberstein

INTRODUCTION

Cyber attacks and their success rate in network breaches are increasing in frequency and sophistication. At the root of many successful cyber attacks are the vulnerabilities that exist within network infrastructure, software applications and the very humans that use those networks and applications. The human element of cybersecurity deals with normal human interactions through email and social media (e.g., vulnerabilities such as email phishing, LinkedIn and Facebook hacking, etc.) and general cybersecurity awareness and good cyber hygiene (e.g., proper use of USB memory devices, remote connections and weak passwords). These vulnerabilities are best addressed through email phishing campaigns to identify gaps in organizational policies and lack of associated email-related security infrastructure, and overall security awareness training. This chapter focuses on vulnerabilities associated with network infrastructure and software applications and leaves the topic of human factors to be addressed separately.

A well-established technique for minimizing and mitigating vulnerabilities within network infrastructure and software applications is the use of vulnerability assessments and penetration testing (VAPT). The use of VAPT is a proven and powerful technique to manage the security risk within an organization or family office. Further, performing a VAPT is very effective in determining your cybersecurity risk profile and general security posture. Understanding and establishing a proven VAPT process and methodology together with utilizing the right tools and techniques will ensure the VAPT accomplishes its goal of improving the overall security of your organization.

Before diving into the details of how to best implement a VAPT, it is important to establish some baseline definitions and the reasons how and why adversaries pursue and exploit vulnerabilities.

Let's start with a simple definition of terms; what do we mean when we discuss a "vulnerability".

> ## vul·ner·a·bil·i·ty (*within general dictionary usage*)[1]
>
> noun: vulnerability; plural noun: vulnerabilities
> The quality or state of being exposed to the possibility of being attacked or harmed, either physically or emotionally.

Refining this definition towards cybersecurity:

> ## vul·ner·a·bil·i·ty (*within cybersecurity*)[2]
>
> Vulnerability is a cybersecurity term that refers to a flaw in a system that can leave it open to attack. A vulnerability may also refer to any type of weakness in a computer system itself, in a set of procedures, or in anything that leaves information security exposed to a threat.

Cyber adversaries look to exploit vulnerabilities everyday with new and innovative techniques. Adversaries come in many shapes and sizes and are looking to steal your sensitive and proprietary information, cause political or reputational damage, acquire financial gain, and simply steal whatever is available to sell to the highest bidder. Adversaries range from the most sophisticated foreign, state-sponsored adversary to organized crime to the ever increasing number of hackers in the world.

Adversaries translate the definition of a vulnerability into two basic approaches: 1) attacking an organization from the outside of a network referred to as an external vulnerability, and 2) attacking an organization from the inside of the network, referred to as an internal vulnerability. Let's have one more definition to help clarify how adversaries execute an attack:

at·tack vec·tor[3]

An attack vector is a path or means by which a hacker (or cracker) can gain access to a computer or network server in order to deliver a payload or malicious outcome. Attack vectors enable hackers to exploit system vulnerabilities, including the human element.

Once the adversary chooses either an external or internal attack (or both), he then decides on specific attack vectors which typically takes on one of two forms: 1) exploiting vulnerabilities within the network infrastructure and/or 2) exploiting software programs and applications. Software programs and applications can be running as an external facing application such as a website or a web-based application or mobile application or a software program/application for internal use running on an internal network server or desktop. It should be noted that an adversary may use an external vulnerability to gain access to the internal network and then exploit the network from within.

With an understanding of how an adversary can attack a network or organization, and the types of attack vectors employed by these adversaries, we can now address the kind of vulnerabilities typically found during VAPT assessments. Network infrastructure (i.e., desktop computers, laptops, servers, firewalls, routers, and switches) and software application vulnerabilities generally fall into a few common categories: 1) infrastructure configuration issues, 2) software and application version control or patching updates, and 3) vulnerabilities resulting from web application code and its development. It should be noted these categories are not inclusive of all possible vulnerabilities but rather common vulnerabilities most often found during a VAPT assessment. Only by performing your own VAPT, will you gain an understanding of your specific security exposure and complete list of network vulnerabilities. In summary, performing regular VAPT assessments will help manage the risk associated with vulnerabilities within your network infrastructure and applications and improve your cybersecurity posture against network attacks and their exploits.

Background

VAPT is essentially two separate testing techniques with their own process, methodology and associated tools. Vulnerability assessment (VA) is a process that inspects the potential points of exploit on network infrastructure and software applications to identify gaps in security. A typical VA uses vulnerability scanning techniques to detect and classify system weaknesses. Further, it provides actionable recommendations to mitigate those vulnerabilities. The VA process employees automated scanning tools that essentially perform a deep and thorough search of a network's infrastructure and software/web-based applications to find and categorize security vulnerabilities. While VA scanning is typically performed with automated software tools, manual vulnerability scanning is also used in certain tests to provide even deeper testing. Manual testing of vulnerabilities requires subject matter experts that can manually navigate through infrastructure configuration parameters and application code. The VA process will generate a report that identifies all vulnerabilities, categorized based on their severity, and provide recommendations to resolve those vulnerabilities. The results of the VA are then used to perform the next step in the overall VAPT process, which is penetration testing. Two important aspects of any VA that should always be considered are: 1) that the VA is performed with a non-intrusive process to ensure IT infrastructure and applications are not affected, and 2) that the VA process does impact the network performance.

A penetration test, or PT, takes a vulnerability and through ethical hacking techniques attempts to exploit the vulnerability through a simulated attack. The PT process verifies, through executing an attack vector, if a vulnerability is present within a network or application and ascertains the level of severity of the specific vulnerability. It acts as a proof point for the VA process and the identified vulnerabilities. With the vast number of existing vulnerabilities and the growing number of new vulnerabilities on a daily basis, the PT is also effective is determining if a particular vulnerability is a "false positive" (a result that incorrectly indicates a specific outcome or condition or how it could impact the network or application). While penetration tests leverage automated techniques, most testing is performed through manual techniques since many application vulnerabilities hinge on logical and semantic flaws (i.e., business logic) which, unlike syntactic bugs, are difficult to identify using automated analysis. While a PT is by definition an obtrusive test, such testing can and is recommended to be performed with similar guidelines to the VA testing, namely to ensure that the PT is performed with a non-intrusive process to ensure the simulated attack does not actually execute the exploit but rather demonstrates its ability to exploit the IT infrastructure and applications.

Undertaking a VAPT process on a regular basis (at least four times per year) has proven to be an effective testing technique to address the need to secure the evolving and increasingly complex IT environment organizations face every day while delivering their business objectives. Performing the VAPT on the three most common attack vectors; external network, internal network, and software applications will increase the probability of identifying security weaknesses that are accidentally exposed or maliciously exploited. Secondary benefits from the VAPT process, once you have secured your infrastructure and applications include:

- Improvements in the overall technical IT environment
- Establishing greater confidence in the security controls within your IT environment
- Understanding areas within the IT environment that require budget allocation for security

VAPT is an involved, sophisticated process that requires the proper methodology, tools and techniques. These are addressed in the following sections.

Testing Methodologies

Vulnerability Assessment

A typical VA methodology uses a four-stage approach for testing and evaluation. The four stages are planning, information gathering, scanning and reporting. The actual testing is either performed from an external perspective without knowledge of accessing the network or testing is performed as an "employee" or "contractor" who has specific information regarding accessing the computer systems but with no physical access to the facilities.

The four stages of the VA methodology are summarized in the following table.

#	Stage	Activities Completed
1	Planning	During the planning stage, a test plan is developed. While vulnerability tests rely to some extent on the knowledge and innovation of the testers, it is critical to create a well-documented plan to focus on achieving the overall objectives of the test. Additionally planning items include: o Development of a customized the general testing strategy, o Finalizing the Rules of Engagement in writing for review and concurrence, and o Determine the testing timeframes and any special considerations.

#	Stage	Activities Completed
2	Information Gathering	The information gathering stage is geared towards obtaining as much information about the organization as possible. During the information gathering stage, the tester gathers and organizes information and updates the vulnerability plan appropriately. Evaluate the organization's network security for confidentiality, integrity and availability. Tests included the identification of the mechanism(s) used for remote access in and out of the perimeter to include encryption methods and other associated controls to protect unauthorized access.
3	Scanning	The scanning stage involves sending packets out on the network to look for responses that indicate that the host is 'alive'. The list of 'live' hosts is used to focus the scanning on specific ports and services. During this stage, various tools are used to perform expanded scanning and to recover as much information from the live hosts as possible. The goal of the scanning stage is to obtain a list of hosts that shows what systems are up and what operating systems and services the hosts are running. This list is used to research the vulnerabilities to which the hosts may be susceptible. Further scans are run to determine known vulnerabilities against the available services and, if necessary, exploitation is attempted.
4	Reporting	In the reporting stage, the Vulnerability Assessment Report is prepared in two sections: (1) the assessment report and (2) detailed findings. Each finding contains the cause of the weaknesses identified, potential or actual effects of the weaknesses identified, the Common Vulnerabilities and Exposure Number or CVE, and information from a particular vendor regarding identified weakness, if applicable.

Penetration Testing

A typical PT methodology uses a five-stage approach for testing and evaluation, many of which are the same or similar to the VA methodology. However, while the four of the five stages are similar, the PT tester performs the associated activities from the perspective of an ethical hacker that will simulate various attack vectors and are repeated here for convenience. The five stages are planning, information gathering, scanning, exploitation and reporting. As with VA, the actual testing is either performed from an as external perspective without knowledge of accessing the network or testing is performed as an "ex-employee or contractor" who has specific information regarding accessing the computer systems and with no physical access to the facilities. The five stages of the PT methodology are summarized in the following table.

#	Stage	Activities Completed
1	Planning	During the planning stage, a test plan is developed. While vulnerability tests rely to some extent on the knowledge and innovation of the testers, it is critical to create a well-documented plan to focus on achieving the overall objectives of the test. Additionally, planning items include: o Development of a customized general testing strategy, o Finalizing the rules of engagement in writing for review and concurrence, and o Determine the testing timeframes and any special considerations.
2	Information Gathering	The information gathering stage is geared towards obtaining as much information about the organization as possible. During this stage, the tester gathers and organized information and updates the vulnerability plan appropriately. Evaluate the organization's network security for confidentiality, integrity and availability. Tests include the identification of mechanism(s) used for remote access in and out of the perimeter and cover encryption methods and other associated controls to protect unauthorized access.
3	Scanning	The scanning stage involves sending packets out on the network to look for responses that indicate that the host is 'alive'. The list of 'live' hosts is used to focus the scanning on specific ports and services. During this stage, various tools are used to perform expanded scanning and recover as much information from the live hosts as possible. The goal of the scanning stage is to obtain a list of hosts that shows what systems are up and what operating systems and services the hosts are running. This list is used to research the vulnerabilities to which the hosts may be susceptible. Further scans are run to determine known vulnerabilities against the available services and, if necessary, exploitation is attempted.
4	Exploitation	Confirmation of the vulnerabilities that were discovered in the previous phases, and provide a proof of concept, which illustrates the impact of severe vulnerabilities. In this phase, the penetration tester also searches in repositories for known exploits for the services, based on the detected versions in order to gain access to the victim's network.
5	Reporting	In the reporting stage, the Vulnerability Assessment Report is prepared in two sections: (1) the assessment report and (2) detailed findings. Each finding contains the cause of the weaknesses identified, potential or actual effects of the weaknesses identified, the Common Vulnerabilities and Exposure Number or CVE, and information from a particular vendor regarding identified weakness, if applicable.

Application Testing/Assessment

A common and recommended application (e.g., software, web-based application) test methodology uses the Open Web Application Security Project (OWASP) which is an organization that provides unbiased and practical, cost-effective information about computer and Internet applications as inputs to an overall methodology. The Application testing methodology is provided below in a seven phase process.

PHASE 1 - Discovery

Proactive information gathering regarding the organization's business logic, features, infrastructure, development technology, profiles, contacts, and sensitive information. Perform additional reconnaissance by using "Google hacking" methods, DNS queries and extracting additional information from other databases and resources.

PHASE 2 – Fingerprinting and research

Identify and analyze the underlying infrastructure, web server, operating system, VM, Services, and DB, data repositories, and software components using automated fingerprinting tools. Manual analysis of HTTP headers, HTTP responses, HTML content, unique behaviors, while verifying the conclusions through an elimination process based on the development technology and infrastructure.

PHASE 3 – Infrastructure scanning

Conduct a vulnerability scan using web server and CMS scanners, and research known vulnerabilities of the underlying infrastructure according to the web server type and version. After the automated scan is complete, perform manual vulnerability research in online and offline vulnerability databases and repositories.

PHASE 4 – Entry point mapping

Map potential entry points in the system (modules that could be used to access information), by using manual and automated scraping tools. This phase is performed on the system public and private zones, while using a combination of chained interception proxies.

PHASE 5 – Metadata analysis

Analyze metadata information using advanced content analysis techniques that are designed to extract hidden information from the files disclosed.

PHASE 6 – Application vulnerabilities scanning and analysis

Proactively scan for web application vulnerabilities using various automated passive and active scanning tools, in addition to using manual testing techniques. Subsequent to the scan, the tester analyses the scan results, and attempts to locate potential attack vectors and leads.

PHASE 7 - Exploitation

Conduct exploitation to the vulnerabilities found, using manual techniques and automated tools. Tools that are typically used in this process include commercial exploitation frameworks and open source exploitation frameworks.

Testing Tools

There are many tools on the market for vulnerability assessments and penetration testing. This section is not intended to serve as a recommendation or endorsement of any particular tool, but rather provide a range of VAPT products that are commonly used for such testing. The testing tools provided in the following two tables are both open source and commercial products.

VA Testing Tools

Tool	Description
Nessus Professional	Nessus® Professional, the industry's most widely deployed vulnerability assessment solution helps you reduce your organization's attack surface and ensure compliance. Nessus features high-speed asset discovery, configuration auditing, target profiling, malware detection, sensitive data discovery and more. With the world's largest continuously updated library of vulnerability and configuration checks, and the support of Tenable's expert vulnerability research team, Nessus sets the standard for vulnerability scanning speed and accuracy

NMAP	Nmap ("Network Mapper") is a free and open source (license) utility for network discovery and security auditing. Many systems and network administrators also find it useful for tasks such as network inventory, managing service upgrade schedules, and monitoring host or service uptime. Nmap runs on all major computer operating systems, and official binary packages are available for Linux, Windows, and Mac OS X. In addition to the classic command-line Nmap executable, the Nmap suite includes an advanced GUI and results viewer (Zenmap), a flexible data transfer, redirection, and debugging tool (Ncat), a utility for comparing scan results (Ndiff), and a packet generation and response analysis tool (Nping).
OpenVAS	OpenVAS is a framework of several services and tools offering a comprehensive and powerful vulnerability scanning and vulnerability management solution. The framework is part of Greenbone Networks' commercial vulnerability management solution from which developments are contributed to the Open Source community since 2009
Metasploit	Metasploit is a penetration testing platform that enables you to find, exploit, and validate vulnerabilities. It provides the infrastructure, content, and tools to perform penetration tests and extensive security auditing and thanks to the open source community and Rapid7's own hard working content team, new modules are added on a regular basis, which means that the latest exploit is available to you as soon as it's published.
THC-Hydra	Hydra is a parallelized login cracker which supports numerous protocols to attack. It is very fast and flexible, and new modules are easy to add. This tool makes it possible for researchers and security consultants to show how easy it would be to gain unauthorized access to a system remotely.
DMitry	DMitry (Deepmagic Information Gathering Tool) is a UNIX/ (GNU) Linux Command Line Application coded in C. DMitry has the ability to gather as much information as possible about a host. Base functionality is able to gather possible subdomains, email addresses, uptime information, tcp port scan, whois lookups, and more.
theHarvester	The objective of this program is to gather emails, subdomains, hosts, employee names, open ports and banners from different public sources like search engines, PGP key servers and SHODAN computer database. This tool is intended to help Penetration testers in the early stages of the penetration test in order to understand the customer footprint on the Internet. It is also useful for anyone that wants to know what an attacker can see about their organization.

PT Tools

Tool	Description
Acunetix	Acunetix is a web vulnerability scanner that automatically checks web applications for vulnerabilities such as SQL Injections, cross site scripting, arbitrary file creation/ deletion, and weak password strength on authentication pages. It boasts a comfortable GUI, an ability to create professional security audit and compliance reports, and tools for advanced manual webapp testing. For downloads and more information.
Burp Suite Professional	Burp Suite is an integrated platform for attacking web applications. It contains a variety of tools with numerous interfaces between them designed to facilitate and speed up the process of attacking an application. All of the tools share the same framework for handling and displaying HTTP messages, persistence, authentication, proxies, logging, alerting and extensibility.
Nikto	Nikto is an Open Source (GPL) web server scanner which performs comprehensive tests against web servers for multiple items, including over 6400 potentially dangerous files/CGIs, checks for outdated versions of over 1200 servers, and version specific problems on over 270 servers. It also checks for server configuration items such as the presence of multiple index files, HTTP server options, and will attempt to identify installed web servers and software. Scan items and plugins are frequently updated and can be automatically updated
Sqlmap	Sqlmap is an open source penetration testing tool that automates the process of detecting and exploiting SQL injection flaws and taking over of back-end database servers. It comes with a broad range of features, from database fingerprinting to fetching data from the DB and even accessing the underlying file system and executing OS commands via out-of-band connections. The authors recommend using the development release from their Subversion repository
DirBuster	DirBuster searches for hidden pages and directories on a web server. Sometimes developers will leave a page accessible, but unlinked; DirBuster is meant to find these potential vulnerabilities.

WebCruiser	WebCruiser web vulnerability scanner, is an effective web penetration testing tool that aids in auditing websites. WebCruiser supports scanning websites as well as POC (proof of concept) for SQL Injection, cross site scripting, local file inclusion, remote file inclusion, redirect and other web vulnerabilities.
ZAP	ZAP is one of the world's most popular free security tools and is actively maintained by hundreds of international volunteers. It can help you automatically find security vulnerabilities in your web applications while you are developing and testing your applications. Its also a great tool for experienced pentesters to use for manual security testing.

The next chapter is focused on understanding the importance of ongoing monitoring, detection, and response (MDR) services, which is vital to cybersecurity. Too often organizations assume that if they perform an annual VAPT, they do not need to conduct continuous MDR, which is clearly a bad assumption. The next chapter discusses the inherent difference and value between observation and intelligent monitoring and detection.

Endnotes

[1] Google definition

[2] Technopedia definition

[3] Internet definition

Chapter 7

CYBERSECURITY MONITORING, DETECTION, AND RESPONSE – TOOLS AND BEST PRACTICES

By: Dori Fisher, CISSP

1. THE RISE OF MONITORING, DETECTION, AND RESPONSE

In recent years, the world has undergone a shift in perception, from focusing on prevention of attacks and breaches, to a resilience focused approach. Simply put, one can stop some of the threats some of the time, but not all the threats, all the time. The rest of the time should be invested in being able to detect and respond to alerts and incidents.

Focusing on the "preventive approach", most of the Cyber security investment budget was traditionally assigned protection and prevention devices, solutions and projects.[1]

Enterprises are transforming their security spending strategy in 2017, moving away from prevention-only approaches to focus more on detection and response, according to Gartner, Inc. Worldwide spending on information security is expected to reach $90 billion in 2017, an increase of 7.6 percent over 2016, and to top $113 billion by 2020. Spending on enhancing detection and response capabilities is expected to be a key priority for security buyers through 2020.

Failing to prevent a successful attack means that the breach should to be detected as soon as possible. According to Verizon DBIR[2] and others, on average, it takes most organizations approximately 200 days to detect a breach, in a few famous cases like that of Heartland Payment,[3] it took years to detect the source breach, even after being aware of information leakage. Responding to a breach starts after an effective detection, thus, the first step to close a breach is to detect and identify it amongst the multitude of logs and network information processed.

Defenders are, by definition, losing the cyber security war - as breach detection is a post breach activity. If prevention systems would have prevented all breaches, all the time, there wouldn't be any need for detection capability. As the adversaries have unlimited tries and the defenders need to be 100% successful, detection needs to evolve and improve. This chapter describes detection status and evolution.

1.1 Seeing is not understanding

Anyone with functional sight can look into a microscope.

Seeing an event does not mean one can understand it. Just like seeing red blood cells through a microscope does not mean one can interpret a blood sample result. Artificial Intelligence (AI) and machine learning is starting to succeed in physician tasks without the "formal training" after being exposed to multiple pictures containing a certain medical condition.[4] The opposing example is a researcher from Carnegie Mellon University proving machine learning face recognition can be misled completely when subjects are equipped with special glasses.[5] The point is that detection requires interpretation and interpretation requires prior knowledge.

According to wired magazine, in the Walmart incident,[6] as in many others, the logs and indicators for the breach existed in the Security information and event management system prior to the incident, but were too minor to arise suspicion or alerts. A few indicators were detected a year before the incident was fully understood, but these were overlooked as a thorough investigation was not conducted at the time of the initial detection.

1.2 Scope of the challenge

A 500-user organization that has a firewall, antivirus, Microsoft Windows Active Directory, a database, and an application, can easily have 100 events (log lines) per second, which amounts to more than 8 million log lines per day. Reviewing these events, sifting for potential alerts and interpreting is not a task for mere humans as analysis of eight million events per day is not effective. Corporations having 5,000 employees can easily produce more than 1,000 events per second, which are more than 80 million log lines per day. The calculation being 1000 (events) x 60 (seconds) x 60 (minutes) x 24(hours).

Collecting these logs is the smallest part of the challenge. Creating the use cases, reducing the alerts to a manageable level, interpreting the meaning and investigating is a task that most organizations cannot handle themselves. Thus, organizations of all sizes are turning to managed monitoring, detection, and response (MDR)" services, which include the people, process and technologies for effective monitoring, detection, and response. These are planned to grow by 2020, according to Gartner's 2017 market guide for MDR.[7] Gartner also estimate that by 2020, fifteen percent of organizations will be using services such as MDR, which is an increase from fewer than one percent today.

Investigating and reviewing cybersecurity breaches concludes that in many cases the alerts are very minor. Dozens of these alerts occur daily, among the popular ones are network scans from internal assets to external (scans from external sources produce hundreds of alerts daily and are usually ignored), failed logins, network access to various irregular ports (high network ports), surfing to low reputation or unknown websites and various firewall and intrusion detection systems that inform on malformed packets and suspicious communications.

24 hours of "alerts" or "events of interest" in a 2,000-user corporate, more than 1400 alerts presented:

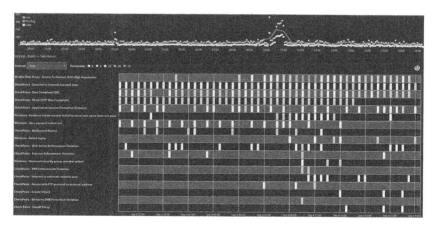

The creation of so many alerts per day explains quotes like "post breach investigation revealed that the alerts were present but ignored, overlooked or were under investigated". Of course, they were overlooked, even if a security operation center (SOC) analyst can resolve 20 alerts per hour (an over estimation), one would require 3 analysts per shift 24x7 hours to triage, (i.e. conduct a short investigation) all these alerts.

According to SANS SOC Survey, reviewing 309 responders,[8] most companies under 10,000 employees have between two to five full time employees for security operation center functions. Three analysts per shift requires at least 15 full time employees, thus there is a gap between alerts created and available analysts for detection and response. Realistically, a 2,000-employee corporate, or even a 10,000 employee corporate, is not going to employ 15 cybersecurity FTEs on security operation center detection and response duties.

The challenge then, is how to deal with more alerts than cybersecurity analysts available to triage and investigate.

1.3 Detection and response general flow

Most books on incident response include the following cycle detailing flow from preparation, through detection, response and documentation. The focus of this chapter is detection as response is not achievable without detection.

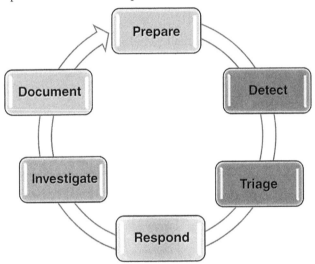

2. COMMON TOOLS FOR DETECTION

Successful detection with a multitude of events and alerts requires strategy, people, process and technology, having the right tools in place and using them correctly is key for detection success.

2.1 Rise (and fall?) of the (Classic) SIEM

SIEM stands for security information and event management. It evolved from early 2000 log management systems. These systems allowed receiving of events, usually via syslog and searching them when needed. The main usage being log retention and forensics.

SIM - Security Information Management - systems, allowed the normalization of the data received from the different devices, thus adding reports and categorized viewing of events mainly for compliance reporting and forensics.

SEM – Security Event Management **-** Although the distinction between SIM and SEM was made more than a decade ago, the functionalities described are still relevant. SEM being – security event management, a solution that allows correlation of events from different sources to reduce alerts to a manageable number that a SOC can use and respond to. SEM is now generally referred as SIEM, due to its having event management capacities, which implies information management functionalities as well.

2.1.1   Network forensics

Less than a month after disclosing that it had been breached, in March 2011, RSA, the security division of EMC purchased Netwitness,[9] signaling the need to go beyond events and into packets for its forensics investigation. Network forensics analysis, data storage and retention produce a "big data" challenge as the volume, velocity and variety of the packets exceeds the SIEM collected events. Even now (2018), most small and medium enterprises are not geared for the volume and complexity of network forensics. Understanding of the gaps that network forensics created led to variations on network data collection, the popular solutions keep metadata only and/or limit the data extract from the packet, reducing dramatically the volume and variety of the data collected.

2.1.2   The endpoint

The classic perimeters matured, hardened, evolved and in the last few years - disappeared, as cloud offering and office-less employment increases, the attack vector has shifted to the endpoint and "the user," adding an extra layer for detection and forensics. All of the new sources of data, combined with the growing awareness for detection and response and growing amount of sensors and data, brought large organizations to adopt a combined "big data" approach to detection, using a classic SIEM for collection and adding big data solutions around it or skipping it all together and using a big data platform.

2.1.3   Big Data, Machine learning and analytics

Different vendors claim machine learning capabilities, which are popular for specific use cases (like malware detection). Security incident response (IR) platforms use machine learning to statistically decide which incidents are related or which analyst is usually resolving which type of incidents. For detection purposes, machine learning offers an opportunity to discover unknown patterns and relations but requires advanced analysts to interpret the patterns. For example: if the system finds a relationship between access to port 7,000 on a server and accessing a bad reputation website, experienced analysts need to analyze and understand the relationship, if exists. Successful use of machine learning for cyber threat detection is reported around identifying similar bad samples after a large number of bad samples have been learned.

The SIEM requirements and knowledge required both to setup, configure and maintain, brought the market to consider other solutions, mainly solutions that are easy to setup and either ignore "classic" rule-based detection or promise automated detection. For mature SOCs who have written "all" the rules, big data systems and analytics is the next step of evolution, as detecting new patterns and receiving new insights from the existing data, is the obvious next step.

For smaller operations, looking for advanced patterns and interpreting them is not achievable considering the growing skill shortage[10] of InfoSec professionals. Deficiencies in detection capabilities (like creating advanced rules and exclusions) in big data platforms do not deter SME's from using them, as advanced rules were not considered in the first place. Some popular platforms are open sourced, easy to use, and provide excellent visualizations and dashboards, thus provide a great alternative for SME's who are satisfied with forensics and visualizations.

Detection platform evolution

As SIEM collects the events, vendors are integrating Big data analytics, machine learning, network sensors, endpoint sensors, automation, incident response, case management, threat intelligence, entity behavior - all within or around (using OEM, plugins or additional modules) the same framework.

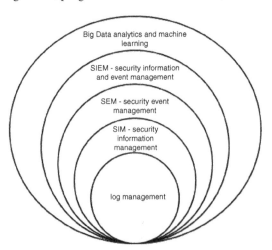

3. DETECTION AND RESPONSE - STRATEGY AND PROCESS

Starting the detection path, how many events and alerts will a corporation have?

Small and medium enterprises will usually have a few security solutions including a firewall, an Antivirus, VPN or remote access solution, Active Directory and sometimes a Proxy. The number of events sent to the SIEM is actually the amount of log lines created by these and additional devices, this amount is first and foremost dependent on the organization decision. One would expect logs to be created based on the organization size, this is also true as 1,000 endpoints produce less logs than 10,000 endpoints, similarly, the alert amount is based on the number and type of rules created for the collected devices.

For example, in most firewalls, the last rule is denying any traffic not specifically allowed and logging it. Prudent firewall admins add a rule before the last one to deny all broadcast traffic which is considered "noise" and not log it. This rule contains all the broadcast traffic stemming from various devices on the network. Removing the pre-last rule in a firewall will increase substantially the events produced by the firewall. Similarly, changing other rules in the firewall from "log" to "not log" will reduce the amount of events created and potentially the alerts. This can be problematic. For example, if threat intelligence information indicates that prior to spreading on the network, a new malware conducted a network broadcast, but this is not logged by the firewall, the behavior will be missed.

In a nother example, one corporate chief information security officer (CISO) was interested in collecting over 10,000 endpoint Windows event logs but was concerned with the amount of logs this action would produce per day. The CISO chose 3 events that would be of value in the collected endpoints:
   a. local login
   b. local group changes
   c. process starting

This decision, saved millions of log lines per day, and subsequently, dollars invested in storage, licensing and computers needed to collect and search these events.

How was that decision made? Why specifically these events were chosen?

3.1 Collecting the "right" events and creating the "right" alerts

What makes an event worthy of auditing and collection?

Before starting to reduce alerts and discussing the techniques to allow effective detection and response, the first step to allow a manageable number of alert is to decide what makes a log line, network connection or email – an alert that needs be investigated. Think of a guard that has 50 television screens showing corridors. Every corridor has motion detectors. what would happen if every movement creates an alert?

In a building that has 100 employees, the guard can handle the alerts, call the relevant people and quickly deal with the alerts, knowing many of the faces. But what if the guard is watching a 1,000 or 10,000 employee building?

Ten thousand employees, moving through corridors would create too many alerts, causing the guard to miss incidents and security breaches, similar to published cyber security incidents discussed earlier in the chapter. After the breach is detected, investigators will find that all the data was available in recordings and alerts were ignored or overlooked.

One possible solution for dealing with many alerts is to choose what to alert about. As the guard is not an expert on the different building functions and facilities, someone will have to decide which alerts are important and which sensors would not alert at all, just record movement.

There are two main approaches to deal with the creation and prioritization of alerts, top-down and bottom-up.

Tip: using a combination of both top-down and bottom-up is a common practice for large enterprises although getting from top to bottom requires several different roles sometimes outside the CISO office, thus making it less common.

3.2 Top down approach

The top-down approach to alert creation is a continuous content creating and evaluation process, in which alerts are created, tuned, published and updated.

The top down approach assures that alerts the SOC handle, are aligned with the requirements and the goals of the organization, and additionally, effectively directs future investment in cyber security detection and response by identifying the gaps between the goals and use cases and the actual sensors and detection capabilities that exist. This point will be detailed in the *SOC detection content creation lifecycle* breakdown.

The first step to create relevant detection/response "content" (alerts, dashboards, reports, response, forensic data) is to understand the main risks addressed. There is a multitude of books discussing risk and cyber risk, so that subject will not be discussed here. For this chapter, we consider risk to be an incident outcome that will cause significant financial, operational, reputational and lately, even physical damage to the organization.

The threats risks entail, are loss of confidentiality, integrity, and availability, and safety (CIAS), that is true for every organization, making the high level risk discussion focus on which CIAS components are more relevant. For example, manufacturing organizations will usually be more concerned about availability, pharma that has production are concerned with integrity, and so on. After having the high-level discussion, additional context would be added to detail threats stemming from the risks detectable by the SOC, as the SOC handles a (growing) portion of the threats.

SOC detection content creation lifecycle

3.2.1   Threat / use case

After having the risk discussion, threat scenarios and use cases should be created, these need to be as detailed as possible to make it technically achievable to detect on later stages.

For example, if the risk is loss of confidential personally identifiable information, the threat can be "personal health records leaked," the use case being personal health records stolen and used unlawfully. Next step would break down the threat to a viable scenario.

3.2.2 Scenarios and indicators

One of the biggest challenges for effective detection and response is getting from a risk, threat or regulation to the details and technical implementation that is actionable by the SOC, this phase is crucial to achieve that, as it provides the linkage between paperwork and technical teams. In this stage, the usage of threat intelligence is effective as new threat scenarios and use cases are created, based on new discoveries and adversaries' tools, techniques, and procedures (TTPs).

Continuing the personal health records example, one scenario could be as follows:

A contractor, in charge of virtual machine infrastructure, creates a clone of a virtual machine containing a database which holds about 5,000,000 personal health records. The contractor copies the machine to an external hard drive to later sold to an unlawful third party.

The technical indicators for SOC detection of the incident can be:
- Clone or copy of a virtual machine
- Cloning or coping of sensitive virtual machine (or any virtual machine)
- Inserting external hard drives to the relevant (all?) servers
- Logging into sensitive virtual machines administration software

Scenario ambiguity or vagueness will result in either overfitting the content, i.e., creating very specific rules, thus missing variations of the scenario (missing a scenario in which the machine is copied over the network to another machine for instance), or under-fitting the content, i.e., creating general rules that will alert on variations of the scenario, which will cause false positives and an overwhelming numbe rof alerts (for example: alerting on every access to the virtual machine management system).

Working with detailed scenarios will create accurate alerts and ease the response creation as there is a definitive alert. Starting with overfitting scenarios and evolving the scenario or adding additional scenario variations will limit the number of alerts created to a manageable number.

Tip: A common question at this stage is "what about the scenarios we haven't thought about?" The short funny answer is – are you ready for an alien invasion or an electromagnetic pulse (EMP)? The real answer is probability and intelligence, understanding what's possible and what's probable should play a key role in detection.

3.2.3 Identify logs, flows and systems

This step furthers the technical achievability of the use case by detailing the actual logs, network flows and systems for successful detection of the scenario. Getting to the details and identifying the specific elements needed to create the detection content, in many cases, reveals gaps, misconfigurations and missing elements in the monitored infrastructure. In this stage, usually, subject matter specialists are consulted to insure the needed configurations and infrastructure are in place and behaving as expected.

Continuing the Health records leakage example, the SOC will require:

- Virtual machine administration auditing to send cloning events of virtual machines to the SIEM
- IT and management help in identifying the sensitive databases and relevant virtual machines
- IT blueprint of the networks, subnets, firewall, systems relevant to the scenario
- Virtual machine infrastructure expert to create and send auditing of external hardware inserting to the Virtual machine infrastructure to the SIEM system
- Virtual machine infrastructure expert to create and send auditing of the VM administration to the SIEM
- IT / CISO should detail the access, change and configuration management of the VM infrastructure

As part of the monitoring capability testing in this stage, it is recommended to conduct the full scenario execution and update detection systems missing elements, logs and visibility. The scenario would initially be played out by one of the IT team members to verify detectability and in the next stage ("build content") using an external red team that execute the scenario with different variations to detect overfitting, missing scenarios and audit deficiencies. For cost-benefit considerations, this activity can be coupled with penetration testing, the amount of knowledge shared with the Pentest team (i.e., black, grey, white box) is dependent on scenario checked.

3.2.4   Build content

After identifying the systems logs and flows relevant to the scenarios, the events are sent or collected by a repository (traditionally a SIEM), in which "content" is created. In addition to this repository, incident management, ticketing systems and knowledge management systems should be updated.

Detection (and response) content is comprised of:

Environment update – Updating the repository with asset information, sensitive accounts, systems, functions, assets, network topologies, conventions etc.

Tip: environment modeling should at least cover the scenarios monitored

Rules – Bases for various functions, mainly alerts, additionally for reporting, dashboards and even threat hunting.

Tip: Rules must produce a manageable number of alerts and be actionable, non-actionable rules should transform to reports or dashboards.

Dashboards – General, for specific systems, products, functions.

Tip: Dashboards are usually used for eye candy. Effective SOCs do not allow any screen to waste energy by presenting irrelevant graphs. Any screen that can be turned off without disabling a SOC capability should be turned off.

Reports – Reviewing non-alert data for anomalies and regulatory needs.

Tip: Reports are invaluable to demonstrate the SOC hard work to management. Case management reports allow measurement and improvement of the day to day operations of the SOC.

Forensics data – Marking events to be retained, anonymized, backed up, sent to other organizational function.

Tip: One of the "Big Data" mindset misconceptions is that everything can be retained indefinitely. Budget limitations limit forensics capabilities, choosing what to collect, aggregate, alert and for how long retain it (and how – real time or backup), is a decision that can change the SOC detection and response capability substantially.

Documentation – Varies between SOC sizes and models, at a minimum a SOC should be updated with incident response procedure, relevant contacts, notification paths escalations paths. Mature SOCs have additional documentation, detailed in SOC maturity model[11] and other MITRE. See, *Ten Strategies of a World Class Cybersecurity Operation Center* (Appendix E).[12]

Tip: Documents become outdated very quickly if not regularly updated. The documentation and updating should be an integral part of the SOC day to day, allowing to quickly and automatically update, revise or evolve documentation. Alternately, usage of external functions to keep the SOC documentation in order, are recommended.

3.2.5   Tune and measure

The SOC usually manages alert tuning and measuring, especially when events become incidents. The standard flow from an event in a system to an incident is:

Event (original system) >>> Alert (SIEM rule) >>> Incident (SIEM or ticketing system)

Some Incidents are created in the ticketing system without going through the SIEM. These can be either alerts from systems not collected by the SIEM, external services, or manually by other teams.

Usually, most alerts are traversing through the SIEM to allow enrichment, contextualizing and correlation (those will be discussed later in the chapter), and these alerts comprise the majority of incidents handled by the SOC.

Incidents intended for SOC handling often go through a report or dashboard phase, in which they are reviewed and tuned down, in sophisticated environments, "events of interest," selected for their potential relevance in detecting "low and slow" incidents, can become bases for anomalies that will become a SOC incident once proven actionability and manageability (i.e. a manageable amount). Not all alerts evolve beyond the dashboard or report phase as tuning often involves other departments and hard decisions around whitelisting and exclusions. Here is a real world (simple) example:

Corporation A has about 15,000 employees in 10 countries. Corporation A decided to create an incident on sensitive accounts failed logins: 3 failed logins in 5 minutes, the incident is born as a report, the report contains 15,234 alerts in 30 days. More than 500 alerts per day. The SOC identifies 25 service and admin accounts that are creating 85% of the incidents. However, the source machines and/or IP addresses are not included in the report as they are missing in the logs, the options are:
1. Management – hire more SOC analysts.
2. SOC – implement automated triage / enrichment to exclude specific correlated events.
3. SOC – leave the alerts as a report to be reviewed periodically by IT.
4. SIEM team – exclude the 25 accounts and get to a manageable number of incidents.
5. SIEM team – increase the number of failed logins to 10 times in 5 minutes and test to reduce it to a manageable account.
6. IT – find the accounts / services and fix the issue.

The best option is six, although experience shows that three, four and five are the most common.

Tuning incidents, beyond being a part of content creation, is an ongoing task and is dependent on collaboration between different teams. Overlooking a multitude of incidents is one task in continuous tuning. Absence of incidents from a certain system or category is more often overlooked as the SOC is usually too saturated to verify that a certain system does not produce alerts or creates less incidents than usual. A different explanation for the SOC missing incidents is the lack of continuous communications with IT infrastructure departments which change and react to needs without notifying the SOC. It is not unusual for IT to change auditing, servers, and/or firewalls without notifying the SOC. In more mature, cybersecurity conscious organizations, the SOC is not only notified of changes, but is an important part of the decision making for new products and services.

Tip: The only real way of checking SIEM content and SOC function is by executing the scenario, this way verification occurs end to end. The original system has relevant audit-defined logs that are actually created and collected by the SIEM, logs are parsed correctly, rules are in place to produce and alert, alerts reach the case management and are handled by the SOC. Anywhere along the way the systems can fail or change, verifying daily that crucial scenarios are indeed monitored is a practice in mature SOCs.

3.2.6 Improve process

Once the content created is tuned to a manageable level, the SOC continues to improve it by enriching the incidents and honing the detection and response process. From a detection standpoint, the SOC strives to increase the accuracy and confidence of an incident. From a response standpoint, the goal to reduce the amount of time and effort to triage (i.e. conduct an initial response) an incident.

Improving the process of detection and response will help to determine the optimal way to deal with an incident; which must be accomplished in the shortest time and with maximum efficiency. One method that is becoming a popular means to increase efficiency is by using automated playbooks.

Playbooks, runbooks, workflows or flows, describe the procedure of triaging an incident, which can be totally manual, describing the logical flow like the one (partial view) offered by CERT Societe Generale.[13]

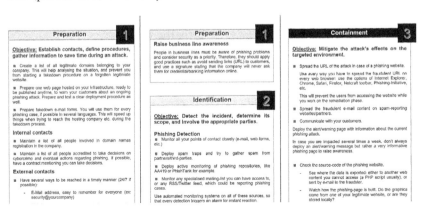

Alternatively, flows can be presented in a tree form and be "half automatic" like many commercial products offer[14], the automation being around common, predictable and cumbersome actions like sending files to a sandbox, deleting suspect email from email boxes, enriching a user identity, etc. In many cases, enrichment tasks occur automatically, leaving the final decision to the analyst, the mature SOC may run a complete process automatically, although usually it will not include destructive measures as these may be exploited.

For example, a corporation has decided to automate the blockage of internet IP's that are scanning the network. Scanning is defined in the SIEM, firewalls and intrusion prevention systems. The flow includes getting the IP address of the scanner and blocking it for 20 minutes in the firewall. The automation system feeds the list as defined in a blocking rule in the firewall. An adversary is scanning the network and detects that after a scan his IP is blocked. The adversary sends spoofed[15] packets that appear to be sent from a major email server or business partner, effectively causing them to be blocked. Automated blocking (account lockout) is common for internal failed logins, but rarely seen for service accounts and administrative accounts for the same reason (adversary abuse), even though these are less popular as they do produce immediate monetary gain like crypto currency mining or ransomware.

Demisto semi-automatic phishing playbook

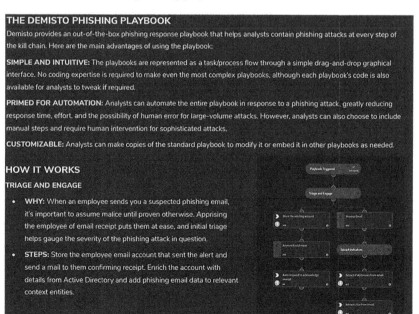

THE DEMISTO PHISHING PLAYBOOK

Demisto provides an out-of-the-box phishing response playbook that helps analysts contain phishing attacks at every step of the kill chain. Here are the main advantages of using the playbook:

SIMPLE AND INTUITIVE: The playbooks are represented as a task/process flow through a simple drag-and-drop graphical interface. No coding expertise is required to make even the most complex playbooks, although each playbook's code is also available for analysts to tweak if required.

PRIMED FOR AUTOMATION: Analysts can automate the entire playbook in response to a phishing attack, greatly reducing response time, effort, and the possibility of human error for large-volume attacks. However, analysts can also choose to include manual steps and require human intervention for sophisticated attacks.

CUSTOMIZABLE: Analysts can make copies of the standard playbook to modify it or embed it in other playbooks as needed.

HOW IT WORKS

TRIAGE AND ENGAGE

- **WHY:** When an employee sends you a suspected phishing email, it's important to assume malice until proven otherwise. Apprising the employee of email receipt puts them at ease, and initial triage helps gauge the severity of the phishing attack in question.

- **STEPS:** Store the employee email account that sent the alert and send a mail to them confirming receipt. Enrich the account with details from Active Directory and add phishing email data to relevant context entities.

Fully automatic enrichment (partial view) using Demisto (SOAR), ArcSight (SIEM) and ELK (Big Data)[16]

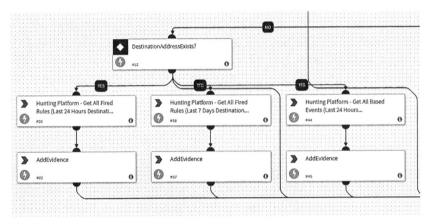

3.2.7   Document and train

Having a well-established, documented process is especially important in a SOC as analyst burnout is high and turnover is frequent. Having knowledge accumulated in analysts' heads without reaching accessible media is a challenge for most SOCs. Effective documentation around the detection response lifecycle must be continuously updated and honed, having the shiniest WIKI without having every analyst contributing, adding and improving will eventually diminish it relevancy as both the internal IT environment changes and adversaries' techniques evolve.

There are several techniques to oppose the deminishing value of SOC documentation, all have pros and cons, a few of the popular ones are:

1. Mandating the updating of the WIKI, assigning the task to a dedicated function
2. Generalizing detection and response procedures (forfeiting detection response details)
3. Automating, using an Incident response platform (or SOAR)

Mandating the updating of the WIKI - The most obvious solution is also a challenging one, as analysts respond to a growing number of incidents, documentation and updating documentation becomes (at least) a second priority, dedicating a function to update the WIKI is a partial solution as the SOC works 24x7 and reaches insights that are not shared beyond the specific analysts who worked on the incident. Combining incident documentation review and analyst interview by the WIKI functionaries can achieve a good coverage latest updates in detection and response within the SOC.

Generalizing detection and response procedures - A document detailing a response to an incident involving a suspicious file, can always contain "check that the file is not malicious," covering a multitude of methods or even more specific, "send the file to a sandbox."

Both methods assume that the analyst understands what a Sandbox is, where a Sandbox can be found, what can be sent to an external Sandbox (maybe suspected financial excel spread sheets are not permitted), which Sandbox to use, what outcome of the Sandbox will conclude the file is malicious and so on.

Generalizing the procedures insures documentation immortality ("verify the file is not malicious" is always true) but would not be effective to train a new SOC employee which will probably need the specific actions and flows relevant to the organization. Some organizations are using SIEM/ Incident response solutions built in categorization or external frameworks to generalize detection and response, building the response procedure based on category, severity, system, technique or attack phase, this is great for management reporting, but needs to be granular enough to allow effective SOC response procedures.

Automating, using an incident response platform (or SOAR) - Recently, platforms for incident response, knowledge accumulation, collaboration and workflows have become available and desired by SOCs worldwide, a phenomenon that is enhanced by the acquisition of two major big data vendors to improve their SIEM capabilities.[17, 18] Predictions are that workflow automation platforms will become popular in the future to the point that Level 1 analysists will be redundant.

The concept behind using automated workflows is "if you know what to do, just do it", i.e., the flow should represent the sum of knowledge available to the organization on alert handling, creating the most efficient response possible, integrating with every available source of context data that exists in the organization. As updating workflows and improving response becomes a part of the daily activities by the SOC, thus keeping the know-how and documentation updated. Incidents are resolved in the platform and with mandatory details on incident resolution, these platforms become the most valuable assets in the SOC. Creating automated, scripted flows ensures the incidents are dealt with in the same manner, every time, and that the SOC succeeds in dealing with many more incidents per shift.

For organizations that do not have resources for detection and response, automated workflows can ask questions, process answers and advance incident resolution. For example, phishing is a popular attack method in which the victim is encouraged the open a document or click a hyperlink. With proper awareness, employees often are cautious in opening suspect emails and send them to the security team. Traditionally, the InfoSec team would review the email, check the links, check the files and decide to allow, or alternatively, deny the email, locate it in all mailboxes and delete it. As this flow is predictable and clear, users are directed to send email to a certain address, workflow automation waits for the email, checks the links with multiple Antivirus, runs the file in a sandbox and either reports bad and deletes the email from all email boxes or reports benign and sends the information back to the employee. The process can be fully automated or half automated, waiting for conformation on deleting emails from mailboxes. Either way, getting 10 phishing emails per day, each validation and deletion takes 30 minutes, saving 5 hours per day(!) for SOC analysts to investigate other alerts. The automated process is documented and reports every step and results of the execution, creating continuous accurate incident reports.

3.2.8 Publish to SOC clients

SOC clients can be internal or external or both. When the SOC is a service to external clients, there are usually contracts in place to mandate the services included. Service level agreements, agreed responses and deliveries, and notification and escalation paths are in place and involve usually a single point of contact on the client side, although this is less common for internal SOCs.

The internal SOC serves different clients within the organization, and being a part of the organization, allows a closer working relationship with the different departments and functions. Some of the SIEM alerts are sent directly to the relevant functions for triage or resolution, bypassing the SOC, and include the recipient's Infosec-related tasks, which adds to the other tasks the department oversees. In some cases, this renders the SOC less popular.

A significant part of promoting the internal acceptance of the SOC is to create use cases and outputs that serve other functions in the organization rather than just adding to their workload.

For example: Creating alerts sent over to the IT infrastructure team regarding service accounts failing login can be useful for early malfunction detection.

In one organization, the SOC monitored the daily backup system logs to automatically alert on errors, saving the system team hours of work each week reviewing logs.

3.3 Bottom up approach

In contrast to the top-down approach, the bottom-up philosophy is to use the already accumulated knowledge: rules, reports, dashboards, source devices, use cases, and response processes. As millions of dollars were already invested in understanding risks, use cases and scenarios, bottom-up proclaims starting with the recommended, proven content is the most effective way to succeed in detection.

Using vendor provided content – SIEM vendors understand that providing a mere platform to detect and correlate events and create alerts is not sufficient as the usability of the platform depends on the integration capabilities, consulting effort and client know-how. Many SIEM vendors offer content updates and marketplaces that contain both free content (rules, reports, dashboards, indicators) and sometimes external specialists who offer paid content with updated use cases, source devices, and intelligence-based alerting. In addition to the vendor content support, consultants, integrators and companies, offer prebuilt content for popular SIEM platforms.

Using best practices – Some detection rules are immortal and use best practices which are well documented and understood is a solid foundation for any detection operation. Example: adding a rule for "a user was inserted to a privileged group and removed within X hours" is a common practice and is relevant for any system or group. It can be effective in detecting rouge privilege escalations and has a low false positive rate. Reviewing every addition to a privileged group (without removal) makes sense in an SME as these are infrequent, furthermore, even the most sophisticated A.I.-based zero-day attack can result in a detectable artifact like group changes.

Using subject matter specialists – In one financial institute, every year, a few of the best hackers from the country are invited to try and get the defined "crown jewels." The SOC is tasked with monitoring every action and verifying sufficient detection capability, level of audit in the abused devices, reporting the events to the SIEM, alerts and response procedure in place. Every attack, successful or not, advances the SOC detection capabilities, focusing on the "crown jewels" use case. Leveraging the already ongoing pen tests and subject matter specialist that understand how to exploit and circumvent systems helps improve SOC detection in both creating use cases and verifying detectability of incidents.

Using threat intelligence – Many SIEM platforms offer built-in or paid threat indicator updates, as most SIEM already collect URL, domain and IP information, cross-correlating these with known bad, or low reputation is common practice. In addition various open source and paid services exist that allow the enrichment of the SIEM.

Going beyond indicators, intelligence allows understanding adversary capabilities and methods. Things that were not thought possible yesterday, are common knowledge today. Most organizations fail in detecting "government grade" incidents. But as tools and techniques are published, detection capabilities are improved when building content based of threat intelligence and latest events. For example, as crypto-based ransomware became popular (2017), and its detection was of great concern to SOCs throughout the world. Prevention was (as it should) the prime focus, but understanding ransomware modus operandi revealed gaps around detecting changes to the network available storage which resulted in organizations changing to permission models for network storage and creating detection capabilities for file creation/writes to the storage. More recently, as crypto mining[19] became popular, the focus shifted to detecting the abuse of resources of internal and cloud systems rather than network storage. In summary, the challenge in using bottom-up approach is losing focus, for example asking, if 50 alerts can be handled per day, which alerts should be selected?

4. DETECTION AND RESPONSE - PEOPLE

Building a detection and response capability for a multinational, 100,000 employee financial institution is very different than what a 2,000 employee corporation needs and can afford. As most literature on the subject[20, 21] deals with NASA-like SOCs,[22] in this section, smaller operations are discussed. Traditionally, small and medium enterprises do not consider having a dedicated team for cyber security detection and response. Detection and response is typically assigned to the CISO, if one exists, and to a technical InfoSec employee, and the SIEM is setup and maintained by an external entity. This is probably still the case for most SMEs.

For an SME the challenge of getting and retaining the talent to be able to detect and respond is greater as it competes with Fortune 500 corporates in a high demand market which is lacking InfoSec employees. One of the growing new models is getting either a fully outsourced SIEM and SOC operation or conducting a hybrid detection and response operation, which includes hybrid technologies and hybrid teams.

Either model requires 3 types of functions (internal or external):

- define, manage and supervise
- build and support
- detect and respond

As most SOCs require a SIEM, it is safe to assume there are more SIEMs than SOCs. Companies that have a SIEM without SOC capabilities usually send the alerts directly to the relevant function (IT, Helpdesk, Infrastructure) for further triage and resolution. For SMEs as a minimum an IT generalist can be used for all 3 following models. The generalist can resolve some of the incidents detected, route others and escalate internally or externally as needed. The models are:

- *Internal SIEM and SOC* – IT generalist manages the SIEM project and the alerts
- *Hybrid SIEM and SOC* – IT generalist and external SIEM SOC are liaising and cross assigning incidents
- *SIEM and SOC as a service* – IT generalist is the point of contact for incident notification and administrative escalation.

The major gap for using only an IT generalist is losing focus on the mission and business priorities and reducing the detection function to detecting viruses and failed logins.

Micro Focus staffing guide[23] offers a minimum of 3 for 8x5 internal SOC operation with after hour MSS support:

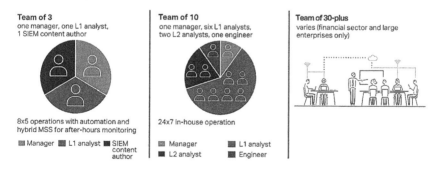

Team of 3
one manager, one L1 analyst, 1 SIEM content author

8x5 operations with automation and hybrid MSS for after-hours monitoring

▨ Manager ■ L1 analyst ■ SIEM content author

Team of 10
one manager, six L1 analysts, two L2 analysts, one engineer

24x7 in-house operation

▨ Manager ■ L1 analyst ■ L2 analyst ■ Engineer

Team of 30-plus
varies (financial sector and large enterprises only)

5. THINKING SMALL – THE NEED TO FOCUS

When everything is a priority, there is no priority.

5.1 Detection costs

On detection costs, SIEM typically vendors recommend every event from every device collected, as their cost model relies on events per second or gigabytes per day. Smaller, newer vendors are trying to change this paradigm and offer new models, like costing based on the organization size, number of employees, etc. Collecting "everything" is also in accordance with the "big data" mindset which is wrongly interpreted as: "storage is cheap, open source big data tools exist, why not." Often, getting all the events from all systems has costs beyond storage. Also, trying to collect and retain all network traffic is not realistic. The main reasons for collecting "everything" from all the devices are forensics and regulation interpretation.

When a breach is detected, the common theme states that one cannot know which data will be key for the investigation, thus all available data needs to be collected to ensure and effective investigation. A different approach[24] claims that, for detection purposes "if you don't know how it looks, you probably won't be able to find it." The question then, is whether collection for forensics purposes justifies the cost. Using the regulation reasoning states that regulation requires collection of all the events from device X, or related to process Y, thus no reasoning should be further discussed.

Collection costs are more than the license required for the SIEM/big data, especially as some popular big data systems are open sourced.[25] The cost of successful event collection is comprised of:
- Hardware for collecting the events
- Networking taps / hardware
- Man-hours to configure the relevant auditing on the source devices
- Software to support event collection (for missing DB audits or storage audits for instance)
- Allow bandwidth to collect events / network from remote location
- Third party brokers to collect clouds and complex applications
- Development time and capabilities to audit internal applications
- Upgrade hardware of certain devices to allow auditing
- Policy changes to allow the correct audit on specific devices
- Storage costs for storing the data
- Compute for searching / using the data

Once collected, many organizations discover that collecting the data is one thing, but searching it is another, as the relevant hardware and architecture must be in place to allow effective searching. The SOC needs to use the tools for triage and to answer questions in a reasonable time, reasonable being seconds to minutes. For SME's, having a full-time employee for detection and response duties is a luxury only some organizations have, the consequence is, that a single person SOC, assuming dealing with an alert takes 30 minutes in average, can handle about 300 alerts per month, additional alerts will result in a backlog that will cause alerts being overlooked or under-investigated.

5.2 Use case monitoring

One of the largest universities in Europe was interested in detection and response capabilities. It had a few employees dedicated to information security but non-dedicated to detection and response. Their first goal was visibility, they wanted to collect all events created by the universities' firewalls and intrusion detection systems. These devices, being standard devices, were simple enough to collect from, but were designated to produce about 20,000 events per second, which are over 1.5 billion events per day and more than 51 billion events per month. An event is a log line, weighing between 500 ytes to 1.5 KB, assuming event size of 1 KB, the amount of data expected was about 1.5 TB per day.

More than a decade ago, event collection projects that were not use case-related were amusingly called "event trash can projects" because organizations would part with millions of dollars to send a lot of events to decay in a large trash can, maintaining and supporting the trash can continuously. Happily for organizations (less for SIEM vendors), those days are mostly over and organizations are realizing that local or managed, a conscious (hard) decision of what to collect and alert about, has to be made.

Going back to the university, due to the costs, it buried the project. However, a different project was offered. Deciding on the content of the monitoring project took a single meeting and resulted in a single question being presented: "What is the University's top risk?"

Interestingly, the top risk did not involve collecting the all the firewall events, the risk was around protecting and monitoring the lifecycle of research documents and included:
- File access to specific folders
- Active directory changes to group allowed to view research documents
- VMware – cloning, moving and copying research VM's
- Changes to document encryption
- Monitor specific assets or top researchers for intrusion

The estimated event collection for the project was 50 events per second, about 4 million log lines per day, effectively saving the university more than half a million dollars per year in licensing, hardware, and maintenance of a large "events trash can." Effective detection, much like life, requires priorities and hard decisions. These decisions need to be made when building local capability or even when outsourcing detection and response to a third party. Hopefully, this chapter provides a few clues on how to achieve that.

Endnotes

1 *https://www.gartner.com/en/newsroom/press-releases/2017-03-14-gartner-says-detection-and-response-is-top-security-priority-for-organizations-in-2017*

2 *https://www.verizonenterprise.com/resources/reports/rp_DBIR_2018_Report_execsummary_en_xg.pdf*

3 *https://www.darkreading.com/attacks-and-breaches/heartland-payment-systems-hit-by-data-security-breach/d/d-id/1075770*

4 *https://www.theguardian.com/society/2018/may/29/skin-cancer-computer-learns-to-detect-skin-cancer-more-accurately-than-a-doctor*

5 *https://www.cs.cmu.edu/~sbhagava/papers/face-rec-ccs16.pdf*

6 *https://www.wired.com/2009/10/walmart-hack/*

7 *https://securityboulevard.com/2018/07/why-you-need-mdr-to-combat-current-and-emerging-threats/*

8 *https://www.sans.org/reading-room/whitepapers/incident/future-soc-2017-security-operations-center-survey-37785*

9 *https://threatpost.com/emc-buys-security-firm-netwitness-040411/75101/*

10 *https://cybersecurityventures.com/jobs/*

11 *https://www.soc-cmm.com/introduction/*

12 *https://www.mitre.org/sites/default/files/publications/pr-13-1028-mitre-10-strategies-cyber-ops-center.pdf*

13 *https://cert.societegenerale.com/en/index.html*

14 *https://go.demisto.com/hubfs/Resources/Playbooks/Phishing%20Playbook.pdf*

15 *https://en.wikipedia.org/wiki/IP_address_spoofing*

16 Created by Moshe Simchon (BDOSOC) using Demisto SOAR platform

17 *https://www.zdnet.com/article/splunk-buys-security-orchestration-provider-phantom-for-350-million/*

18 *https://www.zdnet.com/article/ibm-buys-resilient-systems-aims-to-offer-response-playbooks-to-security-incidents/*

19 *https://www.csoonline.com/article/3269053/security/cryptomining-not-ransomware-the-top-malware-threat-so-far-this-year.html*

20 *http://www.ciscopress.com/store/security-operations-center-building-operating-and-maintaining-9780134052014*

21 *https://www.elsevier.com/books/designing-and-building-security-operations-center/nathans/978-0-12-800899-7*

22 *https://www.nasa.gov/content/security-services*

23 *https://www.microfocus.com/media/white-paper/intelligent_security_operations_a_staffing_guide_wp.pdf*

24 My approach

25 *https://www.elastic.co/elk-stack*

Chapter 8

CYBER RISK ASSESSMENT – TOOLS, TECHNIQUES AND BEST PRACTICES

By: Graham Croock, CISA, AGA (SA)

INTRODUCTION

As the twenty-first century progresses, we are seeing rapid growth and global revision in connectivity and digitalization on a scale never contemplated before. This is, to a large extent made possible by the vast leaps in technology, communication, and globalization fuelling rapid digitalization transformation and automation.

The first decade of the 21st century has been marked by some dark-clouds. During September 2001, catastrophe struck when the World-Trade Centre Twin-Towers in New York were destroyed by two separate passenger aircraft. It was unheard of that a group of extremists would collaborate to perpetuate such a level of mass destruction. It was unbelievable that armed fundamentalists could slip undetected through airport security and board an aircraft. Only one of the Twin-Towers was insured. It was highly unlikely that both towers could be attacked and destroyed all at the same time! At that time risk management was predominantly reactionary, conducted to a large extent as an isolated discipline in business and focussed on business continuity management. Risk management practitioners conducted risk assessments using methodologies based on insurance underwriting principles and to a very large extent were run on spread sheets and primitive databases.

During October 2001, the Enron scandal was exposed, which eventually led to the unexpected bankruptcy of the giant Enron Corporation, an American energy corporation based in Houston, Texas. This was one the largest bankruptcies in American history. It contributed to the introduction of the Sarbanes-Oxley (SOX) Act of 2002, rquiring signing-off of financial controls and, once again, seemed to have been a misjudgement or incorrect risk management approach. During 2008 the sub-prime financial crisis brought the world's financial system to its knees. The Deepwater Horizon oil spill, regarded at that time to be the largest accidental marine oil spill in the history of the petroleum industry, began during April 2010 in the Gulf of Mexico. It claimed eleven lives and caused immense environmental damage.

These events of catastrophic proportion occurred from failure to implement appropriate risk management, rather than the failure of risk management. Without the effective application of suitably designed, configured and implemented risk management tools, techniques and methodologies, effective cyber risk management cannot not be implemented.

Failure to identify, assess, and manage the major cyber risks facing any organization's business model will most certainly and unexpectedly result in a significant loss of stakeholder value or possibly total failure.

Boards and senior leadership must of necessity implement processes to effectively and efficiently manage all substantial cyber risks confronting the organization. This can only be achieved using structured methodologies, appropriate tools and technology, and best practice implementation by suitably skilled specialists.

The diagram set out below depicts the relationship between methodology, knowledge, tools and techniques and how these relate to their respective operational components followed by the overall objectives, which can be achieved by consistent application of best practice principles.

When structured methodologies, based on acceptable codes and standards, with integrated tools are correctly applied to cyber risk management, it is possible to provide key individuals with an understanding of critical cyber risk exposures. This facilitates the balancing of expectations and allows for an increased potential of resilience necessary for survival subsequent to an attack, ensuring uncompromised business sustainability.

The diagram does not purport to be a one-size fits all solution but does represent a basic foundation for design of cyber risk management systems.

WHAT'S IT ALL ABOUT?

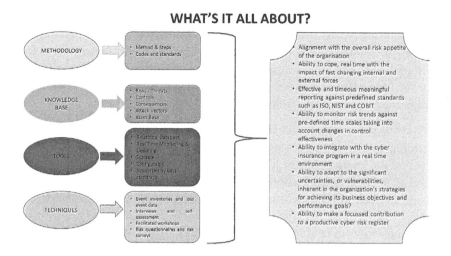

Cyber Risk Management Standards and Codes

Operational risk management is designed and implemented under standards and codes that are set by national or international standards committees or commissions.

Two pillars of operational risk, namely market risk and credit risk were historically well regulated by financial standards of service organisations who relied on mature standards. For example, those set by the Bank for International Settlements. Accordingly, the finance and insurance industries are obligated to hold capital in reserve in order to remain in a solvent trading position. Cyber risk on the other hand, has not yet been effectively subjected to any regulation. This is imperative to enhance business resilience, protection of information and security. Thus it is essential that appropriate tools and techniques are designed, developed and applied to mitigate Cyber risk within organizations to acceptable levels as defined by the organisations risk appetite. Cyber risk management, thus becomes the third key pillar of operational risk management.

Both market and credit risk have well defined and proven methodologies and they have their own mature software applications. Cyber risk management, on the other hand is still very much in its developmental phase, and requires the creation of its own specific tools, techniques and methodologies for effective application of cyber risk management.

Boards of directors and C-suite executives have a strong incentive to adopt appropriate standards and codes as adoption brings the level of rigour that might sustain legal challenges of liability through the courts when adverse incidents occur. Standards continue to assist public and private sector organizations adopt effective risk management. It is recognised that a common platform for risk management addresses issues around jargon that might otherwise be difficult for board members, executives and management to comprehend. The application of effective tools, methods and frameworks for the management of cyber risk, introduces consistency and benefits that are invaluable and measurable.

For cyber risk management to ultimately deliver opportunities whilst addressing the potential downsides, cyber risk management practices and methodologies must not be limited to any specific industry nor any single level of organizational authority or codes and standards. Instead, of necessity, cyber risk management needs to be adaptable to applicable standards such as NIST, CIS, COBIT, ISO and other recognised standards which encourage users to tailor the terminology and measures of risk to reflect the organization's needs. The emphasis is on "application" of the process, not "accreditation," leaving organizations free to develop and implement the most appropriate risk frameworks based on recognised tried and tested standards or combinations of best practice.

Standards and codes contribute significantly to the enhanced credibility applicable to the subject-matter and the effectiveness of the policies and processes that corporations follow. The diagram below is a screenshot taken from an actual tool developed and used by BDO South Africa to assess cyber risk based on mappings to recognised codes, in this case, NIST. Since the risks are mapped against the various NIST Security and Privacy Control families, structured and meaningful reporting by control family is automated for meaningful dashboards with trends based on periodic assessment.

NIST CATEGORIES

- All Risks
  - Access Control
  - Audit and Accountability
  - Awareness and Training
  - Configuration Management
  - Contingency Planning
  - Identification and Authentication
  - Incident Response
  - Maintenance
  - Media Protection
  - Personnel Screening
  - Physical and Environmental Protection
  - Planning
  - Privacy Controls
  - Program Management
  - Risk Assessment
  - Security Assessment and Authorisation
  - System and Communications Protection
  - System and Information Integrity
  - System and Services Acquisition

Performance management has evolved to become one of the leading and stronger business drivers taking shape over the last decade or so. Balanced score card, setting objectives, strategies and measurable key performance indicators (KPIs) all give a tangible outcome to managing performance. Risk management is another support of performance management, with risk management providing corporations with an alternative way of making informed decisions. Through the use of effective cyber risk management tools, techniques and methodologies, compliance with recognised standards can be achieved, leading to reduced exposure to cyber risk. When live real-time reporting is completely aligned to the required outcomes and the associated strategic appetite and values, continuous improvement and return on effort can be achieved. To accomplish this, it is imperative that the techniques and tools utilized for the assessment and management of cyber risk be capable of supporting compliance with the standards and appetite for risk chosen by the organisation. A one-size-fits-all approach is not effective as the methodology adopted needs to be scalable, configurable and adaptable to suit the organization's requirements, goals, capabilities, environment, resources and budget.

The Relationship between Techniques, Methods and Tools.

Throughout this chapter, we will refer to techniques, methods and tools, all within the context of cyber risk management. It is critically important that the reader understands what these are if they are to be used productively:

> **Techniques and methods are synonymous and represent the way cyber risk management is applied, i.e. the steps in the process and the techniques used to effect the methodology. Tools are the software applications used to facilitate the techniques/ methodology.**

Efficient and productive cyber risk management will be achieved when an efficient software platform and appropriate tools exist to support the methodology which is facilitated by the most effective techniques.

Any tool and associated methodology that wishes to achieve the above objective must by necessity be fully configurable without change to the fundamental underlying code. This implies that the methodology deployed for cyber risk management is not hard coded in the tool, but rather the tool allows for easy integration, configuration and optimisation of the methodology by trained users who never have to rely on changes to the application's hard code.

All risk management software stores risks in various databases of some form and these are often distributed throughout the organisation, making it difficult and almost impossible to maintain data integrity. By automating the risk management methodology and separating the standing risk data (knowledge-base) from the organization's data the task of maintaining data integrity becomes relatively easy to manage. The diagram below shows how it becomes possible to separate the standing data from the organizational data. By categorising and mapping between the standing relational risk data base and the organizational structures, the following benefits are derived:

- Data integrity is fully maintained
- Aggregation of risk is easily achieved
- Mapping business unit structures vs categories of risk allows for meaningful dashboard reporting
- Advanced interrogation of the risk and control data is achieved

The mapping of data as depicted in the diagram below facilitated the design of a tool which supports the development of configurable risk management methodologies by the client.

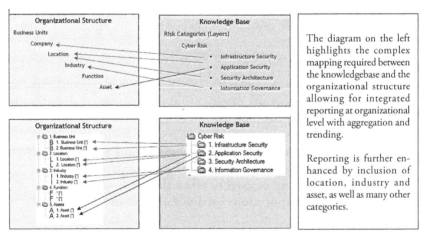

It is impossible for any organisation which is highly digitized, connected and reliant on technology, to deal with all of the more significant risks at the same time. The means to identify **which** risks will be treated and **when** sets the strategic agenda of the cyber risk management framework. As technology progresses with regards to the sophistication, effective analysis leads to prioritisation of mitigating actions. The use of suitable algorithms, often with embedded artificial intelligence integrated within the methodology, is the most effective way to prioritise the application of the efforts required for successful risk mitigation. Given the rate at which technology and the levels of sophistication of cyber threats are developing, there is often insufficient time to manually audit the adequacy of existing controls and institute further appropriate controls to mitigate the key risks and consequences. The process of control enhancement for the mitigation of prioritized risks, must be absolutely automated by using logical routines embedded within the tools and concomitant methodologies.

Methodology (Methods and Steps in the Process)

In-order for cyber risk management tools to operate effectively and achieve the desired outcomes, some basic risk management principles for ensuring an effective methodology need to be applied as defined below:

- Each cyber risk is associated with the context or contexts in which this risk is relevant. This means that the cyber risk may have multiple instances (refer to above diagram).
- The definition and subsequent application of the cyber risk appetite must be an integral process embedded within the methodology applied to the management of cyber risk.
- Aggregation of the key cyber and associated operational risks that combine to reach the thresholds of acceptable appetite must be automated and system driven.
- Aggregation calculations need to be technically sound, providing summarised results based on appropriate realistic scenarios of risk events.
- Data of sound integrity (well-structured and accurate) is an imperative.

A typical methodology of best practices is set out in the diagram below:

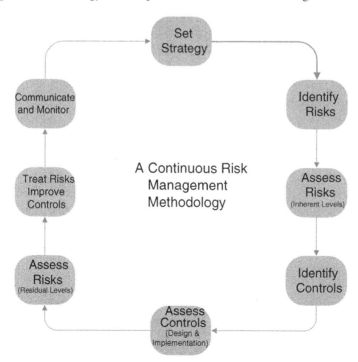

The methodology or as we refer to it as the "methods and steps" must be fully configurable and scalable within the computer application adopted to support the cyber risk management functionality. This means that it must be easy to add or delete steps and to rearrange the order while maintaining integrity of the data.

The initial stages of designing the methodology are the foundation of a sound system and involves the following:

- Definition of the risk appetite in terms of:
    - Probability ranges
    - Levels of consequence/impact
    - Control effectiveness and
    - Quantification of risk outcomes
    - Risk rating levels
- Defining the appropriate standards and codes against which the methodology will be mapped
- Setting the frequency of assessment
- Defining the reporting outcomes including accountability for mitigation
- Defining mitigation strategy
- Setting appetite for insurable risk

Risk Identification

The **identification** of risk involves a review of the risk knowledge base and verification of existence by suitably qualified and experienced executives and management. The knowledge base is developed over time from multiple sources and includes all known and predicted risks, taking into account past experience, threat analysis and other experience.

- **Inherent Risk Assessment**

Assessment of risks at **inherent level** involves valuation of the probability and impact of individual events without taking into account any controls but using frequency of past occurrence as a predictor of future events. Within the fast changing cyber arena, history is often unreliable and thus the frequency of assessment is increased to accommodate the lack of historical information required for accurate predictability.

- **Control Identification**

Identification of controls is usually conducted in a workshop scenario and in discussion with executive and management teams who were and are involved in the design and implementation of the control environment. In the case of cyber risk, this would include the CIRO, the CIO, the CISO, network administrators and ICT service providers.

- **Control Design and Effectiveness Assessment**

Assessment of the controls is conducted by evaluating the design and effectiveness of implementation of the controls. Once again, the same teams of executives are involved and very often input from audits is considered.

- **Residual Risk Assessment**

Having assessed the effectiveness of controls, the inherent risk ratings are re-calibrated to take into account the control effectiveness thus giving the residual risk rating.

- **Recalibration of Controls to Mitigate Risk**

Where it is considered that in terms of the miss-match between the actual residual rating and the defined appetite, additional mitigation is necessary. This is applied by either enhancing controls, which reduces the probability of occurrence or by transferring some or all of the potential impact using some form of insurance to limit the impact. In the case of cyber risk, specific cyber risk policies are available and the ultimate valuations of value at risk (VAR) can be compared with the premiums to accurately establish economic viability. Increasing the effectiveness of controls reduces the probability, while transferring risk using insurance reduces impact. It thus becomes relatively easy to recalibrate towards the defined impact and probability with a balancing mix of both these mitigation tools.

- **Constant Monitoring**

The final stage in the process involves reporting and monitoring on a frequent basis, aligned to the frequency of system configuration changes, and the frequency of application and associated threat changes as well as the maturity of the control environment, while at all times being fully cognizant of the fast and ever changing threat landscape.

With the cyber risk management challenges associated with the fast developing and sophisticated threat landscape, it is imperative that the frequency of iterations of this methodology be increased to align with the defined risk appetite.

Software Tools for Effective Cyber Risk Management

- **Objectives of using appropriate tools and techniques.**

The ultimate goal of enterprise cyber risk management is to assess and evaluate total returns associated with the deployment of digital assets relative to total risks, leading to more informed business decisions. The selection and use of appropriate tools and techniques enables organizations to better understand the effectiveness of their cybersecurity risk management efforts. This assertion forms the basis of nearly all debates regarding the value proposition relating to the selection and deployment of cyber risk assessment and management methodologies and tools deployed to support the chosen methodology.

The key fundamental objectives associated with a choice of tools for integration in the cyber risk management process are described below:

- Alignment with the overall risk appetite of the organisation
- Ability to cope, real time with the impact of fast changing internal and external forces
- Effective and timeous meaningful reporting against predefined standards such as ISO, NIST and COBIT
- Ability to monitor risk trends against pre-defined time scales taking into account changes in control effectiveness
- Ability to integrate with the cyber insurance program in a real time environment
- Ability to adapt to the significant uncertainties, or vulnerabilities, inherent in the organization's strategies for achieving its business objectives and performance goals?
- Ability to make a focussed contribution to a productive cyber risk register

By designing and implementing a cyber risk management process which encompasses a maturity model that allows the organization to adapt and configure its cyber risk management tools to meet the demands for increased knowledge and sophistication, the fundamental objectives set out above can easily be complied with. The constant changes that regulators require, which often result in challenges for cyber risk managers, can be adequately met when the methodology applied is supported by cyber risk management software which can support the changing needs without requiring onerous customization by the software vendor.

Given that cyber risks in the global economy constantly change and evolve, cyber risk management must of necessity, be a continuous process. For optimum results, the process requires strong commitment from C-level executives, an effective process tailored to the organization's unique culture and selection and deployment of effective tools.

Automated cyber risk management software tools are being promoted in the market place as part of the tool kit for instituting a risk management framework using a pre-defined and configurable methodology, while techniques support the implementation process. Until now it has been quite common to use spreadsheets and word processors to capture risk management data that serve as the means to monitor an action plan for risk mitigation. This is acceptable for normal operational risk management but, given the rate at which the cyber threat landscape is evolving, cyber risk management, being more complex and difficult to manage, requires automation and real time monitoring. A well designed and implemented system reliant on a relational database with inputs from real time monitoring services is thus ideal if cyber risks are to be effectively mitigated at affordable cost.

A single cyber risk can lead to several impacts and in turn might require several controls to mitigate the risk and its impacts. In logical terms this is a one too many relationship, which is very difficult to manage using two-dimensional paper-based documents such as spreadsheets and word processors. The reality is that it becomes unproductive to proceed on this basis because it is laborious and unnecessarily complex for staff to become involved with and is likely to be error prone. A relational database with multiple mappings, is the best and most reliable means of managing the capture, assessment and treatment of cyber risks.

One of the challenges of risk management is that the automated tools must be optimally effective in the hands of those who are actually performing the assessments using the techniques set out below. While a dedicated risk manager may be prepared to learn a more complex system, the business unit managers and staff usually want a user-friendly system, which provides immediate results with visual capability. This implies that there are broadly two components here: a methodology that encompasses the risk management framework and a technology platform tool to serve as the repository for risk profiling, monitoring and reporting.

Techniques

Any organization, large or small, public, private, or not-for-profit, U.S.-based or global that has a stakeholder with expectations for business resilience, sustainability and success can benefit from the use of practical techniques set out below.

Before considering some of the specific techniques available for organizations to identify risk, several important factors should be noted about this process and techniques:

- The techniques used should encourage open and frank discussion, and staff should not fear reprisal for expressing their concerns about potential events that would give rise to risks resulting in major cyber attack with the concomitant loss to the organisation.
- By combining the use of a combination of techniques it is often possible to produce a more comprehensive list of cyber-related risks than would reliance on a single method;
- The process followed in dealing with the complex subject matter and associated attack vectors should involve a cross-functional and diverse team of users and cyber experts. Such a group provides additional insight and enhances commitment to effective cyber risk management.
- The process will invariably generate a lengthy list of risks. The key is to focus on the "vital few" rather than the "trivial many."
- The end result of the process should be a risk language specific to the company or the business unit, function, activity or process.

Some practical and proven techniques for effective identification of risk are:
- Brainstorming
- Event inventories and analysis of loss event data
- Interviews and self-assessment
- Facilitated workshops
- SWOT analysis
- Risk questionnaires and risk surveys
- Scenario analysis

For the effective application of these techniques, it is a prerequisite that the methodology is defined and that appropriate tools are in place to support the process. The most practical and proven technique for effective assessment of cyber risks involves the application of sound mathematical formulas based on probability and business impact before and after application of cyber controls. Establishment of probability of occurrence using past history as well as predicted occurrence based on threat analysis and live monitoring of systems, provides a relatively accurate measure if conducted frequently. Concurrent with the establishment of probability of occurrence, business impact associated with attacks is estimated on an ongoing basis and these two factors are applied to quantify values at risk (VAR). The difference in VAR pre-implementation of controls and post-implementation of controls provides insight for executives as to the effectiveness of the cyber control environment.

Having assessed cyber risks in terms of a quantified VAR, it becomes relatively easy to treat or mitigate the risks using what is often referred to as a four "T" approach.

- T1: Treat the control environment with additional control enhancement.
- T2: Tolerate the current situation and leave the controls as is.
- T3: Transfer risk, using appropriately structured cyber insurance products.
- T4: Terminate the risk (in cases where it is beyond appetite and no viable solution is available)

Most organizations find it valuable to capture the direction of the risk over time (trending). This can be labelled on the risk map or communicated separately. The direction of risk movement on a heat map can be defined using terms such as "increasing," "stable," or "decreasing," and relates to the movement of the exposure over time. This is commonly referred to as time trending. Knowing the direction and trend of a risk as well as its monetary impact and likelihood can be crucial to managing that risk. For example, risk trends can reveal that the risk was decreasing over the last several years but has increased recently, suggesting imminent attack.

Organizations can validate the qualitative assessments of initial impact and probability by examining historical data to determine the frequency of events or impact such events had in the past. Events and attacks that happened to other organizations can usually be used to understand how a similar event and attack might impact their own organization. Gathering such data can be time consuming, but it has major advantages given the reliance of organizations on similar / universal application technologies with common vulnerabilities. By automating the risk assessments using constant threat analysis and artificial intelligence-based algorithms, trending has become the best form of reporting for C-suite executives as it provides almost real time information with enhanced predictability.

Knowing the real frequency or likelihood of a major exploit of a known vulnerability, for example, can provide an organization with the information necessary to make informed cost-benefit decisions about potential solutions.

Total Cost of Ownership and Cost of Control

Total cost of ownership (cost of control) is a financial estimate that is calculated to help purchasers and owners of software tools, determine the direct and indirect costs of a product or system. In the case of cyber risk management software and tools, it is a comprehensive measure of running the cyber risk management system with its tools, from inception until the objectives are achieved and cyber risk is considered effectively managed. A reasonable time frame is on average four years.

The total cost of ownership (TCO) of having enterprise-wide cyber risk management (EWCRM) is measured as the cost of purchasing the technology, training and implementing the technology over the life that the technology is used in the business. It is usually the implementation costs that are the most expensive. This is because it includes software support costs as well as the cost of the resources used by the customer. In most cases the latter far exceeds the net cost of the software.

A threat posed to nearly all cyber risk management systems relates to the maturity of the system. Maturity in this context refers to the stage and position of development on the development lifecycle. Our research shows that a substantial body of cyber risk management knowledge is still relatively immature and to a large extent in a developmental phase. Very few organisations can claim complete coverage of cyber risk management across their businesses and where this has reached a perceived maintenance/monitoring mode, it is still work in progress. Additionally, it is unlikely that regulators have reached a stage where their call for industry standards of behaviour, governance and operations in terms of effective cyber risk management is substantially completed. The evidence for this is that there continue to be an increasing number of obligations mandated by various government authorities.

These mandates require some special thinking on the part of cyber risk managers. They must by necessity design a cyber risk management process with an associated analysis that is capable of changing and growing over time. Initially the organisation's approach may be simplistic, to have a common denominator of risk management that all staff can buy into, but over time the process changes to become more sophisticated and some areas of the business require more specialised processes. This impacts directly on the type of tools, methodologies and software needed.

The software needs to be flexible, configurable and sufficiently scalable, to accommodate the fast changing cyber threat landscape, and to prevent the attack vectors and threats from outpacing the functionality of the software and associated tools and methodologies applied. Optimised cost of ownership will be achieved within the organization over the pre-defined time when easily configurable software tools are effectively implemented and constantly used to build a mature system.

Boards, executives and managers are beginning to realise the exposure their organizations have to cyber threats. They are realising that companies make money and increase stakeholder value by engaging in activities that have some risk, yet stakeholders also tend to appreciate and reward some level of stability in their expected returns. With the surge in recent cyber attacks, C-suite executives realise that the failure to identify, assess, and manage the major cyber risks facing the organization's business model, however, may unexpectedly result in significant loss of stakeholder value. In today's globally connected world, quality risk data is a fundamental asset of any organization and for this reason, adequate budgets are beginning to emerge based on the total cost of control.

Conclusion

Following a systematic risk management process using appropriate tools capable of ensuring adequate data integrity and consistency allows for the development and maintenance of useful management data sets. The risk register is essentially the accumulated risk data that is gathered from numerous sources, such as formal risk assessment workshops, continuous threat monitoring, vulnerability assessments, penetration tests, interviews and investigations. By managing the assessment data using an integrated relational database capable of providing mechanisms for continual improvements, valuable data can be maintained, analysed and supported by a well-structured and cost effective methodology. The combination of a well-structured methodology, rich cyber data and the use of appropriate techniques and functional tools ensures that it is possible to maintain a cost-effective cyber risk management process capable of building cyber resilience, to support business continuity.

The next chapter focuses on the importance of identity and access management, which is critical to ensure cybersecurity. At the core of information security is the capability of an organization's information system to be able to (1) confirm the identity of the person seeking access, commonly called authentication, and (2) control of the level of information access to what is deemed appropriate by the organization's leadership, referred to as authorization. It is vital for every organization to implement an effective and efficient information security process for authentication and authorization.

The table below is included for additional reading to demonstrate the capability of some of the tools being used successfully by BDO South Africa.

Tool Application	Functionality	Benefits
CSAT	Collects and analyses policy and security settings on Windows endpoints, Sharepoint, Office 365, and file shares and servers for the purpose of rapidly gaining an understanding and then assessing the cyber maturity of an estate.	Data collected is supplemented with data from easily customizable surveys (CIS, GDPR, and 3 cyber security roadmaps covering 16 tacit modules of structured/ semi-structured and unstructured data protection + cybersecurity.) The solution can be used to rapidly discover endpoints in an estate and relies on pure WMI methods to distribute a survey to target endpoints to complete its scan. Data is returned and presented in an easy-to-use interface that allows for per endpoint or aggregated views of all data across a scan, data stacking to identify outliers, and other forms of analysis. Active Directory (including Azure AD).
Blueliv	Blueliv is a leading cyber threat intelligence provider with a world-class in-house Labs team that scours the web, the dark web and the deep internet to deliver fresh, automated and actionable threat intelligence to organizations across multiple industries to protect their people, networks and brand assets from the outside in.	**The 4 Business Benefits are set out below:** **1.** React faster with actionable and relevant business threat intelligence information targeting the organization's assets at a global level. The Blueliv solution covers a broader range of cyber threats than any other service and enables processing of a higher volume of threat data with its unique capabilities and user-friendly functionality. **2.** Better threat visibility means shorter incident response times. Simplify threat data analysis, reduce false positives, and accelerate threat detection and remediation. Proactive continuous search and monitoring. **3.** The Blueliv Cyber Threat Intelligence Platform is the only solution that continuously delivers real-time information about botnets and malware as well as data obtained from the dark web and deep internet. Reduces required manpower and manual processes with real-time searches and automated incident detection. Easy to deploy, easy to set up, easy to operate:.

		4. A cloud-based platform developed for SOCs conceived as a SIEM. Setup requires no onsite installation and minimal technical training. Provides a ready-to-use API enabling seamless integration with third party systems.
Infocyte	Infocyte Hunt is an application developed by former U.S Air Force cybersecurity officers out of a necessity to fill the gap of real-time threat detection.	Infocyte-Hunt scans and enumerates the entire network to validate all the end-points, thus identifying the malware and suspicious code that may be in your network it will resolve these compromises, using collected forensics gathered from each scan. **Threat Hunting** - Infocyte enables a focused and iterative search for adversaries and malicious programs internal to the defender's networks. Device Validation - By integrating with existing SIEM or network access solutions, Infocyte can effectively scan and validate the cleanliness of devices coming on the network or that have exhibited suspicious behaviour. **Compromise Assessment** - Verify whether a network has been breached or not, independent of the existing security stack. Infocyte is the most effective solution for conducting compromise assessments objectively, rapidly, and affordably. **Incident Response** - Upon confirmation of a breach, Infocyte serves as the initial collector of live incident and forensics data on compromised hosts. Direct access to endpoints enables you to interactively engage and mitigate threats. Infocyte aims to bridge the threat detection gap, saving your company money in detecting malware early. Infocyte will proactively discover active and dormant malware, malicious activity and classify them as un-trusted, until proven trustworthy..

Chapter 9

UNDERSTANDING IDENTITY AND ACCESS MANAGEMENT AS A CYBERSECURITY CONSTRUCT

By: Laura M. Hars, NSA IAM/IEM

INTRODUCTION

Identity and access management (IAM) has become a critical area of concern in cybersecurity. IAM is a framework that includes some specific technology designed to manage identities for a corporation. IAM encompasses both systems and manual processes for securely initiating, storing and managing user identities and access privileges. IAM verifies user access requests and either grants or denies permission to protected company materials. It also deals with various administrative functions including password problems, employee onboarding, employee terminations and overall granting access to employees to corporate applications. IAM ensures that users are who they say they are (authentication) and that they can access the applications and resources they have permission to use (authorization).

The essential components an IAM framework/system are highlighted below:
- Set of processes and a supporting infrastructure for the creation, maintenance and use of digital identities
- Account management
- Identity governance
- Identity federation (single sign on capabilities)
- Role-based design and access control (RBAC)
- Delegated administration for on-boarding and off-boarding employees (provisioning and de-provisioning)
- Audit logging and reporting

The core objective of IAM systems is one digital identity per individual. After the digital identity is established, the goal is to maintain it through it's lifecycle as system access is added and removed depending on the individual's role in the organization.

Why is IAM a Critical Component of a Security Architecture?

The first entry into a software application is usually providing your user id and password. This concept is known as "authentication." The user "authenticates" or identifies that they have the correct credentials to prove they are who they say they are and can legitimately access the software. In a typical corporate environment, employees may need to use more than one or two software applications. Employees frequently have an identity for each software application they access which can translate into five, ten, and even as many as twenty unique user accounts and passwords. This "plethora" of identities and passwords is at the heart of a critical security issue. Because users can't remember all these passwords, they develop "sloppy" password management and write them on sticky notes on their desk, make them simple (so a hacker can crack them), reuse the same password multiple times and are often resistant to changing them. User credentials are usually the entry point into corporate networks and the associated software platforms. Compromised user credentials are the number one cause of security breaches. It is because of this issue coupled with the complex technical environments that are the backbone for most corporate systems, that a user name and password is no longer adequate to protect many corporate systems.

Key IAM Terminology

Authentication

Today, identity management systems often incorporate elements of biometrics, machine learning and artificial intelligence, and risk-based authentication. Thus, regulating user access can involve a number of authentication methods for verifying the identity of a user beyond passwords. Authentication factors such as digital certificates, soft and hard tokens, smart cards and one time passwords (OTP) are now every common forms of authentication. Hardware tokens and wallet size smart cards serve as one component in two-factor authentication, which combines something you know (your password) with something you have (the token or the card) to verify identity. A smart card has an embedded integrated circuit chip that can be either a secure microprocessor or a memory chip alone and functions like the magnetic strip or chip on a credit card. Software tokens, can exist on any device with storage capability, from a USB drive to a cell phone. OTP tokens are frequently software-based, and the passcode generated by the token is sent to the user's smartphone usually in a text message. Software tokens make it easier for mobile users to enter authentication information and not have to keep track of handwritten passwords or use a separate piece of hardware.

Authentication patterns can be defined simply by three high level types: direct authentication, brokered authentication and multi-factor. With direct authentication (using a user id and password), the user makes a request to access a resource, their credentials are validated by a directory/database look up and request is denied or accepted. Brokered authentication involves the following steps:

1. The client submits an authentication request to the authentication broker.
2. The authentication broker contacts the identity store to validate the client's credentials.
3. The authentication broker responds to the client, and if authentication is successful, it issues a security token.
4. A request message is sent to the service; it contains the security token that is issued by the authentication broker.
5. The service authenticates the request by validating the security token that was sent with the message.
6. The service returns the response to the client.

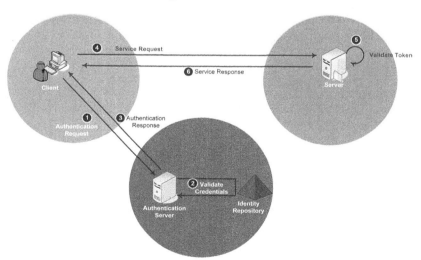

Multi-Factor Authentication adds an additional layer of security. It requires the following:

1. Something you know (such as a password)

2. Something you have (token, smart card)
3. Something you are (biometrics such as fingerprint, retinal scan, voice print etc.)

Authorization

Authorization is the process of deciding which system resources a user should be allowed to access. For example if the user is a financial analyst he would normally be granted access to all the relevant finance applications that he might use in his daily activities and it would be unlikely he would have access to the human resource applications.

Access Management

Access management is the process responsible for allowing users to make use of IT services, data or other assets. Access management helps to protect the confidentiality, integrity and availability of assets by ensuring that only authorized users are able to access or modify the assets.

Role Based Access

Role-based access control is a method of regulating access to computer or network resources based on the roles of individual users. The access for the user should be based on "least privilege" and "need to know" and limit the ability of the user to only access information appropriate to their role within the organization. In this context, access is the ability of an individual user to perform a specific task, such as view, create, or modify or delete a file.

Active Directory

Active Directory (AD) is a Microsoft technology used to manage computers and other devices on a network. It is one of the key features of the Windows Operating System. One characteristic of Active Directory is that is provides a robust database that allows for the storage of user profiles and accounts. The directory services feature of Active Directory has a centralized reporting feature for auditing user activity and for producing access management reports required for compliance with regulations like HIPAA. One feature of its directory services is that they can integrate with two-factor authentication systems such as one time password, hard and soft tokens and biometrics. Additionally tools such as Group Policy Objects (GPO) in Active Directory make it easy to enforce consistent authentication polices for all members of the Active Directory domain. Examples of these policies are password complexity, history and expiry, limiting the number of user logins and limiting the time length of active user sessions. There are many other security restrictions that can be uniformly administered to through the use of GPOs. Active Directory is most notably used to accomplish single sign on (SSO) so that enterprise users ideally only have one password to remember.

Auditing

Auditing is the process of maintaining detailed, secure logs of critical activities in a business environment. These activities could be related to security, content management, business transactions, or other such activities. For example, the following activities could be audited:

- Login failures
- Unauthorized access to protected resources
- Modification to security policy
- Digital signatures for non-repudiation

Access management auditing and reporting approaches can be broadly divided into two critical areas: security investigations and IT compliance. Audit logs are one of the most critical pieces of evidence that is needed to retroactively provide proof of specific user activity needed for security incident investigation in the event of a breach. Relative to compliance and IT controls, if an employee violates a corporate policy, proof generally is provided by an audit log of that user's activity.

The Organizational Benefits of IAM

One primary driver of implementing an IAM strategy for an organization has been the need to safely authenticate and authorize external users (contractors, suppliers, customers etc.) of corporate internal systems. Giving these external users seamless access to systems generally drives down the operational costs of faxing, emailing and making phone calls by empowering the external user to retrieve the information themselves. Additionally, a well-defined IAM strategy can drive down help desk calls as corporate users are granted access to the systems they need bsed on their role at the time of hire. This is accomplished by warning of their password expiration and ensuring they understand it and are educated that attempting to access data that they are not "legitimately" authorized to view or change may be audited/monitored and can have adverse consequences for them from a disciplinary standpoint.

Additionally many different compliance and regulatory standards require some form of IAM standardization. Sarbanes Oxley (SOX), PCI/DSS, Health Insurance Portability and Affordability Act (HIPAA), Gramm Leach Bliley Act (GLBA), Family Educational Rights and Privacy Act of 1974 (FERPA) and North-American Electric Reliability Corporation (NERC) all require some form of streamlined IAM business processes and/or IAM systems solutions. Thus healthcare, financial services, insurance, utilities, education and retail industries all require some form of IAM standardization due to the aforementioned regulatory standards. These standards require proof of the following types of security controls: user access reviews, audit trails of user activity, role based access, separation of duties and least level of privilege. Penalties for noncompliance can be in the millions, even billions, of dollars when the loss of reputation and operational costs of a security breach are considered beyond the regulatory fines.

IAM Systems and Automation

There are many different types of IAM system solutions designed to automate provisioning and deprovisioning users, establish a single sign-on environment, establish role-based access and control entitlements (permissions regarding what a user can view/modify or delete in an application). Listed below are some of the different types of identity and access concepts that are addressed by software solutions. Some of these concepts may be stand- alone software solutions or may be combined in An IAM application.

- Identity and Access Provisioning - This type of software solution provides a variety of options for account creation for system users. Generally it provides an SSO capability by establishing connections between the many software applications and access to a centralized directory store which is the "source of authority" for all identities. Frequently software solutions provide their own account creation and password repository. The security concern arises when users have multiple unique accounts and passwords for the many different software tools they use in performing their daily tasks. Many corporations use Active Directory (defined above) as the directory or "source of authority" that stores all of their network accounts and passwords. When a user terminates employment with the corporation, all of the user's accounts must be disabled. An IAM software solution makes this possible. It also has the ability to create enterprise user roles which makes provisioning a new user with the appropriate access a seamless event.

- Identity and Access/User Access Management (UAM) – Access management is a critical component of any IAM software solution. After a user is authenticated to the system, the software solution must authorize the user for access to applications, file shares and network resources. There are two forms of authorization: coarse grain and fine grain. Coarse grain defines what web pages and applications a user can access, while fine grain defines the application modules a user can access and can also define what functions (add, view, edit, delete) the user can perform in those modules. There is no industry standard for these authorization concepts so their application may vary from one organization to another. The UAM feature in an IAM tool can also define role-based access. RBAC, if designed correctly, provides assurance that the employee is limited to access only the information they need to perform their specific job duties. Users in the organization will be placed in a particular role upon their hire and this role will contain a particular set of entitlements. The entitlements define the applications the role can access and what functions the role can execute (as stated above: add, delete, view etc.).

- Privileged Identity Management (PIM) - These software solutions track, secure, and audit privileged credentials used by administrators, computer services, and applications when accessing sensitive or confidential information and computing assets. These applications are usually enterprise password management tools, as opposed to a user account management system, and generally these systems use a password vault where the privileged users can check out the password for a period of time. This type of system monitors the user activity of the user accounts that have the highest level of access in an organization. These are built in "super user" accounts, such as "admin" and "root" but usually it is more than just those as most applications require some type of administrative privilege for installation, updates and general maintenance. Accounts such as "Oracle" and "SA" are examples. Accounts are needed to run system jobs, access and change the database, and delete system files are examples of these type of accounts. The accounts may be a default part of the operating system or application or are created for the purpose of high level system functions. They are often "shared" and used by system, network and database administrators and application owners. This is what creates the security concern as multiple individuals know and share the passwords for these accounts.

Why Use Privileged Identity Management?

Use Case	Challenges	Solution
Administrator accessing shared privilege identity	• Limit the use of privilege identities for non-administrative tasks	• PIM can allow administrators to access the system and perform privileged duties without a password
	• Achieve accountability and auditability for the administrators accessing shared privilege identities	• PIM can facilitate the session monitoring and audit recording for compliance and investigations

Discover privilege identities on the applications/systems	• Difficult to manually identify privileged users and accounts without a system or solution	• PIM can auto-discover these privilege identities on the systems and maintain them in its repository
	• Requires monitoring, administration and reporting	• Audits and logs the activities performed by the privilege identities
Applications need access to privilege identities	• Achieve accountability and auditing proof	• PIM can change the password frequently based on the enterprise password policy
	• Reduce the risk of sabotage by internal actors	• Eliminate the need for hardcoded credentials
	• Maintain compliance and controls	
Administrators accessing emergency privilege identities	• Passwords are not changed for these privilege identities according to corporate policy	• PIM can change the password frequently based on the enterprise password policy
	• Achieve accountability	• Audits and logs the activities performed by the privilege identities
Administrators need ad-hoc privileged access	• Control access requests for privileged access	• PIM can provide workflow capabilities for approval of access requests requiring elevation of access
	• Ensure accountability and an audit trail of privileged access by individual administrators	• Audits and logs the activities performed by the elevated administrator

■ Federation – This is a type of SSO use case that is actually broader in scope as it is for multiple enterprises and users across multiple security domains. A trust exist between these organizations and a user's credentials are stored by the identity provider (IdP). One scenario is that multiple service providers (SPs) trust the one IdP, but there are many variations of the interactions between the IdP and the SPs. The term "SSO" is truly an umbrella concept meaning a user can log into multiple applications but only authenticates once. Federation does not require the user to remember a password whereas SSO does require the user to have that knowledge. Federation uses digital identities otherwise known as security tokens. The federation server knows the username and password for each application and presents the application with a security token that says "this is maryjones@domainabc.com." The server accepts the token because of the trust that was previously established. The token is passed using an identity protocol. An identity protocol is a method of passing authentication data between two entities. Some of the common identity protocols are listed below:

- SAML1.1
- SAML2
- WS-Federation
- OAuth2
- OpenID Connect
- WS-Trust
- Various proprietary protocols

The main challenge of federation is determining how to "trust" (i.e., mutual confidence, liability, risk, and compliance) another organization with proprietary and confidential data. The table below outlines some of the critical considerations for federation.

Component Architecture	• Creation of a federated identity relationship with an external entity requires an assessment and comparison of the entity's security architecture, policies, IT, and authentication techniques.
Risks and Liabilities	• A federated identity link exposes the potential exploitation through a business partner, the result of which may be a severe economic or reputational loss or both.
	• Agreements must be negotiated with partners to assign and manage financial risks and liabilities associated with federated identity.
Audits and Assessments	• An important aspect of federated identity management is ensuring that the basic principles of audit ability, security and business controls are upheld.
Privacy Considerations	• The federated identity relationship must comply with applicable federal, state and local privacy regulations.
	• Restrictions must be preserved and enforced in a federated relationship across entities.
Trust	• A key issue in federation is ensuring that external business partners manage their IT environment judiciously and according to accepted industry standards.

The Challenges of Designing an IAM System in a Corporate Environment

As discussed the benefits of having an IAM system include:

1. Account provisioning and deprovisioning to streamline on-boarding and off-boarding employees
2. Establishing RBAC to control and limit employee access to applications/ corporate resources
3. Password management for privileged access
4. SSO to limit the number of passwords users have and make authentication seamless
5. Enhanced auditing capabilities which can serve as alerts for security events
6. Increased productivity because many manual tasks are now automated

With so many benefits, it would seem optimal for all companies and corporations to implement an IAM system by purchasing IAM software. So what are the obstacles?

The first obstacle for a smaller to mid-size company is that the cost of IAM software might be prohibitive with a limited IT budget and competing software and infrastructure needs. However, some of the IAM benefits can still be achieved by developing solid IAM business processes. The development of these processes are great steps to prepare for the future deployment of IAM software. Listed below are some critical processes:

- Role development – Develop standard roles for each department (HR, Finance, IT etc.) for system access. For example, an HR a recruiter may have access to different software than a benefits analyst but they also might have some applications they both use. The role definitions should include even fine grain access such as what that role can do in the application (software modules – add, change, delete etc.).
- On-boarding IAM checklist – Develop a list for new employees of all the standard applications they should have access to and the level of access within each application.
- Off-boarding checklist – Define all the physical items the employee should return. Request the manager list all the accounts the employee has access to. The manager can use the list of software defined for the role the employee had in the onboarding IAM checklist and include any additional software or file shares that were added to their access profile over time. For involuntary terminations this may not be possible before the employee leaves, but, this is a critical task that should not be forgotten. Terminating access to applications used by the employee that are web based and could potentially be accessed by the employee when they are not on the corporate intranet are particularly important. Unauthorized access and hacking using web based applications account for 41% of breaches (according to Verizon Data Breach Investigations).

- Password management – Plan to integrate applications to Active Directory to accomplish an SSO capability if the applications are capable of this integration. If a GPO does not exist for or AD passwords, create one with strong complexity, length, strength and expiry parameters. This integration may be a longer term initiative as it involves account investigation into many software platforms and many migration activities. If AD migration is not possible then as an interim measure, require that the application passwords meet the same length, strength, complexity and expiry criteria as the employee's AD account.
- Access Reviews – Define and institute a business process for access reviews. This process involves both IT and the application or file share owner. The application owner should interrogate the application database for a list of application accounts and passwords (if not integrated with AD). Compare these accounts to a list of all "active employees" from an AD listing. Identify any terminated employees and remove/disable those accounts. Verify that the employee has the correct access commensurate with their role. Identify any employees who may have transferred to other positions and no longer need access to the application. Document all actions taken.

Other IAM Obstacles to Consider

Although there are many advantages to establishing IAM processes, procedures and implementing solutions, the journey can be challenging. Over time, lack of documentation and standardized procedures with account management and access controls often leads to the "unknown factor." The following areas are some of the common problems corporations encounter as they try to set up a comprehensive monitored IAM environment.

- Orphan accounts – During access reviews these accounts are always discovered. They may be in AD or could be local accounts on servers or in an application database. The person who created them has long since left the company and there is no documentation to indicate who owns them or what they are used for. The danger of disabling or deleting these accounts is that they could be embedded in a script that runs a monthly or annual job, they could be buried in an application performing some process or perhaps they are used once a year for some exchange of information that is critical to the business. Because their owner is unknown, understanding their criticality or need is a mystery. The issue is these are usually systems or service accounts that have a high level of privilege and could be exploited by a hacker. They generally have weak passwords that are easily cracked.
- Profile cloning – In the absence of standardized roles, cloning the access of one user to create a new employee's user profile is a common practice.

The issue with this is that most employee's access "grows" over time. Thus the profile that is being "cloned" could have administrative access or access to applications and network resources that are inconsistent or unnecessary for the new employee's role.

- Lack of control over privileged access – Often privileged access is granted simply because it is requested and the person granting the access does not understand the reason for the access and is not required to understand it or challenge the need for access. At the heart of this issue is the lack of an approval process that involves the stakeholders who would understand the need for access and also the security implications of granting that access. Often administrative access is granted for a brief period of time for a user to install an application or run a report and then because there is no process to approve, track or terminate the access, the person who was granted the "temporary" access retains it for the length of their employment. Privileged access accounts are the most dangerous as these can be used to extract data from the database, change core system parameters, modify software code and even bring down entire systems.

Business Case for IAM

IAM may be one of the most important security programs a corporation or enterprise can deploy to combat cybercrime. The simple reason for this is that the primary goal for hackers is to appear like legitimate users within the corporation. They want to log in and be completely undetectable while performing malicious tasks, taking critical data or pilfering intellectual property. Controls on what information employees have access to and how they authenticate to the corporate network have become hot topics in the cybersecurity world and constitute the core business problem that a well-developed IAM system solves.

The biggest challenges for corporations are complexity and disparate business processes due to the diverse computing environments. IT professionals are charged with so many challenges that didn't exist even ten years ago. Most corporations now have so many different system platforms in use from cloud computing that could be SAAS or PAAS, and also on premise and legacy systems. Even social media use and telecommuting present challenges for the IT staff as they have to control how social media is used (often it infects the corporate environment) and telecommuting means that the remote employee must have the same security controls in place that the on-site employee has. Due to this diversity, the margin for error has radically increased, especially when it comes to managing identities in larger enterprises. Also, different cloud applications and environments have increased the complexity for IT administrators regarding the number of processes and polices they have to be intimately familiar with.

The key to solving these issues is a universal IAM strategy and governance process that encompasses all environments from the local data center to SAAS and PAAS. None of these environments should be an island governed by a different set of rules and processes. IAM software, policies and processes need to be designed in a universal manner that eliminates complexity and achieves the ultimate goal of certifying employees access based on the core security principles of "separation of duties" and "need to know." IAM is not a quick fix but a foundational element of a solid cybersecurity program. The time it takes to get it right can be substantially reduced by careful planning, selection of the right technologies and partners and strategic communication to the business to achieve the "buy-in" and commitment needed.

Chapter 10

CYBERSECURITY FOR FINANCIAL SERVICES – CHALLENGES AND BEST PRACTICES

By: Michael C. Stiglianese

INTRODUCTION

Stating that the financial services industry is, and has always been, a target for cyber criminals is stating the obvious. Legend has it that in the early 1950's when a reporter asked the famous bank robber, Willie Sutton, "Why do you rob banks?" Sutton's response was simply "Because that's where the money is." In 2018 little has changed. Financial institutions still have a lot of money available for stealing. Cyber criminals try to breach financial intuitions because that is where the money is. But now, criminal do not have to physically go to a bank to try to steal. They can be anywhere in the world, as long as they can connect to the internet. Nor do they have to worry about restricting their efforts to banking hours; cyber breaches can occur 24 hours a day, 7 days a week. They do not have to wear a mask, they can hide their identity rather easily. And most importantly, they have little chance of getting caught. The cyber world has made robbing a financial institution much less risky than it is in the physical world.

The fact that financial institutions are an attractive target makes managing cybersecurity very difficult. While in many industries it is possible to isolate a cyber adversary to specific groups targeting the institution (threat actors), financial institutions need to assume all threat actors are targeting them. They also need to assume they are under attack 24/7/365. Finally, they have to understand that the threat actor who is actively attacking only needs to be successful once. The financial institution needs to stop every attack. Having to manage this risk is very challenging. Financial institutions face so many challenges that discussing each one could fill this entire book. However we will only focus on three. And while the three we focus on are far from the ones which create the most risk, they are the ones that may in fact create the most headaches for those who manage cyber risk. These challenges are:

- The regulatory compliance challenge - With high profile security breaches continuing to hit the headlines, regulatory agencies are taking an ever increasing role in trying to determine that financial institutions are secure. This results in the need for institutions to comply with various guidelines and/or regulations. It also results in situations where a single institution may have to answer to multiple regulatory agencies and be compliant with potentially conflicting requirements.

- The being complaint vs. being secure challenge – While institutions need to make sure that they are compliant with all appropriate regulations, being complaint with a regulation does not, by itself, make an institution secure. Institutions are often faced with the challenge of deciding whether they should focus limited resources on improving compliance or improving security.

- The risk management challenge – Finally, the key to cybersecurity is to focus on it as a typical risk discipline. The goal should be to manage risk to an acceptable level. Financial institutions need to determine the proper balance across preventive, detective and responsive controls. Understanding the inherent risk of threats and vulnerabilities and establishing the level of residual risk that meets the institution's risk appetite is necessary to properly manage cyber risk.

Each of these challenges impact all financial institutions. The cyber challenges identified above often make the role of managing cybersecurity risk difficult because, in an environment of limited resources to focus on cybersecurity, the above stated challenges often cause the institution to make trade-offs which, ideally, would not be necessary. Let's take a deeper look into each of these challenges.

THE REGULATORY COMPLIANCE CHALLENGE

The Challenge

Cybersecurity is a primary consideration of regulators around the globe. In fact it is a growth industry, with regulators worldwide increasing their focus on the issue. Similar to attempting to address all the challenges facing financial institutions, addressing all the global regulators and regulations would fill its own book. So let's focus on the United States regulatory process.

For the United States financial services industry, passage of the Gramm-Leach-Bliley Act (GLBA) in 1999 was a defining moment for how they would need to address information security in the future. While Financial Institutions were always concerned with the safeguarding of information, for the first time there was a law which mandated certain specific actions. Under GLBA, financial institutions were required to:

- Ensure the security and confidentiality of customer information;
- Protect against any anticipated threats to the security or integrity of such information; and
- Protect against unauthorized access to or use of such information.

The Act went further in that it provided guidelines which outlined specific measures financial institutions should use in designing their information protection program. First and foremost was the need to develop a written plan containing policies and procedures intended to identify, assess and control the risks that might threaten customer information systems. In addition, GLBA required that the plans be implemented, tested for effectiveness and adjusted to take into consideration changes in technology and the overall threat environment. With the passage of GLBA information security became a key element in how U.S. regulatory agencies examined and rated financial institutions. Initially, the regulatory effort was mainly focused on banks and driven by the Federal Reserve System, The Federal Deposit Insurance Corporation and the Office of the Controller of the Currency. Over time other federal agencies got involved in regulating cybersecurity, expanding coverage beyond banks to insurance companies, brokerage firms, investment bankers and all other types of financial institutions. The table below shows the principle federal agencies which now have a role in regulating cybersecurity.

Principal United States Federal Regulatory Agencies

Securities and Exchange Commission (SEC)	Financial Industry Regulatory Authority (FINRA)
Commodity Futures Trading Commission (CFTC)	National Credit Union Administration (NCUA)
Federal Reserve System (FRS)	Consumer Financial Protection Bureau (CFPB)
Federal Deposit Insurance Corporation (FDIC)	National Association of Insurance Commissioners (NAIC)
Office of the Comptroller of the Currency (OCC)	National Futures Association (NFA)
Financial Crimes Enforcement Network (FinCEN)	

In addition to the above, each state has at least one agency which regulates state chartered institutions. In 2018 alone at least 36 states, D.C. and Puerto Rico introduced or considered more than 265 bills or resolutions related to cybersecurity.[1] Keeping on top of this is often a daunting task for even the largest of institutions.

While some coordination across these organizations takes place, typically a financial institution is left to navigate overlapping requirements. In addition, these requirements impact all financial institutions, regardless of size. This often leaves smaller institutions in a position where compliance is difficult because of a lack of appropriate resources, both skills-based and financial.

A Suggested Approach

Addressing compliance will never be simple for financial institutions. For all the reasons stated previously it will always be a challenge which will require active management. However there are things which can be done to help simplify the task. Let's take a look at a few of these.

1. Have Clear and Achievable Policies

The first step in determining compliance to regulatory guidance is to review an institution's policies and procedures. This will be the first thing that is covered in a regulatory examination. It is important that an institution have appropriate, documented policies and procedures which cover all aspects of the regulatory guidelines. Most importantly, these policies need to be implemented and followed by the institution. Having detailed, best in class policies which either are not followed or are too advanced to be followed by the institution are as much of a problem as having no policies at all.

It is also important that policies and procedures are properly documented. Informal policies and procedures are not sufficient. Even beyond policies and procedures, it is important that the institution has a formally approved cybersecurity plan which properly documents the decision making processes, roles and responsibilities and foundational elements of the cybersecurity program.

2. Conduct an Organizational Cyber Risk Assessment

A key element in achieving regulatory compliance is being able to demonstrate that the management of the institution is aware of the cyber risks they face (inherent risk) and is comfortable that the risk which remains after reasonable controls are implemented (residual risk) is within the overall risk appetite of the institution. The best way to demonstrate this is to perform an organization-level cyber risk assessment.

While there are many ways of conducting this assessment, the regulators themselves have provided financial institutions with an approach which is quite effective. In fact, they have actually taken this approach and developed an assessment tool which is available to financial institutions free of charge and is very good at identifying inherent and residual risk. This is the Federal Financial Institutions Examination Council (FFIEC) Cybersecurity Assessment Tool.[2] The FFIEC is a formal U.S. government interagency body composed of five banking regulators (FED, FDIC, OCC, NCUA, and CFPB) that is empowered to prescribe uniform principles, standards, and report forms to be utilized in the examination of financial institutions.

Rather than focusing on the tool, let's focus on the approach. The latter being the product of the institution's cybersecurity inherent risk profile and cybersecurity maturity. Cybersecurity inherent risk is the level of risk posed to the institution by the following:

- Technologies and connection types
- Delivery channels
- Online/mobile products and technology services
- Organizational characteristics
- External threats[3]

The inherent risk profile includes descriptions of activities across risk categories with definitions for the least to most levels of inherent risk:

FFIEC Cybersecurity Assessment Tool Overview for CEOs and Boards of Directors

The approach's second part is to measure the maturity of an institution's cybersecurity controls (cybersecurity maturity). This is step is designed to help management measure the adequacy of the controls an institution has in place to address its inherent risk. The levels range from baseline to innovative. Cybersecurity maturity includes statements to determine whether an institution's behaviors, practices, and processes can support cybersecurity preparedness.[4]

Finally by taking into consideration the inherent risk calculated above and the cybersecurity maturity, an institution can calculate its residual risk. Regardless of the methodology utilized, understanding residual risk is a key component to achieving regulatory compliance.

3. Define What Is Necessary for Compliance

Understanding the difference in what is necessary to be compliant with regulatory guidance and what is best in class security is one of the most important aspects of being able to manage compliance. An institution can be in compliance with a regulation without having best in class security in place. Compliance typically allows for a wide range of solutions. The appropriate solution for an institution needs to be in compliance with the regulatory guidance but appropriate for the institution based upon residual risk and risk appetite. This differs on an institution by institution basis.

As a first step, an institution should define what it will consider is compliance with each aspect of a regulation and document this definition. Defining compliance does not mean an institution might not strive for better than just being compliant. It just means that the institution is separating the mandatory actions being taken to achieve compliance from the optional actions being taken as a business decision to go beyond just being in compliance.

4. Be Transparent With Your Regulators

There is a natural tendency to try and hide problems from regulators. That is the wrong approach. The worst thing you can do is to surprise a regulator. Determining compliance with a regulation is somewhat subjective. Time and time again, regulatory examiners take a more stringent point of view simply because they have the perception that management is not being forthright with them and might be hiding things. The best way to avoiding this situation is to have an ongoing dialogue with the regulator. Don't make them find problems; inform them of your problems and focus the conversation on what you're doing to mitigate risk as you perform remediation.

While following the four suggestions above will not eliminate the difficulty of addressing the compliance challenge, using them will greatly assist in traveling the road to compliance. Now let's focus on the next challenge.

THE BEING COMPLIANT VS. BEING SECURE CHALLENGE

The Challenge

One of the little understood facts of cybersecurity is that being compliance with regulations does not guarantee you are secure or that you are properly managing your cyber risk. In fact, you can be out of compliance with regulations but be very secure and properly managing cyber risk.

Typically, compliance requirements change slowly and predictably. Compliance normally is meant to satisfy external requirements and facilitate business operations, is driven by business needs rather than technical needs and is considered achieved when the third party is satisfied. Essentially compliance is a point-in-time snapshot that demonstrates you meet the minimum, security-related requirements of specific regulatory standards.

Security on the other hand is the unique ecosystem of policies, processes and technical controls that defines how an institution effectively protects data from cyber threats. Contrary to changing slowly and predictably like the compliance landscape, the security/threat landscape is in a perpetual state of change. Security is not meant to satisfy a third party's needs. It is driven by the need to protect against constant threats to an organization's assets and is never finished but is continuously maintained and improved.

Since there is considerable overlap in being compliant with being secure, in a perfect world a financial institution would just do both. However, in reality every institution has limitations in available resources, whether from the perspective of qualified personnel or adequate funding. This creates the need to prioritize and identify trade-offs. Let's look at some things which can be done to help facilitate that trade-off.

A Suggested Approach

Understanding the potential conflict between the requirements of being compliant with regulations and the actions which are necessary to make sure the institution is secure, there are certain things which can be done to help an institution address the challenge.

1. Find a Balance

Security and compliance need to be viewed as going hand in hand, and complementing each other by filling the gaps in areas where one may fall short. Compliance should be used to establish a comprehensive baseline for an organization's security posture. Based upon a robust risk assessment process, security practices should be built on that baseline to ensure that the business is covered as completely as possible. By maintaining an equal focus on both of these concepts, an institution will be empowered to not only meet regulatory guidelines, but also demonstrate that it goes above and beyond baseline requirements when it is warranted by risk.

2. Avoid a Checklist Approach

Institutions can be tempted to take a checklist approach to compliance. The temptation to do this is further enforced by a search of the web which will reveal numerous compliance checklists for every regulatory requirement. While checklists are useful tools, overreliance on them can hinder security. Being compliant should be viewed as a result of having good security practices rather than as a check-the-box exercise that is expected to guarantee security.

By their very nature, checklists are generic in nature. Security on the other hand needs to be risk based in order to be most effective. A risk-based security approach cannot be generic; it needs to be customized to the actual risks being incurred by the financial institution.

Being compliant needs to be viewed as a result of having good security practices rather than as a check-the-box exercise that is expected to guarantee security. The focus needs to be on conducting good cyber due diligence and assessments, implementing proper detection controls, having effectively enforced third-party risk and insider risk programs and conducting testing designed to simulate the institution's response in the event of a serious attack.

3. Take a Managing Risk Approach

We will expand upon how to manage risk in the next section. For now, it is sufficient to say that by recognizing that being cyber secure is really about managing cyber risk, an institution will position itself to best coordinate the requirements of being compliant with the requirements of keeping the institution secure.

THE RISK MANAGEMENT CHALLENGE

The Challenge

Cyber risk is a broad-reaching, enterprise-level risk, and financial institutions are in the challenging position of having to manage this risk in an ever changing environment. The push for digital innovation, disruptive technologies, and delivery of more personalized customer experiences continuously introduces new threats.

Financial Institutions need to understand that cybersecurity is about managing risk. Security is simply another business risk like shareholder, credit, market, and customer risk. Just like any other risk discipline, risk will never be fully eliminated. It must be managed. By its very nature it is never black and white, but gray. In dealing with risk-based decisions, institutions must use the best available information and make the most reasonable decisions given the current situation.

Cybersecurity is an evolution of information security in the context of an institution's risk management program. Cybersecurity needs to be managed consistently with other risk disciplines. Negative events are inevitable. That's why it's important to have controls in place to minimize the impact of those events, processes to quickly recognize they have occurred, and a plan to manage their impact and recover.

When an organization narrowly focuses on cybersecurity it oftentimes mistakenly considers it to be a technology responsibility. Cyber risk management is a business responsibility. Let's look at how a financial institution can approach cybersecurity as a risk discipline.

A Suggested Approach

A financial Institution should take a holistic approach to managing cyber risk. The core of any cybersecurity program should be designed to maintain the confidentiality, integrity, and availability of data. Cyber risk management also encompasses principles to defend an institution's reputation and financial resources, while at the same time protecting the security of client's sensitive information. Therefore, in addition to core information security principles covering data protection, access control and entitlement and security monitoring, other aspects of a cyber risk management program are as critically important.

In order to manage risk, you need to assess your risk. This assessment, combined with your institution's appetite for risk, will define your strategy and dictate the design of your risk management program. Once your program is defined you begin to get into the operational aspects of cyber risk management.

Information security also includes the processes and tools you utilize to protect against cyber attacks and to detect if you have been attacked. Cyber threat intelligence keeps you abreast of the ever changing cyber environment and provides a basis for adjusting your protection and detection techniques.

As important as protection and detection are to the process which will be utilized when a cyber incident actually occurs, having a robust incident response plan for both pre- and post-event is key to minimizing the impact of an event

Finally, cyber insurance helps to manage the financial impact of a cyber event on your institution. While cyber insurance does not make you more secure, it does help in managing the impact that residual risk has on the institution.

BDO USA LLP's HOLISTIC APPROACH TO CYBERSECURITY

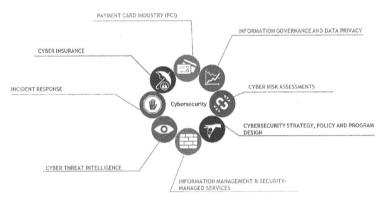

In addition to what has been already covered a holistic approach also addresses how your cyber strategy needs to align with your business strategy. A holistic approach recognizes that people, and thus culture, is an important element. Since people represent one of the biggest security weaknesses, making sure the institution's program and strategy are acceptable within the institution's culture is equally important.

Finally, a holistic approach understands that managing risk has a cost and must be funded. It is important to display that the benefits of making investments in cybersecurity in a manner which is understandable by the institution's business units.

SUMMARY

As the result of operating in a highly regulated industry, financial institutions are required to have structured cybersecurity programs. Regulatory requirements for financial institutions have become more extensive, and institutions are burdened by the need to interpret what a complex regulatory landscape means for their individual situation. When new requirements or frameworks come out, financial institutions must determine their current security state and identify deficiencies.

Simply staying ahead of compliance requirements does not equal security. Security cannot be approached as a one and done exercise.

Cyber risk is dynamic and enterprise-wide. Security is an ongoing process that financial institutions must maintain by taking a holistic approach to managing cyber risk.

The next chapter will focus on the cybersecurity challenges and best practices of the fastest growing industry in the world, the global healthcare industry.

Endnotes

[1] National Conference of State Legislatures

[2] The Federal Financial Institutions Examination Council

[3] FFIEC Cybersecurity Assessment Tool Overview for CEOs and Boards of Directors

[4] FFIEC Cybersecurity Assessment Tool Overview for CEOs and Boards of Directors

Chapter 11

CYBERSECURITY IN THE HEALTHCARE INDUSTRY – CHALLENGES AND BEST PRACTICES

By: Gregory A. Garrett, CISSP, CPCM, PMP

INTRODUCTION

The U.S. and international healthcare industry is valued at trillions of U.S. dollars, it is growing in size each year with an aging society worldwide, and it provides an incredible valuable service. The global healthcare industry has access to extremely sensitive and valuable information, including:

- personal identifiable information (PII)
- payment card information (PCI), and
- protected health information (PHI) via
- electronic medical records (EMR)

As a result, the healthcare industry which varies significantly in size, complexity, regulatory, requirements, quality of care, and cost by country is the target of cyber attacks by:

- nation-state cyber warfare groups
- cyber criminal groups
- hacker groups
- insider threats

In this chapter, the focus is on understanding the nature of the cyber challenges facing the healthcare industry and recognizing the proven effective cybersecurity best practices related to healthcare organizations.

Recent Cyber Events in the Healthcare Industry

Following the trend of the last couple of years, most of the reported attacks in this industry are based on ransomware; either spear-phishing targeted attacks or "scattershot attacks" (i.e. unfocused, and often generic attacks). The vast majority of malware attacks in the healthcare industry are delivered via file attachments or URLs that link the user to malicious code. In 2018, the preferred vehicle was via malicious URLs. Note that most common malware that plague the healthcare organizations worldwide, to a large degree overlap with other sectors (e.g. Locky, The Trick, Global and Imposter).

The relatively large number of successful cyber attacks in the healthcare industry, in comparison to other industries such as the financial-services for example, indicates that the computer systems in the healthcare sector are systematically ill-protected across the industry. This matter is further compounded by continual developments and adoption of artificial intelligence (AI) and the Internet of Things (IoT) systems. Accordingly, it may take several years for the healthcare industry to fully address this matter. According to International Data Corporation (IDC), in 2017 alone, AI investments were US $12.5 billion. Yet, that investment amount pales in comparison to IoT investments which are expected to exceed US $800 billion in 2018, and are forecasted to reach US $1.4 Trillion in 2021. Moreover, according to healthcare cybersecurity firm Cynerio, the number of connected medical devices alone, is currently estimated at 10 billion, and is expected to reach 50 billion within the next 10 years.

The industry is currently in its early stages of re-evaluating its operation with regards to new cyber threats and adequate integration of AI and IoT systems with life supporting technologies. Accordingly, it is imperative to insure that medical devices connected to the internet are well-deployed and operated properly. This concern is relevant to any company or organization, but is particularly pertinent to the healthcare industry as any disruption, failure or security breach may result in injury or loss of life.

"Orangeworm" Threat Group Launches Campaign Against Healthcare Industry

A new threat actor known as Orangeworm has been deploying malware in a campaign targeting the healthcare industry and its supply-chain in the United States, Europe and Asia, according to a report by Symantec from April 23, 2018. Orangeworm, has been observed installing a custom-made backdoor called Kwampirs across the healthcare sector, including pharmaceutical companies, IT solution providers for the healthcare industry, and medical equipment manufacturers, as part of a supply-chain attack designed to reach deliberately and meticulously chosen targets within the health sector, likely for espionage purposes. The origin of Orangeworm is currently unknown, as there are currently no technical or operational indicators. The group likely consists of an individual or a small number of individuals, as opposed to being a nation-state actor. It appears to conduct well-planned strikes on its targets.

According to Symantec, almost 40 percent of Orangeworm's confirmed victims operate within the healthcare industry, while attacks on other industries such as manufacturing, information technology, agriculture, and logistics were also intended to reach targets in healthcare. Notably, the group has deployed the backdoor on medical imaging devices such as x-ray and MRI machines, as well as machines used to assist patients in completing consent forms. Once deployed, Trojan.Kwampirs allows the attackers to remotely access the compromised host. After ensuring its persistence, the malware collects initial information on its victim to determine whether the target is of high-value. If the victim proves to be of interest to the threat actor, then Kwampirs collects additional network information to facilitate its propagation, which the malware carries out by copying itself over network shares. This method is suitable for older operating systems such as Windows XP, which are in prevalent use across the healthcare industry. Despite slightly modifying itself while moving across a network to evade detection, Orangeworm does not appear too concerned about being discovered and uses "aggressive" and "loud" methods to propagate the malware and communicate with servers.

Medical Device Recalls Increased by 126% in 2018 Predominantly Due to Software Issues

According to the Stericycle Recall Index, the first months of 2018 saw an increase of 126 percent in recalls of medical devices, primarily for reasons relating to software, which is often run on vulnerable legacy systems. According to this index, the number of medical devices recalled in the first quarter of 2018 is the highest it has been since 2005. Software issues caused a total of 22.7 percent of recalls - more so than any other cause.

To demonstrate the impact of compromised medical devices on patient care, a pair of researchers at University of California (UC) San Diego and UC Davis in the U.S. researched breaches of various medical devices, including pacemakers, light scopes, and insulin pumps. To do so, they simulated medical emergencies and provided the doctors in the experiment with the breached devices. The hacked devices significantly hindered the ability of the physicians in the experiment to provide medical care. At the end of the test, the researchers asked the doctors whether they thought the devices were hacked - all of them replied that they did not. According to the research team, this indicates an implicit trust in medical infrastructure, as well as a lack of awareness at the inherit risk of using digital devices.

Health Equity Data Breach Compromises Records of 23,000 Individuals.

On June 13, 2018 it was reported that on April 22, 2018 the financial services provider HealthEquity, which manages millions of health savings accounts (HSAs), suffered a data breach affecting 23,000 individuals. According to reports, the breach occurred when a HealthEquity employee's email account was unlawfully accessed, compromising clients' full names, their HealthEquity member IDs, as well as their employers' Health Equity IDs. Furthermore, the stolen data also contained various types of healthcare accounts, payment records, and social security numbers (SSNs) for some employees.

Massive Data Breach Affects Australian Software Provider PageUp

A multinational human resources (HR) software provider in Australia announced in June 2018 that the personal data of thousands of its clients was potentially compromised, after discovering on May 23, 2018, that an unauthorized entity had accessed the provider's system.[1] PageUp is a company with about two million active users spread across 190 countries. It provides services to companies and organizations across multiple sectors, and among its clients are Australian firms and institutions such as Telstra, NAB, Coles, Australia Post, Aldi, and Medibank.

On May 23, 2018, PageUp detected "unusual activity" on its systems. The provider immediately launched an investigation to determine what had occurred. On May 28, 2018, PageUp discovered that client data may have been compromised in this event, including client names, street addresses, email addresses, and telephone numbers. The company also said it believes certain data such as placement agencies, applicants, references and lists of employees was accessed. Information such as resumes and financial details was not affected. PageUp said it is confident that the incident has been successfully contained and the threat has been removed. Meanwhile, the provider is employing the services of third-party security teams and the

Australian Cyber Security Center (ACSC) for assistance in its investigation. While speaking to reporters on June 6, 2018, head of ACSC Alastair MacGibbon claimed that "malicious code" was executed inside PageUp's systems, although he did not provide any additional details on this matter.

As the investigation progresses, companies and organizations using PageUp's services are notifying employees and customers about the incident.[2] Australia Post has warned its employees that their personal information may have been compromised, and Telstra announced it has suspended the use of PageUp services while the investigations are ongoing. Medibank, a national private health insurer in Australia, likewise suspended its PageUp-powered recruitment site during the investigation process, and went further to claim that the amount of compromised data was greater than what was disclosed by the HR company. According to the health insurer, the compromised information may also include financial details, tax file numbers, diversity and health information, and emergency contact information.[3]

Two Data Breach Incidents Hit Arizona's Dignity Health Group

Dignity Health, a non-profit healthcare corporation that operates medical facilities in three U.S. states, has recently experienced two data security incidents impacting certain patient information.[4] On June 2, 2018, the Dignity Health Group's St. Joseph's Hospital and Medical Center in Phoenix, Arizona, announced that it had experienced a data security incident compromising 229 patient medical records. The records, which were accessed in an unauthorized manner by a hospital employee from October 13, 2017 through March 29, 2018, contained certain sensitive information, including patient names, dates of birth, clinical data such as nurses' or doctors' notes and diagnostic information. The compromised data did not include social security numbers nor billing or credit card information. The hospital clarified that impacted patients do not need to take any further action to protect themselves against identity theft.

On April 24, 2018, Dignity Health and its affiliates Dignity Health Medical Group Nevada, LLC, and Dignity Health Medical Foundation, discovered that an email list formatted by Healthgrades, one of its business associates, contained a sorting error that resulted in Dignity Health inadvertently sending misaddressed emails to a group of 55,947 patients. The emails contained the wrong patient's name and, in some cases, his or her physician's name. No other information was included in the email. There was no financial, insurance, or medical information included. Upon learning of the incident on April 25, 2018, Dignity Health and Healthgrades launched an investigation to determine what had occurred, and the companies said they are implementing appropriate measures to prevent a reoccurrence.

Data of 500K Patients Exposed in LifeBridge Health Breach

LifeBridge Health, a nonprofit healthcare corporation based in Baltimore, Maryland has recently experienced a security breach potentially impacting the personal information of over 500,000 patients.[5] LifeBridge Health operates four hospitals in the greater Baltimore area. On March 18, 2018, LifeBridge Health detected malware on the server that hosts electronic medical records of Potomac Physicians, one of its physician practices, as well as on a shared registration and billing platform used by other LifeBridge Health providers. After the discovery, LifeBridge promptly launched an investigation into the incident and engaged the services of a forensic firm. The probe revealed that an unauthorized third-party gained access to the organization's network on September 27, 2016.

On May 16, 2018, LifeBridge Health issued a press release about the incident and said it was notifying all potentially affected patients. The organization did not disclose the type of malware found on its systems, nor the nature of the 2016 breach. However, it said the incident compromised certain sensitive information, including patient names, addresses, dates of birth, diagnoses, medications, clinical and treatment information, insurance information, and in some instances, social security numbers. LifeBridge Health and LifeBridge Potomac Professionals said they have no reason to believe that the patient information has been misused in any way, and have established a dedicated call center to answer any questions patients may have on the incident.

Allied Physicians Hit by SamSam Ransomware

On May 17, 2018, the Allied Physicians of Michiana in South Bend, Indiana, was hit by a variant of the SamSam ransomware, a prolific strain of malware known to target the healthcare sector. The practice immediately took steps to shut down the network and successfully restored its data in a secure format without causing significant disruption to patients and daily operation.[6] The Allied Physicians practice did not disclose whether a ransom was in fact demanded in this incident, nor if any sum was ultimately paid, but clarified that the incident was contained with the help of internal IT staff, its incident responder, outside assistance and other professionals. The company would not disclose any additional information about the incident.

First appearing in 2016, SamSam is a ransomware strain that exploits vulnerable systems to gain access to a victim's network, or uses brute-force tactics against weak passwords of the Remote Desktop Protocol (RDP). Upon gaining access to a system, the malware holds the victim's data hostage using RSA-2048 encryption. The bitcoin addresses associated with SamSam have received over $1 million in ransom payments just this year, making it a highly prolific ransomware strain.[7]

Misconfigured FTP Server Compromises Data of 205,000 Patients

A misconfiguration of a public FTP server maintained by the Arkansas-based MedEvolve, a practice management software provider, exposed the protected information of 205,000 patients from two separate healthcare providers. While a number of clients had files on the FTP server, two had stored the medical files without password-protection.[8] One of the clients, Premier Urgent Care in Pennsylvania, had a SQL database with 205,000 patient records that was not secured. Around 11,000 of those records contained social security numbers. The second client was Texas-based dermatologist Dr. Beverly Held, who with three .dat files compromised an estimated 12,000 social security numbers stored in the files. On May 3, 2018 DataBreaches. net notified the two medical practices and MedEvolve, the files were consequently removed that same day.

Responding to the questions of DataBreaches.net researchers, President and CEO of MedEvolve Matthew Rolfes said:

> Our IT team, along with our healthcare lawyers, are aggressively investigating the situation. We have, and will take any necessary steps in order to mitigate any adverse effects to the extent within our control. We are also aware of HIPAA requirements applicable to covered entities and business associates in the event of a breach. Our company will comply accordingly. I know you will understand that we cannot, on the advice of counsel disclose to you all aspects of the investigation.

Ransomware Hits Associates in Psychiatry and Psychology

Between the evening of March 30, 2018 and the morning of March 31, 2018, threat actors breached the servers of Minnesota-based Associates in Psychiatry and Psychology (APP) and encrypted all data files and disabled all system functions. The attackers demanded ransom in exchange for system restoration.[9] The attackers, who are believed to be located in Eastern

Europe, infected several of APP's computers with a TripleM ransomware variant, which encrypted the files with an RSA-2048 encryption protocol. They also disabled the system restore function on all affected computers and reformatted the network storage device where the practice maintained its local backups.

After the discovery of the attack, APP's servers were taken offline for four days so that the practice could assess the situation. The attackers initially demanded 4 Bitcoin, but APP successfully negotiate the sum down to 0.5 Bitcoin, which was paid to the specified Bitcoin wallets provided by the threat actors. The compromised server stored certain demographic information such as insurance claim processing data and medical details. Credit card information was stored in a separate cloud-based bucket and was not part of the breach. APP said it had found no evidence any patient information was accessed or copied.

Misconfigured $3 Bucket Exposes Personal and Medical Data

A misconfigured Amazon $3 bucket maintained by a Chicago-based insurance startup has exposed a large amount of client data, including sensitive medical information and personal identification documents.[10] AgentRun, a software startup that provides customer management software to independent insurance brokers, inadvertently compromised sensitive client information after it stored files in the misconfigured bucket.

Compromised information included client data, among them information belonging to such companies as Cigna, Transamerica, SafeCo Insurance, Schneider Insurance, Manhattan Life, and Everest, as well as the medical information of thousands of insurance policyholders. In addition, the breached bucket contained scans of customer identification documents such as social security cards and numbers, medicare cards, driver's licenses, armed forces and voter identification cards. According to Andrew Lech, the company's founder, the permissions on the bucket were erroneously flipped during an application upgrade and during migration, leaving the bucket unprotected and accessible to anyone. The bucket was secured one hour after disclosure of the breach. The company said it is notifying all potentially impacted individuals and has contacted the relevant authorities.

Phishing Attack Compromises Medical Data of 42,600 Aultman Hospital Patients

Attackers used credentials gained from a phishing attack to access several email accounts belonging to the Aultman Health Foundation, including its Ohio-based Aultman Hospital, as well as its occupational medicine division AultWorks, and 25 of its physician practices.[11] The Aultman Health Foundation notified about 42,600 patients of a data breach potentially affecting their medical information after several employee email accounts were accessed by unauthorized individuals. The unknown attackers gained access to the accounts via a phishing attack that occurred earlier in 2018.

The breach was first detected on March 28, 2018, after which Aultman launched an investigation to determine how the incident had occurred and what information was impacted. The probe revealed that access to the email accounts occurred on several occasions starting mid-February 2018, and continued until the breach was detected in late March 2018. The system that stores electronic medical records was not compromised in this incident, as the breach was limited to the hacked email accounts. Compromised accounts belonging to Aultman Hospital and several practices contained various types of patient data, including names, addresses, clinical information, medical record numbers and names of physicians. The accounts belonging to AultWorks Occupational Medicine had a greater range of information exposed, including names, addresses, dates of birth, patient medical history, reports on physical examinations, results of drug, hearing, and breathing tests and other lab test results.

After discovering it was hit by a phishing attack, the Aultman Health Foundation reset and strengthened passwords used across its practices. In addition, the foundation hardened its security protocols to prevent future incidents, and employees were provided further training on detection of phishing attempts. The Aultman Health Foundation said it had not received any reports suggesting that any of the compromised information was misused in any way. However, it was not possible to determine whether any sensitive information was viewed or accessed. The Foundation is notifying all potentially impacted individuals and advised patients to monitor their credit reports.

Healthcare Organizations Fail to Adopt DMARC Standard to Prevent Impersonation

Despite the prevalence of email-based cyber attacks in healthcare and across other industries, a recent study by mail authentication vendor Valimail found that the majority of healthcare organizations are not sufficiently protected against impersonation and phishing attacks and do not employ DMARC, an open standard designed to detect and prevent email spoofing and domain abuse.[12] The Domain-based Message Authentication, Reporting and Conformance (DMARC) standard, an email-validation system that is designed to detect and prevent email spoofing was found to be rarely used in any capacity across the health sector, according to the report. Valimail discovered that 98.3 percent of the healthcare companies analyzed were susceptible to being impersonated by phishing attacks directed at employees, partners, patients or others.

DMARC is designed to fit into an organization's existing inbound email authentication process. When a DMARC record is created for a domain, the receiving server checks to determine whether the sender of the message is authorized to use the domain. For the study, the vendor analyzed the domains of 928 healthcare companies around the world (with annual revenues of over US $300 million). These include hospitals, medical equipment suppliers, pharmacies, physicians and health practitioners. Just 121 of those companies (13%) have adopted DMARC to secure their domains and prevent email spoofing. These findings are concerning, as phishing emails have been cited to be responsible for more than 91 percent of all cyber attacks.[13] The majority of successful phishing attacks employ email impersonation techniques that can be more easily prevented by incorporating DMARC.

Medical Transcription Service Suffers Breach Affecting 45,000 Patients

Nuance Communications, a Massachusetts-based software company that provides medical transcription platforms to hospitals, has experienced a security incident potentially affecting the medical records of 45,000 individuals.[14] The compromise occurred from November 20, 2017 to December 9, 2017, when a former employee successfully breached Nuance's servers and accessed the personal information of thousands of individuals from several of the company's clients. After discovering the breach, Nuance Communications promptly shut down the affected platforms and notified law enforcement of the incident.

The company said it had notified its clients of the breach and moved them to an alternative platform while it resolved the issue. So far, the San Francisco Department of Public Health is the only one among Nuance's clients to notify impacted patients. The department sent letters to 895 individuals whose personal information was compromised. This information includes patient names, dates of birth, medical record numbers, patient numbers and medical information such as patient condition, assessment, diagnosis, treatment, care plan and date of service. The impacted patients visited the

Zuckerberg General Hospital and Laguna Honda Hospital in San Francisco. In a press release,[15] the Health Department said that it delayed notifying patients at the request of the FBI and Justice Department, which have been investigating the breach. The U.S. Department of Justice said there was no evidence that the compromised information was used or sold, as well as that the data had been recovered from the former employee.

The Oregon Clinic Notifies Patients of Data Security Incident

The Oregon Clinic has recently disclosed that on March 9, 2018, it learned that an unauthorized third party accessed an email account that contained certain protected health information.[16] The Oregon Clinic, a private specialty physician practice in Oregon, has been notifying patients about a company email account breach that may have compromised their personal identifying information. In a press release, the clinic said the account was disabled immediately after the breach was discovered. It did not disclose the number of patients affected by the breach or the exact method used by the third-party individual to gain access to the account.

The clinic said it had launched an investigation along with a digital forensics firm and other cybersecurity experts to determine what exactly had occurred. This investigation revealed that the exposed information included patient names, dates of birth, medical record numbers, diagnosis information, medical condition, diagnostic tests performed, prescription information, and/or health insurance information. Moreover, for a small subset of patients, social security numbers may also have been affected. The Oregon Clinic clarified that the breach was restricted to the one email account alone and did not affect any of the practice's infrastructure. The Oregon Clinic is providing impacted patients with additional information about steps to can take to protect their personal information and is also offering credit and/or identity monitoring services for 12 months free of charge.[17]

Malware Hits Three Florida Hospital Websites

Malware was recently discovered on three websites belonging to the Florida Hospital. The incident potentially compromised certain patient information to malicious actors. The hospital is notifying all impacted individuals.[18] In a statement released on May 2, 2018, Florida Hospital said the impacted websites (*FloridaBariatric.com*) FHOrthoInstitute.com and FHExecutiveHealth.com potentially exposed patient names, email addresses, phone numbers, birthdates, height, weight, insurance carriers and the last four digits of individuals' social security numbers. No financial information was compromised. The malware did not affect any other hospital infrastructure.

In addition, the hospital said that it had found no evidence that patient information had been misused. Meanwhile, all three websites have been taken down while the malware was removed. It is unclear how long the malware was present on the hospital's websites nor what type of malware was involved. Florida Hospital did not disclose the number of affected patients, but clarified that it is implementing the appropriate measures to ensure similar breaches are prevented.[19]

Medical Transcription Service Compromises Medical Records

MEDantex, a Kansas-based medical transcription service, has recently removed its web portal after it exposed thousands of patient medical records that were not password protected.[20] The company was notified on April 20, 2018 by KrebsOnSecurity, a security blog run by journalist Brian Krebs, that a portion of its website, reserved for physicians, was completely accessible online. Moreover, visitors were capable of adding and deleting user information and searching for records according to patient or physician name.

After being notified of the breach, MEDantex confirmed that it had recently rebuilt its online servers after being hit by ransomware, suspected to be a variant of WhiteRose malware.[21] According to the company's founder and chief executive Sreeram Pydah, the exposed pages were inadvertently incorporated into the rebuild after the attack. The exact number of compromised documents remains unclear; while in some cases, records date as far back as 2007, the majority are quite recent. Among the clients receiving MEDantex services are the New York University Medical Center, the San Francisco Multi-Specialty Medical Group and Jackson Hospital in Montgomery.

Texas Health Experiences Breach Impacting Nearly 4,000 Patients

The Texas Health Physicians Group recently announced that on January 17, 2018, it was informed by law enforcement that an unauthorized third party may have gained access to a number of Texas Health email accounts in October 2017, potentially exposing sensitive patient information.[22] Texas Health clarified that it was requested to refrain from immediately contacting patients so as to not impede the investigation of the incident, which was part of a wider cyber event that affected multiple entities in the

U.S. Meanwhile, the organization launched its own internal investigation with the help of a forensic security firm. The investigation revealed that the affected email accounts may have included information such as patient names, medical record numbers, birth dates, addresses, social security and driver's license numbers, and insurance and medical information. According to Texas Health, the breach affected some 3,808 patients that received treatment in 2017. The organization said it had no indication that the exposed information has been misused in any way.

California Center for Orthopedic Specialists Hit by Ransomware

The Center for Orthopedic Specialists (COS) in California announced that it has been hit by a ransomware attack affecting three of its facilities across the state. The attackers succeeded in encrypting the medical records of some 85,000 former and current patients that were stored on the system of a third-party IT vendor.[23] The encrypted patient data potentially included patient's names, birth dates, medical record information and social security numbers. COS clarified that all the information was taken offline before the threat actors could remove it from the system. However, COS did not indicate whether it had paid the demanded ransom and did not reveal what strain of ransomware had infected its systems. Upon launching an investigation with the affected IT vendor, COS discovered that the attackers began their attempts to access its systems on February 18, 2018. Consequently, the compromised system has been permanently taken offline and all potentially affected patients have been notified.

Billings Clinic Notifies Patients of Data Breach

Montana-based healthcare center Billings Clinic is notifying 949 patients about a data security incident potentially impacting personal information that was stored in the clinic's email system. The incident did not affect the center's medical or financial record systems.[24] After detecting suspicious activity on its email system, Billings Clinic recently launched an investigation that determined that un unauthorized party had accessed a number of emails containing personal information, including patient names, dates of birth, contact numbers and listings of sums owed to the clinic's Atrium Pharmacy. A small amount of the compromised information included payment details and limited medical information. The clinic clarified that it had found is no evidence that any patient information has been misused and that it is providing patients with information and steps they can take to monitor and protect their personal information.

"Billings Clinic takes threats to the security of its systems and patient information very seriously." Billings Clinic said in statement. "We are constantly investing in and strengthening our system's security."

Scenic Bluffs Health Centers Email Account Hacked

Wisconsin-based nonprofit healthcare provider Scenic Bluffs Health Centers is notifying 2,889 patients of a potential breach of personal information after it discovered on March 1, 2018, that an employee email account had been accessed by an unauthorized-party on February 28, 2018.[25] The unauthorized entity had set up an automatic forwarding mechanism that succeeded in forwarding only 44 emails before being disabled. None of the emails contained any sensitive medical information, but may have exposed some personally identifying patient information. The account was subsequently closed and the provider said it had resolved the breach. Scenic Bluffs Community Health Centers notified all potentially impacted individuals on April 23, 2018. The health center said it is working with a security firm to strengthen its systems and identify solutions to any underlying problems.

63,500 Patient Records Compromised-Due To a Misconfigured Database

On April 12, 2018 it was reported that New York based healthcare provider Middle Town Medical has issued a notice to 63,551 patients regarding a misconfigured radiology interface that exposed medical data. As reported by Healthcare IT News[26] on April 12, 2018, the incident was detected on January 29, and was resolved the following day. Currently it is unknown how long the data was exposed. However, the provider did disclose that unauthorized actors could potentially access only a limited, yet not specified, number of patient data. The database contained patient names, client identification numbers, dates of birth, as well as dates and types of medical procedures provided to the patients.

Following the breach, Middle Town Medical stated that they implemented additional security measures and provided their staff additional training on securing systems and modifications to interfaces. This breach is the latest in a long series of data breaches caused in recent years due to misconfigured databases and servers; many of which concern healthcare providers. These include amongst many others Emory Brain Health Center, and Long Island based Cohen, Bergman, Klepper, Romano MDs which notified 42,000 affected patients in late March 2018.[27] In early April 2018, Virtua Medical Group was fined US $418,000 after confidential data of 1,654 patients was compromised[28] due to misconfigured database in January 2016.

Medical Records Exposed by Flaw In Telstra Health's Argus Software

A vulnerability in medical software called Argus, which is used in Australia's health sector and distributed by Telstra, has potentially exposed sensitive medical information of thousands of Australians.[29] On Thursday, March 22, 2018, a Fairfax Media report revealed that Argus has left computers with remote desktop software accessible to exploitation. That is, Argus created a separate username with a static default password that was stored in plain text when it was used by health practitioners on their home computers. According to a source speaking to Fairfax Media, attackers have already exploited this vulnerability, although there has been no evidence they have used the access to steal medical records.

In January 2018, Telstra has officially confirmed that several customers with unsecured remote desktop configurations and open internet access were impacted by this vulnerability. Since then, a security patch has been issued and the company urged its current and past users to remove the associated accounts from their active directories and uninstall the software. No additional incidents have been reported since the issue was addressed in late January 2018.

Cybersecurity for Healthcare Industry

Ten Best Practices

1. **Prepare for complexity:** Criminals are increasingly employing advanced evasive techniques, and more nation-state standard tools are being used for high profile cyber attacks. This is likely to spread quickly through many industries and countries, and raises the importance of continual monitoring and detection of an organization's information technology environment.

2. **Be ready for the unexpected:** Unanticipated outcomes during an attack are also factors that should be addressed in scenario planning. This is particularly important which establishing cyber defense procedures to handle multi-vector attacks against several systems either simultaneously or as part of an escalation. Notably, reviewing the implementation of a 'kill-switch' for various systems in cases of large-scale and sophisticated

destructive attacks is important to consider, particularly if an organization may be required to react quickly when required.

3. **Take time to review and approve budgets:** It is highly recommended to allocate additional resources for emergency scenarios. Typically emergency scenarios are under-budgeted for by a factor of x3 and during an emergency situation many firms cannot or do not bring the appropriate skills and teams within an appropriate timeframe. This delay can and does lead to significantly higher impact from attacks.

4. **Create a cybersecurity culture:** Developing a cyber security culture is vital in helping improve an organization's security posture by intertwining security practices with business operations. Creating a cybersecurity culture demonstrates that security is not only an IT department function, but a key part of the strategy at all levels.

5. **Employ an effective communication plan:** Organizations are incredibly diverse therefore different forms of communication is fundamental in ensuring employees know and understand the threats and measures that are in place to protect against them.

6. **Implement cybersecurity for medical devices:** Medical devices provide an increased level of value for patients and doctors, but also introduce cybersecurity vulnerabilities that could impact clinical operations and/or put patient care at high risk. Medical devices are typically network-connected, which often involves interaction through websites and the transmission of sensitive data. Encrypted data transmission and multilayered authentication are necessary to prevent unauthorized access.

7. **Gather threat intelligence:** It is important to gather information of potential cyber threats from both internal and external sources. External sources include the Department of Homeland Security (DHS), the Federal Bureau of Investigations (FBI), Information Sharing and Analysis Organization (ISAOs), and the National Council of Information Sharing and Analysis Centers (NC-ISACs).

8. **Provide cybersecurity education and training:** Cybersecurity education and training should be provided via classroom sessions, webcast/webinars, or streaming videos on topics including:
   - cyber awareness on handling PHI, PII and PCI
   - cyber spears phishing exercises
   - social engineering tactics
   - ransomware
   - incident Response – via table top exercises

9. **Perform third-party/vendor cyber risk assessments:** Maintain a business associate agreement (BAA) inventory. Perform adequate due

diligence prior to initiating a relationship to ensure that third-party partners are fully aware of all relevant threats and they are consistently auditing and managing their own information security programs consistent with HIPAA or HITRUST cybersecurity risk management framework.

10. **Conduct timely incident response** – Put business continuity plan (BCP), incident response (IR) plan, and disaster recovery (DR) plans in place. IR/DR teams should be implemented, as well as internal and external escalation and notification processes.

Prepare for the Breach

The following Cybersecurity Preparedness Pyramid (below) illustrates the importance of the actions which organizations should perform to reduce the probability and potential negative impacts of a cyber data breach.

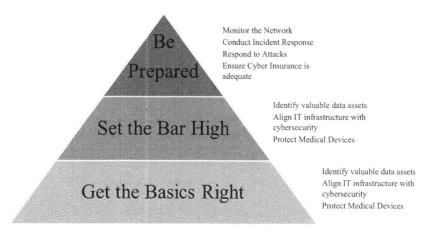

Cybersecurity Preparedness Pyramid

Top Ten Cybersecurity Questions For Healthcare Leadership

	Top Ten Cybersecurity Questions
1.	Does the organization treat cybersecurity as a business or IT responsibility?
2.	Has the organization identified and protected our most valuable processes and information?
3.	Does the organization's culture support cybersecurity?
4.	Does the organization have the basics of cybersecurity in place and documented?
5.	Does the organization focus on security compliance or security capability?
6.	Is the organization certain the business associates are securing their information?
7.	Is the organization vigilant about cyber defense via monitoring, detection, and response?

8.	Does the organization regularly evaluate the effectiveness of cybersecurity?
9.	Does the organization have an incident response plan in place?
10.	Does the organization have adequate cyber liability insurance coverage?

SUMMARY

In this chapter, the focus has been on understanding the real and significant cybersecurity challenges currently facing the healthcare industry each and every day. Further, a top ten list of cybersecurity best practices for the healthcare industry has been provided to help organizations counter the increasing cyber attacks. Lastly, a list of the top ten questions each healthcare services organization's leadership should ask about their information security practices has been provided to spur discussion. Remember, the healthcare industry is in cyber war, thus preparation and defense are essential to success.

The next chapter is focused on the unique cybersecurity challenges and best practices of the private equity industry and the potential impacts of cyber data breaches on companies involved in the mergers and acquisition process – before, during, and after the deal.

Endnotes

[1] *https://www.pageuppeople.com/unauthorised-activity-on-it-system/*

[2] *https://www.bleepingcomputer.com/news/security/maware-infection-at-hr-company-tr1ggers-flurry-of-data-breach-not1ficat10ns/*

[3] *https://careers.medibank.com.au/data-security-incident/*

[4] *https://prod.cms.dignityhealth.org/arizona/locations/stjosephs/about-us/press-center/press-releases/2018-06-02-data-breach*

[5] *https://www.prnewswire.com/news-releases/lifebridge-health-and-lifebridge-potomac-professionals-notify-patients-of-a-recent-security-incident-300649922.html*

[6] *https://www.apom.com/content/uploads/2018/05/FINAL_Allied-Physicians-News-Release_May-21-2018-C2-1-e1526932385481.jpg*

[7] *https://healthitsecurity.com/news/samsam-ransomware-attacks-focus-on-victims-who-will-pay-up*

[8] *https://www.databreaches.net/more-than-200000-patients-records-were-expose-on-medevolves-public-ftp-server-researcher/*

[9] *https://www.appmn.com/faq/*

[10] *https://www.zdnet.com/article/insurance-startup-leaks-sensitive-customer-health-data/*

[11] *https://www.healthdatamanagement.com/news/hackers-access-email-of-aultman-hospital-occupational-medicine-branch?brief=00000157-c311-d2b6-af57-cb9929c60000*

[12] *http://www.healthcareitnews.com/news/despite-email-attacks-healthcare-still-not-using-dmarc-protect-against-spoofing*

[13] *https://www.darkreading.com/endpoint/91--of-cyberattacks-start-with-a-ph1shmg-ema1-/d/d-1d/1327704*

14 https://www.bankinfosecurity.com/nuance-communications-breach-affected-45000-patients-a-11002

15 https://www.sfdph.org/dph/alerts/files/DPH_Release_notification_of_security_incident_5_11_18.pdf

16 http://www.oregonclinic.com/dataincident

17 https://www.healthdatamanagement.com/news/the-oregon-clinic-notifies-patients-after-data-breach

18 https://www.hipaajournal.com/malware-tnstalled-o--flori a osp1 k-florida-hospita1-may-have-compromised-patient-data.html

19 https://www.beckershospitalreview.com/cybersecurrty/malware-attacat

20 https://krebsonsecurity.com/2018/04/transcription-service-leaked-medical-records/

21 https://www.bleepingcomputer.com/news/security/the-whiterose-ransomware-is-decryptable-and-tel!s-a-strange-story/

22 https://www.thpg.org/Pages/A-Notice-to-Our-Patients.aspx

23 http://www.cos-orthopaedics.com/web-notice/

24 http://www.kulr8.com/story/38061238/billings-clinic-reports-data-security-incident

25 https://www.databreaches.net/scenic-bluffs-community-health-centers-notifies-patients-of-security-breach/

26 http://www.healthcareitnews.com/news/63500-patient-records-breached-new-york-providers-misconfigured-database

27 https://dashealth.com/dr-news-item/long-island-provider-exposes-data-42000-patients-misconfigured-database

28 http://nj.gov/oag/newsre1eases18/pr20180404b.html

29 https://www.smh.eom.au/technology/medical-records-exposed-by-flaw-in-telstra-health-argus-software-20180322-p4z5k0.html

Chapter 12

CYBERSECURITY FOR THE PRIVATE EQUITY MARKET – CHALLENGES AND BEST PRACTICES

By: Gregory A. Garrett, CISSP, CPCM, PMP

INTRODUCTION

Cybersecurity is a growing risk factor in the private equity (PE) marketplace within the U.S. and worldwide. Cyber attacks are increasing in sophistication and magnitude of impact across all industries globally. All organizations possess valuable information assets, which may include: intellectual property, financial payment information, client information, supply chain partners information, personal identifiable information (PII), protected health information (PHI), and/or payment card information (PCI) just to mention a few. It is vital for the buyer in the merger and acquisition (M&A) process to ensure they fully understand both the value of the information assets they are looking to acquire and the level of cyber threat and vulnerability facing the company they are considering to acquire. Further, the buyer must be able to determine the potential financial impact of the company's cybersecurity preparedness or lack thereof upon the deal price.

Likewise, it is imperative for the seller in the M&A process to take appropriate actions to reduce their organization's probability of a cyber breach and the potential negative impacts post-breach to optimize their sale price and ensure appropriate cyber defense. The focus of this chapter is to highlight the key questions and appropriate actions which both buyers and sellers involved in the M&A process can take before, during, and after the deal to mitigate the potential negative impacts of cyber attacks and optimize the financial aspects of the deal. Plus, to identify the challenges and best practices of implementing cybersecurity for the PE market.

Cybersecurity for the PE Market Ten Key Questions to Consider

1. What reputational risks do potential or actual data breaches and cyber attacks present to companies before, during, and after the M&A process?

   All companies, especially publicly traded companies face significant reputational risks as a result of both potential and/or actual data breaches and cyber attacks. Companies are increasingly being negatively impacted by class action law suits by investors following major cyber breaches, when investors believe the company was negligent in providing appropriate internal information security controls, effective monitoring, detection, cyber incident response, and disaster recovery planning.

2. Do any recent high-profile data breaches demonstrate the financial impacts which companies face as a result of cyber attacks?

   Clearly, both the Equifax and Uber data breaches demonstrate the significant reputational risks that companies face following a data breach or cyber attack. Equifax lost billions of dollars in stock value as a result of a lack of consumer confidence in the company as a result of their massive data breach impacting 143 million Americans. Likewise, Uber's massive breach impacting over 50 million customers and employees worldwide caused the company to lose billions of dollars of market value, as demonstrated in the reduction of their sale price of a portion of their company to Japan's Soft bank.

3. Is it only companies of a certain type or size, or operating in certain sectors, that should be concerned about cyber-related reputational risk, or do all companies need to plan for this eventuality?

   All companies need to plan for the potential reputational risks associated with actual cyber data breaches. We consider the following market sectors to be the highest targets for cyber attacks:
   - financial services
   - healthcare services
   - government contractors
   - automotive and manufacturing
   - private equity
   - retail

4. What methods can private equity companies adopt to effectively align their risk management strategies with operational realities to reduce exposure to data breaches and cyber attacks?

Seven Best Practices to Optimize Cybersecurity and Reduce Exposure to Data Breaches

(1) Provide practical and timely cybersecurity education and training from the top of the company on down to every employee and supply chain partner.

(2) Ensure multi-factor authentication to protect access to the network.

(3) Provide 24x7x365 monitoring, detection, and rapid incident response.

(4) Conduct timely and effective software patch management.

(5) Implement effective business continuity planning/disaster recovery.

(6) Conduct periodic vulnerability assessments and penetration testing.

(7) Ensure the adequacy of cyber liability insurance.

5. Are more .companies turning to cyber insurance to mitigate the financial effects of a data breach?

Many companies are turning to cyber liability insurance to mitigate the financial impacts of a data breach. However, companies are learning that not all cyber liability insurance is the same. In fact, cyber liability insurance coverage varies widely so it is important to understand what is covered, what is not covered and what documentation is required in order to prepare a proper claim for damages as a result of a cyber breach.

6. In the event that a company suffers a significant attack during the M&A process that exposes data, what strategies can it deploy to reduce the negative fallout?

Six Cybersecurity Best Practices

(1) Conduct an independent cyber investigation to determine the source of the attack, impact of the attack, and appropriate remediation actions.

(2) Gather cyber threat intelligence via social media analysis, dark web recon and much more . . . .

(3) Implement 24x7x365 monitoring detection, and incident response.

(4) Ensure appropriate back up plans and disaster recovery process.

(5) Provide follow-up cyber security education and training.

(6) Assess cyber liability insurance coverage, prepare a claim, and submit a well-documented claim for damages.

7. Are data breaches likely to become more frequent?

Yes.

If so, should companies devote more resources to dealing with cyber threats in order to safe guard their reputation as much as possible?

Yes.

8. What is the average cost of a data breach in the U.S.?
   According to the U.S. Security Exchange Commission (SEC) February 2018 report, the average cost of a cyber data breach is now $7.5 million, not including the cost of the impact on the company's reputation and loss of potential revenue.
9. What are the most common cyber attacks methods impacting organizations in the PE market?
   - spear-phishing
   - ransomware
   - spoofing
   - trojan-horse malware
   - waterholing
10. What are the most common sources of unauthorized access into a company's network?
    - inside threat – current or former company employee, either inadvertently or malicious access
    - third-party/subcontractor
    - spear-phishing and/or spoofing campaign

Cyber Threats to Merger and Acquisition Deals

Numerous businesses, organizations, and governments have found their digital data imperiled by a world-wide dispersal of two waves of malware. The first wave, a ransomware attack dubbed "WannaCry," began on May 12, 2017. Globally, it infected an estimated 230,000 computers in 48 hours, locking down the computers it infected, and encrypting and rendering inaccessible all of their stored data. The WannaCry worm caused kinetic effects, "paralyzing hospitals, disrupting transport networks, and immobilizing businesses." *WannaCry Should Make People Treat Cyber-crime Seriously,* The Economist, May 20, 2017.

The second wave of malware, called "Petya," began on June 27, 2017, and severely disrupted operations of "some of the world's largest companies, including WPP, Roseneft, Merck, . . . AP Moller-Maersk[,] . . . Saint-Bobain and the DLA Piper law firm." *Global Groups Hit by Fresh Ransomware Cyber Attack,* Financial Times, June 28, 2017. For example, one day into the Petya attack, integrated global transport and logistics company A.P. Moller-Maersk "tweeted" on June 27, 2017, that the malware had brought down its "IT systems . . . across multiple sites and select business units." By the second day, Maersk had "shut-down many of its ports around the world." WannaCry and Petya vividly demonstrated the vulnerability of many companies to a crippling cyber attack.

The experience of the Target Corporation provides insight into the costs of a major breach. In 2014, the Target Corporation experienced a breach of its networks affecting 40 million credit and debit-card numbers and personally identifiable information for up to 70 million individuals. The remediation costs had a material impact on the company. Target eventually reported that it "incurred $252 million of cumulative data breach-related expenses, partially offset by $90 million of expected insurance recoveries, for net cumulative expenses of $162 million."

Despite the ubiquity of cyber incidents, and the cost and disruptive impact of cyberattacks, such risks appear to remain "below the radar," underestimated, or belatedly addressed in many M&A deals. Yet, with the value of so many enterprises dependent upon the condition of their high-value digital assets, and with so many of those assets vulnerable to cyber attack, consideration of adding a cybersecurity due diligence review would seem a good and prudent precaution at the start of any proposed M&A deal.[1]

Illuminating the Impact of Cyber Incidents on M&A Deals

The cybersecurity experiences of two companies involved in recent M&A transactions demonstrate the critical importance of cybersecurity due diligence.

Neiman Marcus

Luxury department store Neiman Marcus experienced a cyber incident that began as early as July 16, 2013. The incident involved injection of malware into the retailer's customer payment processing system, ultimately compromising data on about 350,000 customer payment cards. Seven weeks later, on September 8, 2013, as the intruders operated undetected within the retailer's networks, Neiman Marcus agreed to be acquired by a group led by Ares Management and a Canadian pension plan. On October 25, 2013, the acquisition of Neiman Marcus closed. Five days later, on October 30, 2013, the card-scraping activity of the malware inside the retailer ceased. No report of the incident suggests that Neiman Marcus or its acquirers knew, as of the closing, that the digital assets of the retailer had been compromised by intruders.

On December 17, 2013, Neiman Marcus received the first of several reports indicating fraudulent use of customer credit cards at its stores. On January 10, 2014, Neiman Marcus publicly disclosed the incident. Shortly thereafter, affected customers filed class-action complaints alleging the retailer failed to protect them adequately against the breach and to provide them timely notice. Although Neiman Marcus sought to dismiss the suit by arguing that there was no harm to the plaintiffs, and thus no standing to sue, the U.S. Court of Appeals for the Seventh Circuit allowed the case to proceed, holding that:

> [i]t is plausible to infer that the plaintiffs have shown a substantial risk of harm from the Neiman Marcus data breach. Why else would hackers break into a store's database and steal consumers' private information? Presumably, the purpose of the hack is, sooner or later, to make fraudulent charges or assume those consumers' identities.

In so holding, the Seventh Circuit pointed to the continuing risk, noting that "stolen data may be held for up to a year or more before being used to commit identity theft. Further, once stolen data have been sold or posted on the Web, fraudulent use of that information may continue for years." In March 2017, Neiman Marcus entered into a settlement with the class-action plaintiffs and agreed to create a settlement fund in the amount of $1,600,000 to cover claims, legal fees, and other litigation-related expenses. Apparently, neither the buyer nor the seller knew that Neiman Marcus digital assets had been compromised as of the closing, nor did they foresee the future risk of harmful use of such data. As the Neiman Marcus incident illustrates, there is a growing need to assess a target's cyber vulnerabilities and the potential repercussions from incidents so that they can be given their appropriate weight in the negotiations of a deal.[2]

Yahoo!

In late 2014, senior officers and legal staff of Yahoo!, Inc. learned that unauthorized access to its computer network had been gained by what Yahoo! identified as a "state-sponsored actor." Yahoo! did not, at that point in time, publicly disclose the incident. Yahoo!'s board apparently did not receive a report of the incident or learn of it until almost two years later.

On July 23, 2016, Yahoo! and Verizon Communications Inc. entered into a stock purchase agreement by which Verizon agreed to acquire "one or more subsidiaries of Yahoo holding all of Yahoo's operating businesses, for approximately $4.83 billion in cash. . . . "The acquisition of Yahoo! was "expected to close in the first quarter of 2017." Verizon Communications Inc., Form 10-Q for the period ending June 30, 2016, filed Jul. 29, 2016, at 10.

Around the time that Yahoo! and Verizon signed their agreement, "a hacker claimed to have obtained certain Yahoo! user data. [T]he Company could not substantiate the hacker's claim [but] . . . intensified an ongoing broader review of the Company's network and data security, including a review of prior access to the Company's network by a state-sponsored actor that the Company had identified in late 2014." Yahoo, Inc., Form 10-Q for the period ending September 30, 2016, filed Nov. 9, 2016, at 40.

Thereafter, Yahoo! issued a statement to the U.S. Securities and Exchange Commission (SEC) that said it had no knowledge of "any incidents" of "security breaches, unauthorized access or unauthorized use of its IT systems." Yet less than two weeks later, in September 2016, Yahoo! disclosed to Verizon, and shortly thereafter to the public, that a "copy of certain user account information for at least 500 million user accounts was stolen from Yahoo's network in late 2014 (the First Security Incident)." After disclosing the incident, Yahoo! began notifying potentially affected users, regulators, and other stakeholders.

On December 14, 2016, five weeks after Yahoo! filed its Form 10-Q with the Security Exchange Commission (SEC) that addressed the First Security Incident, Yahoo! disclosed on its website and in a Form 8-K that analysis of data by Yahoo!'s outside forensic experts convinced Yahoo! that a separate cyber incident involving almost 1 billion accounts had also occurred (the Second Security Incident).[3] After further negotiations and as a result of the two cyber incidents, Yahoo! *agreed with Verizon to modify* the terms of the deal as follows:

- the purchase price was reduced by $350 million, down to $4.48 billion;
- Yahoo! would be responsible for all liabilities arising from shareholder lawsuits and SEC Investigations related to the two cyber incidents; and
- Yahoo! and Verizon would each be responsible for *"50% of any cash liabilities incurred following the closing related to non-SEC… government investigations and third-party litigation related to the breaches."*

As the cyber incidents at Neiman Marcus and Yahoo! demonstrate, cybersecurity now deserves to be an integral part of M&A due diligence, and to be done properly, it must begin at the earliest practicable time in the transaction. Omitting cybersecurity assessments in M&A due diligence, conducting superficial evaluations, or limiting such due diligence to a company's IT systems rather than treating cybersecurity as a risk category in its own right means ignoring the serious risks that cyber threats pose to all companies and to M&A deals involving them.[4]

M & A Cybersecurity Due Diligence Lessons Learned

To accomplish its goal, the acquirer's M&A cybersecurity due diligence process should address six categories of topics, as follows:

1. Identify the target's high-value digital assets and evaluate the relative importance of those assets to the target's business.
2. Evaluate the target's Internal cybersecurity program to protect those high-value digital assets, e.g., whether it Is appropriate for the business; whether It is complete, etc..
3. Assess the target's cyber-risk-management efforts as they relate to third parties on which the target depends for goods, services, data, outsourced business functions, and joint business initiatives.
4. Identify the target's prior breaches and assess its Incident-response capabilities.
5. Evaluate the status of the target's cybersecurity regulatory compliance, i.e., identify applicable compliance requirements, determine whether the target is in compliance with its cybersecurity legal obligations, and evaluate the risks posed by any failure of such compliance.
6. Consider and evaluate the target's overall resilience and general ability to withstand a direct cyber attack on its digital assets.[5]

Private Equity (PE) Market Cybersecurity Best Practices for Buyers

For buyers, whether a private equity firm or strategic company buyer, it is essential to take the following actions as appropriate for the industry, size, and complexity of the acquisition target including:

Before the Deal

- Select one or two independent firms with extensive cybersecurity advisory services, cyber threat analysis capabilities, vulnerability assessment and penetration testing services, and managed security services.
- Once a potential M&A target is selected engage one of the independent cybersecurity advisory firms to do the following:
  o Conduct a dark web analysis for the company, key personnel, and selected supply chain partners .
  o Conduct a social media analysis of the company and key personnel.
  o Conduct an extensive internet search of the company and key personnel.

All actions taken should be focused on identifying potential negative or damaging information, which could lead to cyber vulnerabilities including: ransom, malware, ransomware, spear-phishing, spoofing, and other attack modes.

During the Deal (Due Diligence)

- review the company's information security policies, plans, and procedures, including: incident response (IR) plan, business continuity plan (BCP), and disaster recovery (DR) plan.
- Evaluate the company's cybersecurity education and training program
- Assess the most recent cyber vulnerability assessment and penetration testing findings.
- Conduct a new vulnerability assessment and penetration tests, preferably via an independent cybersecurity services firm.
- Assess the information technology infrastructure, people, hardware, software.
- Evaluate the company's compliance with industry required cyber security risk management framework.
- Conduct a cyber liability insurance coverage adequacy evaluation.

After the Deal is Done

- Take the following cybersecurity remediation actions as necessary and appropriate:
  - o Conduct a cyber risk assessment.
  - o Enhance IT technical operations.
  - o Engage a managed security services provider (MSSP) to:
    - Provide managed monitoring detection, and incident response services- 24x7x365 and
    - Provide threat intelligence services.
  - o Provide cybersecurity education and training to all employees.
  - o Assess third-party vendor cyber risks.

Private Equity (PE) Market Cybersecurity Best Practices for Sellers

For sellers, the key to improved cybersecurity is to take all of the aforementioned actions as necessary and appropriate before engaging in the M&A process, including:

- Cyber risk assessment,
- Cyber threat assessment,
- Vulnerability and penetration testing,
- Cybersecurity education and training,
- Information security documented policies, plans and procedures,
- Multi-layer cyber defense system with encryption, multi-factor authentications, and 24x7x365 monitoring, detection and incident response
- Cyber liability insurance coverage, and
- Business continuity plan.

SUMMARY

The risk of a massive cyber breach negatively impacting a company's reputation and market value is ever increasing. Thus, both buyers and sellers
engaged in the PE marketplace need to fully understand the value of the
information assets they are looking to acquire, the cybersecurity related risk,
and then factor the benefits and risk variables into their respective business
equation and pricing. Once all of the aforementioned actions are taken, then
informed business decisions can be made by both parties to reduce the potential negative impacts of a cyber breach and the post breach consequences
on a deal. Said simply, spending thousands of dollars on a cyber threat assessment, cybersecurity risk assessment, and/or a vulnerability assessment
up-front in the M&A process, could save millions of dollars for both parties
at the end of the process.

The next chapter of this book will focus on the cybersecurity challenges and
best practices involved in the public sector, including U.S. federal government agencies and government contractors.

Endnotes

[1]   Roland Trope and Tom Smedinghoff, *Guide to Cybersecurity Due Diligence in M & A Transactions*, ABA, 2017

[2]   *Id.*

[3]   *The Importance of Cybersecurity Due Diligence in M & A Transactions*, Business Law Today, September, 2017

[4]   *Id.*

[5]   *Id.*

Chapter 13

CYBERSECURITY FOR THE PUBLIC SECTOR AND GOVERNMENT CONTRACTORS – CHALLENGES AND BEST PRACTICES

By: Gregory A. Garrett, CISSP, CPCM, PMP

INTRODUCTION

With cyber attackers growing increasingly sophisticated in their methods and the number of data breaches on the rise, it is no wonder that cybersecurity is top of mind for both public and private sectors. In fact, the numerous attacks in recent years have been serious and costly enough to prompt action at the federal level of the U.S., and internationally, with government departments and agencies/ministries all over the world creating cybersecurity strategies, policies, plans, and procedures to protect their national vital information from cyber attacks.

For example, the European Union (EU) has developed and begun to implement a standardized cybersecurity risk management framework (RMF). Likewise, the state of Israel has formed a National Cyber Security Authority (NCSA) to oversee cybersecurity efforts from Israeli Civilian Ministries and private sector businesses across all industries. Further, China has enacted a federal law on cybersecurity with a wide-range of policies and mandatory information security requirements for all Chinese government agencies and businesses. In this chapter, the focus is on understanding U.S. federal cybersecurity challenges and best practices of government agencies and government contractors.

UNDERSTANDING U.S FEDERAL GOVERNMENT CYBERSECURITY CHALLENGES

U.S. federal government networks are attractive targets for foreign intelligence services and other malicious actors in cyberspace. Networks serving over 100 agencies and millions of employees enable government missions and operations, handle sensitive internal communications, and store personal data on millions of Americans. The level of threat faced by the U.S. federal government networks has few parallels, and agencies have been unable to keep up.[1] U.S. federal government cybersecurity is a dense, inaccessible topic to those outside the information security community and even to some inside it. Information is scattered across a variety of U.S. federal government departments and numerous regulatory requirements, with no "one stop shop" to understand the topic.

Securing U.S. federal government civilian agencies networks and systems is a complex and daunting prospect. Several systemic factors contribute to a challenging environment:

1. **Difficult tradeoffs between centralized and decentralized management.** The overall U.S. federal government structure is largely decentralized, with each agency managing its own risk, and implementing its own security solutions. Full centralization would bring its own challenges, such as limiting agencies' ability to develop tailored, agile solutions to their cybersecurity challenges.

2. **Varying levels of engagement of agency top leadership on cyber risk management.** Successful agency heads develop an awareness of cyber risk and actively manage it. Within agencies, the authorities of chief information officers vary widely.

3. **Varying effectiveness of levers to direct, incentivize, and enforce action by nonperforming U.S. federal government agencies.** The Department of Homeland Security (DHS) and Office of Management and Budget (OMB) have some levers to drive action by individual agencies, and DHS' increasing operational authority has been critical.

4. **Resource constraints and a rigid U.S. federal government budgeting cycle.** Properly resourcing cybersecurity priorities can be expensive, and the structure of the government budgeting process poses challenges for agency cybersecurity efforts.

5. **Scattered U.S. congressional oversight.** No single congressional body has the full picture of U.S. federal government cybersecurity measures, and legislative requirements are spread across many bills, making it complicated for U.S. federal government agencies to adapt to threats.

In developing approaches to better manage cyber risk to U.S. federal government systems, policymakers, agency leaders, cybersecurity professionals, and congressional staff should consider the following best practices:

- **Sound risk management underpins all U.S. federal government cybersecurity efforts**. Federal agencies cannot and will not prevent every incident or intrusion. Agencies must identify the most important missions and assets, then craft strategies to reduce, mitigate, or accept the risks.

- **Sustained, high-level leadership from agency heads is critical to success**. Agencies with engaged department heads or deputies are much more likely to use resources strategically, force mission or business owners to attend to cybersecurity, and empower chief information officers to take steps needed to protect systems and enforce standards.

- **Effective management demands clarity on roles and responsibilities**. The U.S. federal government cybersecurity system is complex. This is not inherently bad but it does demand constant effort to refine, clarify, and institutionalize roles and responsibilities to ensure coherence.

- **Steady, incremental progress makes a difference**. The Cyber Sprint in 2016, modest as it was, demonstrated that agencies can make progress when held accountable for discrete milestones, especially on issues of basic cyber hygiene often exploited by intruders.

- **Some areas, however, require constant innovation, or even a fundamental "rethink."** The most advanced agencies have policies that reward and implement innovative ideas on topics like workforce, procurement, and executive education.

- **Congress plays a critical role**. Congress authorizes and appropriates agency missions, authorities, and budgets. Very little can be done without strong support and engagement from the legislative branch.

- **Resources matter**. Skimping on resources for modernizing networks or attracting cybersecurity talent will reduce the ability of agencies to secure their core missions, with real impacts to both government and citizens.

- **Evolving technology will change the game**. Innovation in the digital ecosystem, like automation, will bring both new threats and new defensive applications. The government will need to plan 5- to 10-years ahead to keep from lagging behind.

There are no silver bullets for U.S. federal government cybersecurity. The system will retain its inherent complexity, necessitating close coordination and partnership. U.S. federal government cybersecurity will be an enduring mission, always evolving and changing to stay ahead of the threat. In other words, there is no "finish line" only continual improvement, adaptation, and cooperation to secure the federal government and those it serves.[2]

U.S. OFFICE OF MANAGEMENT AND BUDGET AND DEPARTMENT OF HOMELAND SECURITY– CYBERSECURITY RISK REPORT (MAY) 2018

OMB and DHS determined that 71 of 96 agencies (74 percent) participating in the risk assessment process have cybersecurity programs that are either at risk or high risk. OMB and DHS also found that U.S. federal government agencies are not equipped to determine how threat actors seek to gain access to their information. The risk assessments show that the lack of threat information results in ineffective allocation of agencies' limited cyber resources. This situation creates enterprise-wide gaps in network visibility, IT tool and capability standardization, and common operating procedures, all of which negatively impact federal cybersecurity.

OMB and DHS examined the performance of 96 agencies across 76 metrics, and this risk report identifies the following four (4) core actions that are necessary to address cybersecurity risks across the federal enterprise:

1. Increase cybersecurity threat awareness among federal agencies by implementing the Cyber Threat Framework to prioritize efforts and manage cybersecurity risks;
2. Standardize IT and cybersecurity capabilities to control costs and improve asset management;
3. Consolidate agency Security Operation Centers (SOCs) to improve incident detection and response capabilities; and
4. Drive accountability across agencies through improved governance processes, recurring risk assessments, and OMB's engagements with agency leadership.

FINDINGS AND PLANNED ACTIONS

Finding 1: Limited Situational Awareness -

Agencies do not understand the current cyber threats and do not have the resources to combat the current threat environment.

Action: OMB, DHS, and the National Security Agency will disseminate and help implement the cyber threat framework to prioritize efforts and manage cybersecurity risks.

U.S. federal government and industry cybersecurity reports and news headlines describing cybersecurity incidents continue to underscore that threat actors employ persistent and increasingly sophisticated techniques to attack and compromise information systems. Nevertheless, U.S. federal government agencies' and private organizations' ability to determine threat actors' motivations and methods for staging cyber attacks has not improved. The risk assessment process revealed that those charged with defending agency networks often lack timely information regarding the tactics, techniques, and procedures that threat actors use to exploit government information systems. In fact, situational awareness is so limited that Federal agencies could not identify the method of attack, or attack vector, in 11,802 of the 30,899 cyber awareness incidents (38 percent) that led to the compromise of information or system functionality in FY 2016.

Improving Situational Awareness

For the better part of the past decade, OMB, the Government Accountability Office (GAO), and agency inspector generals (IGs) have found that agencies' enterprise risk management programs do not effectively identify, assess, and prioritize actions to mitigate cybersecurity risks in the context of other enterprise risks. Furthermore, OMB found that only 59 percent of agencies reported having processes in place to communicate cyber risks across their enterprises. OMB has repeatedly emphasized that managing risk effectively requires timely data reporting and communication flows so that employees at all levels in the organization have the information necessary to block attacks in their area of responsibility.

Finding 2: Lack of Standardized IT Capabilities -

U.S. federal government agencies do not have standardized cybersecurity processes and IT capabilities, which impacts their ability to efficiently gain visibility and effectively combat threats.

Action: Agencies will continue standardizing their IT offerings and cybersecurity capabilities in FY 2019.

An agency's ability to mitigate security vulnerabilities is a direct function of its ability to identify those vulnerabilities across the enterprise. Agency risk assessments show that this issue becomes more complex in federated agencies that lack standardized procedures and technology across the organization. The lack of standardization and access to common capabilities means that these agencies cannot apply a single solution to address specific cybersecurity challenges and eventually reduce their overall attack surface. Although congress and the executive branch have taken steps to enhance CIO authorities and visibility into IT spending across the organization through the Federal Information Technology Acquisition Reform Act (FIT ARA), the risk assessments demonstrate that additional actions are necessary to modernize and standardize IT solutions across the government. Additionally, while agencies plan to utilize DHS's Continuous Diagnostics and Mitigation (CDM) program, which provides standardized capabilities aimed at enhancing visibility and eventually control costs, the risk assessments show there are considerable capability gaps across government that must be closed to ensure CDM's effectiveness over time.

Improving Access Management

One of the most significant security concerns that results from the current decentralized and fragmented U.S. federal government IT landscape is ineffective identity, credential, and access management (ICAM) processes. Fundamentally, any organization must have a clear understanding of the people, assets, and data on its networks. Effective access management provides a governance structure that allows organizations to limit users' access to only the information required to perform their jobs, and therefore minimizes the risks of unauthorized access or information disclosures. To this end, federal agencies have made tremendous progress enforcing the use of multi-factor authentication personal identity verification cards in recent years. Through increased oversight, and accountability for implementing this control, agencies now enforce the use of this control among 93 percent of their privileged users, who have access to large tranches of sensitive agency and citizen data.

To continue progress, the U.S. federal governmnet agencies must improve their ICAM architecture through the centralization of such solutions. In particular, agencies need to move toward a single, authoritative solution for establishing and managing attribute or role-based access controls for their users. OMB found that, across government, agencies employ fragmented ICAM programs, solutions, and user directories. This structure prevents agencies from achieving a comprehensive understanding of their users, managing those users' access to the agency network, and effectively safeguarding sensitive government information. For example, one agency noted that it maintains a decentralized environment with 23 domains and over 300 unique user groupings based on geographic location, which precludes the agency from effectively managing users' access to information across the enterprise.

Furthermore, the IGs report that only 55 percent of agencies limit access based on user attributes and roles and only 57 percent review and track administrative privileges. Although effective ICAM is a foundational step to ensuring that the right users have access to the right data at the right time, only half of federal agencies have processes in place to restrict users' access to information. Over the next year, OMB and DHS will work to enhance agencies' access management programs, starting with efforts to provide enterprise-wide views of who is on their networks.

Email Consolidation

Email, by way of phishing attacks, remains one of the most common attack vectors across both the U.S. federal government and industry. The 23 CFO Act agencies account for nearly 2.2 million email inboxes, with hundreds of thousands of additional inboxes across 100+ smaller agencies. Standardizing and consolidating email at the enterprise level is a key element of the strategy for securing users, and yet some agencies report several separately managed email services inside their organizations. For example, one U.S. federal government agency lists no fewer than 62 separately managed email services in its environment, making it virtually impossible to track and inspect inbound and outbound communications across the agency.

Standardizing email services across the agency enhances the ability to provide phishing protection by inspecting inbound and outbound messages, disabling and quarantining malicious attachments, and validating the sender and receiver in email exchanges. At least nine of the 23 CFO Act agencies have already consolidated their enterprise email and note that associated complexities stem from the size of the organization, rather than from cost or technical challenges. In fact, the largest of these agencies, with over 100,000 users, estimates a 10-month timeframe for consolidating all of their users into a single email solution. Additionally, agencies of varying size that have consolidated, or are in the process of consolidating, identify cost savings in the $1 million to $4 million range per year. Accordingly, over the coming year, OMB will work with agencies to develop enterprise-wide email consolidation plans in support of the activities set forth in the IT modernization report to the president.

Standardized Software and Applications

Several industry reports identify software application whitelisting as one of the most critical cybersecurity controls for preventing, or minimizing the impact of, cyberattacks. Software whitelisting is a process by which agencies list applications and application components that are authorized for use in an organization. This capability is especially effective for those attacks that employ malware and malicious code. IGs consistently find that agencies are limited in their ability to detect and whitelist the software running on their systems, with only 49 percent of agencies having this capability. In addition to not actively whitelisting software, many agencies have multiple versions of the same software tools in place, or they have tools with overlapping functionality. Different versions of the same software will often have distinct vulnerabilities and require unique efforts from an agency's security team(s), whose time is better spent on standard implementations. In the absence of this capability, agencies do not have a clear picture of the applications running on their networks.

To address the difficulty and complexity of securing multiple versions of the same software tool, or competing tools in the same environment, OMB and the General Services Administration (GSA) will work with agencies to move to standard configurations or versions through shared services and new government-wide marketplaces. This effort will augment the software application whitelisting capability that DHS is providing to agencies in CDM Phase 1. These initiatives are critical to allocating resources effectively during the acquisition process and, more broadly, in securing the U.S. federal government environment as a whole.

Finding 3: Limited Network Visibility -

Agencies lack visibility into what is occurring on their networks, and especially lack to ability to detect data exfiltration.

Action: Agencies will begin consolidating their security operations center capabilities and processes, or migrating to a SOC as a Service in FY 2019.

U.S. federal government agencies do not have the visibility into their networks to effectively detect data exfiltration attempts and respond to cybersecurity incidents. The risk assessment process revealed that 73 percent of agency programs are either at risk or high risk in this critical area. Specific metrics related to data loss prevention and exfiltration demonstrate even greater problems, with only 40 percent of agencies reporting the ability to detect the encrypted exfiltration of information at government-wide target levels. Only 27 percent of agencies report that they have the ability to detect and investigate attempts to access large volumes of data, and even fewer agencies report testing these capabilities annually. Simply put, agencies cannot detect when access large amounts of information leave their networks, which is particularly alarming in the wake of some of the high-profile incidents across government and industry in recent years.

The risk assessments also reveal that agencies have a low level of maturity on incident response as a whole. Only 52 percent of agencies reported having validated incident response roles during testing over the past year. Agency IGs also found that only 30 percent of agencies have predictable, enterprise-wide incident response processes in place, with as few as 17 percent of agencies actually analyzing incident response data after an incident has occurred. This indicates that agencies are not adequately developing incident response processes and, when incidents occur, they are not able to respond in a consistent manner.

The current situation is untenable, as agencies lack both the visibility into their networks to determine the occurrence of cybersecurity incidents and the ability to minimize the impact of an incident if one is detected. In the near term, the DHS CDM program seeks to provide agencies with greater insights into what is occurring on their networks. Specifically, the program will include access management capabilities, as well as boundary protection and event management capabilities in Phases two and three, respectively.

Finding 4: Lack of Accountability for Managing Risks -

Agencies lack standardized and enterprise-wide processes for managing cybersecurity risks.

Action: Hold agency heads accountable for their organization's security and governance processes, by conducting quarterly risk assessments that track agencies' progress implementing cybersecurity controls.

Both FISMA and Executive Order 13800 identify the agency head as the official ultimately responsible for each agency's cybersecurity. FISMA also requires agencies to report their cybersecurity program performance to the OMB Director. OMB uses this information as part of its oversight processes to ensure that agency heads efficiently and effectively safeguard their networks and protect taxpayers' information from cybersecurity risks. While such top-level accountability is important to drive measurable improvements agency-wide, agency heads often delegate cyber risk management responsibilities to the CIO and CISO. While most agencies noted in their responses to Executive Order 13800 that their leadership was actively engaged in cybersecurity risk management, many did not, or could not, elaborate in detail on leadership engagement above the CIO level.

This finding is concerning because the assessments show that CIOs and CISOs often lack the authority necessary to make organization-wide decisions despite direction to centralize authority in statutes such as FITARA and FISMA. This is particularly true in federated agencies, which employ multiple component CIOs who often control their own budgets. OMB and the IGs have repeatedly found that senior-level visibility and authority is necessary to drive consistent improvement in agency cybersecurity, and requires the agency head, Deputy Secretary, and CXOs to be involved and prepared to hold underperforming components accountable. However, the agency risk assessments, OMB's oversight processes, and IG and GAO reports all show that awareness and accountability for managing cyber risks is uneven across the federal enterprise.

Additionally, IGs report that federal agencies possess neither robust risk management programs nor consistent methods for notifying leadership of cybersecurity risks across the agency. In contrast to federal agencies' approach to transparency and accountability, the Securities and Exchange Commission requires every publicly-traded company to file quarterly and annual reports to inform shareholders of risks, including cyber risks that could affect their business. These reports are meant to demonstrate the due diligence and due care companies undertake to safeguard their business operations and shareholder's investments. U.S. federal government agencies would benefit from a similar process that tracks quarterly performance against strategic performance targets, communicates the resulting risks to stakeholders, and provides a sense of the return on investment for cybersecurity protections over time.

Report Conclusions

At a time when the world's reliance on technology is becoming greater and the nation's digital adversaries are growing more adept, we must ensure that the U.S. federal government can secure citizens' information and deliver on their core missions. To this end, the Risk Report has identified four core actions to enhance government-wide cybersecurity risk management practices in a timely manner. In the near term, OMB will take necessary actions to implement the Cybersecurity Threat Framework, standardize IT capabilities and tools, consolidate or migrate SOC operations, and drive accountability for cybersecurity risk management across the enterprise. These actions will help shape agency budgets for FY 2019 and beyond. OMB will continue to work with its cross-agency partners, including DHS, NIST, GSA, and others to ensure that agencies are aware of expectations and available resources. Additionally, OMB will work through the Federal CIO and CISO Councils to ensure that the federal government is moving together toward improved security outcomes.

U.S. GOVERNMENT CONTRACTORS – CYBERSECURITY CHALLENGES AND BEST PRACTICES

The Trump Administration released an Executive Order (EO) in 2017 mandating that all U.S. federal government agencies plan, develop and submit formal cybersecurity risk management plans to help safeguard their sensitive information and controlled unclassified information (CUI). This cybersecurity EO was signed to promote cyber risk mitigation across the entire government by holding each agency head personally responsible for network protection and requiring all agencies to modernize their information technology (IT) systems. In addition to the cybersecurity EO, each agency is also expected to use the National Institute of Standards and Technology's (NIST) Cybersecurity Risk Management Framework to enhance its controls and management of CUI.

The U.S. Department of Defense (DoD) has required government contractors to be held accountable to similar cybersecurity standards, dictated by the NIST Special Publication (SP) 800-171, *Protecting Controlled Unclassified Information in Nonfederal Information Systems and Organizations*. NIST SP 800-171 provides 109 individual controls categorized under 14 families of information security requirements designed to help companies control the security of their CUI (see chart below). This set of cybersecurity requirements is expected to be implemented across government contractors via a new final rule to the Federal Acquisition Regulation (FAR), which is an expansion of the Defense Federal Acquisition Regulation Supplement (DFARS) requirements that were issued in December 2017.

With these additional regulations on the horizon, it's not surprising that many government contractors feel overwhelmed; after all, they must now comply with several new federal requirements on top of the numerous industry-specific and international cyber standards, such as ISO 27001, already in place. As a result, many government contractors are experiencing numerous pain points related to the implementation of cybersecurity information governance, risk management and compliance.

Based on our discussions with more than 100 government contractors in recent months, we have outlined the top six cybersecurity questions they should address below.

Cybersecurity NIST SP 800-171 Requirements	
Information Security 14 Categories	Subject to Audit and Reviews by DCAA and DCMA
• Cybersecurity Awareness, Education and Training	• System Security Plan (SSP)
• Incident Response	• Incident Response (IR) Plan
• Audit and Accountability	• Information Security Policy documents
• Configuration Management	• Information Security Procedures
• Identification and Authentication	• Reports and Cyber Incidents
• Maintenance	• Flow-down of DFARS 252.204-7012 requirements to all subcontractors
• Media Protection	• Review of actual information security controls
• Personal Security	• Audit of costs incurred for information security
• Physical Protection	
• Risk Assessment	
• Security Assessment	
• System and Communications Protection	
• Systems and Information Integrity	

THE TOP SIX CYBERSECURITY PAIN POINTS FOR GOVERNMENT CONTRACTORS

1. How can government contractors accurately and cost effectively assess their cybersecurity compliance to NIST SP 800-171?

First, it is important to understand that NIST SP 800-171 is a set of guidelines established to help companies protect their CUI and DOD covered defense information (CDI) in non-federal systems and organizations. CUI is a result of the Obama Administration Executive Order 13556 issued in November 2010. The CUI system aims to standardize and simplify how the government handles unclassified information that requires safeguarding. There are 22 approved CUI categories of information, covering everything from agriculture, transportation and energy to defense technical drawings and product specifications provided by federal government agencies to government contractors.

Second, according to NIST, there are two classifications of security requirements: basic and derived. The basic security requirements are obtained from the Federal Information Processing Standard 200 (FIPS 200), which provides high-level fundamental security requirements for federal information and information systems. The derived security requirements, which supplement the basic security requirements, are taken from the detailed security controls contained in NIST Special Publication 800-53.

Third, for a government contractor to ensure it receives an accurate and cost-effective assessment of its cybersecurity capabilities in comparison to the NIST SP 800-171 guidelines, it should competitively evaluate and select an independent professional services company with the ability to perform a high-quality and timely cyber risk and gap assessment.

Currently, it appears that many government contractors do view the NIST 800-171 guidelines as a mandatory rule that requires full and strict compliance. It is expected that the new DFARS 252.204-7012 cybersecurity and information security management systems will be treated in the same manner as the six current major contractor business systems: accounting, cost estimating, material management and accounting system (MMAS), government property management and earned value management system (EVMS).

2. What actions have U.S. government contracting officers taken when government contractors have failed to comply with the DFARS 252.204-7012 (NIST SP 800-171 compliance requirement) since the Dec. 31, 2017 deadline?

So far, government contractors have been advised via updates from the DOD chief information officer (CIO) that the Defense Contract Management Agency (DCMA) may request a copy of their system security plan (SSP) for purposes of evaluation for compliance with the NIST SP 800-171 requirements and that the Defense Contract Audit Agency (DCAA) may audit their related information security management systems' cost.

Concerns to consider:

- Currently, neither the DCAA nor the DCMA have the necessary cybersecurity expertise to assess the contractor's compliance with the standard. Without certified information system security professionals (CISSPs), certified information technology auditors (CITAs) or the like, they cannot accurately evaluate government contractors' SSPs to fairly assess their compliance with NIST SP 800-171.
- If the federal government decides to outsource the SSP evaluation to assess compliance with NIST SP 800-171, it is imperative to ensure that the selected companies are free of organizational conflicts of interest (OCI) and personal conflicts of interest (PCI).
- If a government contractor is non-compliant with all or part of NIST SP 800-171, then the government contracting officer will have to decide on a number of actions. He or she can:
  o Withhold contractor payments up to 20 percent;
  o Issue a stop work order;
  o Issue a suspension of work; or
  o Terminate the contract for default.

3. How should government contractors pay for this additional cybersecurity compliance expense?

The DCAA has not yet provided specific guidance on how the new cybersecurity compliance-related expenses will be audited. Nevertheless, these costs will likely be audited in a similar manner to the six existing DFARS contractor business systems. Compliance-related business expenses may be categorized as a direct or indirect cost, depending on the contract requirements and the contractor's accounting system. Often, these DFARS contractor business system requirements are considered indirect costs. Thus, if these cybersecurity management system-related compliance costs are charged as indirect costs, properly allocated and considered fair and reasonable in both nature and amount, they should be deemed as allowable costs.

4. Do I have to purchase cybersecurity liability insurance?
Currently, the FAR and DFARS do not require government contractors to purchase cybersecurity liability insurance.

Concerns to consider:

- If a government contractor does purchase cyber liability insurance, will the cost of the insurance be considered as an allowable cost on a government contract?
- How much cyber liability insurance will be considered sufficient by the federal government and deemed an allowable cost?
- If a government contractor experiences a cyberattack that results in a network breach and its insurance provider denies some or all of the security-related breach remediation costs, will costs, if fair and reasonable in nature and amount, be deemed an allowable cost on a government contract?

5. Will prime government contractors be held contractually responsible and financially liable for cyber-related damages caused by their sub-contractors and/or third-party partners' failure to comply with NIST SP 800-171?

The FAR states that prime contractors are responsible for the selection, administration and performance of their subcontractors.

Concerns to consider:

- The contract between prime contractor and a subcontractor is a commercial contract. Subcontractors have no privity of contract with the government. Often, prime contractors do not communicate all the appropriate government requirements to their subcontractors.
- Prime contractors often attempt to contractually transfer all responsibilities and financial liabilities to their subcontractors.

6. How can government contractors staff and retain high-quality cybersecurity talent to meet the increasing number of government information security compliance standards when considering the highly competitive marketplace and global shortage of cybersecurity professionals today?

The recruiting, staffing, training and retention of cybersecurity talent is a significant challenge for nearly every organization. The global shortage of experienced cybersecurity professionals is expected to increase over the next three to five years. Thus, the need to create the right balance of cybersecurity employees, tools and managed outsourced services becomes vital to all public and private organizations, especially for small to mid-sized companies.

Cybersecurity – What is Next for U.S. Government Contractors?

1. Expect the Defense Contract Management Agency to begin conducting information security reviews/assessments of major defense contractors and selected mid-sized defense contractors.

   It is expected that DCMA may request a copy of the contractor's system security plan (SSP), incident response (IR) plan, and a copy of their information security policies and procedures for each of the 14 information security categories contained within NIST SP 800-171.

2. Anticipate the Defense Contract Audit Agency (DCAA) to develop audit guidelines related to information security management systems' cost accounting and begin conducting audits for cost allowability and reasonableness.

   It is expected that the new DFARS 252.204-7012 cybersecurity and information security management system will be treated in the same manner as the current six major DFARS contractor business systems: accounting, cost estimating, material management and accounting system (MMAS), government property management, and earned value management system.

3. Expect a few large and mid-sized defense contractors to be determined to be noncompliant with all or part of the DFARS 252.204-7012 and NIST SP 800-171 requirements in 2018 - 2019.

   It is expected that some contractors will be given a variety of remediation actions and/or penalties as deemed appropriate by the respective government contracting officer, as previously discussed.

4. Anticipate the issuance of a new FAR final rule creating cybersecurity requirements for all U.S. government contractors by 2019.

   It is expected that the Federal Acquisition Regulatory Council will enact a new FAR cybersecurity final rule for all government contractors, which will be quite similar in nature and content as the current DFARS clause.

5. Expect a new wave of government contractors conducting internal cyber risk assessments and compliance gap analysis per NIST 800-171 information security requirements by late 2018 and early 2019.

It is expected that a new wave of government contractors will conduct internal risk assessments, after the DCMA information security system reviews and DCAA audits on defense contractors are conducted containing numerous negative audit findings. Plus, the issuance of a new FAR final rule for cybersecurity requirements for all government contractors will further increase the demand for independent cybersecurity risk assessments and compliance gap analysis. Many government contractors will become highly focused on improving their respective information security policies, processes, and procedures, with increased focus on monitoring, detection, incident response, business continuity planning, disaster recovery, and third-party information security management.

6. Anticipate a new public law (PL) for cybersecurity to be established for consistency in cyber incident response reporting and timely remediation actions for cyber breaches for all publically traded companies in 2019.

   Based upon the increasing number of cyber attacks and the growing financial impact of recent cyber breaches, especially upon large publicly traded companies, it widely expected that the U.S. congress will enact a new public law to establish some consistency in cyber incident reporting with specific requirements for timely remediation actions post-breach with appropriate penalties for non-compliance.

SUMMARY

As government contractors are required to comply with new U.S. regulatory requirements, they are experiencing a rise in compliance related costs. It is well known that many government contractors will sometimes decide to defer these additional compliance related costs to see if the government will enforce the new information security requirements. If the cybersecurity requirements are enforced by the government, as we expect they will be, the government contractors will often wait to see how much the penalties are and if the cost of the penalties are greater than the cost of compliance to decide whether they should bear the additional expenses.

Government contractors now find themselves facing a growing business dilemma: they must figure out the best way they can properly safeguard their CUI, ensure regulatory compliance while continuing to remain competitive in the federal marketplace, and achieve a fair and reasonable return on investment. Meanwhile, we fully expect the U.S. federal government to continually evolve and expand their cybersecurity regulatory requirements for government contractors.

The next chapter will focus on the unique cybersecurity challenges and best practices of the retail sector as controlled by the specific cybersecurity requirements of the payment card industry, which can only be evaluated by organizations deemed by the PCI as a qualified security assessor (QSA) office staffed by well-trained and certified pci quality security assessors.

Endnotes

[1] *Understanding Federal Cybersecurity*, Belfer Center For Science and International Affairs, Katherine Charlet, April 2018

[2] *Id.*

Chapter 14

CYBERSECURITY FOR THE PAYMENT CARD INDUSTRY

By: Fred Branter

INTRODUCTION: THE COUNCIL

The Payment Card Industry Security Standards Council (PCI SSC) is a governing organization that develops and maintains security standards for the protection of cardholder data. The standards are a global framework that was introduced in 2006 and was derived from the individual data security compliance programs of five major payment brands: American Express, Discover Financial Services, JCB International, MasterCard, and Visa Inc.

The PCI SSC is independent of the payment brands and is responsible for the development, management, education, and awareness of the PCI Security Standards. The Council's standards include the following:

- PCI Data Security Standard
- Payment Application Data Security Standard
- Point-to-Point Encryption Standard
- PIN Transaction Security Point of Interaction
- Hardware Security Module Standard
- PIN standards
- Card Production standards

Here is a brief overview of the security standards that are developed and maintained by the council.

PCI Data Security Standards (PCI DSS) is the standard for the security of the cardholder data environments that process, store or transmit account data. This also includes systems that could affect the security of the cardholder data environment. PCI DSS compliance validation is required every 12 months. PCI Payment Application Data Security Standard (PA-DSS) is the standard for securing payment applications and is used to support PCI DSS compliance. An application with the PA-DSS certification only denotes that the application can be configured to meet PCI DSS requirements. A PA-DSS application does not mean the organization is PCI compliant.

PCI P2PE (point-to-point encryption) is the standard for the secure encryption, decryption, and key management for point-to-point encryption solutions. If an entity chooses to use a P2PE solution, which is listed on the PCI SSC's website, they may qualify for a reduction in scope of their assessment. PCI PTS (PIN Transaction Security) is the point-of-interaction (POI) standard that covers device tamper detection, cryptographic processes, and other mechanisms used to protect the PIN and other sensitive data, such as cryptographic keys.

PCI PIN Security is the standard for the secure management, processing, and transmission of personal identification number (PIN) data during online and offline payment card transaction processing. The PCI PTS HSM is the standard for the design of hardware security modules and for securely protecting those devices until they are deployed.

The card production standards establish minimum security levels for card vendors involved in payment card manufacturing, card personalization, pre-personalization, chip embedding, data preparation , and fulfillment.It should be noted that each of these PCI standards is independent from the others and has their own program and requirements. Adherence to one standard does not imply or affect an organization's compliance to any other standard.

In addition to the security standards, the council maintains a list of frequently asked questions, new material pertaining to the security standards, and a roster of internal security assessor (ISAS), qualified security assessor (QSAS), payment application qualified security assessor (PA-QSA), point-to-point QSAS, PCI professional (PCIPS) and qualified integrators and resellers (QIRS). For additional information regarding the council and the supported resources of the council, visit their website at *https://www.pcisecuritystandards.org/.*

PCI DSS Applicability Information

PCI DSS applies to all entities involved in payment card processing including merchants, processors, acquirers, issuers, and service providers. PCI DSS also applies to all other entities that store, process, or transmit cardholder data and/or sensitive authentication data.

Cardholder data and sensitive authentication data are defined as follows:

Account Data	
Cardholder Data includes:	**Sensitive Authentication Data includes:**
• Primary Account Number (PAN)	• Full track data (magnetic-stripe data or equivalent on a chip)
• Cardholder Name	• CAV2/CVC2/CVV2/CID
• Expiration Date	• PINs/PIN blocks
• Service Code	

PCI DSS requirements apply to organizations where account data (cardholder data and/or sensitive authentication data) is stored, processed or transmitted.

Data Security Standards

The Payment Card Industry Data Security Standard (PCI DSS) is a set of controls developed and maintained by the PCI SSC. These controls are referred to as requirements and apply to both merchant and service providers. There are six primary domains and twelve PCI DSS requirements. The primary domains and PCI DSS requirements are:

PCI Primary Domains	PCI DSS Requirements
Build and Maintain a Secure Network and Systems	1. Install and maintain a firewall configuration to protect data. 2. Do not use vendor-supplied defaults for system passwords and other security parameters.
Protect Cardholder Data	3. Protect stored cardholder data. 4. Encrypt transmission of cardholder data across open, public networks.
Maintain a Vulnerability Management Program	5. Protect all systems against malware and regularly update antivirus software or programs. 6. Develop and maintain secure systems and applications.
Implement Strong Access Control Measures	7. Restrict access to cardholder data by business need-to-know. 8. Identify and authenticate access to system components. 9. Restrict physical access to cardholder data.
Regularly monitor and test networks	10. Track and monitor all access to network resources and cardholder data. 11. Regularly test security systems and processes.
Maintain an information security policy	12. Maintain a policy that addresses information security for all personnel.

Each requirement has their own set of controls to be tested and the number of controls to be tested depends on the scope of the assessment. An example for this would be, if an organization does not perform system development and the QSA verified through interviews, observations and testing procedures that the organization does not develop software, then a majority of requirement six would not apply.

The PCI DSS requirements are broken up into different sections: testing procedures, reporting instructions, assessor's responses and summary of assessment findings. Within each requirement, there are sub-requirements. See below for an example of requirement 5.1.

PCI DSS Requirements and Testing Procedures	Reporting Instruction	Reporting Details: Assessor's Response	Summary of Assessment Findings (check one)				
			in Place	in Place w/CCW	N/A	Not Tested	Not in Place
5.1 Deploy antivirus software on all systems commonly affected by malicious software (particularly personal computers and servers).			☐	☐	☐	☐	☐
5.1 For a sample of systems components including all operating system types commonly affected by malicious software, verify that antivirus software is deployed if applicable antivirus technology exists.	Identify the sample of system components (including all operating system types commonly affected by malicious software) selected for this testing procedure.						
	For each item in the sample, **describe how** antivirus software was observed to be deployed.						

Think of the testing procedure as a control objective. The PCI DSS is validated against this control objective or requirement. The reporting instruction is to be viewed as the individual guidance to be assessed to meet the objective of the testing procedures. The reporting instructions could be a review of a policy or procedure, an interview with an applicable individual, or an observation of a procedure. In many cases, the reporting instructions will require all these processes to meet the requirement of the testing procedure.

The reporting details are the assessor's (QSA's) response where the assessor will document who they interviewed, which policy and procedure they reviewed, and what are the results of their observations. This is the section where the assessor documents the result of their testing to satisfy the testing procedures.

The summary of the assessment findings is simply a check box where the assessor will note if the requirement is in place, in place with a compensating control, not applicable, not tested, or not in place. The assessor will mark one box and the mark must align with what the assessor wrote under the assessor's response section.

The following is a high-level summary of the twelve requirements of the PCI DSS. For additional information on these requirements, visit the PCI council's website at *https://www.pcisecuritystandards.org/*.

PCI DSS Requirement 1

Requirement 1 was developed to assess firewall and router configuration standards. Firewall and routers control the traffic in and out of an organization environment, including the cardholder data environment (CDE). Organizations must have documented firewall and router configurations standards that require current network diagrams and current data flow diagrams. The data flow diagrams must include the flow of the cardholder data, the systems the data passes through and the systems that cardholder data is stored on. These diagrams must also include any wireless networks even if wireless is out of scope for the assessment. The diagrams should confirm that wireless networks are in fact out of scope. The firewall and router configuration standards must also document all the applicable ports, services and protocols that are in scope (both inbound and outbound) for the CDE. This includes any insecure protocols that are in use. If an organization is using telnet, then a business justification must be documented in the firewall and router configuration standards as to why the organization is using an insecure service.

Requirement 1 also addresses controls for DMZ testing as public facing systems should be in an external facing segment of the network and systems that store cardholder data should be placed on an internal private segment that is only accessible to the organization staff with a need to know privilege.

An example of this would be to place the organizations public facing web server that is used to take merchandise orders in the DMZ where it is accessible by external consumers and place the database server, used to store transactional data (including primary account numbers) on the internal segment. The firewall and router rules will be assessed to make sure ingress and egress rules are defined and that the documented rules align with the actual configuration of the devices.

PCI DSS Requirement 2

Requirement 2 was developed to assess an organization's configuration standard for all systems components including, but not limited to firewalls, routers, switches, servers, and workstations. An organization must configure their systems according to an industry accepted standard: Center for Internet Security (CIS), International Organization for Standardization (ISO), Systems Administration Audit Network Security Institute (SANS), National Institute of Standards Technology (NIST), etc. As known vulnerabilities are identified, the configuration standards should be updated to make sure the vulnerability are not introduced into the environment. The configuration standard must also require the organization to change all vendor supplied defaults and remove or disable any unnecessary default accounts before installing a system on the network. An example of this would be system accounts, passwords, Simple Network Management Protocol (SNMP) community strings, etc. This includes wireless environments connected to the cardholder data environment. An organization must also remove all unnecessary services, ports and protocols and document the services, ports and protocols that have been approved and are in use.

PCI DSS Requirement 3

Requirement 3 was developed to assess organization's that store cardholder data. As noted earlier in the chapter, there are two primary classifications of account data, cardholder data and sensitive authentication data.

Cardholder data consists of the primary account number (PAN), cardholder name, expiration data and service code. These are considered data elements that can be retained as long as the retention adheres to the PCI DSS requirements. Sensitive authentication data on the other hand, cannot be retained after authorization unless the organization is an issuer or an organization that performs issuing services. When an organization stores cardholder data, they must have a record retention policy that documents the business or legal purpose for storing the data. The organization must also determine the applicable length of time that the data can be stored for and have a process in place to verify that cardholder data is not retained after the retention period.

Requirement 3 also has guidance for organizations that receive sensitive authentication after authorization and the assessor must validate that these data elements (track data, CVV, PIN or PIN block) are not retained. In addition, the primary account number must be masked when displayed and encrypted when stored. Sub requirements 3.5 and 3.6 pertain to encryption standards for encrypting cardholder data at rest.

PCI DSS Requirement 4

Requirement 4 was developed to assess organization's that transmit cardholder data over open public networks.

Examples of open, public networks include but are not limited to:
- The Internet
- Wireless technologies, including 802.11 and Bluetooth
- Cellular technologies, for example, Global System for Mobile communications (GSM), code division multiple access (CDMA)
- General Packet Radio Service (GPRS)
- Satellite communications

The assessed organization must use strong cryptography and security protocols to safeguard sensitive cardholder data during transmission over open, public networks. This includes end-user messaging technologies (for example, email, instant messaging, SMS, chat, etc.). If an organization allows the transmission of cardholder data through end user messaging technologies, then the transmission must be encrypted. If the organization does not allow the transmission of cardholder data through end-user messaging technologies, then the organization must state in policy that this type of action is forbidden.

PCI DSS Requirement 5

Requirement 5 was developed to assess an organization's antivirus deployment to make sure an antivirus program is installed to protect all in-scope systems that are commonly affected by malicious software. The organization must use an antivirus program that will detect, remove and protect against all known types of malicious software. The antivirus program must be configured to be periodically updated to be kept current, perform frequent scans, alert a systems administrator of an event and retain the log data for at least one year.

PCI DSS Requirement 6

Requirement 6 was developed to assess an organization's patch management, change management and software development processes. Critical patches must be installed within 30 days from the manufacturer's release date. System changes must be approved and include testing procedures, back-out plans and a documented impact analysis. Software development is to verify that application code is following a system development life cycle (SDLC). The SDLC includes segregation of duties, such as different development and production environments, and requires the code to be reviewed and approved by an individual that did not do the coding.

In addition, the coding and code review process must follow the OWASP top ten to protect against common coding vulnerabilities. The OWASP top ten are:
- Injection flaws, particularly SQL injection. Also consider OS command injection, LDAP and XPath injection flaws as well as other injection flaws.
- Buffer overflow
- Insecure cryptographic storage
- Insecure communications
- Improper error handling
- All "high risk" vulnerabilities identified in the vulnerability identification process
- Cross-site scripting (XSS)
- Improper access control (such as insecure direct object references, failure to restrict URL access, directory traversal, and failure to restrict user access to functions)
- Cross-site request forgery (CSRF)
- Broken authentication and session management

PCI DSS Requirement 7

Requirement 7 was developed to assess an organization's user and administrative access controls. Users and administrators must be set up on the network and applications using least based permissions and per the individuals job responsibilities.

PCI DSS Requirement 8

Requirement 8 was developed to assess an organization's user and administrative authentication controls. Login accounts must have a unique identification for each account to identify the individual accessing the account and to hold them accountable for their actions.

Passwords are also used to further validate the authenticity of an individual logging into the network or an application. Passwords must be complex and changed periodically to ensure their effectiveness against an attacker that will try brute force to crack the password. Password requirements are:

- Require a minimum length of seven characters
- Complexity must contain both numeric and alphabetic characters
- Change user passwords/passphrases at least once every 90 days
- Do not allow an individual to submit a new password/passphrase that is the same as any of the last four passwords/passphrases he or she used
- Limit repeated access attempts by locking out the user ID after not more than six attempts
- Set the lockout duration to a minimum of 30 minutes or until an administrator enables the user ID
- If a session is idle for more than 15 minutes, require reauthentication to reactivate the terminal or session

Multi-factor authentication (MFA) is also a requirement. MFA is when an individual authenticates using any two of the three methods:

- Something I know (password, passphrase or an answer to a security question, etc.)
- Something I am (biometrics – finger print, retina scan, face recognition, etc.)
- Something I have (Fob with a random generated token, thumb drive with a code, certificate, etc.)

MFA is required for all users connecting to the organization network originating from outside the organization's network. This applies to both user and administrator and includes any third-party entity access for support or maintenance.

MFA is also required inside the network for any administrator that is authenticating to the CDE via non-console access methods for administrative purposes. This could be achieved by installing MFA per device or by setting up a bastion host where the MFA authentication takes place on the jump server allowing access into the CDE.

PCI DSS Requirement 9

Requirement 9 was developed to assess an organization's physical security controls. PCI does not focus on disaster recovery or environmental controls, but rather on the physical access to the facility and data centers/computer rooms where cardholder data is stored. Organizations must have an access control system in place to track employees and visitors access to the facility. The access systems can be electronic or a manual process if the access to secured areas can be tracked to an individual. Access must be monitored either through a badge access system, camera systems or both. The retention of the recordings is to be retained for at least three months.

Employee and visitor badges should be part of the organizations user provisioning process where employees are assigned an access badge at the time of hire and the access only allows access to the applicable areas of the organization based on the employee's job responsibilities. Access must be approved at the time of hire and revoked at termination. Organization badges must also be easy to distinguish between an employee and a visitor's badge. If the organization does not have visitor badges, then the visitor must be escorted at all times. Visitor badges must be set to expire at the end of the visitor's stay.

This requirement also covers the physical control of electronic and hard copy media that contains cardholder data. This media (backup tapes, thumb drive, hard drives, paper receipts, paper reports, faxes, etc.) must be inventoried and secured to make sure the data on the media are protected from unauthorized use. This includes destruction of the media when no longer in use.

Organizations that have point of interaction (POI) devices must implement additional controls to make sure the POI devices are not tampered with or swapped without proper authorization. Employee training is also required for all employees that interact with POI devices. The training should educate the employees on how to inspect the POI devices and how to identify suspicious individuals.

PCI DSS Requirement 10

Requirement 10 was developed to assess an organization's log management and monitoring controls. Requirement 10 is essential if an organization were to sustain a breach. The logs from the security incident and event management (SIEM) system will be used by the PCI forensic investigator (PFI) as a means to determine the root cause of the breach and the data elements potentially compromised. The PCI Council list approved PFI's on their website; however, the PCI Council does not investigate compromises, as this is the responsibility of each payment brand to manage. With this bit of background information, Requirement 10 focusses on gathering relevant log data from the cardholder data environment and also requires and organization to have non-cardholder data systems reviewed periodically based on the organizations risk assessment and risk tolerance.

To adhere to Requirement 10 an organization must configure its systems to gather the following log events:

- All individual access to cardholder data
- All actions taken by any individual with root or administrative privileges
- Access to all audit trails
- Invalid logical access attempts
- Use of and changes to identification and authentication mechanisms, including:
    o All elevation of privileges
    o All changes, additions, or deletions to any account with root or administrative privileges
- Initialization of audit logs
- Stopping or pausing of audit logs
- Creation and deletion of system level objects

The logs that are captured must also record the date and time of the events, source and destination, type of event and the authentication method of the event. This information is also critical for an PFI investigation. The logs must be reviewed on a daily basis to identify anomalies or suspicious activity. If suspicious activity is suspected, the organization must have a process to notify key individuals responsible for following up on the alert and escalate if necessary. In order to protect the log data for the PFI investigator, the logs should be secured, unalterable, limited access and backed up. The log data should be readily available for a minimum of three months and should be maintained for at least one year. Change detection or file integrity monitoring software must be configured to protect the log data as well. The change detection application should generate an alert if log data modified.

PCI DSS Requirement 11

Requirement 11 was developed to assess an organization's vulnerability management processes. Subrequirement 11.1 often gets marked as not applicable; however, this requirement must be tested and validated for compliance. Requirement 11.1 provides that an organization must perform wireless scans on a quarterly basis. An organization may state that they don't have wireless technologies in the cardholder environment or that they don't have wireless operations in general. For these reasons, organizations and some security assessors will document requirement 11.1 as not applicable. However, the intent of this requirement is to scan for wireless devices at least quarterly to search for any potential rogue wireless devices. Does the organization have any outside or connected to wireless devices that are not part of the organizations approved wireless access list? By performing a wireless scan at least quarterly, an organization will know which wireless devices are authorized and not authorized, will be able to respond to any unauthorized wireless access points minimizing the exposure to the organizations and their cardholder data environment.

The other scanning elements of requirement 11 are to perform internal and external vulnerability scans on a quarterly basis and to perform internal and external penetration test at least annually unless the organization is a service provider and is relying on segmentation controls to protect the cardholder data environment. In that case, the organization is required to have a penetration test performed at least twice a year. Another caveat to the vulnerability and penetration tests are that the scans cannot have any high or critical vulnerabilities. High and critical vulnerabilities must be remediated and rescanned until a passing result is achieved. Scans are also required to be performed whenever an organization makes a significant change to a system, process or environment. The organization must determine what signifies a significant change based on their risk tolerance as a significant change in one organization may be classified as a standard change for another organization.

The scans noted above can all be performed by an internal resource if the resource is qualified to perform the scans and is also reasonably independent of the individual or department that configures the systems being scanned. There is one exception to this; the quarter external scans must be performed by an approved scanning vender (ASV). The PCI Council, certifies, approves and lists the ASV's on their website. Organizations are also requested to submit certified passing ASV scan reports to the appropriate party; usually their acquirer or payment brand. See "Validation Levels" later in this chapter to better understand the reporting requirements an organization should follow as each payment brand requires different validation documents to be submitted.

Like Requirement 10, Requirement 11 also includes a change detection or file integrity monitoring (FIM) component. FIM must be configured to monitor changes, additions, and deletions to system executable files; system and application executables, configuration and parameter files and critical files determined by the organization's risk assessment. If an unauthorized change is detected, FIM is required to alert the appropriate individual or distribution group of the change so the incident can be investigated and followed up on.

PCI DSS Requirement 12

Requirement 12 was developed to assess an organization's governance controls. This requirement assesses the organizations policies and procedures for information security and acceptable use of the organizations systems and processes. Note that each of the previous requirements discussed above also includes a subrequirement for the organization to have policies and procedures in place for that requirement. Policies and procedures must be published and made known to all relevant personnel.

The organizations risk assessment should be for the whole organization, not just the cardholder data environment, and reviewed and updated at least annually or after a significant change to the environment. This is an area where organizations struggle and is a critical component to an organization's information security program. The following is a way an organization can view their risk assessment process. To start, the organization must first identify the assets they are trying to protect (example, cardholder data, SSN, account number, servers, firewalls, etc.).

Definitions:
- Organization risk - Is when a threat exploits a vulnerability that wholly or partially damages the asset and breaks business processes.
- Risk assessment - A process used to identify and evaluate risk and potential effects. Risk assessment includes assessing the critical functions necessary for an organization to continue business operations, defining the controls in place to reduce organization exposure and evaluating the cost for such controls. Risk analysis often involves an evaluation of the probabilities of an event.

An organization should identify its assets and focus on the confidentiality, integrity and availability (CIA) of these assets. By identifying the assets, determining the risks to the assets and putting CIA controls in place to safeguard the assets, the organization is building a risk assessment. Examples of risk assessment methodologies include but are not limited to OCTAVE, ISO 27005 and NIST SP 800-30.

Requirement 12 also focuses on accountability and holds the board and management responsible for the oversight of the organizations PCI program. Service providers are required to have a PCI charter with status reports being delivered to management. The responsibilities for information security should be defined in policy so information security individuals are aware of their responsibilities and daily tasks. Roles and responsibilities must be documented and assigned to prevent gaps in processes that could lead to protentional compromise.

Entities should also consider transition and/or succession plans for key personnel to avoid potential gaps in security assignments, which could result in responsibilities not being assigned and therefore not performed.

Security awareness training is a sub-requirement of Requirement 12 and applies to all personnel, not just personnel with access to the cardholder data environment. Security awareness training should be relevant to the employee's job-related roles and responsibilities and should be administered at time of hire and at least annually. Employees are also required to acknowledge their completion to security awareness training and adherence to the organizations information security policies.

As organization outsource security controls (log management, firewall configuration, physical security, etc.) to third party service providers (TPSPs), they rely on the controls of the TPSPs to achieve PCI compliance. Since an organization cannot outsource responsibility for their PCI compliance, they must have a process in place to make sure their TPSPs are PCI compliant or include their TPSPs in their own PCI compliance assessment process. Clear policies and procedures should therefore be established between an organization and its TPSPs for all applicable security requirements. Requirement 12 has several subrequirements organizations must follow to monitor their TPSPs. These are:

- Maintain a list of service providers including a description of the service provided.
- Maintain a written agreement that includes an acknowledgement that the service providers are responsible for the security of cardholder data the service providers possess or otherwise store, process or transmit on behalf of the customer, or to the extent that they could impact the security of the customer's CDE.
- Ensure there is an established process for engaging service providers including proper due diligence prior to engagement.
- Maintain a program to monitor service providers' PCI DSS compliance status at least annually.
  - o Organizations should reach ouch to their TPSPs at least annually and request to obtain their attestation of compliance (AOC) and review the AOC to determine if the PCI DSS requirements tested at the TPSPs align with the PC DSS requirement the organization is expecting to be assessed.
- Maintain information about which PCI DSS requirements are managed by each service provider, and which are managed by the entity.
  - o Organizations and TPSPs use a matrix to identify the PCI DSS requirements that an organization is responsible for and the requirements the TPSP is responsible for.

The last subrequirement in Requirement 12 is to assess the organizations incident response plan, make sure the plan has the required wording, verify that the organization is training the appropriate personnel to respond to a breach and test the plan at least annually.

Report on Compliance

Organizations classified as a level 1 entity (see below for validation level explanations), are required to complete a report on compliance (ROC) that is accompanied by an attestation of compliance (AOC). The QSA company will assess the organizations PCI DSS requirements and issue the ROC and AOC to the organization if they are a merchant and will issue only the AOC to the acquirer or payment brand if the assessed entity is a service provider. The QSA will provide the ROC to the acquirer and payment brand when requested.

The ROC is a completed assessment of an organizations cardholder environment and includes the following sections:
- The executive summary.
  - o The executive summary section of the ROC is a description of how the entity accepts payment cards for business transactions and includes how and why the organization stores, processes, and/or transmits cardholder data.
  - o Lists the various payment channels and whether transactions are a card-not-present or card-present transaction.
  - o Documents the TPSPs that the organization shares cardholder data with, including payment processor relationships.
  - o A high-level network diagram showing all connections in and out of the network. A card data flow diagram must be included in this section.
  - o Individuals interviewed, and documents reviewed during the assessment are also documented in the executive summary.
  - o Compensating controls are documented if they are used to satisfy a requirement.
  - o The results of the 4 quarterly ASV scans are documented at the end of the executive summary.
- The 12 PCI DSS requirements/subrequirements.
  - o This is the backbone of the ROC. This is where the organizations cardholder data environment is assessed against the twelve PCI DSS requirements.
  - o The twelve PCI DSS requirements will include the assessors documented results from their testing and will denote whether the requirement is in place, in place with a compensating control, not applicable, not tested, or not in place.
- The appendix.

o   Appendix A1 of the PCI DSS is intended for service providers that provide shared hosting environments for multiple clients on the same server.

o   Appendix A2 must be completed if SSL or early TLS are in use.

o   Appendix C is used to document compensating control worksheets if compensating controls are used.

Self Assessment Questionnaire

Merchant organizations classified as a level 2, 3 or 4 (see below for validation level explanations), may perform a self-assessment of their PCI environment as long as the self assessment questionnaire (SAQ) and accompanying AOC are signed off by an authorized officer of the organizations. The SAQ does not need to be completed by a QSA; however, a QSA can assist and sign off on an organizations SAQ. The SAQ is like a ROC in that it has an executive summary, 12 PCI DSS requirements and sub-requirements and an appendix. The SAQ uses the same PCI DSS questions and testing procedures; however, the results of the testing procedures are not written out in detail. The results are recorded in a check box to indicate if the requirement is in place, in place with a compensating control, not in place or not applicable.

SAQs come in multiple versions and are based on how an organization processes, stores or transmits cardholder data. The number of PCI DSS requirements also varies depending on the SAQ an organization uses. Before beginning the self-assessment, the organization should confirm that their environment is accurately scoped and that it meets all the eligibility criteria for that particular SAQ. Each SAQ has a section called "Before You Begin." This section explains the purpose for the SAQ and then asks several questions that the organization must be able to answer "yes" to. If the organization answers no to one of the questions, then that SAQ does not apply to the organization and they must choose a different SAQ. The following are the SAQ options:

- SAQ A is intended for merchants that accept only card-not-present transactions (that is, e-commerce, mail order or telephone order), and that outsource all their cardholder data functions to PCI DSS compliant service providers. SAQ A is not applicable to face-to-face payment channels.
- SAQ A-EP was developed for e-commerce merchants with a website that does not itself receive cardholder data, but that directly affects the security of the payment transaction.
- SAQ B is for those merchants who process cardholder data using only imprint machines or using only dial-out terminals.

- SAQ B-IP has been developed for merchants who process cardholder data only via standalone, PTS-approved point-of-interaction devices that have an IP connection to the payment processor.
- SAQ C is for merchants with dedicated payment application systems segmented from all other systems and connected to the Internet for the purposes of transaction processing. SAQ C is not applicable to e-commerce payment channels.
- SAQ C-VT is for merchants using only web-based virtual payment terminals, where cardholder data is manually entered into a secure website from a single system.
- SAQ D is for all other SAQ-eligible merchants that do not fall into any of the other SAQ categories, and for any service providers defined by a payment brand as eligible to complete the SAQ.
- SAQ P2PE is for merchants using a validated P2PE solution that is listed on the PCI SSC website.

Merchants are advised to consult with their acquirer or payment brand to determine whether they should submit an SCAQ, and if so, which SAQ to complete. SAQ's and their corresponding AOC's are submitted to the merchant organization at the completion of the PCI DSS assessment. The merchant provides the AOC to their acquiring bank.

Compensating Controls

Compensating controls maybe used to help meet the intent of the requirement as long as the compensating control adequately addresses the risk, meets the intent and rigor of the original PCI DSS requirement and is above and beyond the existing PCI DSS requirement. PCI DSS applies to people, processes, and technology, so if there is a business or technical constraint preventing implementation of one of the non-technical PCI DSS controls, compensating controls may be needed to address these also. A compensating control must be documented using the compensating control worksheet in Appendix C and also summarized in the executive summary.

PCI DSS Assessment Scoping

As noted above, PCI DSS applies to people, processes, technology and systems that could affect the security of the cardholder data environment. The key to scoping the cardholder data is to create a very detailed data flow diagram that maps the path of the cardholder data. Ask yourself the following questions:

- What is the incoming transactions file (web application, SFTP server, point of interaction device, payment application, call center, etc.)?

- When the cardholder data enters the organization's network, what systems does the data pass through? What systems does the data reside on?
- What systems are involved with cardholder data processes?
- Who has access to or could impact the security of the cardholder data environment?

Once the organization has a clear understanding of the people, systems and process that are involved with cardholder data security, they should create a clear data flow diagram to assist in determining the scope of the environment. One caveat to scoping a PCI assessment is that all systems that are in the same network zone (segment) as systems that process, store or transmit cardholder data are also in scope for the assessment. For this reason, all systems in the same segment must be held to a heightened security standard.

Reducing the Scope

Since the scope of a PCI assessment is focused on the security of cardholder data, one possible means to reduce the scope of the cardholder data environment would be to not store cardholder data. The majority of Requirement 3 does not apply when an organization is able to change their processes to prevent the storage of cardholder data. The organization could rely on a PCI compliant TPSP to store the data on their behalf.

Another way an organization can reduce the scope of the cardholder data environment would be to implement segmentation and segment the cardholder data environment from the corporate office. The PCI Council's definition of segmentation is isolation. This means isolating the system that processes, stores or transmits cardholder data from the systems that perform everyday functions for the organization. The scope of the PCI assessment would focus only on the systems within the cardholder data environment and the organization would only need to have the 12 PCI DSS requirements applied to the cardholder data environment, not to the entire corporate network.

Note that segmentation is not a PCI requirement, but is a way to reduce the scope of a PCI assessment. If an organization implements segmentation to reduce the scope of their cardholder data environment, it's still advisable to implement strong security controls to the entire network.

Implementing a point-to-point encryption (P2PE) process also reduces the scope for an organization as the cardholder data is encrypted at the point of interaction and not decrypted until it reaches the processor. If the organizations cannot decrypt and get access to the cardholder data, minimal requirements are necessary to validate PCI compliance.

Validation Levels

Validation levels determine the reporting requirements for merchants and third-party service provider. The reporting requirements govern the PCI report to be used when assessing an organization's cardholder data environment against the PCI DSS. Each payment brand's validation levels and reporting requirements differ from the other payment brands and they are also different between a merchant and a TPSP. To illustrate this concept a little further, the following are the validation levels and reporting requirements for Visa and MasterCard. Please keep in mind that the payment brands determine the validation levels and the acquiring banks determine the transaction volume for the merchants they do business with.

Visa's validation level for merchants:

A merchants total Visa transaction volume (inclusive of credit, debit and prepaid) over a 12-month period determines their merchant level and the necessary requirements for validation.

- Merchants processing over 6 million Visa transactions annually across all channels or global merchants identified as level 1 by Visa region are categorized as a level 1 merchant.
- 1 to 6 million Visa transactions annually across all channels are categorized as a level 2 merchant.
- 20,000 to 1 million Visa e-commerce transactions annually are categorized as a level 3 merchant.
- Merchants processing less than 20,000 Visa e-commerce transactions annually and all other merchants processing up to 1 million Visa transactions annually are categorized as a level 4 merchant.

Visa's reporting requirements for merchants:
- Level 1 merchants
  - o Are required to file a report on compliance by a qualified security assessor or internal auditor if signed by an officer of the company. visa recommends the internal auditor obtain the PCI SSC internal security assessor certification.
  - o Submit an attestation of compliance form.
  - o Conduct a quarterly network scan by an approved scan vendor.
- Level 2 merchants
  - o Are required to complete a self-assessment questionnaire.
  - o Submit an attestation of compliance form.
  - o Conduct a quarterly network scan by an approved scan vendor.
- Level 3 merchants
  - o Are required to complete a self-assessment questionnaire.
  - o Submit an attestation of compliance form.

o   Conduct a quarterly network scan by an approved scan vendor.
- Level 4 merchants
  o   Are required to complete a self-assessment questionnaire.
  o   Submit an attestation of compliance form.
  o   Conduct a quarterly network scan by an approved scan vendor (if applicable).

Visa's validation level for service provider:

Service providers are organizations that process, store, or transmit Visa cardholder data on behalf of Visa acquirers/issuers, merchants, or other service providers. Visa issuers and acquirers are responsible for ensuring that all of their service providers comply with the PCI DSS requirements. Visa has prioritized the compliance validation based on the volume of transactions, the potential risk, and exposure introduced into the payment system. Service provider levels are defined as follows:

- VisaNet processors or any service provider (TPA) that stores, processes and/or transmits over 300,000 Visa transactions annually are categorized as a level 1 service provider.
- Any service provider that stores, processes and/or transmits less 300,000 Visa transactions annually are categorized as a level 2 service provider.

Visa's reporting requirements for service providers:
- Level 1 service providers
  o   Are required to file a report on compliance by a qualified security assessor.
  o   Submit an attestation of compliance form.
  o   Conduct a quarterly network scan by an approved scan vendor.
- Level 2 service providers
  o   Are required to complete a self-assessment questionnaire (SAQ D).
  o   Submit an attestation of compliance form.
  o   Conduct a quarterly network scan by an approved scan vendor.

MasterCard's validation level for merchants:

All merchants that store, process or transmit cardholder data must be PCI compliant. Each merchant that is categorized as a level 1, level 2 or level 3 merchant is required to report its compliance status directly to its acquiring bank.
- Level 1 merchants
  o   Any merchant that has suffered a hack or an attack that resulted in an account data compromise (ADC) event.

- o   Any merchant having more than six million total combined Master-card and Maestro transactions annually.
- o   Any merchant meeting the Level 1 criteria of Visa.
- o   Any merchant that Mastercard, in its sole discretion, determines should meet the Level 1 merchant requirements to minimize risk to the system.
- o   MasterCard recommends the internal auditor (if being used for the onsite assessment) obtain the PCI SSC internal security assessor certification.
- Level 2 merchants
  - o   Any merchant with more than one million but less than or equal to six million total combined Mastercard and Maestro transactions annually.
  - o   Any merchant meeting the Level 2 criteria of Visa.
  - o   MasterCard recommends the internal auditor (if being used for the self-assessment) obtain the PCI SSC internal security assessor certification.
- Level 3 merchant
  - o   Any merchant with more than 20,000 combined Mastercard and Maestro e-commerce transactions annually but less than or equal to one million total combined Mastercard and Maestro e-commerce transactions annually.
  - o   Any merchant meeting the Level 3 criteria of Visa.
- Level 4 merchant
  - o   All other merchants.

MasterCard's reporting requirements for merchants:
- Level 1 merchants
  - o   Annual onsite assessment.
  - o   Quarterly network scan conducted by an ASV.
- Level 2 merchants
  - o   Annual self-assessment.
  - o   Onsite assessment at merchant discretion.
  - o   Quarterly network scan conducted by an ASV.
- Level 3 merchants
  - o   Annual self-assessment.
  - o   Onsite assessment at merchant discretion.
  - o   Quarterly network scan conducted by an ASV.
- Level 4 merchants
  - o   Annual self-assessment.

o   Onsite assessment at merchant discretion.

o   Quarterly network scan conducted by an ASV.

MasterCard's validation level for service provider:

Service providers are categorized as level 1 or level 2 based on service provider category and annual MasterCard transaction volume. Service provider levels are defined as follows:

■   MasterCard processors or any service provider that stores, processes and/or transmits over 300,000 MasterCard transactions annually are categorized as a level 1 service provider.

■   Any service provider that stores, processes and/or transmits less 300,000 MasterCard transactions annually are categorized as a level 2 service provider.

MasterCard's reporting requirements for service providers:

■   Level 1 service providers

o   Are required to file a report on compliance by a qualified security assessor.

o   Submit an attestation of compliance form.

o   Conduct a quarterly network scan by an approved scan vendor.

■   Level 2 service providers

o   Are required to complete a self-assessment questionnaire.

o   Submit an attestation of compliance form.

o   Conduct a quarterly network scan by an approved scan vendor.

PCI DSS Validation Requirements Overview:

	Merchants		
	Level 1	Level 2	Level 3 and 4
Type of Assessment:	Onsite Assessment	Self-Assessment	Determined by Payment Brand or Acquirer
Reporting Requirements:	ROC and ASV Scan Report	SAQ and ASV Scan Report	Determined by Payment Brand or Acquirer

| | Service Providers | | |
	Level 1	Level 2	Level 3 (American Express)
Type of Assessment:	Onsite Assessment	Self-Assessment	Self-Assessment
Reporting Requirements:	ROC and ASV Scan Report	SAQ and ASV Scan Report	SAQ and ASV Scan Report

Merchants and service providers should consult with their acquirer, or applicable payment brands, to determine their level and reporting requirements. This is not to be determined by the QSA.

Resources and Guidance

The PCI DSS was written to apply to both large and small organizations; therefore, the standards were written with specific requirements that are sometimes vague and difficult to determine if the requirement applies to a certain process from organization to organization. For this reason, the PCI Council have published supporting information on their website to help guide assessors, merchants and service providers. The Council has published frequently asked questions (FAQs), supplemental documents, quarterly news articles, quarterly conference calls, annual conferences and has a venue where the assessor can directly email the council for guidance. In addition to emailing the Council, assessors, merchants and service providers can contact the payment brands for support.

The next chapter is focused on the unique cybersecurity best practices when forming and implementing public/private partnerships to foster enhanced cybersecurity practices in both the public and private sectors within the Netherlands, the European Union, and globally.

References

https://www.pcisecuritystandards.org/

https://usa.visa.com/

https://www.mastercard.us/en-us.html

Chapter 15

CYBERSECURITY FOR PUBLIC - PRIVATE PARTNERSHIPS – BEST PRACTICES

By: Sandra J.C. Konings MSc

PUBLIC AND PRIVATE CYBERSECURITY INTERESTS INTERFERE

Early in 2018 it was disclosed that Cambridge Analytica was suspected to have collected personal information from millions of Facebook users in 2014 and built a system that could profile individual U.S. voters in order to target them with personalized political advertisements. In this digital age people all over the world store sensitive data in applications they trust. These people are willing to share information via questionnaires, including information about how they feel about certain products or topics and information about how they would react in certain circumstances. The reward for sharing this information is a kind of personalized response; like the color, animal, name or city which fits their profile best. It looks harmless and trustworthy for the respondent, since the questionnaire is presented to the respondents via applications they trust, like Facebook, and is promoted by their friends who have already completed the questionnaire and are now proudly sharing their results. The gathered data can be used to create profiles of people and use these profiles to further influence their opinion by exposing them to certain advertisements, news articles or photos. In this way, it is possible for activists to influence people's thoughts and behavior and even the outcome of a democratic election! Trust in applications owned and built by *private* companies is used to influence *public* decisions and has public and political consequences. Enforcing by law proper protection of data stored in these privately owned applications, and regulations about profiling, might prevent or at least limit these type of activities.

Another example where public and private cybersecurity interests interfere is when local governments would like to gain access to information from individuals stored in privately owned applications or databases, and circumvent the data protection rules. This happens for instance when national intelligence or investigative agencies would like to gain knowledge to prevent (or solve) a crime or terrorism. After all, in this digital age, crime and terrorism take place in a combination of our physical and our digital world. In order to protect their citizens, local governments request regularly access to certain privately owned data transfer and data storage systems to learn what a criminal or terrorist is about to do. The purpose is to protect the safety of their citizens and to prevent downtime of critical infrastructure like energy, telecom and water management.

These two examples show current situations in which public and private cybersecurity interests interfere. A third example is the need of countries to protect their economy and dictate by federal law that technology designed in that country should not leave the country or the intellectual property should at least be owned by the a local company. In this way all Intellectual Property rights, and the financial transfers involved, are for the benefit of the inventing company and therefore beneficial to the country and economy where the (parent) company is based. The law dictates that innovative information and/or intellectual property should be owned by local companies for economic benefit. These countries require by law up-to-date cybersecurity protection mechanisms to keep this valuable information within the country.

Because public and private interests interfere and cooperation between public and private parties is needed to prevent unwanted meddling with democratic decisions, to help prevent or solve a crime, to protect critical infrastructure, and to protect valuable intellectual property, governments have created laws and regulations to stimulate the desired behavior. Examples of these laws and regulations include the European General Data Protection Regulation (GDPR), the United States' Foreign Intelligence Surveillance Act, the European Directive on Security of Network and Information Systems (NIS Directive), and the United States' Critical Infrastructure Cybersecurity Framework (voluntary for now).

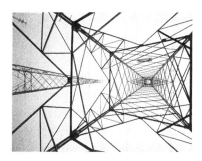

The next section explains why governments and private parties need close cooperation on cybersecurity. The third and fourth sections describe the best-practices on public-private partnership.

THE NEED FOR PUBLIC-PRIVATE COOPERATION

The current society depends heavily on the Internet of Things (IoT) solutions. Key processes are automated and tools are connected with the Internet. IoT downtime of critical infrastructure, like energy, water management and healthcare, might cause immediate effect on the society. These IoT systems are an attractive target for terrorists to cause disruption and chaos. A deliberate interruption of vital processes can lead to significant economic damage and social disruption. In the cold December month of 2015 about a million people in the Ukraine were cut off from electricity for about 6 hours.[1] It is suspected that the IoT systems of the electricity company were hacked and proper electricity delivery was interrupted. Cyberattacks private companies with critical infrastructure have influence on the economic well-being and safety of citizens, countries and enterprises.[2] This is the reason why public parties need to cooperate with private parties to limit the impact of cyberattacks.

The need for public-private cooperation to protect critical infrastructure and the urgency to get this organized is best displayed by the European Committee who created EU-wide legislation to enforce cooperation regarding cybersecurity on critical infrastructure. This effort resulted in the EU Directive on Security of Network and Information Systems (*https://ec.europa.eu/ digital-single-market/en/network-and-information-security-nis-directive*). The NIS Directive provides legal measures to boost the overall level of cybersecurity in the EU by ensuring:

- Member states' preparedness by requiring them to be appropriately equipped, e.g. via a computer security incident response team (CSIRT) and a competent national NIS authority;
- Cooperation among all the member states, by setting up a cooperation group, in order to support and facilitate strategic cooperation and the exchange of information among member states. Members also need to set a CSIRT Network, in order to promote swift and effective operational cooperation on specific cybersecurity incidents and sharing information about risks;
- A culture of security across sectors which are vital for the economy and society, and moreover, rely heavily on IoTs, such as energy, transport, water, banking, financial market infrastructures, healthcare and digital infrastructure. Businesses in these sectors that are identified by the member states as operators of essential services must take appropriate security measures and provide notice of serious incidents to the relevant national authority. Also, key digital service providers (search engines, cloud computing services and online marketplaces) must comply with the security and notification requirements under the new directive.

Member states were required to incorporate the directive into their national laws by May 9, 2018 and identify operators of essential services by November 9, 2018.

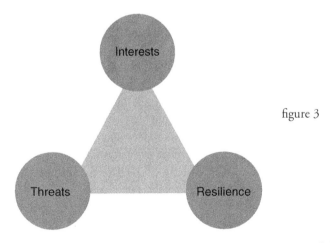

figure 3

To prevent cyberattacks it is important to understand the interests of the attackers, the latest threats (including the latest approaches of cyberattacks and newly discovered vulnerabilities) and how to increase resilience to attacks. This is displayed in figure 3.[3] The best way to do this is to share threat intelligence and knowledge about vulnerabilities and attack paths. But also to warn each other when discovering suspicious internet traffic. When national cybersecurity centers, national intelligence services, national police and enterprises all share their knowledge about threats and breaches with each other, society will become more resilient to cyberattacks. With this knowledge an attack on critical infrastructure (like an electricity company) might be prevented. Or when the attack has occurred this knowledge will help ensure a quick recovery.

Several countries in the world organized this cooperation between the government and enterprises via the so called information sharing and analysis centers (ISACs). These are public-private partnerships organized per critical sector to exchange information and experiences about cybersecurity. More about these public-private partnerships is explained in the following paragraphs on best-practices.

BEST-PRACTICES

We have identified six best-practices for public-private partnerships.

1. Information Sharing and Analysis Center

The most commonly known and installed public-private partnerships are the information sharing and analysis centers (ISACs). An ISAC consists of private companies within a certain sector of critical infrastructure and public parties. The companies and parties are "the ISAC members." The first ISACs were formed in the United States in the late 1990s.[4] Now many other countries have installed ISACs for different critical sectors. Most ISACs have a national focus, but for some sectors there are also international ISACs like the ISAC for financial services, the FS-ISAC (*https://www.fsisac.com*). The financial ISAC operates internationally since cyberattacks can be cross-border. The FS-ISAC was established in 1999 by the financial services sector in response to Presidential Directive 63. That directive, issued in 1998 and updated by 2003's Homeland Security Presidential Directive 7, mandated that the public and private sectors share information about physical and cyber security threats and vulnerabilities to help protect the U.S. critical infrastructure. Focus of the FS-ISAC was U.S. financial services. In early 2013 the FS-ISAC was extended to share information between financial services inside and outside the U.S. (world-wide).

Usually an ISAC operates like a member-owned non-profit entity. The purpose of an ISAC is to share threat intelligence and best practices to increase the knowledge of all representatives (of the private and public parties who are members), and teach all representatives how to increase the resilience of their company to cyberattacks.

" When a meeting, or part thereof, is held under the **Chatham House Rule**, participants are free to use the information received, but neither the identity nor the affiliation of the speaker(s), nor that of any other participant, may be revealed. "

Members share information based on trust and under the Chatham House Rules. This means that participants are free to use the information received, but neither the identity nor the affiliation of the speaker(s), nor that of any other participant may be revealed (see *https://www.chathamhouse.org/chatham-house-rule*). This is important, since companies and public parties usually do not want their clients or their citizens to know all recent cyberattacks since it might lower their reputation and/or cause companies to loose customers. Therefore the information is shared under strict confidentiality rules.

Countries have established ISACs for different sectors of the national critical infrastructure. For example, figure 5 displays the current ISACs within the Netherlands (*https://www.ncsc.nl/english*). Each sector ISAC consists of representatives from organizations in the particular sector and the following public entities:
- National Cyber Security Center (NCSC) which is the national NIS authority as dictated by the EU NIS directive.
- General Intelligence and Security Service (Dutch abbreviation is AIVD).
- National Police Team High-Tech Crime (THTC).

2. Governmental cyber defense and intelligence teams

Apart from ISACs, there are other public-private cooperation entities on cybersecurity. Several countries have their own cyber defense army with cyber reservists working in their day to day job as cybersecurity experts within different private organizations and offering their capacity and knowledge to the public cyber defense team. In exchange, these cyber reservists are trained by the government and can use the gained knowledge to increase the cyber resilience of the companies they work for. Also country specific services like

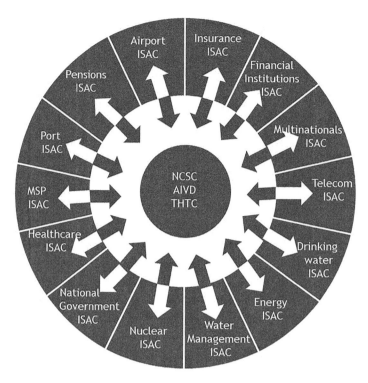

Figure 5: *Example of current ISACs in The Netherlands*

CIA and FBI have established closed and trusted communities in which information related to certain types of attacks is shared. Of course these public services do not share all they know, but sometimes it is important that organizations are aware of a certain threat or attack in order to prevent a cyberattack and therefore prevent a denial of service or data loss.

3. Cyber Security Council

In some countries, like in the Netherlands, a cyber security council has been established which is an advisory body of the government composed of representatives from public and private sector organizations and the scientific community.

4. Cyber Research Agenda

Several countries, like the Netherlands have their own cybersecurity research agenda. Public and privacy sector organizations sponsor cybersecurity research programs and use the results to further improve the cyber resilience of public services and private sectors.

5. International Cyber Security Awareness Month (October)

Installing sector ISACs, a cyber security council, a cyber research agenda and CIA and FBI trusted communities is not sufficient. It is important to involve all citizens and teach them how to recognize and prevent cyberattacks. Every year in October the United States (since 2003) and countries in Europe (since 2012) run national awareness programs to teach citizens and small and medium enterprises how to prevent, recognize and recover from cyber attacks. Every year public and private parties work together to define the main theme of that year and draft the program.

6. National network of Cyber Resilience Centers for Supply Chains

Proper prevention of cyber attacks and resilience to cyber attacks can only be achieved when a whole supply chain is taken into account. Even large enterprises operating in the critical infrastructure (like an electricity company) depend on other (sometimes smaller) companies in their supply chain. It is important to have a clear picture of all parties involved in the supply chain and their dependence on ICT. This is explained in a white paper created by five Dutch energy companies and the elements are shown in figure 6.[5] For supplier N to supply an energy product to consumers, it needs several process steps to be executed by companies A, B, C and D. Each of these process steps is supported by critical and non-critical processes. The critical processes are supported by critical and non-critical ICT systems. A denial of service of a critical ICT system at one of the companies (A, B, C, D or N) will result in a delay of delivery of energy to consumers. The same applies for other companies like telecom or financial institutions.

Another example is when this supply chain figure is not about the supply chain of an energy company but of a company producing machines with embedded software. When for instance company B is infected by malware, the embedded software in the article created by process step 2 will contain malware. Even the end product of process step N might still contain this malware. When the client of company N receives the infected product and connects it with her network, it will introduce malware within the network. In August 2018 this happened with chip manufacturer TSMC. When the WannaCry virus affected TSMC, production facilities were probably shut down to remove the infection. According to German magazine elektroniknet. de[6] "The WannyCry variant that infected TSMC appeared to have been on a machine before the manufacturer delivered it to TSMC. When the people at TSMC integrated the new machine into the production environment, WannaCry remained undetected, allowing the worm to spread."

These examples show it is important to understand the cyber risk within the supply chain. Partners within a supply chain should cooperate to increase resilience to cyberattacks. With help and knowledge from public parties the supply chain can be further secured. This will limit the likelihood of a disturbance of the critical infrastructure and strengthen the economy of a country, since less companies will be affected by cyberattacks.

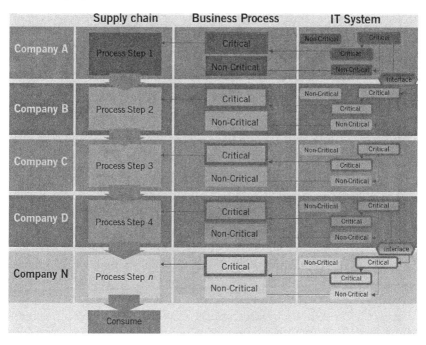

Figure 6: Critical process and IT systems in a supply chain[4]

A good example of a cyber resilience for supply chains is the recent initiative of the Ministry of Economic Affairs and Climate Policy (EAC) in the Netherlands to install a network of cyber resilience centers focusing on supply chains. This network of centers will cover the whole country and is steered by the Digital Trust Center of the Ministry EAC. This network focuses on all sectors and all companies from very small (1 employee) enterprises to large SMEs and even corporate multinationals. The network consist of certain nodes. Each node is one cyber resilience center focusing on a particular branch and/or region. See figure 7. It starts small with the creation of certain nodes and after two to three years the whole country will be covered by cyber resilience centers in such a way that every organization is able to become a member of one of the centers.

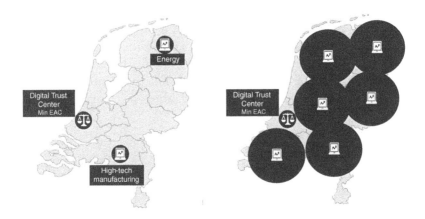

Figure 7: *Dutch National network of cyber resilience centers steered by Digital Trust Center from Ministry of Economic Affairs and Climate* Policy

At the moment of writing this book (Autumn 2018) Ministry EAC is supporting the design and build of the first six sector oriented cyber resilience centers (nodes) in the Netherlands. The design of the first node has started in 2013 and this node functions as blueprint for all other nodes in the Netherlands. This first node is the Cyber Resilience Center for High-Tech Manufacturing initiated by BDO Advisory B.V. together with Ministry EAC, Brainport Development N.V. and Brainport Industries Cooperatie U.A. This center will consist of about 300 companies within the high-tech manufacturing industry in the Netherlands with similar cyber resilience needs. Members vary from start-ups (four employees) to multination companies with over 15,000 employees). This is different compared to the ISACs where members are of comparable size with comparable needs. The Cyber Resilience Center for High-tech Manufacturing will support companies with a professional security operating center (SOC), companies without a SOC but with a certain ICT operations team, and companies with no ICT employees at all, but just an external consultant who supports their IT systems for a couple of days a month.

The cyber resilience center for the high-tech manufacturing industry is created in a three step approach (see figure 8). First a network of representatives of the larger (and comparable) companies in the sector is created. This is similar to the set-up of ISACs. This network is built on trust. The purpose is to share best-practices and warn each other in time when new threats are discovered. Threats and incidents are shared ad-hoc. The next step is to share threats, incidents and other knowledge more structural and real-time and with more companies. Also all companies in the supply chain of the group of step one are involved now, from very small enterprises to large ones. For this step two the digital trust center shares threat intelligence from the government with the companies within the cyber resilience center through a portal. This is information sharing from public to private. These threat warnings will be filtered in such a way that they are of interest to the high-tech manufacturing industry. Every warning is accompanied by a risk explanation and instructions on how to prevent these threats from happening. Also, threat intelligence sharing from private back to public is organized. Threat intelligence from the companies within the cyber resilience center will be shared with the DTC. This information is of value to the DTC since it might be of value to other branches and/or region in the country and will be shared by the DTC with other cyber resilience centers. The portal of the DTC in step two is also used to share knowledge and good-practices between the companies within this cyber resilience center.

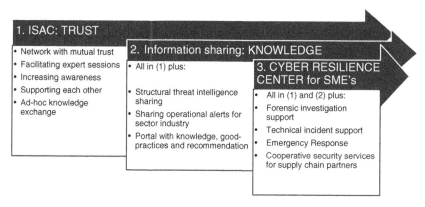

Figure 8: *Creating Cyber resilience center for Supply Chains*

Step three is a more cooperative way of working for the members of the cyber resilience center. This is especially created for the smaller companies in the supply chain with smaller budgets and less knowledge about cybersecurity. Members of the center can choose for a collaborative subscription on forensic investigation support, technical support, emergency response and other security consultancy services. Each member of the center has to pay an annual membership fee. They can choose for the basic fee which supports only services of step two or choose for extra services from step three. The fees are suitable for all type of companies, since the larger companies at the end of the supply chain (for example, company N in figure 6) are willing to pay a higher fee to increase cyber resilience of their smaller suppliers. The first cyber resilience center, the one for the high-tech manufacturing industry is expected to be fully operational (steps one, two and three) by February 2019.

The next paragraph contains an overview of best practices and their main purpose including some results from the financial industry.

Type of public-private partnership:	ISACs with Nat Cyber Security Center	CIA/FBI trusted communitees	Cyber Security Council	Cyber Research Agenda	Cyber Security Awareness Month	Cyber Resilience centers for supply chains
Purpose:						
Prevent influencing citizens		✓	✓	✓	✓	
Solving a crime/prevent terrorism	✓	✓		✓	✓	✓
Protect critical infrastructure	✓	✓	✓	✓	✓	✓
Protect national Intellectual Property	✓	✓		✓	✓	✓
Protect Supply Chain		✓	✓	✓	✓	✓
Protect privacy		✓	✓	✓	✓	

Figure 9: *Contribution of public-private initiatives*

OVERVIEW AND RESULTS

In the first section of this chapter six purposes are described for which there is a need for public-private partnerships on cybersecurity. These are:
1. Protect the citizens from unwanted influence on their way of thinking or decision making.
2. Collect all intelligence needed from different sources to prevent or solve a crime or terrorist attack.
3. Protect critical infrastructure like water management, energy, telecom, healthcare and financial services.
4. Protect valuable national intellectual property created within local universities or local companies.
5. Protect the supply chain.
6. Protect privacy sensitive data of citizens.

In figure nine, the contribution of the six best practices as described in the previous paragraph is shown. All six forms of public-private partnership contribute to more than one purpose. It is of high importance to increase awareness of all citizens and keep attention on cyber security research.

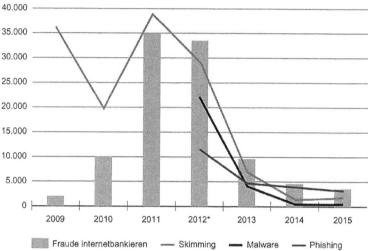

Figure 10: Damage by internet banking fraud (x 1,000 euro)
* since 2012 the fraud report distinguishes phising, maleware and other types of fraud.
Source: Nederlandse Vereniging van Banken (2016), 'Factsheet Veiligheiden Fraude'

One of the oldest public-private partnerships it the financial institutions ISAC. The main reason is that criminals are always looking for financial gain, which is most likely to be obtained when attacking financial services. The financial services industry is now, together with defense industry, one of the best protected private sectors. Figure ten shows how the damage from certain types of attacks has decreased in recent years as a result of these efforts. The energy industry is catching up and nearly on the same level due to an increased threat of attacks on that industry.

With a growing amount of products connected to the Internet and increasing digitalization, like self-driving cars, it is often more important to share threats, interests of attackers and best-practices to improve resilience. This information should not only be shared with the critical infrastructure sectors and public parties but should be available for all SMEs and all supply chains. Governments should find ways to share this type of sensitive information with a network of (SME) companies in such a way that the connected companies and therefore society, will benefit, without increasing the knowledge of the attacker.

The next chapter discusses the lessons learned and proven best practices for planning and implementing a successful strategy for achieving enhanced cybersecurity and ISO 27001 certification at the same time.

Endnotes

1 Kim Zetter, *Inside the Cunning, Unprecedented Hack of Ukraine's Power Grid*, March 2016.

2 Geert Munnichs, Matthijs Kouw and Linda Kool, *Een nooit gelopen race - Over cyberdreigingen en versterking van weerbaarheid*, Den Haag, Rathenau Instituut, 2017.

3 National Coordinator for Security and Counterterrorism (NCTV), *Cyber Security Assessment Netherlands–SCAN 2018*, The Hague, The Netherlands, August 2018.

4 Koen van Impe, *How Can an ISAC Improve Cybersecurity and Resilience?*, July 2018

5 Wam Voster, Jeffrey de Bruijn, *Cyber Security Supply Chain Risk Analysis*, January 2016

6 *https://www.elektroniknet.de/markt-technik/halbleiter/wannacry-legte-tsmc-fertigung-lahm-156501.html*

Chapter 16

ISO 27001 CERTIFICATION – LESSONS LEARNED AND BEST PRACTICES

By: Bart Jenniskens, CISSP, CISM

INTRODUCTION

There are plenty of examples where someone has begged a manager for security tooling that would be beneficial to the whole wellbeing of the organization. But often good security governance is missing in the organization so it is difficult to make the business case and the tool just seems to be an expensive toy for the information technology (IT) staff. Convincing managers and C-suite executives to invest in cybersecurity is a battle as old as the invention of the Internet.

Yet, behavior does evolve in every organization to a certain degree. At a given time, each organization generates a relative level of common sense and a feeling that now is the right time to improve information security (IS). This feeling of needing to improve IS usually is generated when either a security incident occurs, the organization has clients who demand more visibility into an IS assurance, or the organization has specific cybersecurity regulatory or contractual requirements. This momentum generates the perfect moment to start thinking about an information security management system (ISMS).

The best practices for an information security management system are laid down in the ISO 27001 standard. ISO 27001 has gained popularity over the years. It is a tool that helps users implement a robust system to manage information security. The continual cycle that is embedded in ISO 27001 assures that the organization will improve itself over time.

This chapter is focused on the lessons learned and best practices that we have seen when implementing ISO 27001 from scratch to certification.

These lessons learned, and best practices will provide each organization the confidence needed to succeed in the implementation of ISO 27001 and/or improve the organization's current information security management system.

THE GOAL

The first step in achieving ISO 27001 certification for any organization is to gain senior leadership (management) commitment. Management commitment is key to the success of the implementation progress. Throughout the implementation the ISO 27001 project manager needs to work closely with senior management to guide them through the processes.

While getting the management commitment, it is wise to think about the end goal that comes with the implementation of ISO 27001. What is the real goal? Is it ISO 27001 certification with the minimal amount of effort? Or is it to improve the organization by embedding information security in its core, with certification as icing on the cake? Both directions will take you to your final goal, certification, but the direction determines your implementation path. Typically, the information security professional serving as the ISO 27001 certification project manager (PM) will select organizational improvement. In this role, one quickly learns that senior management needs convincing to achieve this goal. During the implementation, the ISO 27001 certification PM will typically notice that senior management will eventually become believers as they see and experience the benefits derived from the IS improvements that flow out of the project. Certification is the result of the implementation effort. During the external certification audit, the management commitment becomes priceless, it can literally make or break the audit.

STARTING THE PROJECT IMPLEMENTATION

A work breakdown structure (WBS), a master integrated schedule (MIS), and a process road map are key elements to a successful ISO 27001 project implementation. In every organization there are certain ways to successfully run projects. Use known processes for your project implementation and avoid reinventing the wheel. Start your project implementation with the work breakdown structure, a project schedule, and a process roadmap and use these tools to create a short-term project plan and long-term project plan. There is no perfect blueprint available for the project implementation of ISO 27001. Below a list of key actions that will guide the assigned PM in the right direction.

Use the following steps to create a successful ISO 27001 certification project plan or roadmap to victory.

a. **Quick scan and scope** – If the PM is new to the organization, then they should make an initial quick scan of the organization to understand the structure and hierarchy. If the PM has been working with the organization for a long period of time, then they will already be familiar with the organizational structure, departments, and team structure. It is also important to understand the organization's goals and values. Once all the information is known, then start building the project scope of work and, if possible, draft the first ISMS. Define the project goals, compose a WBS, and conduct an official project kick-off meeting for the ISO 27001 implementation with full management attendance and commitment.

b. **Organizational context** – Create a full definition of the organization. Obtain an inventory of the organization and if not available create an inventory process. Start classification processes for processes, services, assets and data repositories. Verify, complete or create an overview of all laws and regulations that apply to the organization.

c. **Policy and manual** – Start drafting the ISMS policy and manual. These two documents are the cornerstones of the ISMS.

Describe in the policy the following topics;
- goal of the ISMS
- scope statement (as it will be printed on the certificate)
- management process, management accountability, staff accountability
- information security and risk management
- policy framework
- quality controls

Describe in the manual the following topics;
- scope of the ISMS
- the organization and its structure
- tasks, responsibilities and accountabilities of roles in the organization
- meeting and communication structure
- risk identification methodology
- objectives and performance indicators
- audit methodology
- continued improvement, reporting and continuous management method

d. **Risk assessment** – Prepare and start the first internal risk assessment. The scope of the risk assessment is determined by the scope of the ISMS and the process and/or assets it contains. During this risk assessment you also determine or review the process classification. For each process a business impact analysis and threat analysis must be conducted, taking laws and regulations into account. This risk assessment will lead to a measure proposal and a clear overview of risk owners. The measure proposal will be used to draft a corrective action plan containing an overview of mitigating tasks. This is also a good time to think about and draft the statement of applicability.

e. **Embedment** – The real implementation starts within this step. Proposed measures are planned for implementation, processes and procedures are integrated into the operational processes and missing or incomplete procedures and guidelines are created and updated. Processes like configuration, incident change and service level management will see changes to assure alignment with the standard. Overall this step requires a very hand-on approach. Working closely together with teams and coaching staff. Workshops are a great example of how to work together interactively. Awareness is typically addressed separately during the implementation, with the hands-on approach and workshops, the PM will notice that this will be generated automatically.

f. **Monitoring, logging and reporting** – Quality management will help the PM keep a consistent delivery. For the ISMS it is important to establish applicable KPIs. The KPIs are also part of the audits you must walk-through and are the basis for reports to management. Establishing the KPIs is important, but assuring consistent and trustworthy numbers in reports is equally important. The PM must work with the KPI owners to assure that they can deliver the input for the reports. Once the ISMS quality monitoring process is defined the PM can create the ISMS logging and reporting structure. The reporting process is the gateway to keeping management up to date with the latest developments. It also is a great tool for addressing issues early and assuring management commitment for planned improvements.

g. **Audit** – When all implementation tasks are completed, and the full ISMS is up and running an internal audit should be planned. It is advised to plan the first internal audit with a trusted auditing entity who understands your line of business. Use the internal audit as a rehearsal for the real external certification audit. The internal audit report will provide a list of findings that are weaknesses, strengths and improvements. Use the internal audit report to further improve the ISMS.

The implementation of ISO 27001 is not a serial process. Activities can be started and run parallel from each other. Make a backlog that contains all the activities. Add a responsible deadline and effort estimation to each activity. Visibility of the backlog is important, it should be accessible by everyone who is involved in the implementation. Use the backlog also for reporting to senior management. It will help to prioritize work.

Communication

Setting up a complete ISMS is a real team effort. Communication is therefore very important and part of a successful implementation. When management commitment and the project approval are received organize an ISO 27001 project kick-off meeting. The meeting should be available to all staff that will be involved in the implementation. Ideally, senior management will talk about the importance of ISO 27001 for the organization and the improvements it will bring. This is a great demonstration of management commitment. Throughout the implementation the PM should inform the applicable teams and departments about the progress. Use message boards, flyers, newsletters, posters, team meetings as your communications channel around the office floors and be creative. Make it a living thing until it starts buzzing around the water coolers and coffee machines.

Workshops

Involvement of organization team members is highly underestimated for a successful ISO 27001 implementation. As management commitment is essential, involvement of the staff can make or break the external certification audit. During the certification audit it is vital to show that information security is fully embedded in the organization. It is important to demostrate this capability during the audit interviews. When staff has been involved in the implementation they will know exactly the scope, what has been implemented, what has been improved, and where to find the needed documentation. With this approach, the auditor will see that knowledge and understanding of information security does not only reside with the information security professionals.

Workshops are the best method to engage the team or staff. In the organizational context step of the implementation, workshops can drive the conversation within teams. It is critical to set up workshops with groups of staff or teams in a specific areas, in this example, IT infrastructure. In the workshop, the PM discusses the ISO 27001 standard and makes the group familiar with its contents. It is a best practice to select a specific list of measures from the standard that apply to this group and then conduct a debate with the group about each measure. Often the PM or group facilitator will be surprised with the feedback. The desired outcome of the workshop is a validation of existing measures, the maturity of the existing measure and the subject matter expert who you will work with to get measures implemented or improved.

The Certification Audit

It is normal to get nervous about the certification audit. The ISO 27001 implementation PM works long and hard to setup the ISMS. He or she knows the ISMS by heart and so do colleagues who have been involved since the beginning of the creation of the ISMS. The following checklist is useful in helping to prepare for the certification audit:

- Print all applicable documentation on paper and organize it nicely in a binder. Have at least two copies, one for yourself and one for the auditor.
- Based on the audit agenda, select the persons who will be interviewed by the auditor. Run try-outs with these persons to prepare them for the audit interview. Make sure they know the scope and come prepared to the interview.
- Let the auditor lead the conversation during interviews. Only intervene in the conversation when applicable. When others talk about information security with the same passion it shows great embedment in the organization.
- Assure that someone takes notes that include all remarks from the auditor. It is useful to evaluate the remarks after the interviews.
- Do not let the auditor go out of scope. When this happens be very clear about the scope and follow the agenda provided by the auditor.
- Always ask for clarification from the auditor when a question or remark is not understood correctly. In many cases the auditor will rephrase its sentence to make an easier question or remark.

Give It Time to Develop

For information security professionals, implementing ISO 27001 from the ground up to certification is a great experieice and opportunity. After the first external certification audit, the maintenance begins and one can focus on improving the ISMS accordingly. Also these phases of the ISMS life cycle should not be underestimated. It is easy to fall back into previous habits or shift priority for the maintenance of the ISMS. It is important to allow adquate time during implementation and leading up to certification. If the implementation requires extra months to complete documentation, improvement tasks or other activities, then allow this delay and postpone certification audit. Investing the extra time will improve the ISMS and will provide greater confidence going through the audit.

Celebrate Success

The last and final lesson learned that must be addressed before closing this chapter, is to celebrate success. By demonstrating enthusiasm during the implementation, workshops, and communications, other will follow your direction. Don't shy away from celebrating achieved milestones. The implementation of ISO 27001 from scratch requires a great deal of time and personal commitment, plus a lot of energy and often, real perseverance. It is therefore a good practice to take a step back and evaluate what has been achieved!

The next chapter discusses the power and value of software tools to help organizations enhance their cybersecurity governance, risk management, and compliance.

Chapter 17

CYBERSECURITY SOFTWARE FOR IMPROVED ORGANIZATIONAL RISK AND COMPLIANCE

By: Jason Gottschalk

BACKGROUND

Risk practitioners are all critically aware of the pressure mounting on organizations, due to the ever increasing competitive marketplace. Organizsations have been and continue to embrace improved mobile connectivity and available technology and the ever "silver bullet" of moving data into the cloud. Overlay this with an ever increasing compliance and legislation burden leaving organisation with fear and uncertainty as to how best to ensure adequate risk management and compliance.

Traditionally consultants have in the past advised clients on how best to manage risk and compliance by designing frameworks which were implemented through policies and process. Given the pace at which business is moving, there is only so much effective risk mitigation one could achieve through this mechanism. Evolution of the consultant's toolbox to now include the design of technical solutions/effective technical controls implemented by the organisation are a step in the right direction. Clients are becoming more expectant of working with organizations that can not only help remediate issues identified but also understand issues in context of the compliance and legislative requirements.

This chapter explores two high risk areas and describes feasible and industry accepted approaches to mitigating the associated risks and achieving the desired regulatory compliance:

- Privileged Access Management (PAM) - Creating visibility and control over privileged access for Administrators of Information Technology (IT) and Business systems.

- Cloud Access Security Brokering - Creating visibility and control over the movement of data to and from the cloud as well as data stored on the cloud.

Where applicable, vendors are mentioned purely as reference to the nature of the technology and should be considered for that context only. Each subsection contains a clear understanding of the business challenge that the solution is attempting to resolve.

INTRODUCTION TO PRIVILEGED ACCESS MANAGEMENT

A recent breach responded to wrung true a statement often flouted within cyber security "that a breach often occurs from the exploitation of a vulnerability within a key third party." A well-known example of this is the Target breach that occurred in 2013, which resulted from the compromise of its own key third party environment.

Breaches such as the Target Corporation as well as a number of others often originated through the compromise and escalation of unauthorised use of privileged accounts. Privileged user accounts include:
- database administrators
- network engineers
- developers
- persons employed by any other organisation that have privileged access to any part of one's environment

General IT control auditors will share countless examples where audited environments have yielded results depicting control failures where administrators and developers (privileged users) have unmonitored access to production environments (this is often referenced as the insider threat/risk). This control failure is further aggravated by a lack of any compensating controls that would monitor the access and, more importantly, monitor the activity while the sessions are active.

It must also be considered that privileged users are not necessarily the only or key driver for wanting to have improved PAM controls. Drivers could include the strategy of mitigating the risk of external breaches that utilise malware and complementary techniques that target privileged accounts. Insisting that privileged users themselves be the driver for the PAM requirement is a smart strategy as it helps repudiate concerns as to their own position during breaches and fraud-related incidents.

Adoption of PAM solutions has been slow within organisations, mostly due to the following challenges:

- cost of solution and associated implementation costs
- flat network architecture with the inability to adequately segregate necessary systems
- lack of awareness
- other information security/cyber security urgencies
- misconception that password vaulting removes the requirement for PAM solutions.

Privileged access management should not be confused with identity and access management/governance (IAM/IAG). The two are very different, with IAM/IAG focusing on access to systems/data for *joiners*, *leavers* and *movers*, while PAM focuses on managing and monitoring privileges users' access and activities when performing administration activities on resources.

PRIVILEGE ACCESS MANAGEMENT TECHNOLOGY

Commonplace, especially among outsourced technology providers, are the frequent use of jump servers to form the bridge between the support organisation and the environment being maintained. By design (quite essential to the design) is the ability of the jump server to be the bridge and ensure that all activities traverse it.

Usually this jump server is a Citrix, Windows or Unix based environment that a privileged user will access to and from that server will *jump* to the target environment. In some instances the jump server is not as secure as it should be due to the lack of a multifactor authentication approach, meaning the compromise of a username and password will provide direct access to the remote environment at a network level (the jump server itself does not have privileged access to the target environment, but rather provides the bridge (see figure one below)).

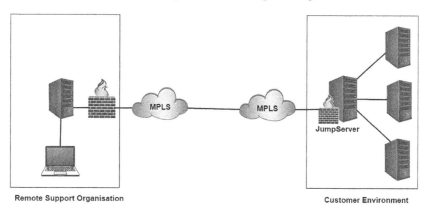

Figure 1: Jump Server Depiction

While the above design/implementation achieves segregation through the requirement to traverse via the jump server, the actual activities and access goes mostly unmonitored. Furthermore, the key challenge is that the actual privileged credentials are known to the users and if compromised in conjunction with the jump server, the attackers have access to privileged credentials.

By the contrast, implementing a PAM solution, the available controls that an organisation can implement are quite extensive. Functionality includes the ability to remove actual known privileged credentials from target resources as well as ensure the monitoring of sessions.

Below are the three main common components of a typical PAM solution:

- **Session Manager** – The session manager enables an organisation to monitor session activity as performed by a privileged user. This would essentially include all activity performed including most protocol support such SSH and RDP. Key feature sets across the PAM vendor listing include:
  - 1. **Workflow Driven Access** – Depending on the type of access model being implemented, users could be granted access to an administration function via workflow driven access request forms. See the below example.
  - 2. **Real-Time Monitoring Using Behaviour Analysis** – All sessions traversing the PAM solution, including a number of supported protocols (RDP, SSH, etc.), provide real-time activity monitoring which include OCR recognition (useful in highly graphical applications). Session whitelisting/ blacklisting can prevent (or just alert) incidents by alerting security teams about high risk commands being executed (Select * from table or SUDO commands). Blacklisting can be extremely useful to stop specific type of command that may be deemed high risk in certain environments.
  - 3. **Reporting and Auditing** – This is particularly useful when detailed activity can be linked to a specific user, at a specific time and could include all the actions executed as part of the session. Logs absorbed into your SIEM/SOC could be configured to identify high risk alerts in a real-time manner thereby alerting security teams in real-time, mitigating potentially high risk activities. Reporting could include connection tracking, activity reporting and the recorded user sessions.
- **Password Vaulting/Manager** –The password vault (sometimes referred to as password manager) is a critical component of the PAM solution. Its primary purpose is to ensure the security of the actual privileged accounts for the relevant resources (servers, routers, firewalls, etc.). When password vaulting is implemented, typically the privileged users' credentials on the target resources are removed and replaced with the vaults credentials (it

Remote Support using Jump Servers

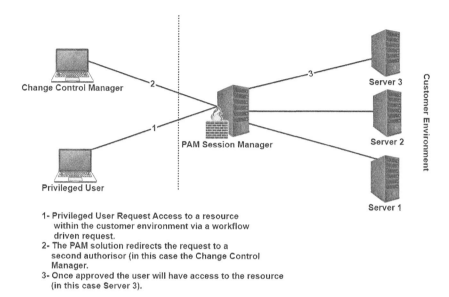

1- Privileged User Request Access to a resource
   within the customer environment via a workflow
   driven request.
2- The PAM solution redirects the request to a
   second authorisor (in this case the Change Control
   Manager.
3- Once approved the user will have access to the resource
   (in this case Server 3).

Figure 2: Example of workflow driven access request

is important to note that there are nuisances to how the vault is implemented). The vaults credentials can be infinitely stronger (more complex and longer) than a traditional password that is manageable by the user. Furthermore the vault can automatically cycle its passwords to mitigate the risk of man-in-the-middle attacks.

- Typically the privileged user will access the password vault that, in turn, will log the users into the target resource, with the target resource password never known nor revealed in the process. Vault encryption typically supports AES-256, RSA-2048 and FIPS 140-2 validated cryptograph (reducing the risk of Overpass-the-Hash, Golden Ticket, Overpass-the-Hash and other related vulnerabilities), as well as replication to support disaster recovery scenarios.

Successful PAM implementations are not only about the technology but also about understanding the problem being solved and that being captured by strong PAM governance framework, including defined and relevant policies that focus on the people and change component. Many PAM implementations fail due to low adoption and resistance by privileged users.

The next section discusses some of the key components that will enable a structured and ultimately successful PAM implementation.

INITIATING A PRIVILEGED ACCESS GOVERNANCE PROGRAM

A strategy for implementing a successful PAM program should start by answering the following questions which in turn will be used as the basis for the strategy:

1. What are the key risks being mitigated and what are the key business drivers for doing so? Buying a PAM solution without understanding the business risk and ultimate drivers will result in a lack of business support and potentially poor adoption within the IT/development environments. Once a clear understanding of this is formed, the ability to derive the technical requirements becomes much easier and having a defined technical specification will help in identifying the appropriate solution.

2. Identifying the crown jewels – Identifying all your key data and systems they reside on is a key. After doing so, a risk based approach should be taken as to understanding the risks associated with the privileged user and the assess they have to the underlying data and systems. Key criteria that increase the risks associated are:

   o Customer data, especially where the data is quite sensitive. Intellectual property risks are often thought of as patents but also consider other forms of intellectual property such as custom code which is proprietary.

   o Consider the regulatory drivers and applicable legislation, as this may increase the requirement to secure the environment and not only from a PAM perspective.

   o In legacy environments, where patches and updates are no longer provided, a PAM solution may offer an opportunity to secure the environment and may actually serve to set the priorities for system within the scope for environment. This may also include resources that don't support multifactor authentication or complex passwords.

3. Who has access to what and what are the detailed permissions? This includes creating a view of the number of privileged accounts across the technology environment. Be careful not to leave out PaaS, IaaS and SaaS environments from this analysis. A number of PAM vendors will provide access to a platform that can scan your estate and identify privileged accounts. This should be taken advantage of as manual identification can be tiresome and is prone to errors.

4. What model of access will be implemented as part of the PAM solution? There are some nuisances with each one but at a high level it could influence the implementation. For further definitions of these principles, please refer to NISTIR 7657,[1] which covers the following access control models:

   o IBAC - identity-based access control
   o RBAC - role-based access control
   o ABC - attribute-based access control

5. Requirement for access certification, monitoring and reporting.

   o **Access Certification** - Access certification deals with the re-attestation of access for all privileged users. The concept and process is not similar to that of re-attestation of access for standard users (movers, leavers). Depending on the PAM solution chosen, it may be possible to workflow and automate the process of re-attestation. Generally privileged users will be assigned to a group and each group could be assigned a head of department or team leader that will be responsible for confirming that access is valid and appropriate. The frequency largely differs from environment to environment, however one should consider that frequent re-attestation will add an unnecessary burden to an environment that will be highly managed and monitored.

   o **Monitoring** – The greatest advantage with PAM solutions is the ability to monitor the activity on a granular level. Some PAM solutions support the implementation of compliance rules that can limit actual commands/actions being executed. This functionality will be useful but not unless the appropriate use cases are adequately defined. Be sure to spend sufficient time defining these use case.

   o **Reporting/Alerts** – Having reporting or rather a requirement of reporting for the sake of it is not the best route to follow. When it comes to privileged users, backwards looking reports have limited value especially in breach or fraud instances as the damage has largely been done and the purpose of the PAM solution was to prevent or early detect these risks. Focus should rather be made on ensuring that the reporting or rather alerts are integrated real-time into a SIEM or SOC. In the absence of a SIEM or SOC, high risk alerts should be escalated directly to persons outside of the group responsible for triggering the alert. Spend the time testing to ensure the alerts are functioning correctly and in a real-time manner to maximise the effectiveness of the PAM solution.

6. Security architectural, licensing and other requirements – Some key considerations are explored which are largely based on lessons learned:

o **Authentication** – It is strongly recommended that the solution be implemented with multifactor authentication. It is commonplace today and without question, implementing a PAM solution without it will result in mitigation of only half the problem.

o **Architectural considerations**
  - Segregation of environments - Attackers traverse latterly through environments with a PAM solution offering the ability to enforce a segregated environment for critical data (example of a PCI zone for credit card data). The ability to do this is not very common and in some cases it may be possible to VLAN specific systems. Consider these requirements upfront as there will be dependencies which may impact timelines.
  - Cloud Services – Organizations will have different strategies relating to whether resources are in located data centres, on premise, in the cloud, or a hybrid between them. Additionally resources may be scattered across multiple geographic locations. These requirements should be considered when defining the requirements.

o **Licensing Model** – PAM vendors offer different licensing models which have been driven out of the ever changing IT architecture landscape. Consider the number of privilege users within your organisation vs the number of concurrent sessions. Depending on the numbers it may be more advantageous to go with concurrent sessions vs number of users.
  - With hybrid architectures, it's important to understand how each vendor licenses the actual bastion (session manager). If you have a highly distributed environment, you may choose to have a number of bastions with the same number of users per bastion. In this case it may be more sensible to go with a vendor that charges per user/session independently of the number of bastions.

o **Additional Security Requirements** – Consider the following additional requirements:
  - Support for password rotation with automation capabilities
  - Ability to integrate with business as usual (BAU) utilities
  - Provide independent assurance relating to the testing and security hardening of their platforms (SOC2, ISO 27001).

In summary, the success of a PAM program is based on an understanding of the requirements and expectant challenges across people, process and technology. Ignoring one of those areas will most likely impact the overall success of the PAM program. A successful program is one that begins with a limited scope, with meaningful and achievable milestones and builds upon on each success while expanding the resources in scope with each iteration.

INTRODUCTION TO CLOUD ACCESS SECURITY BROKER

Cloud access security broker (CASB) platforms provide an ability to manage and control the movement of data into the cloud as well as some of the some of the unique risks associated with data stored in the cloud. When risk assessments are performed for organisations wanting to identify the use of cloud services, there is consistent surprise as to the very active cloud adoption strategy being embraced by the users even though the organisation has not mandated one. The array of cloud services and their functionally is increasing every day, with vendors embracing users' desire to adopt cloud services enabled by bring your own device (BYOD) strategies, high speed broadband and mobile connectivity.

Commonplace in organisation are the use of cloud services (such as or similar to a non-corporate version of Dropbox) to share and store company information without approval (also known as unsanctioned apps). While at face value this may not necessarily be considered a risk, organizations may reconsider when they realise that they have no control over visibility of:

o   Who that information is shared with.
o   Whether adequate security controls have been implemented, such as encryption at rest and multi factor authentication.
o   When that employee leaves the organisation they leave with corporate information and the organisation may have little control/influence to compel the user to delete information. In most cases without the necessary controls, organisation may not even be aware of the data residing in the cloud.

The CASB solutions promise to solve this issue by centrally driving and managing the compliance burden through its feature rich capabilities. Some high level functionality of a CASB include (more detail is provided further in this chapter):

o   **Enabling Compliance** – The requirements of regulation can be mapped and driven through the creation and implementation of aligned CASB rules. A key example would be the European Union (EU) General Data Privacy Regulation (GDPR) legislation which has strict requirements as to where EU related data resides. In this case the CASB could detect the movement of data outside of EU approved environments and restrict this.
o   **Improved Security and Threat Detection** – CASB vendors comb the internet identifying different cloud services locations and in some case assessing the security posture. Some vendors have also

implemented malware detection within the CASB, enabling the detection of malware for data moving to and from the cloud, reducing the risk of infection reaching the target environment.

Locational awareness and machine learning of user behaviour is further improving threat detection and providing an additional level protection. Consider if you are a United Kingdom-based organization accessing a specific cloud service, should you allow the cloud service to be accessed from unusual locations? The CASB could be configured to block that access attempt, reduce the ability to download data and/or produce an alert for action by the SIEM/SOC team.

o **Discovery** – The ability to identify data moving into the cloud is critical. A number of CASB vendors allow for firewall/proxy logs to be assessed and a report to be produced to identify the cloud service being utilized. This service could also be implemented as a shadow IT implementation, where activity is monitored but no actual actions are performed by the CASB. The discovery process is also valuable when trying to determine the uptake of cloud services and assessing the risk of cloud services. Consider the discovery capability as a usual tool as the foundation to form a view when motivating for the purchase of a CASB solution.

SANCTIONED VS UNSANCTIONED CLOUD APPLICATIONS

Understanding of the difference between a sanctioned vs unsanctioned application is important. A sanctioned cloud application is simply an application that has been approved for organisational use but importantly is managed by the organisation. Typically the organisation would procure the service and therefore have control over the management thereof.

An unsanctioned application is a non-approved cloud application that is not approved for storing organisational information. There may be slight nuisances for the definition of unsanctioned applications. For example, if a user obtained permission to use a cloud application to store customer data but the application was not centrally managed then technically the organisation still has no direct control over who has access to the data. As such that is still considered to be an unsanctioned application.

CASB technology and cloud services

CASB vendors utilise a number of methods to manage and monitoring cloud activities. These include API's, ActiveSync proxies, reverse proxies, forward proxies. The reason for so many options is simply because of how cloud vendors themselves dictate and drive the level of integration into their platforms and therefore in turn the level control a CASB can exert over that service.

Selecting the correct CASB vendor is not the only consideration for effective cloud risk management as using a cloud provider with limited integration for a CASB may limit the overall control your organisation can exert (especially a BYOD environment).

Key Cloud Challenges

CASB vendors offer some unique functionality that promises to resolve a number of risk/challenges with the movement of data into the cloud:

Challenge	Solution Offered
Lack of encryption of data at rest	• Not all cloud services offer encryption at rest natively and that functionality may incur additional costs as well as result in decentralized management. • CASB's offer functionality which includes the ability to enforce encryption of data at rest.
Reliance on end point malware detection	• CASB provide an additional layer of malware analysis by inspecting all data moving to and from the cloud. The key benefit is that data is analysed and quarantined prior to the data reaching the target environment.
Overhead of ensuring a uniformed approach to compliance across different cloud services (SaaS, PaaS and IaaS)	• CASB solutions provide an opportunity to centrally manage, monitor and drive compliance across cloud services in a uniformed and centralised manner by applying consistent governance rulesets
Social media awareness – Organizations have employees that have access to confidential information which could find its way onto social media.	• CASB vendors offer an ability to play in-line with SSL traffic and are aware of social media activities. Configuration of rules will enable the CASB to detect potential violations via both sanctioned and unsanctioned services. CASB can be highly configurable and many support the use of regular expressions with Boolean operators which can focus on specific use cases.

Challenge	Solution Offered
Lack of visibility for the use of cloud services and deviation of policy	• Configured use cases can alert suspicious or high risk activities across cloud services. This could be in-line, real-time or as a shadow IT implementation.
	• Alerts can be integrated in a SIEM/SOC solution to enable easy management, investigation and remediation. Regulatory requirement mappings are often provided by CASB vendors which enable out the box configuration. An example would be the ability to detect the movement of PCI, social security details and other standard formatted data.
Unmanaged Devices – Balancing agility with security is challenging especially when it relates to unmanaged devices and ensuring usability.	• A major risk is users being able to download data from the cloud onto unmanaged devices (any device that is not under the control of your IT department). This could include a member of staff's personal device or a when a contractor accesses services on their corporate machine for which you have no visibility or control or level of protection applied. CASB's offer a number of solutions but would require that the cloud service support management via the CASB either through reverse proxy and/or API.
	• Should this be possible the CASB would detect the device accessing the cloud service as being unmanaged and limit the functionality. Feature set dependent, this could include read only mode and view online only being possible via unmanaged devices.

CASB Implementation/Configuration Strategies

As mentioned earlier in this chapter, a CASB can be implemented in a number of different ways and specifically with a combination of the available configuration/implementation options. This is largely due to the nature of cloud applications and their available functionality. A key component is also whether or not the organisation has control over the user's end point device or not.

Before we go into implementation strategies, it's important to understand the different configuration options:

o **API (Application Program Interface) Integration** – In its most basic form API's enable an application to interact with another application. Cloud services that provide API functionality, with advanced integration, enable CASB's to obtain increased visibility and control over data stored within the cloud environment (at a file level). Specifically the API's enable the CASB to inspect files stored within the environment and enable to initiation of compliance scans to identify sensitive data (providing visibility for the organisation). From a data loss prevention (DLP) context, API's can enable a CASB to redact, watermark or encrypt data at rest. API integration also offers improved governance relating to sharing of information as well as managing cloud based activities from unmanaged devices. It is important to note that not all cloud services provide API integration, some applications provide APIs that give a limited set of functionality to the connecting CASB and where available, the cloud service is usually a sanctioned application and paid for by the organisation.

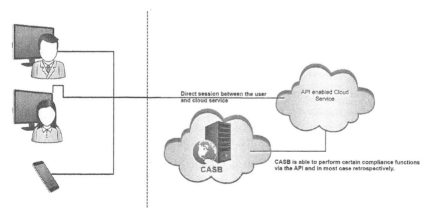

Figure 3: CASB topology using API integration

o **ActiveSync Proxies** – This configuration option is applicable for mobile end point devices. ActiveSync functionality enables users to securely access the organisations data without a client side agent (agentless). ActiveSync enables the session to be automatically redirected via the CASB when the session is initiated, resulting in a seamless useless experience. It's worth noting that activity usually occurs within the native mobile application.

o **Forward Proxies** – Forward proxies are particularly useful in instances where cloud services do not support a reverse proxy (e.g. when you are trying to control access to unmanaged applications). The key challenge with this implementation strategy is that the agents have to reside on the end point, which can prove difficult if you have implemented a BYOD strategy. Forward proxies have similar capabilities to reverse proxies but have limitations when unmanaged cloud services (that contain organizational information) are accessed on non-managed end point devices and can also cause complications when integrating with any existing corporate proxies (e.g., for more traditional web content blocking services). More detail is discussed later in this chapter

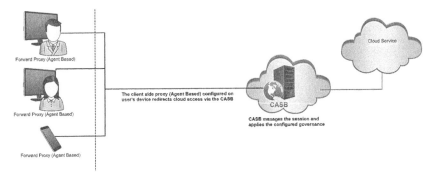

Figure 4: CASB topology using forward proxy

o **Reverse Proxies** – By configuring a cloud service to use a CASBs through a reverse proxy configuration, this enables data governance across managed and unmanaged end points. This is probably the key differentiator between the different configuration options. Given the adoption of BYOD, this functionality is critical as it provides the greatest level of control and is what the industry will term as "agent-less" compliance. In practise the CASB proxy resides between the endpoint device and the cloud service, redirecting the active session once authentication is completed. Because the CASB resides on the server side, no configuration is required on the end points device with redirection occurring through the cloud service automatically (although some service configuration is required and this often means the application must support such functionality).

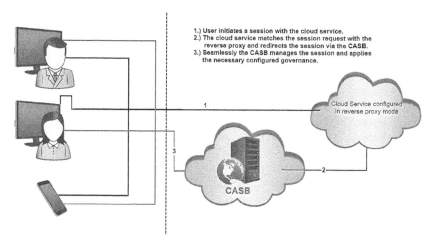

1.) User initiates a session with the cloud service.
2.) The cloud service matches the session request with the reverse proxy and redirects the session via the CASB.
3.) Seamlessly the CASB manages the session and applies the necessary configured governance.

The summary table below is quick reference guide to the key differences between the different configurations options:

Configuration Type	Agent Required	Configuration Efforts	Level of governance achievable	Applicability	BYOD Friendly
API	No	Medium	Limited	Cloud application specific	Yes
Active Sync	No	Low	High (limited to specific clouds)	Cloud application specific	Yes
Forward Proxy	Yes	High	Medium (and only on managed devices)	All cloud services used from the managed device	No
Reverse Proxy	No	Low	High (limited to supported applications)	Cloud application specific	Yes

The table below indicates some configuration strategies to ensure compliance across the different supported configuration types:

Configuration Type	Additional Forward Proxy Required (Agents)	Active Sync Required	API Required	Key Benefits/challenges
Sanctioned application with reverse proxy support	Recommended - The requirement for the client side agent will enable the detection and prevention of organizational data moving into unsanctioned cloud applications.	Optional – Features and benefits vary across cloud applications	Optional - Features and benefits vary across cloud applications	Data residing within reverse proxy enabled cloud applications can be managed and controlled regardless of whether the service is accessed from a managed or unmanaged device. Governance is applied in a real-time manner
Sanctioned/unsanctioned application without reverse proxy support	Mandatory - The ability to apply governance controls is purely dependant on the deployed CASB client side agents (In certain cases API functionality may provide some control)	N/A	Recommended – API may enable key governance controls.	• Data residing in these cloud applications may be accessible on non-managed devices, leaving organisational data at risk. API controls may limit exposure and functionality will vary across providers. • The implementation of client side agents will limit the leakage of organisational data through unsanctioned applications but block such activities

			• Access to sanctioned applications outside of the organisation should be restricted to only managed devices.
Sanctioned application without reverse proxy support but with API support	Mandatory - The ability to apply governance controls through API functionality is limited. The service is heavily dependent on the API functioning in a real-time manner which may not always be the case.	N/A	N/A	• API functionality varies across cloud providers but usually the API is particularly useful when scanning files at rest for compliance requirements • Access to sanctioned application outside of the organisation should be restricted to only managed devices.

Initiating a Cloud Compliance Program

Implementing a Cloud Compliance Program should start with identifying the cloud risk profile of the organisation, regulatory requirement and drivers. The following areas offer guidance which should help form a cloud compliance program:

1. What are the key risks being mitigated and what are the key business drivers for doing so? Implementing cloud governance could have a significant impact of the average user within an organisation as it could limit cloud-based functionality, which could impact critical processes. The key is to understanding the drivers for compliance such as legislation and regulatory requirements. This can include HIPAA, GDPR, PCI-DSS and similar requirements.

2. Compliance requirements – Different vendors offer different capabilities and matching those with your business requirements will help guide the selection of an appropriate vendor. Also consider the people and change impact as well as policies relating to end point devices (laptops, workstations and mobile phones). CASB's can implement policies that potentially will impact users' abilities to work with non-sanctioned applications and that may be contrary to existing policies.

3. Identifying the crown jewels – Identifying all your key data and systems they reside on is a key, the focus at this stage would not only be identifying what is migrating into the cloud as a strategic decision but more importantly what is already residing in the cloud. Focus on understanding the use of sanctioned vs unsanctioned applications. Key criteria that increase the risks associated are customer data, especially where the data is quite sensitive. Intellectual property risks are often thought of as patents but also consider other forms of intellectual property such as custom code which is proprietary and similar assets.

4. Implementation strategy – Features are great but the inability to implement them will impact the success of the project. Discuss the ability to implement agents on endpoint devices vs. the use of sanctioned vs non-sanctioned application functionality. A common example is where BYOD is in use which may not enable you to install agents. Sanctioned applications may not offer sufficient control and an agent may be required, which may impact your BYOD policy.

5. Requirement for access certification, monitoring and reporting.

o **Monitoring** – The greatest advantage with CASB solutions is the ability to monitor the activity on a granular level. Spend the time upfront to define the appropriate use cases.

o **Reporting/Alerts** – Focus on ensuring that the reporting or rather alerts are integrated real-time into a security information and event management system or a security operations center.

Endnote

[1] *https://nvlpubs.nist.gov/nistpubs/Legacy/IR/nistir7657.pdf*

Chapter 18

IMPERATIVES FOR BUILDING AND MANAGING A CYBER RESILIENCE PROGRAM

By: Danny Solomon

INTRODUCTION

To achieve resilience, firms need to establish a cyber defense that will enable them to repel advanced attacks, and enable a rapid return to normal operations, with minimal impact, or with a tolerable range that had been recognized as the organization's acceptable risk posture. While perspectives on how to approach to the cyber problem have been shifting from static and reactive measures, to more proactive and pre-emptive mind-sets enabled by advances in technology, the emerging priorities are evolving beyond simply focusing on the availability of data and systems: and now need to assure clients of the confidentiality and integrity of the information it holds, as well as the security and the integrity of the systems. Firms are learning from the near daily reporting of cyber breaches that an attacker's process can last for days or may have been ongoing for months, that *low and slow attacks* and persistent threats are becoming the norm, that insider threats or interconnected supply chain partners are a common source of risk, and the realization that advanced attacks are not based on a single piece of malware.

Defense as a concept, is the activity of defending oneself and as such is dynamic. It differs from "security" which is more static in nature, though it does encompass forms of controls that can provide protection, detection, and prevention around a suite of tools and technology like firewalls, and antivirus, etc. Defence conceptually requires a doctrine that defines how you will defend yourself, and is built on an appreciation of how you could be attacked, and how you could respond. As with any combative pursuit, a defense is or should be prepared for different scenarios in which you could be attacked, and a response is put in place for different forms of attack that could be used against you. Scenario-building therefore lies at the heart of preparing a defense, or a developing a playbook for defensive methods and tactics.

The adoption of a dynamic concept of cyber defense which incorporates the principle of detection and response in real time, with the ability to detect anomalies in activity and behavior, and differentiate between good and bad by applying multiple sources of threat intelligence are now critical to early identification of potential compromise and to the response capability which is absolutely central to cyber resilience.

While good security requires acute awareness and preparedness, resilience requires the ability to detect, react, defend and recover with a minimal impact to the organization. Developing security has been addressed in previous chapters of this publication, and the principles of maintaining awareness and preparedness are consistently broadcast through the industry, but resilience is a concept that cannot be developed into a single technological solution, or a program or enlightened policies or procedures. As this chapter will explore, cyber resilience is a more complex configuration of technology, processes, and skills essential for the survivability of an organization in the digital age.

Unsurprisingly the process for establishing a requisite resilience-building program, maintaining its relevance, and managing the many 'moving parts' is both complex, and a step further advanced from the current typical activities of a chief information security officer in most companies. The management of a cyber resilience program demands more of both security management and organizational leaders, and with many firms reporting that the cyber threat now represents the number one risk, the need for effectively defined and implemented cyber resilience is an absolute requirement.

PART ONE: RESILIENCE: THE GROUNDWORK

PREPARING TO DETECT, DEFEND, AND DETER CYBER ATTACKS

Improving resilience with the development of a more evolved detection and response capability, should be initiated by a staged-process of resilience and readiness assessment that form an integrated and holistic strategy. Effectively defining, managing, and directing this process is complex, but critical to success. This chapter aims to offer targeted guidance to detect, defend, and deter cyber attacks.

There are three aspects which must be in place for an effective resilience development program:

- 1. Capability development comprises ongoing investment in technology, staff, skills, and planning. This is invariably the priority that is first established and tends to garner most attention, and requires the ability to evaluate and introduce new capabilities and improve the effectiveness of existing measure.

- 2. Maturity development comprises the evolution of experience, expertise, and effective performance. This is emerging as a priority, because maturity describes not only the complete picture of tools and methods, but also the ability to apply, and adapt, according to the requirements of a changing threat landscape. It therefore provides a more relevant method for measuring progress over time, and benchmarking organizational posture.

- 3. Oversight development, comprises a system of management roles, processes and functions that drive progress. Oversight is the most problematic of the three aspects, is only now starting to receive attention but still lacks a blueprint for a comprehensive approach. There is a chronic absence of formalized and structured oversight in most organizations, and the root causes of weakness and failure can often be traced to the lack of coherent and effective oversight.

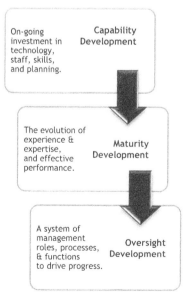

This chapter sets out prerequisites for tackling each of these three aspects, introducing the principles of each, with specific focus on the priorities for managing resilience building.

Developing resilience must be firmly rooted in the needs of the business, and driven by a risk-informed assessment of the organization, before defining an appropriate risk appetite, and thereafter a target end-state that the resilience-building program will work towards. Most organizations are familiar with security assessments for the purpose of compliance, but the need to assess cyber readiness, and cyber resilience is more complex and dynamic because it is aligned with the more multi-faceted nature of resilience.

The need to evaluate organizational readiness extends beyond traditionally accepted vulnerability assessments and penetration testing methods, because they are too narrow in focus, and address systems devices and networks. In order for evaluations to be relevant, they need to dynamically assess how *appropriate* the organizational readiness posture is. Essentially is the organization as a whole ready for the right threats, and the next attacks rather than the last ones? A broad-base testing program will identify whether you are ready for the current threats as well as new and emerging threats that you need to be ready for in the future. Testing systems ensures they are *effective*, a full evaluation incorporating a red team exercise will demonstrate human, process, and procedural weaknesses to provide a complete view. In examining the outcomes, the process will highlight where your cyber defense measures are *incomplete*, and where current planning reveals gaps and blind spots, which the evaluation may have demonstrated, in order to illustrate the weaknesses under real world conditions.

This assessment process is complex in its requirement to generate a hierarchy of measures that need to be introduced as part of a cyber resilience program, or even to remediate failings in a long establish cyber security/ readiness plan. To achieve a workable structured program of operational, tactical, and strategic aspects you will need to assimilate inputs from all the different functions of the business, translate judgments into both qualitative and quantitative outputs, and synthesize both security and risk into a commonly understood language. Thereafter, formulating a macro strategy to achieve the end-state of cyber resilience is no less complex as it requires the amalgamation of several subcomponent strategies which may have been developed by different units at different times, with different priorities. Therefore the consolidation requires an open intrastrategy dialogue, which coordinates and de-conflicts between different workstreams.

Based on an agreed resilience posture, the organization needs to launch parallel initiatives for remediation. One initiative is invariably to develop more strength around technology, methods and staff, or capability development. The second is to reinforce existing capability to make it more appropriate and effective to the changing threat landscape, and rendering the firm better able to cope and adapt to the environment or maturity development. Decisions on investment in capabilities such as a security operations center, the propagation and limits of cloud use, outsourcing, and the buy-or-build consideration of introducing any capability, will all have fundamental implications for the different strategy components and in turn, consideration of each is likely to impact the overall definition of the overall approach.

However the development of capability and maturity are essential inter-linked. By introducing new capability, the firm is improving its underlying maturity because it is capable of deploying greater means to defend itself. By developing greater maturity in *how* the firm maintains cyber readiness, and therefore a higher probability of being resilient to cyber attack is clearly determined by the utility it achieves from capability. This essentially is the is basis for establishing an *effective* defense. Senior leadership consensus is an essential outcome from a top-down and bottom-up reconciliation of what is to be attained in investing for cyber resilience, with how it will be introduced and managed, which are both critical to implementing a cyber resilience strategy and a cyber defense framework.

AIMS OF A 4-STEP APPROACH TO ASSESSING CYBER READINESS AND BUILDING RESILIENCE

Evaluate	Examine	Identify	Introduce
the degree to which organizational readiness is appropriate, complete and effective, and how you maintain yourreadiness	how appropriate your resilience planning and measures are, and under which conditions they are more likely to fail	a hierarchy of operational, tactical, and strategic imperatives for establishing the correct resilience posture	a structured program to build strength in technology, methods, procedures and people aligned to best practices

FROM DEFINITION TO IMPLEMENTATION

Senior management involvement in directing these processes, allocating priorities, and building consensus is imperative to moving forward with genuine organizational commitment. If there is a disjoint at any stage, from conception and formulation through to the implementation phase, there is every chance that the organization will not identify the real problem, the solution will not address the problem, and the organization will not support the solution.

- The process of determining a cyber resilience strategy and its essential components, raises complex decisions requiring trade-offs between investment, security, risk and the efficient functioning of the enterprise, so as not to compromise sales and profit generating activities. This fact alone requires the full engagement of executive management, and introduces one of the main reasons why governance and oversight of the process needs to be rigorous to ensure that the desired end-state achieves business requirements, and is sensitive to the operation priorities of the different parts of the organization.

- Implementation can often be undermined, despite efforts to identify the appropriate process, for a number of reasons, not least because the process is typically long, laborious, and requires significant change. Moreover, several elements require continuous evolution and validation like vulnerability and threat management and awareness and training, while others require more periodic refining and adjustment like detection and response.

- Like any change management program, adequate time and management attention needs to be invested to ensure that change happens and the value is recognized. The more unique challenges for a cyber resilience program are generally greater where a high level of awareness needs to be established, and a high state of readiness needs to be maintained. These factors make appropriate oversight processes all the more critical to the program's success.

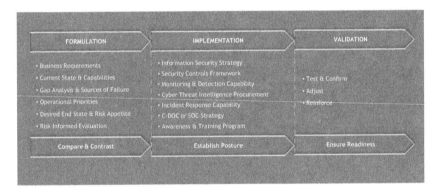

Buy vs. Build-In Resilience

The more straightforward route to rapidly establishing resilience and maturity is now to procure them as managed security services (MSS), in particular monitoring, detection and response (MDR). There are clear advantages of this approach for accelerating resilience-building, and for managing the associated processes.

The MSS provider leads firms through the process of assessment and evaluation, so their input from the start ensures the right diagnostic process. In doing so, the definition of the correct posture would be agreed to, followed by the customization of a solution that will fill the gaps in technology, procedures and people.

For an effective monitoring, detection and response service this will combine a vulnerability and threat management program, a security incident event management (SIEM)-as-a-service and a security operations center

(SOC)-as-a-service with all the associated intelligence, hunter, and forensic analyst capabilities that would be required.

The essence of customization is to best align client needs with the budget, which can be a small fraction of the cost of a self-build and drastically reduce management time and challenges required. This highlights the value of introducing specialist vendors and service suppliers into your portfolio, organizations who have an effective and long established professional services consulting experience to accompany their technical services. While many firms have been working in the field of information technology (IT) outsourcing for years, the issues of security and resilience are relatively new to the outsourcing model. Many IT directors and chief information officers (CIOs) have spent recent years dealing with IT procurement, and professional services for cyber risk, audit, and compliance purposes. The advent of the cloud has highlighted the need for CIOs to be more conversant with the security implications, and there is evidence that the security posture and strategy of organizations cloud usage are poor.

More recently the evolution of the role of the chief information security officer (CISO) has highlighted the need for more C-suite level management and planning skills. This is increasingly evident in the challenges companies face in management intensive tasks, like supply chain security management, and vendor management. Both these key cybersecurity issues raise the concern of how to wield effective governance of third parties and vendors. Clearly, vendor management needs to be effective in order to best leverage the advantages of outsourcing and not to be disadvantaged when dealing with managed security service providers (MSSPs).

DEVELOPING ORGANIZATION AND MANAGEMENT

The organization and structure of the different aspects that deliver cyber resilience, require the integration of very different components. In their own right, each of the functions for handling a cyber intrusion is complex from identification of a threat through defense and response to an attack and to recovery from an incident. Some functions are more technology-heavy, some more procedure-centric, and some are very reliant on human skills, but all need to contribute to a common aim and effective management of this mission is essential.

When this is considered within the context of the staff that have to collaborate effectively to deliver cyber resilience in a large organization, there are different types of teams, with different perspectives and roles. They may be in different parts of the world, may speak different languages, and some longer established, or with different perceived seniority than others.

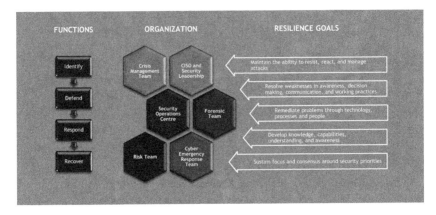

Managing the effective working of six individuals on a complex task is not simple. Likewise, directing six teams to work together, understand each other, and report or communicate effectively when they may only do so infrequently or under duress can often be very problematic.

It is vital for the organization's leadership to establish information resilience goals and to decide exactly what the security principles need to accomplish. It is quite reasonable to expect that not all these objectives will be fully achieved. This illustrates the challenge for any CISO tasked with the mission of achieving cyber resilience, and the challenge of governance and oversight at an organizational level. In many cases, the challenge is too great for CISOs without the necessary experience of organizational senior leadership, and there are instances where a board-level mentor can contribute significantly to facilitating organizational processes. Whether this translates into oversight or not, there are many causes of failure, roadblocks, and reasons for inertia in running a cyber resilience program. The potential roadblocks need to be recognized in advance in order to be avoided.

Irrespective of the goals or stepping stones that need to be achieved along the way, the establishment of the correct collaborative framework, budgetary understanding, and management mechanisms for making decisions and taking action, the CISO needs to ensure continuity of understanding and momentum in pursuit of those goals, while remaining engaged with the business leadership.

Developing and maintaining capability, awareness, and a high state of readiness is very management intensive, and very resource intensive. There are rarely adequate resources to support all parallel initiatives. In most cases the regular assessment and testing are sacrificed. Many firms are relatively unaware of the point-in-time effectiveness of security and defense. This highlights the problems in tackling some of the objectives set out in figure four above. Commonly, addressing weaknesses, developing knowledge, or remediating problems, are certain to be limited when firms do not conduct the requisite type of assessments regularly, to prioritize their efforts.

Building consensus, and sustaining focus and commitment to a proactive approach to cyber defense is always a major challenge. This is one area where resilience is undermined by a tendency to focus on the wrong security priorities, particularly in regard to preparing for lower probability scenarios. This becomes clear when firms are faced with a threat they were not prepared for, and are forced to address the costs and causes of failure. Invariably, much of the responsibility lies with the management and oversight function. Much of the accountability lies with the CISO, and usually the explanation is underfunding of the program overall, or the over-allocation of investment to capability development at the expense of other program workstreams.

DEVELOPING CAPABILITY

When security and resilience fail, the causes can be grouped as lack of capability, lack of maturity, and lack of oversight, the three core themes of this chapter.

When examining a weakness due to inadequate capability, it is straightforward to identify a specific technology that was lacking or a specific process or management task that underperformed. When assessing how resilience may have failed in a particular instance, it is important to recognize that technology in itself can fail to meet expectations. Often the failure occurs in the processes that are supposed to keep that technology effective. For example, a firewall that is not properly configured, or a SIEM that was not fully deployed.

Processes describe how capabilities are to be deployed and maintained, and poor technology performance often stems from poor implementation of processes, procedures, or policies. The example of poor implementation is symptomatic of a lack of maturity in the organization, or simply, weak management of the processes. Failures in oversight can cover a plethora of failings that can be traced back to the functions of management and governance that should ensure the effective maintenance of the overall system. When we look to the real reasons why resilience fails, it can often be simplified to a lack of capability, however it often *should* identify important lacking of maturity such as: how the organization deals with a threat or incident that it had not anticipated, or how seriously it considered the problem to be, and how it functions under pressure of a security breach.

Whether addressing maturity or oversight, a human tendency towards complacency is one of the most toxic forces that can affect resilience posture and its management. Resilience programs therefore require formalized components that will specifically anticipate and counteract this. Developing human capabilities and skills in tandem with investment in cyber defense technology is paramount to accelerating maturity, and must receive adequate attention within the oversight program.

For example, when faced with a serious cyber incident, staff ultimately determine actions based on advanced technological capabilities for detection and response. Together operators and systems need to enable these key skills:

- Recognition: The ability to recognize the problem, differentiate between its symptoms or causes, and recognize the scope of the problem for what it is and what it is likely to be, or what it could be now, or as the problem escalates.
- Interpretation: The ability to correctly interpret what should have been recognized, accurately analyze potentially confusing signals and indicators, make effective use of intelligence, and correlate with reality.
- Decision-making: The ability to take the right decisions, for the right reasons, at the right time, and based on the right evidence and according to the right protocols.
- Taking Action: After decisions are made there are often failures attributed to their actionability. So determining appropriate action needs to ensure that decisions can be actioned fully, correctly, and in a time-sensitive manner.

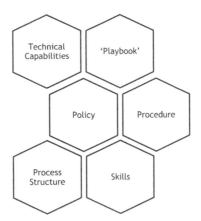

Capability Development

There are several routes to defining a roadmap for capability development. Invariably the end vision is one that the CISO subscribes to which is born of his own experience and exposure to systems and solutions. It can also be limited by the scope of the CISO's experience. Therefore, the recruitment of a new hief can often lead to a change of view, in the same way that most organizations experience a radical shift in perspective immediately after a major breach has heightened their sensitivity to the potential impact, and concentrate attention on a specific aspect of cyber defense, as was seen after distributed denial of service (DDoS) attacks first appeared in the mainstream.

Some routes are therefore independent of a maturity model, and driven by other visions and views of short-to-medium term priorities. Sometimes this is somewhat improvised by a CISO that is trying to engage with business leadership over priorities, and budgets. This make-do approach is problematic when a firm is trying to move forward form simply achieving compliance standard to adopt a more proactive approach of cyber defense. One of the main differences between being compliant and being resilient is that the capabilities required for real defense or effective security are considerably greater and more complex and require more funding.

One of the more effective methods of illustrating the relative cyber defense posture of the organization is a maturity model that describes what different levels of maturity entail and what capabilities they require. This is described further in the next section. The use of a maturity model to define a target end-state and a road map for achieving it, ensures a consistent narrative to the senior management who define budgetary limits, about where the firm stands on its journey towards resilience, and what it needs in order to progress.

After recognizing that resilience is built around being able to defend against a cyber attack, and resolve a major cyber incident or breach, the key aspects of building capability to detect, respond and recover from a breach can be summarized as follows:

- A technological capability-building/sourcing program based around a maturity roadmap and supported by continuous threat intelligence gathering, and regularly updated scenario analysis.
- An optimized and integrated range of technological capabilities for conducting security operations to provide situational awareness, and the ability to interpret and respond.
- Playbooks for core scenarios incorporating technological and human capability into formalized and structured response or survival plans.
- Processes and procedures, aligned to the playbooks and integrating all detection, response and recovery components.
- Relevant planning and documentation associated with the new and integrated detection, response, and recovery capabilities, methods and techniques.
- Training and skills development program specifically around the blue team or cyber defenders, with an appropriate regime of simulations and tests.
- Continuous monitoring of performance and process to improve performance with appropriate evaluation.

DEVELOPING MATURITY

There is huge variability in levels of maturity within any industry, and the degree of commitment to improvement varies widely as well. Enterprises that are serious about resilience undergo a regular maturity assessment which provides a proper framework for asking and answering many difficult questions about what they are capable of, and what they are incapable of.

Besides testing and evaluating capabilities, it highlights what firms need to know about potential causes and characteristics of failure, and what they need to prioritize about improvement, with an emphasis on preparation that is appropriate to their real-world threat profile. The many different aspects presented below in each of five core capabilities need to be examined under appropriate test conditions to identify their limits, and conditions under which they fail.

A maturity model defines a full set of capabilities required for the resilience organization. Segmented into five elements, each of differing degrees of complexity. Many firms still struggle with the first stage capability of being able to **Plan and Prepare** appropriately and effectively. Organizations that are in the process of developing a resilient posture by adopting a cyber defense doctrine will invariably have started to develop the ability to **Identify and Recognize** threats, **Interpret and Analyze** the characteristics of threats in real time, and ultimately the ability to **Respond and Recover** in a manner which minimized the impact to the firm.

Under normal circumstances, firms may be fully capable of performing a task, but under differing conditions of pressure and uncertainty, some simple tasks become complex. The model evaluates whether there is a 'maturity' to the organization's grasp of how to use certain capabilities or skills. A static audit approach may recognize skills and abilities, but under more dynamic assessment conditions, a maturity assessment will do more than provide recognition that a capability exists. It will go further to identify whether the organization and its staff operate with the skills of an advanced user rather than a novice. This provides a very different perspective when compared to an audit of the evidence of deployed technologies, methodologies, plans and policies.

Maturity assessments, and in particular, the technical aspects like red teaming and war games are a way of finding your breaking point or identifying how sophisticated an attack needs to be, or how much escalation can be managed, before organizational resilience fails. Measuring this regularly provides a very tangible view of an enterprise's endurance, or ability to withstand a potentially escalating cyber crisis.

There is prevalent recognition of the futility in being simply reactive to cyber risk, and a broader acceptance of the need to be threat-aware and use risk-informed processes, but this is slow to translate into a truly risk-focused posture. Equally valid are initiatives to draw more attention to proactive approaches, adopting an attacker perspective, being more intelligence-informed, and being more self-aware.

But progress is slow. Compliant firms still struggle to follow basic pre-scripted processes based on limited capability, and risk-focused companies struggle to follow the book so their basics can fail when it really matters. Risk-focused firms are becoming increasingly common in the industrial/commercial world but they lack sophisticated capabilities and take a risk-informed approach to their limited investment in security and resilience. They have well established governance, risk and compliance programs but their cyber defense doctrine is very elementary and built around robust security, with little incident response or forensic capability. These organizations tend to focus their attention on retaining situational awareness, maintaining an optimum level of readiness, and following a proscribed methodology for high probability and high frequency events.

Conversely, cyber defense is rooted in a proactive approach to confronting the cyber problem and being prepared to deal with the many manifestations thereof. Anticipatory organizations are typically within the upper levels of maturity found in commerce are typically among the defense industry and large banking sector. Invariably they have most of the capabilities on the maturity model with a defined defensive doctrine and a very low tolerance for data leakage, with a resilience program to suit. These advanced cybersecurity organizations tend to have well established programs that ensure continuous readiness and an in-depth understanding of their internal and external threat environments, and they tend to focus their resources on maintaining a high level of readiness based on their ability to apply foresight and insight to their security operations, with teams of security professionals.

CYBER DEFENCE MATURITY MODEL

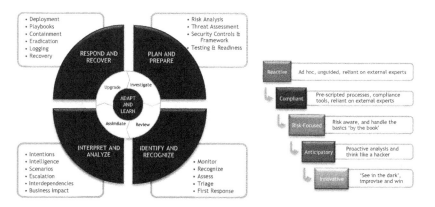

The key aspect to applying a cybersecurity maturity model is that it is a mode of measuring position and progress for any organization, and a yardstick that management can refer to when assessing posture against changes in risk (such as a shift in the threat landscape); and when assessing risk against changes in posture (such as a major change in organizational set-up after acquisition or merger).

For senior management this reference point is central to any process of governance and oversight, whether it is for internal purposes, to ensure continuous improvement and progress towards better cyber security, or is to represent the company's present status, or intent, to relevant external parties, stakeholders and shareholders that need to know how resilient the organization is.

This chapter will address the priorities for the governance and management of a resilience program, a key differentiator is the process by which maturity gains are achieved and managed. This differs in some ways from other implementation and change programs that are based in the main on the implementation and integration of capabilities. A poor grasp of maturity will dilute the objectives to solely achieving advances through the introduction of capability, whereas a solid appreciation of maturity will ensure that governance does not lose sight of the softer but critical aspects that differentiate between a immature defensive team and a mature one. One of the main differentiators is the fifth element: the ability to adapt and learn which is outlined next.

THE FIFTH ELEMENT: ORGANIZATIONAL LEARNING AND CONTINUOUS IMPROVEMENT

The inherent complexity in constructing and maintaining a full-spectrum capability as described in the maturity model, requires a significant program of learning. While capability can be acquired in terms of technology and skilled staff, the integration of the many moving parts into a finely-tuned resilience operation is a long process. The effort to maintain a high level of readiness also requires ongoing learning as the threat landscape is ever-changing.

The ability to adapt and learn is the fifth capability that is required to achieve maturity, and the central element in ensuring that the organizational maturity increases in line with investment. The creation of a continuous monitoring and improvement system requires embedded processes of assessment and evaluation based on appropriate criteria, and techniques for investigation.

Gaps in performance and weaknesses need to be investigated and fully acknowledged as part of a timely review. This may be set periodically or the need may become apparent after a security event. However minor the event that triggers managerial scrutiny, a structured approach to evaluating the strengths and weakness of the organization's process, procedures, and staff can reinforce good performance as much as it establishes focus on aspects that need further attention. This requirement establishes a strong need for objective oversight particularly to ensure that there is a formal assimilation of lessons learned, which is established as organizational knowledge to be applied in the future, for example updating playbooks and circulating updated procedural documents to ensure team-wide awareness. Poor governance will invariably neglect performance gaps at a micro level unless these are under specific observation, to identify the causes and priorities for remediation. Moreover it may fail to trigger the correct actions, and mobilize the required resources required to ensure an effective continuous improvement process which is seen within the context of increasing maturity.

CONTINUOUS LEARNING AND IMPROVEMENT

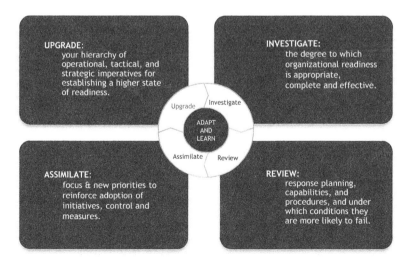

UPGRADE: your hierarchy of operational, tactical, and strategic imperatives for establishing a higher state of readiness.

INVESTIGATE: the degree to which organizational readiness is appropriate, complete and effective.

ASSIMILATE: focus & new priorities to reinforce adoption of initiatives, control and measures.

REVIEW: response planning, capabilities, and procedures, and under which conditions they are more likely to fail.

Upgrade / Investigate

ADAPT AND LEARN

Assimilate / Review

One of the most important functions of oversight and governance is to identify *when* changes are required in the program. Invariably a thorough planning process will establish consensus around a program plan, and with a broad base of involvement in that process there should be a firm organizational commitment to it.

This however, creates a tendency towards myopia among those managers that were involved in the planning process, and it limits the objectivity they bring when assessing whether the program is working and on track. Over-prescriptive planning can be quite rigid, and it can limit and even discourage room to maneuver, when it is recognized that the plan needs to adapt to varying degrees of success or difficulties. This highlights one of the most crucial missions for the oversight function, that it can remain objective, facilitate change, and reinforce initiatives when it is clear that an intervention is required. The greater the level of maturity, the less challenging this function will be, as the process of continuous learning and improvement is an engrained part of the culture in the organization.

Program Principles to Remediate Weaknesses In Methods, Procedures and People

Delivering resilience differs from managing the effectiveness of a security controls framework, which all CISO's typically apply themselves, specifically because of the focus on non-technology issues like staff, skills, and methodologies. The concept of controls is in fact quite absent from *this* aspect of cyber defense implementation so it poses new challenges for CISOs and their senior security officers because of the need to objectively evaluate their own procedures and softer skills of the teams, and individual team members. Invariably some of these tasks ask new questions of the CISO and the security leadership, and it is essential that oversight is provided that will positively mentor and encourage the adoption of new process and practices. In summary -

The organizational ability to learn, and adapt that learning is the most critical to accelerating maturity and capability development.
- Leadership and governance of the continuous-improvement process needs to be formalized and proactive to avoid 'drifting' off course.
- Closing capability gaps in skills, methods and procedures requires closer supervision and scrutiny than when introducing new technology or changes in doctrine, e.g. deception.
- Failures in organizational learning, and the inability to overcome roadblocks in developing maturity tend to indicate poor oversight and organizational commitment.
- A structured program should provide an honest view of capability, and clear, ongoing visibility of readiness.

PART TWO: THE MANAGERIAL PRIORITIES FOR A RESILIENCE PROGRAM

A FRAMEWORK FOR EFFECTIVE PREPARATION

A common reason for poor implementation of programs is poor management, and more urgent or complex programs can be so resource-intensive that insufficient management time and attention is factored into the overall process to ensure the right checks and the right time. The temptation to hurry a process or take shortcuts, even if justified by allocating more budget, is usually at the expense of proper process for monitoring and measuring progress towards the ultimate goal or even intermediate objectives. In order to ensure that a program is set up to succeed, it is important to establish an appropriate framework for managing the process. Essentially this alludes to establishing a framework for oversight as an essential part of preparing for a process of change.

Conceptualizing a program that will improve maturity or build resilience needs to be three dimensional in that it balances what is done, when, and how it is done. Program goals are stated around improving or establishing capability which are defined in six clusters (as outlined in previous section). These are a function of specific decisions regarding a desired end state, and the security strategy for achieving that end state. The process of achieving the programs objectives over time should then be defined as two parallel tracks. One is the series of steps that should be taken on an annual basis as a matter of course. The second is through program workstreams that provide continuous guidance, steering, and governance for the process.

These workstreams often lack formalization, and structure, the absence of which can lead to weaknesses in cyber resilience programs and their failure to deliver the desired objectives. The following sections focus on the characteristics of these workstreams.

- The **monitoring** of status, conditions, and change is about generating knowledge. At any time it is imperative to know the progress and effectiveness of new security measures and initiatives that will become central to establishing a high state of readiness. This program awareness provides managers the control and insight they need to keep the program on track, particularly in respect to developing greater maturity.
- The awareness that this generates should then feed into the **continuous improvement** of capability where it falls short of requirements. Where the monitoring function must be trusted to identify failings and potential causes of failure, the continuous improvement function must

be trusted to identify where and how to prioritize remediation, learning and development.

- The third field of responsibility is the **management** of the overall process based on formalized processes, and relevant artifacts, rather than more *ad hoc* and judgment based evaluation. This encompasses not only the oversight of the aforementioned monitoring and continuous improvement workstreams that are to introduce change to the organization, but also to manage the impact of change within the organization including the expectations, and the interests of internal and external stakeholders that will be affected by changes in different ways. Furthermore the role of program management to provide direction also establishes accountability to the most senior leadership and crisis management teams that are, in effect, the end clients of a cyber resilience program.

The parallel track of key steps (on the left of the diagram below) is one that all three functions provide input into, and receive outputs from, hence the undeniable interdependence of the two parallel tracks. A rolling process of capability and performance assessments should feed into a constantly evolving roadmap for the program and inform the initiatives for remediation. The utility of these steps should be clear to managers that need to monitor progress in developing capability. Thereafter, a series of training exercises should be specifically timetabled to bring together the different capabilities to build expertise and familiarity with plans and their implementation against simulated threats. These steps play a key role is identifying progress to a higher level of maturity. By identifying gaps this way between the theory vs. reality, the main goal of effective oversight is established to ensure the efficacy of the program's measures, and ultimately to momentum towards cyber resilience.

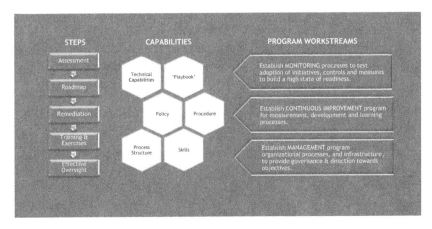

DEVELOPING PROGRAM OBJECTIVES

Ensuring Monitoring

The starting point for the program must be appropriate board endorsement for achieving a target state of resilience. The importance of this being a risk-informed process cannot be understated, and the process of establishing the necessary understanding about the approach to be adopted, and the steps that are required, tends to be long and drawn-out if not translated into the language of board-level risk, and aligned with the priorities of the business as the board views them. Invariably, this requires a considerable investment in time and attention to develop the relevant appreciation and requires buy-in at the highest levels to ensure ongoing support.

The first priority for senior management is to ensure that there is a true view of the firm's situation and it is almost the first test of the oversight function to ensure that this is conducted thoroughly. The bedrock of both tactical and strategic development processes is the integrity of assessment. The core of a well structured program must be the tools and components which will provide structure to rolling evaluations and remediation. Without objective transparency, there will always be gaps in remediation, and hence, vulnerabilities.

Moreover, the monitoring processes, and initiatives for continuous improvement must be driven by regular and targeted assessments to provide for evidence-based evaluation of progress, and a real-world performance review that should be required for oversight functions. The task for senior leadership is to ensure that these principles are accepted and adhered to, while monitoring the organization's changing security posture and its journey towards resilience.

Building consensus around a desired end state is often the more challenging aspect of establishing a program, as the aim needs to be accepted as relevant and achievable within the scope of acceptable resources constraints. Developing effective monitoring of the program must be based on a balanced view of the core objectives. More on this issue has been set out earlier in this chapter. As a specific constraint on the program can be the availability of suitable management resources to lead the program, and provide oversight throughout in parallel to existing pressures and missions, the role of program management and governance will itself be subject to some debate in terms of scope, accountability, authority, and reporting structure. Once this is overcome the role of governance, whether this is performed by singular or group leadership, is to ensure that the right steps are introduced and that the plan for each receives the proper scrutiny and attention.

Ensuring Improvement

The structure of the program must transpose from monitoring onto improvement, because each defines the other. This interdependency should be clear and instinctive, but it still requires oversight to ensure that observations are translating into actions, and remediation leads to appropriate retesting. Setting objectives for improvement needs to be based on three principles discussed below.

Organizational readiness needs to be appropriate to the threat, and complete and effective in combating the threat. These are principles that leadership should be asking continuously of it cyber security principles. In order to achieve improvement it is vital to prioritize what is being targeted, and what performance is being judged against. By defining a hierarchy of priorities as either strategic, operational, and tactical, senior management needs to establish a balance of the criticality of each objective and ensure that the sequencing of steps is most suited to the pace and trajectory of the program over time.

The value of questioning how workflows are being defined and implemented in parallel cannot be understated as it ensures that unexpected gaps, overlaps, and clashes are avoided that could translate into program inefficiencies, and temporary blind spots in effective security. An effective roadmap will not only establish the capabilities that are being introduced, but also the criteria for judging their efficacy, and the tools and metrics that will be used to establish judgments. It is important to differentiate between exercises that are designed for the purpose of learning/training, and tests that are designed for assessment/judgement of progress. It is therefore crucial that the structure of the improvement program deconstructs overall capability into tasks or batches.

This raises the question for managers tasked with program oversight of how to conduct an effective question and query process without exerting inappropriate intrusive pressures on managers that have been tasked with the more tactical aspects of program improvement. The use of metrics and key performance indicators (KPIs) is increasingly common but can be found to be hollow if the process behind their measurement lacks depth, and it is important to identify those that are meaningful.

The progress achieved against the roadmap can be articulated once KPIs are in place, but the softer aspects of improvement like staff skills development, and assessing organizational learning requires more qualitative assessment of improvements and refined processes and not simply based on a review of procedural documentation to identify changes that may reflect an upgrade on last year's approach or playbooks.

Ensuring Day-to-Day Management

The key to managing the resilience program is about knowing where to focus management attention and to what effect. This will vary at different stages of progress through the roadmap, and between building new capability and improving existing capability. One of the main principles of oversight is to ensure that there is clear sight of goals, progress, and weight of emphasis, and how to use that information effectively in support of the implementation.

This visibility is absolutely key to supporting junior managers tasked with implementation, working with external consultants that are brought in to facilitate change, and maintaining understanding about the multi-faceted aspects that are being pursued in parallel and the potential for change and disruption to the program's schedule and budgets.

Junior and middle management face considerable challenges with time-tables for achieving goals and invariably there are unforeseen obstacles to overcome. The need for appropriate management infrastructure is often underestimated, with insufficient management hours allocated, and often lacking representation of the required skills, functions and seniority across risk, security, BCM, and operations. This balance is crucial so as not to establish bias in approach or perspective on the fulfilment of the program and factors affecting its delivery. While the program must be sensitive to operations and the risk calculations of the executive management, it is imperative that the management has a clear vision of what resilience is, and the real world implications beyond the theoretical.

The senior leadership tasked with governance and oversight need to be sensitive to the challenges of operationalizing a resilience program while accepting that they will never have a deep understanding of the details. They also need to sustain the positivity and drive towards the goals established, and ensure that management set-up is seen to be objective and independent of potentially contentious bias in background or function that often contribute to silos in many organizations.

The final point of emphasis for the senior leadership is the underlying need for continuity of reporting and buy-in of all stakeholders in improving the organizations resilience. Maintaining their understanding and support for the program is vital for such long term initiatives, and it is important to represent different interests, reflect fairly the progress and status, and manage the visibility of the program to build confidence in the initiatives being taken. As the ultimate aim is to reduce cyber risk and reinforce the organization's resilience against cyber attack, it is important to constantly refer back to this aim and provide the metrics that describe progress in a form that is understood by all stakeholders.

MONITORING	IMPROVEMENT	MANAGEMENT
STAGE ACTIVITIES		
• Program Objectives • Desired End State View • Embed Evaluative Processes • Regular Testing • Assessment Schedule • Current State of Readiness • On-going Gap Analysis • Operational Priorities	• Program Metrics: Question & Query • Skills Development Program • Reinforce Awareness of Objectives • Establish Progress against Roadmap • Assimilate Learning & Reprioritize	• Reinforce Goals • Confirm Progress • Planning & Accountability • 'Stakeholdership' • Visibility & Reporting
STAGE OBJECTIVES		
• **Investigate:** the degree to which organizational readiness is appropriate, complete and effective. • **Evaluate:** Cyber-defense planning, capabilities, and procedures, and under which conditions they are more likely to fail. • **Test:** adoption of initiatives, control and measures to build confidence in security and a high state of readiness.	• **Define:** a hierarchy of operational, tactical, and strategic imperatives for establishing a higher state of readiness, and the correct resilience posture. • **Upgrade:** structured approach to remediate weaknesses in technology, methods, procedures & people	• **Know:** where to sustain focus & prioritize long-term attention to reinforce posture
STAGE IMPERATIVES		
• To develop organisational awareness, preparedness and resilience according to a roadmap for achieving the target level of maturity. • To establish organisational requirements, and program components for descriptive, operational, and evaluative processes. • Board-level endorsement and sponsorship of program	• To introduce a structured approach to remediate weaknesses in technology, methods, procedures & people. • To establish program components for measurement, development and learning processes necessary for continuous improvement.	• To introduce management infrastructure, and program procedures that will provide direction towards organisational goals.

MANAGING PROGRAM MONITORING

With objectives set, and imperatives in place, the weight of emphasis now falls on effective governance to make sure the program succeeds. This needs to be viewed as a function distinct from the hands-on management of the processes, and it is important to ensure that the oversight of the management does not become involved in day-to-day process and inadvertently encroach on fulfilment at an operational level with excessive review, deliberation, and approvals.

The central tenet of oversight is to be continually asking more strategic or macro questions of the process. So less emphasis is placed on the details of how these processes are being conducted but more attention is given to whether goals are being achieved. This can be split into three distinct areas of questioning.

Questioning Objectives:

Are the program's objectives still relevant?

Once a program is running it should generate a momentum of its own, and one function of oversight is to ensure that this is the case and that it is on course. Maintaining momentum can often translate to ensuring that roadblocks are removed in whatever form they may take. One reason why resistance can be encountered within an organization to different aspects of the program is that the changes and implications can be seen or perceived, to negatively affect operations and operational efficiency, especially among managers that are not associated with the program at all. To these managers there may be little obvious relevance to their department, and the objectives are not relevant to their part of the business. Often, the details of daily operations of the business may change, and they may certainly need to adapt in a way that is less visible to top management or among the leadership that aligns the cyber resilience program's objectives with business overall. This is particularly the case with multinational operations that have different characteristics between different regional or national businesses.

This is especially the case where conglomerates are concerned with a variety of different international businesses or business divisions, and organizational change growth and restructuring is a continuous process. If there are changes in the shape of the business that affect priorities or scope of cyber resilience building, then it is vital to anticipate the implications and be able to steer the program. Invariably this leads to complexity in terms of the realistic timing or sequencing of implementation or initiatives, particularly where different parts of the business have different levels of maturity and capability. This is particularly the case when integrating business with long-established capability, or legacy technology for example. More simply there may be parts of the business that are committed to existing programs with less scope to integrate into a broader corporate program. Alternatively there may be different divisions with very specific priorities, like manufacturing, and production industries with very different automation and process control technology to secure. These scenarios can all pose difficult questions for program management in justifying the pace, direction, and objectives of the resilience program, irrespective of the potential reason.

Questioning Methods:

Are the tools and methods properly deployed?

This is a valid question to ask at every stage of the program as the integrity of the process relies on objective assessment, which in turn relies on the consistent use of the tools to provide comparability. It is often easy to criticize methods for generating results that managers cannot relate to, or do not reflect the complexity of the issue being measured. Many issues can be characterized as not being black or white and some forms of metric can fail to reflect the changes in grey which generate frustration, disillusion, and resistance to the program and its initiatives.

For the purpose of monitoring implementation of the program and the introduction of change the more important issue is that the agreed tools and being used properly, agreed methods are being applied, and consistently. Irrespective of whether some of the results are surprising or as expected, program oversight needs to ensure that the evaluation processes are effective, and this often translates into scrutiny of managers that are tasked, and the processes they are entrusted with. In complex situations this can simply boil down to ensuring schedule and budgetary discipline reflected in the reporting, but this needs to be balanced with ensuring that management tools and methods are being utilized and applied properly. Visibility is a core facet required for effective oversight, and ineffective reporting can negate parallel efforts to manage budgets, resources, and processes which need to be viewed top-down by leadership.

Questioning Judgments:

Are correct judgments being reached?

Beyond validation of the methods, oversight needs to be aware of the outcomes and the evaluations that are being reached, looking for errors in interpretation and potential subjectivity by those that are deriving conclusions and defining appropriate actions.

It is often tempting to sit back and watch the show as various initiatives are introduced with faith in those managers or parties that are leading them. It can be similarly easy to see activity and accept subordinates reporting that all is well. It can be positively exciting when a manager reports that an initiative is ahead of time and budget, and all should require a degree of cross-examination to identify the basis for judgments and assessments. To an experienced senior executive this may be instinctive and common practice, but a common failure of cyber security in general, and program management in particular, is the tendency towards complacency, which can manifest in the unquestioning belief in staff judgments when they present good news that was hoped for.

Conversely, there may be negative judgments or assessments being presented, or reports of challenges that may be inaccurate in identifying reasons for delay or problems. These judgments will naturally draw attention but objective review of the assessment or judgment needs to be applied before conclusions are reached. Resist the tendency to reflect judgments as black or white, or to attribute multiple symptoms to a single cause. The role of program governance is to ensure that processes are not being shortcut or summary judgments reached without proper process. Furthermore, the partly detached and therefore more objective perspective that senior oversight can bring will balance the potential for error and natural bias in managerial assessment. This is especially true where human judgment is based on tools, methods, or processes that are open to misinterpretation, or have potentially significant consequences. Generally speaking, the greater potential consequence for impact of the program overall, the greater the need for scrutiny. While this would be instinctive to most experienced managers, it is also important to recognize the boundaries of expertise and experience of each manager. Then one can appreciate why views and assessments may differ, how to attribute weighting to the differences or factors, and how to guide the program accordingly.

Top 10 Topics for Self-Questioning

1. Are tools and components for monitoring the program all effectively deployed?
2. Have the business objectives changed and require a reassessment of the target level of maturity?
3. Do the program's priorities need to change in line with the business?
4. How effective are program evaluation processes? Have they prompted a review of assumptions?
5. Is progress and implementation being identified objectively?
6. How does top-down view of progress reconcile with the bottom-up view of achievements?
7. Which aspects of the program's progress are surprising you?
8. Where are emerging roadblocks and can you anticipate them?
9. If an evaluation is too subjective, where are decision-makers likely to be erring?
10. Have you articulated the mistakes you do not want to see?

MANAGING PROGRAM IMPROVEMENT

After establishing the essentials of ongoing or continuous monitoring of the organization's situation at any point, primarily aimed at driving the introduction of capabilities, the second work-stream is to manage improvement to ensure they are measured, recognized, achieved and understood. This work-stream aims more directly than others at what I have coined as the fifth element of the cyber maturity model focused on organizational learning based on changes to policy, processes and procedural aspects of security, defense, response, and resilience.

For senior management, continuous improvement is more challenging to provide direction and guidance for as it is somewhat less tangible than working with technology. This raises specific challenges in how improvement is measured and achieved especially when examining improvement in human performance in isolation, or the human performance of process or procedure. It also requires astute judgment about true causes of fault: is it the human or the definition of the task that you want this person to perform?

- Some problems in improvement can be traced to poor training or introduction of change, while others are in the process itself which is not easily or naturally achievable. Specifically, some templated policies, processes and procedures are not easily transferred from one organization to the next for different cultural, or operational reasons even if they are accepted as a best practice, and trying to enforce them without appropriately adapting them to suit will lead to poor rates of adoption.

- A second issue is the *persistence* of a weakness, or evidence of poor improvement, i.e., is this a temporary poor result, or is the inability to improve due to a persistent cause or failing? To contextualize this, managers must also ask whether the adoption expectation (in terms of time) is realistic given the complexity of the change, or degree of learning in relation to the nature of the skill, procedure, or process being targeted.

- A third is the *volatility* of performance, or why early evidence of learning can suddenly be followed by symptoms of lost learning. Managers need to be sensitive to the reasons why learning can be lost, for example because the process of reinforcing new learning, and practicing new procedures may insufficient; or because of changes to key members of staff or team leaders that have exerted a strong influence on others. This can be especially important in small specialist teams, and it highlights the challenge in institutionalizing knowledge and learning so that a loss of personnel does not lead directly to a loss of learning and knowledge retention in critical teams like a security team, incident management and response team or a crisis management team.

These are very real illustrations of the difficulty in measuring improvement achieved, and recognizing the true nature of that learning or change, and whether the learning is retained, and how. Understanding these key aspects of continuous improvement and whether change is happening are essential in order to decide how to respond to the results, reach the correct judgments, and guide the activities required to adjust or refocus planned efforts. There can be clear evidence of new processes and procedures being introduced, and the monitoring of the company posture will regularly assess progress in introducing change. The greater challenge is to identify that the changes lead to the anticipated outcomes, and those outcomes can be articulated as improved security and resilience.

The onus of the oversight function is to ensure that these evaluations are informing the appropriate changes to roadmap/plans, and that appropriate action is taken. It is important to restate that the oversight of the process should not become involved in day-to-day process, and encroach on fulfilment at an operational level, and it is equally important that the taskforce examines improvements from both an outcome-focused perspective and process-centric perspectives. So while reinforcing the importance of the plan and ensuring that the improvement process is effective, it is equally important to ensure that the outcomes are apparent.

Questioning Objectives

Are the program's objectives still relevant?

Roadmaps should be refined on an ongoing basis, and priorities can change in line with the reprioritization of different initiatives. This is specifically relevant when new technical capability is introduced for detection or incident management for example, which should trigger immediate reprioritization of planning and learning associated with procedures and playbooks that reflect the new capability. The greater challenge is to synchronize evaluations across different aspects of the introduction, implementation, and improvement of cyber defense and resilience because of the potential for overlapping priorities and conflicts in priorities. This can happen when managers attempt to introduce some capabilities simultaneously, but cannot effectively orchestrate the training and development programs around the technology, or new doctrine. At this stage the questioning of interim goals particularly on the continuous improvement aspects need to be assessed carefully. Invariably some de-prioritization of improvement goals can be justified while attention is focused on implementation of new tools and methods, but the temptation to do so should be curbed because this can lead to loss of focus on the need for learning and improvement that is required to ensure the efficacy of new technology or procedures that have been introduced. This is a common flaw, whereby the existence of capability is clear for the purpose of an audit, but testing against real world scenarios exposes the lack of organization ability to effectively defend itself, and ultimately to relatively poor resilience gains even after considerable investment. The most common example is the investment in a SIEM without the associated learning around how to use it, and the changes that a SIEM enables the organization to make to its security procedures.

Questioning Methods:

Is implementation and improvement 'happening'?

Some capabilities are less tangible than others, so while the introduction of a technical capability can be clearly viewed, the softer skills and learning associated with it may be much harder to introduce effectively in order to operationalize it. The first aspect is evidence-based measures of improvement that are sufficiently repeatable to be reliable within a margin of error. Here, it is also important that an objective external view of the implementation is in place to determine whether objectives are achievable, and learning and change programs are delivered correctly. The nature of these subprograms can differ considerably between introducing new processes to a security team, implementing new procedures for incident management based on new technology or capability, to security awareness training for high risk individuals, and to preparing for new business continuity scenarios across different teams.

This is complex as it requires a consistent view of the training methods and tools, and a regular feedback loop from both managers and staff about the training, change or delivery of different aspects of this program, as well as understanding the underlying attitudes towards new technology, changes in policy, or resistance to new procedures.

Questioning Judgments:

Are correct judgments being reached?

If there are roadblocks to operationalizing improvements, what is at fault, and should the process be paused to allow for extra or repeated efforts to introduce improvements? The attribution of cause or fault is important and specific to different aspects of the continuous improvement process, and the executives tasked with oversight need to balance outcome-focused vs. process-centric examination. This can be a challenge as the governance function must be distinct from planning and implementation staff who will be much more familiar with the challenges of sustaining improvement. So there is frequent reason for misunderstanding and misinterpretation of explanations to the complex questions of: Are we getting better at this?, How long will it take?, and Why aren't we doing better? when oversight may be non-technical, but the answers are essentially too technical. Nevertheless, a seasoned senior executive will appreciate that implementing improvements according to a plan requires balance between doing the right thing vs. doing things right vs. doing things right now. Sometimes the essence of the role of governance is to work with the CISO to make sure that he or she is getting that balance right and that balance is manageable.

Asking distinct questions:

a. Is the roadmap/plan still fit for purpose?
b. Is implementation in sync with planning?
c. Have objectives changed post-introduction of new capability?
d. Have priorities changed in line with most recent evaluation?
e. Is improvement being operationalized?
f. How does improvement in security measures, reconcile with resilience?
g. Is learning really happening?

MANAGEMENT OVERSIGHT

The crux of a resilience program and its success, is its management at both an operational level and a strategic level. The complexity of the program in its many facets can pull the strategic management functions or oversight too far towards a process that resembles simple risk management. While this is a natural default position, and these functions need to be performed they should not *characterize* the governance of the program. Although it is inevitable that governance will be perceived as detached from the daily realities of the program, and unable to understand the intricacies of some parts. They should not be cause for a schism between those overseeing the program and those tasked with delivering daily improvements in maturity and resilience.

Furthermore, the conceptual distance of the strategic managers from the daily challenges and hurdles that different lower-to-middle managers face in implementation can easily create a situation in which the oversight is seen as a function that polices the lower management of the program components to delivery to schedule and budget. These are dangerous tendencies that can obscure the real purpose of oversight. It is less to provide a form of governance that drives compliance to a set of program parameters, but more to ensure success of the program in delivering its goals in its most holistic sense, and facilitate the processes that enable the program. For governance to offer real benefits and be able to value its contribution to the program's success, it needs to ensure the management of people, processes and problems is positive, coordinated, and mission-focused with a clear sense of purpose.

The role of oversight is very much two-directional in its accountability. It is held accountable for the success of the program and therefore most of its focus is to ensure that process and content are both complete and effective. It also has a very important role in reflecting the progress and value of the program to others among the highest echelons of the organization, and to stakeholders outside the organization. Representing the progress of the organization in pursuit of a more resilient posture, both within the organization and to the markets, industry peers, and regulators, is important to sustaining the backing, goodwill and faith of executives who are not associated with the program directly, but have supported its introduction. It also builds the reputation of the organization with its customers, partners and suppliers which is typically one of the main arguments for justifying the program.

The oversight function also owes a responsibility to the managers that are tasked with delivering the program. This speaks to the role of senior management in assisting the team in circumnavigating the roadblocks that can hinder progress, and to facilitate the resources, relationships and understanding that needs to be fostered across different divisions, and units to move the program forward. While a CISO or any executive responsible for a complex technology program is being increasingly challenged to be an ambassador for the value that the program delivers, the delivery is built upon the diverse range of skills and knowledge that comprises cyber defense and digital resilience in the twenty-first century, and a seasoned executive will recognize the importance of nurturing the teamwork and collaborative attitudes that the program requires.

An important factor to the cohesion of the team is creating the sense throughout the different levels of staff that oversight is there to help and not to judge. Hence the role of the executive leadership as the impartial cheerleader, is as important when presenting achievements to the board as it is when reflecting achievement back to the security team. Providing a strategic view to all parties helps to maintain their perspective on progress and achievement. Having the right balance of expertise in a management or governance taskforce is important as it can rarely be effectively driven operationally by a single cyber tsar alone. The CISO role requires continuous visibility at board level, and the configuration of the program's oversight must properly accommodate the inputs and agenda of the CIO in the overall picture.

The key to achieving effective oversight and delivering value to the process is perspective. Invariably the source of weak resilience-building programs can be traced back to organizational and managerial faults. Ultimately the faults are often determined to result from the resilience concept not being completely understood, never fully supported or properly funded, and therefore resilience was never properly established. It should come as no surprise in such circumstances that resilience is not planned or developed properly, and even if it has, it is not fully implemented.

Many of the main causes of security failure can be traced to attitudinal aspects of senior managers or a poorly calibrated perspective on the nature of the problem. Research continues to show that board-level consideration of the cyber threat is still deficient. This recognition brings the issue of developing an effective oversight program into sharp focus. In order to maintain integrity, independence and objectivity must be seen, in order to sustain a more macro perspective in order to actively avoid flaws in security thinking.

This chapter has outlined a process for establishing a real-world view of company security posture and identifying the steps for introducing capability and increasing the levels of maturity to suit. The misalignment of strategy can result in the pursuit of the wrong objectives that are inappropriate to the reality of the risk that organization faces, and it can lead to a poorly defined program for security and resilience building. This raises the question of what errors commonly lead to wrongly defining strategy.

Common failures can be traced back to poor or amateur analysis, often based on outdated assumptions about the nature of modern threats. The mistaken perception of the organization's capabilities, and a poor appreciation for the impact of a breech also contribute to failures. This all tends to lead to an under-justification for the information security budget, and therefore to the limited investment in capabilities. Some of the failure to conduct proper risk analysis can be based on outdated analytical methods, simplistic risk models, and human error. Human error often incorporates a degree of analytical bias when not performed by an external third party, and an inability to properly assess risk against the probabilities of attack or an accurate calculation of the risk based on various impact scenarios. Whether this is due to ignorance or complacency is immaterial when expertise is available to conduct proper risk assessments.

A further reason for error in organizational security is that some managers still adhere to outdated concepts of what should or could be introduced. Many firms still rely on what are essentially reactive approaches to the cyber problem and based on outdated concepts of information security which demonstrate a lack of understanding. More often these should be seen as symptoms of delusion when it comes to the cyber problem. Typically the belief that being compliant is sufficient to demonstrate that the organization had taken sufficient steps to secure its data and systems has been disproved endlessly with attack beats audit headlines even among large enterprises.

The increasing belief that cyber insurance now offers a route for executives to demonstrate that they have addressed risk is also worrying, but this is often a result of the fact that executives cannot handle the complexity of understanding or managing cyber defense, or working with the uncertainty and unknowns that are inherent to interpreting and anticipating the constantly evolving cyber problem. This touches upon more complicated and common challenges in managing cyber risk, such as the lack of intelligence on the issue and threat, and the belief that there will be some form of forewarning. This is exacerbated when managers focus their attention on technological solutions that claim to defend against known threats already common, without really appreciating how the threats could evolve, and underestimating the persistence and sophistication of the adversary and his tools.

Finally, the various interdependent reasons for poor decision-taking about cyber resilience is often hidden behind an explanation of the organization having taken a risk-informed decision on cyber defense, whereby managers claim to have assessed the risk and decided to accept the risk, when in fact they have chosen to disregard the risk. When their assessment has been conducted on flawed analysis of threat and impact, the assertion that decisions on budgets and programs being based on an assessment of risk are of no value. In fact, they essentially describe the fact that managers felt that cyber attack was low probability, and low impact and therefore would not justify budget for mitigation in the context of other competing investment priorities. Whether this is delusion, reckless, or ignorant, it displays poor insight and weak leadership at the highest levels of management that are tasked with ensuring the healthy growth of the organization, while ignoring one of the most toxic and complex threats to its future and reputation.

Oversight must be characterized by "managing through questioning" and it is asking the right questions, at the right time, that is critical. If errors are made and it transpires that no-one thought to question a decision, then fault will be found with the governance of the program as ineffective. Even if the onus in a large program is to ensure that oversight is prompting *other* program managers to ask the right questions, this is an alternative illustration of the same principle. Oversight is not established to manage, but to ensure effective management, and by maintaining awareness about the causes of error and failure, management can continually ask the more challenging questions of itself and the individual steps of the program.

The most valuable reflection on the many potential causes of failure, most of which are forms of management and planning failure, is to regularly articulate the errors that you don't want to make. For a CISO this could start with "today I do not want to have to report a breach to the board." Simplistic as it may be, it should trigger a simulated process in the mind of the manager of why that might happen and where the fault lies. Questioning regularly of the program's objectives is less productive than questioning the plan to make it a reality. Is the plan still appropriate and relevant? Have the circumstances changed significantly? Is the plan complete, and being pursued completely? Are managers managing? Is technology effective? Are processes happening? These are all basics that a CISO can become overwhelmed with compared to a more fundamental one of "What am I missing?".

One challenge, which is central to effective oversight is to translate the answers that these questions promptly. Particularly when questioning assumptions upon which the program is built, or where the answers are based on outcomes which need to be traced back to causes. Some of the answers may be indistinct, hard to articulate, or conceptual, while others may be easy to dismiss or ignore. In these cases there is the potential for management error, and specific steps should be taken to ensure that these tough answers are explored fully. One key throughout the management chain is to know where to find guidance.

Program oversight must provide a channel for managers to seek guidance without prejudice and fear of judgment. Even the most senior and executive leaders should be encouraged to seek external expertise whenever required, as it is rare that all the experience required to implement and manage a complex program will reside within the organization. This type of external assistance can be provided by a CISO-as-a-service model through a trusted cyber defense consulting company that should be retained and engaged throughout the process for different professional advisory and technical services to support the program. One of the more important characteristics of program governance is to maintain an independent view of the program and, where required, be able to enlist external third party experts to reinforce or validate that view.

Finally, it is important to restate the need for oversight to remain strategic, particularly when there is a natural tendency for managers to revert to more tactical views based on their immediate role and tactical responsibilities, or to default back to fields of expertise and knowledge that are longer established, whether this is technical or not. Maintaining a balance of focus between internalities and externalities is a common challenge when reflecting on an organization's weaknesses with older attitudes focused on vulnerabilities and controls needing to be usurped by a more relevant concept to cyber defense that requires greater situational awareness, and scenario-based preparation with threat intelligence at its core. To remain strategic, the ultimate goal of effectively reducing the organizational risk of a breach by establishing incident readiness and ensuring an effective response needs to be restated constantly when engaging with the complexities and intricacies of operational challenges.

Transmitting a strategic view throughout the organization and supporting a CISO that is leading a resilience program must reiterate that the development and management of effective cyber defense and resilience is an ongoing process and effective management cannot be performed on a strategic, operational and tactical level without a balance of security, risk, technology and business understanding across the management taskforce.

Appendix A

UNCLASSIFIED

DEPARTMENT OF DEFENSE
DEFENSE SCIENCE BOARD

Task Force on

Cyber as a Strategic Capability

Executive Summary

June 2018

CLEARED FOR OPEN PUBLICATION
March 27, 2018
DEPARTMENT OF DEFENSE
OFFICE OF PREPUBLICATION AND SECURITY REVIEW

OFFICE OF THE UNDER SECRETARY OF DEFENSE FOR RESEARCH AND ENGINEERING
WASHINGTON, D.C. 20301-3140

UNCLASSIFIED

DEFENSE SCIENCE
BOARD

OFFICE OF THE SECRETARY OF DEFENSE
3140 DEFENSE PENTAGON
WASHINGTON DC 20301-3140

MEMORANDUM FOR THE UNDER SECRETARY OF DEFENSE FOR RESEARCH
AND ENGINEERING

SUBJECT: Final Report of the Defense Science Board (DSB) Task Force on Cyber as
a Strategic Capability – Executive Summary

I am pleased to forward the final report executive summary of the Defense Science Board Task Force on Cyber as a Strategic Capability, co-chaired by Mr. Chris Inglis and Mr. James Gosler.

This study is one in a long line of cyber-related studies, but it is the first to specifically address how cyber capabilities can and should be used to pursue strategic objectives and protect strategic interests. The United States is currently years behind its rivals in cyberspace, both conceptually and operationally. The findings of this study illuminate the scope of the problem. The recommendations proposed in this report will, if implemented, create the necessary conditions for the Department of Defense to possess cyber as a strategic capability.

The asymmetry between the United States and its rivals in the cyber domain contributes to escalation and leaves the United States increasingly vulnerable to theft, sabotage, espionage, and subversion. Remedying this strategic inadequacy must be a priority for DoD military and civilian leadership over the coming years.

I fully endorse all of the Task Force's recommendations contained in this report, and urge their careful consideration and soonest adoption.

Craig Fields
Chairman, Defense Science Board

Attachment:
As stated

THIS PAGE LEFT INTENTIONALLY BLANK

OFFICE OF THE SECRETARY OF DEFENSE
3140 DEFENSE PENTAGON
WASHINGTON DC 20301-3140

MEMORANDUM FOR THE CHAIRMAN, DEFENSE SCIENCE BOARD

SUBJECT: Final Report of the Defense Science Board (DSB) Task Force on Cyber as a Strategic Capability – Executive Summary

The final report executive summary of the DSB Task Force on Cyber as a Strategic Capability is attached.

The Cyber as a Strategic Capability Task Force examined the threats and opportunities posed by the employment of cyber capabilities to pursue strategic objectives. Previous DSB studies have addressed cyber vulnerabilities to specific systems and the strengthening of deterrence against cyber attacks; however, they did not examine the strategic-level implications of information operations (IO) and information warfare (IW) pursued by U.S. adversaries, nor did they consider how the United States might benefit from using cyber capabilities to achieve strategic effects and outcomes. Over the course of the year-long study, the Task Force absorbed multiple briefings from a wide array of experts and practitioners. The findings and recommendations of the Task Force are detailed in this report.

The Task Force determined that the Department of Defense must move beyond tactical applications for cyber and realize cyber as a strategic capability. To accomplish this, the USG and DoD need to revamp cyber strategy, to ensure we are not self-limiting or focused on only tactical outcomes. The adoption of a comprehensive cyber strategy oriented towards strategic effects and outcomes is essential for changing the current culture that often slows down or halts cyber options.

Stronger defenses in both the public and private sectors will be necessary to ensure offensive options are routinely considered as part of the trade space. The DoD must view cyber offense and defense as interdependent.

Cyber operators will need more experience in actually undertaking cyber operations and greater readiness before an effective and credible strategic cyber capability is achieved. At present, cyber operators do not get the exposure they need to make them proficient at their craft. Additional training can help, but there is no substitute for actual contact in the field. Allowing cyber operators to "see action" will also help stem the brain drain from the government to the private sector as cyber operators take their training they receive from the USG and seek more lucrative opportunities elsewhere.

The DoD must integrate its cyber strategy with the rest of the USG, creating a whole-of-nation approach that will align all factions of the USG with the same strategic goals. This includes closer cooperation and integration with the private sector and the defense contractors who own a large share of critical infrastructure and perform important functions for the government.

Lastly, the current policies that guide and govern cyber operations must be revised to incentivize the development of desired skills and the execution of effective cyber actions that promote U.S. strategic objectives. The authorization practices of cyber action currently impede (or at least this is the perception among practitioners) the USG's ability to execute cyber operations in a useful timeframe or manner. The United States will need to align our policies to reflect the constant contact nature of cyberspace.

If the DoD fails to harness cyber as a strategic capability, the United States will not be able to maintain its current global posture. The U.S. homeland and the military will be left unacceptably vulnerable to adversary coercion and meddling. It is our sincere hope that the recommendations provided in this report are implemented with the seriousness of purpose that they deserve.

Mr. Chris Inglis
Co-Chair

Mr. James Gosler
Co-Chair

DEPARTMENT OF DEFENSE | DEFENSE SCIENCE BOARD

Table of Contents

THIS PAGE LEFT INTENTIONALLY BLANK

DSB Task Force on Cyber as a Strategic Capability
Executive Summary

During the writing of this report, Dr. James Babcock, a distinguished member of this Task Force, passed away. The members would like to dedicate this report in Jim's memory. His selfless service to our Nation spanned many decades and his contributions were of high impact. His friendship and wise counsel will be deeply missed. He was a truly great American.

Introduction

The Defense Science Board (DSB) Task Force on Cyber as a Strategic Capability was established to assess how cyber capabilities are being used by U.S. competitors and adversaries to achieve strategic effects, and provide recommendations for how the United States can develop and employ a strategic cyber capability of our own. While the United States retains significant advantages in most military domains, the United States has fallen behind its competitors in the cyber domain, both conceptually and operationally. The threat that adversary nations and non-state actors pose is not a hypothetical one – the United States has witnessed the effectiveness of strategic cyber operations, both against other countries and against the United States itself, on multiple occasions. Given the degree to which U.S. civilian and military infrastructure depend on cyber-enabled technologies, U.S. risks in the cyber domain present a serious and growing challenge to the Nation's ability to defend itself at home and advance its interests abroad.

The DSB report on Cyber as a Strategic Capability concludes that U.S. strategic competitors and other states possess effective strategic cyber capabilities and doctrine. These may, in certain scenarios, stress U.S. ability to deter adversary cyber aggression. The study, therefore, examines the laws, governance structures, and culture that impair the United States from fully possessing strategic cyber capabilities. The United States must act quickly to enable strategic cyber as an option in the spectrum of effects. Doing so will help ensure the United States maintains its current global posture and the U.S. homeland is protected against adversary blackmail and aggression.

Scope of Study

From October 2016 to September 2017, the Task Force held monthly meetings to deliberate and receive briefings about the cyber threat landscape. Experts and practitioners from a wide array of backgrounds, including the DoD, the Intelligence Community, other U.S. government agencies, think tanks, academia, and the private sector shared their insights and information.

The breadth of knowledge and expertise shared with the Task Force throughout the study ensured that the Task Force made its findings based upon the most complete and accurate information available. Those findings, and their associated recommendations, are detailed in the Task Force's classified report. The Task Force believes that if these recommendations are acted upon, the United States will be able to leverage cyberspace to accomplish strategic objectives, defend U.S.

vital interests dependent upon digital infrastructure (i.e., cyberspace), and defend against adversary actions in cyberspace.

A classified full version of the report on Cyber as a Strategic Capability can be obtained through the DSB office.

Findings and Recommendations

The Task Force deliberations resulted in the following five overarching findings.

Finding 1: **Current cyber strategy is stalled, self-limiting, and focused on tactical outcomes. The DoD must build and adopt a comprehensive cyber strategy.**

Finding 2: **Defense is a necessary foundation for offense. Effective offensive cyber capability depends on defensive assurance and resilience of key military and homeland systems.**

Finding 3: **Cyber forces, including leadership, require more experience and readiness. Sustained experience in operations is essential to readiness of U.S. cyber capability.**

Finding 4: **The DoD must integrate cyber into a whole-of-government approach. Cyber capabilities developed by DoD must be integrated into a whole-of-government approach, and integrated with private sector and coalition efforts to most effectively defend our collective interests.**

Finding 5: **Current policies often thwart cyber capability. Policy guidance is both essential and currently at odds with effective use of cyber capabilities.**

Based on these findings, the Task Force has put forward the following recommendations for adoption by the DoD.

Recommendation 1:
- The Secretary of Defense direct the Commander of U.S. Cyber Command (USCYBERCOM), working with the Assistant Secretary of Defense for Homeland Defense and Global Security, to develop a comprehensive cyber strategy to be widely adopted and operationalized. This strategy will contain the following components:

    - *Tactics* that are actionable, reliable, and precise on short notice (Commander USCYBERCOM action);

    - *Strategic effects* as measured by direct and timely impact to digital systems of interest (Commander USCYBERCOM action); and

    - *Strategic outcomes* as measured in terms of the advancement of U.S. objectives (Secretary of Defense articulation through the interagency).

Recommendation 2:

- The Secretary of Defense and the Chairman of the Joint Chiefs of Staff, working with the Under Secretary of Defense for Intelligence and the Under Secretary of Defense for Policy, direct the Combatant Commanders, working with the Under Secretary of Defense for Intelligence, to compile a prioritized list of targets that can be held at risk with cyber capabilities.

Recommendation 3:

- The Secretary of Defense, through the National Security Council, working with the Department of Homeland Security's Assistant Secretary for Cybersecurity and Communications, direct the Commander USCYBERCOM lead and expand the DoD support to the protection of private sector and critical infrastructure in advance of contingency and crisis:

  - promote DoD-sponsored institutions to share unclassified/classified situational awareness information that informs DoD actions in the conduct of its authorized missions;

  - deem DoD-derived vulnerability information of private sector infrastructure shareable to the appropriate private sector entities;

  - deem DoD-derived threat information (e.g., adversarial targeting information) shareable to the appropriate cross-U.S. and private sector entities (important information should not be held close by just a few and unavailable to those who need it most); and

  - critical infrastructure providers should be offered direct monitoring services and tools by DoD assets.

Recommendation 4:

- The Secretary of Defense direct the National Security Agency to establish an independent Strategic Cyber Security Program to perform cyber red teaming on DoD critical systems and critical infrastructure. This recommendation is consistent with *Recommendation 2.2* of the DSB Task Force Report on Cyber Deterrence.

  - The Strategic Cyber Security Program analysis should include both current critical systems as well as future acquisitions before the DoD invests in/employs new capabilities.

  - The Secretary of Defense should receive quarterly updates on identified challenges, plans, and progress.

Recommendation 5:

- The Commander USCYBERCOM direct and ensure development of a portfolio of cyber military capabilities/effects, focused on adversary military targets, which:

  – includes the development of infrastructure and tools to support the Cyber Mission Forces;

  – ensures operational experience and an exquisitely skilled workforce; and

  – creates agility to respond to dynamic situations/opportunities.

Recommendation 6:

- The Commander USCYBERCOM develop a deliberate plan and acquisition strategy that leverages existing infrastructure and identifies where new infrastructure and tools are required.

Recommendation 7:

- The Commander USCYBERCOM, with the advocacy of the Secretary of Defense within the National Security Council, develop a plan for joint training and exercises—and ultimate operations—with and alongside other U.S. organizations, operating as joint teams.

  – Operating deliberately "joint," not on an ad hoc basis, will improve effectiveness and efficiency.

Recommendation 8:

- The Secretary of Defense direct the Chiefs of Staff of the Army and the Air Force, the Chief of Naval Operations, and the Commandant of the Marine Corps to direct their personnel staffs (i.e., the "1s") to treat the cyber mission career field as a national security priority, where promotion boards understand the cyber mission as a priority and facilitate recruitment, retention, and career-long professional development in cyber expertise.

Recommendation 9:

- The Commander USCYBERCOM establish and expand professional military education opportunities, at all levels, to allow military personnel to work in cyber-related private sector positions. Offer greater commercial exchange opportunities to allow both military and civilian personnel "commercial tours" to improve skills and operational understanding.

Recommendation 10:

- The Secretary of Defense lead, through the National Security Council, the creation of a coordination and collaboration authority or entity that coordinates national cyber priorities and private-public collaboration across the spectrum of peacetime, contingency, and crisis:

DEPARTMENT OF DEFENSE | DEFENSE SCIENCE BOARD

- USCYBERCOM should play a key and unique role within the proposed entity;

- an ultimate goal must be to integrate the private sector/industry into this collaborative enterprise; and

- UK and Israeli cyber entities can serve as models for U.S. efforts to build private-public sector collaboration, yielding mutually supporting collaboration amongst government, industry, and academia in the design, operation, and defense of U.S. critical infrastructure.

Recommendation 11:

- The Under Secretary of Defense for Policy, in coordination with the Director of National Intelligence, the Department of Homeland Security's Assistant Secretary for the Office of Cybersecurity and Communications, counterparts in the Department of Justice, the Chairman of the Joint Chiefs of Staff, and the Commander USCYBERCOM, lead the effort within the National Security Council to codify new policy and establish a new U.S. policy directive.

  - This new policy framework would replace existing Presidential Policy Directives 20 and 41 guidance and provide guidance on the use of cyber capabilities that acknowledges we are always at some level of conflict or competition in cyberspace. The framework would clearly address the DoD's role in protecting critical infrastructure (especially in those cases where military missions are dependent), identifying actions DoD may take under standing rules of engagement, and ensure decision making is streamlined and, where possible, delegated to Commander USCYBERCOM.

  - Furthermore, a new operations approval framework should be developed to incorporate the concept of a standing small cadre of National Security Council and interagency "approvers" to streamline decision making around both offensive and defensive cyber operations abroad. This cadre should utilize specific techniques to proactively gather and manage policy precedents; the current approval process is too long and bureaucratic.

Recommendation 12:

- The Secretary of Defense authorize USCYBERCOM leadership to engage early with the interagency to brainstorm proposals before options or proposals reach the Principals Committee or the Deputies Committee or the level within the interagency. Nothing is prohibiting this action from taking place now, except culture.

Recommendation 13:

- The Director of the Office of Net Assessment in the Office of the Secretary of Defense, in coordination with the Under Secretary of Defense for Policy, the Director of National Intelligence, the Chairman of the Joint Chiefs of Staff, and the Commander USCYBERCOM, establish a continuous strategic net assessment process to support U.S. campaign planning against strategic competitors, adversaries, and rogue regimes. This process should leverage the Intelligence Community, industry, and allied partner capabilities and incorporate persistent red team assessment activity for measuring our effectiveness in cyberspace.

Recommendation 14:
- The Deputy Secretary of Defense work with counterparts at the Department of Homeland Security and the Office of the Director of National Intelligence to expand the scope of the Enduring Security Framework to better promote private sector collaboration for protecting and promoting national interests in cyberspace.

  - This expanded Enduring Security Framework charter should include representatives from other critical infrastructure sectors such as energy, telecommunications, and transportation where defense and national security have clear dependencies and where threats from competitors and adversaries can be reasonably anticipated, if not already observed.

  - This expanded charter should also take into account the evolution of industry partner roles to support the synchronized U.S. campaign planning, standards development, and information sharing.

Recommendation 15:
- The Secretary of Defense (Office of General Counsel), in coordination with the Under Secretary of Defense for Policy, the responsible leadership in the Department of Homeland Security, Department of Justice, the Joint Staff, and USCYBERCOM, review existing statutes governing DoD and U.S. action in cyberspace (e.g., Electronic Communications Privacy Act and Computer Fraud and Abuse Act), and update or draft replacement language to enable continuous offensive and defensive actions for protecting and promoting national interests in cyberspace.

  - Specifically, this task should include drafting legal statutes for enabling anticipatory defense, active defense, and other countermeasures in cyberspace in accordance with national and international law, and providing liability protection and other legal incentives for robust private sector participation to support national interests in cyberspace.

Recommendation 16:
- The Under Secretary of Defense for Policy, in coordination with counterparts in the Departments of State, Commerce, and Homeland Security, lead bilateral and multilateral activities to support the development and operation of an International Cyber Stability Board of like-minded nations and industry partners for the purpose of protecting cross-border critical infrastructure, creating common standards, and enabling coalition campaigning.

Appendix A: Terms of Reference

THE UNDER SECRETARY OF DEFENSE
3010 DEFENSE PENTAGON
WASHINGTON, DC 20301-3010

ACQUISITION,
TECHNOLOGY,
AND LOGISTICS

JUL 1 5 2016

MEMORANDUM FOR CHAIRMAN, DEFENSE SCIENCE BOARD

SUBJECT: Terms of Reference – Defense Science Board Task Force on Cyber as a Strategic Capability

Over the past several years, numerous cyber-related studies have been commissioned to identify the national security issues resulting from the confluence of our staggering dependence on Information Technology and the corresponding exploitable vulnerabilities of the technology. The Defense Science Board (DSB) Task Force (TF) on "Resilient Military Systems and the Advanced Cyber Threat," the Naval Studies Board Committee on "A Review of U. S. Navy Cyber Defense Capabilities," and the DSB TF on "Cyber Deterrence" are three examples of the more recent efforts. The combination of these studies, various DoD Red Team exercises, and recent aggressive/impactful adversarial operations have significantly raised senior level awareness and concern relative to our defensive shortcomings.

While the tactical benefits and challenges of offensive cyber capabilities and operations are understood, how they could provide support to strategic objectives is inadequately characterized. The role of full-spectrum cyberspace operations in supporting shaping, deterrence, constrained military objectives, and full-scale conflict is not adequately appreciated or understood. It is the principal objective of this TF to investigate the opportunities for, and limitations of, offensive cyber capabilities in support of overall U.S. strategy and provide actionable recommendations to enhance those capabilities. In particular, the TF should address:

- Within conventional military operations, the U.S. targeting process for kinetic engagements considers two categories of targets within relatively short and predictable timelines— deliberate (which normally supports future operations planning) and dynamic (which supports current operations planning). How can this construct be applied to delivery cyber effects and as part of integrated or stand-alone capabilities? How may the United States identify areas where a cyber capability provides a unique advantage in the targeting process that occurs early enough in the planning process to inform requirements and capability development?

- To what extent, and under what conditions, can offensive cyber capabilities rise to the level of a "Strategic Capability"? What are the technical or policy limitations on the development of strategic cyber capabilities, and how can they be overcome or, conversely, imposed?

- Related, what intelligence tools and production requirements will be needed to support both deliberate and dynamic targeting for cyber offensive capabilities and to sustain the utility of those capabilities over time?

DEPARTMENT OF DEFENSE | DEFENSE SCIENCE BOARD

- Knowledge of, and experiences with, a wide-range of U.S. kinetic weapons allows for holding at risk a very diverse set of physical targets that, if then engaged, likely result in predictable effects. How can we develop similar analyses of anticipated effects resulting from the use of current or future cyber capabilities? Based on this review, in what areas should the United States be investing to increase its offensive capabilities and assess forecasted effects? To what degree can the unintended consequences and collateral damage be estimated and managed?

- In any military campaign, having a wide range of effects against targets is desirable. While the cyber domain provides a broad spectrum of potential effects, the ability to develop and deliver certain effects requires great specificity, which increases the perishable risk to the capability if or once revealed. What measures can be taken to maintain capability effectiveness once it has been employed and its effects revealed?

- Given the likely need to specifically tailor cyber capabilities to achieve strategic effects, how should the United States pursue development of the capabilities? What protections should apply, and how should they be tested?

- Identify other issues/challenges that should be addressed in order for offensive cyber capabilities to be effectively integrated in support of U.S. strategy.

I will sponsor the study. Brigadier General Chris Inglis and Mr. James Gosler will serve as Co-chairmen of the study. Rear Admiral T.J. White, U.S. Navy, will serve as the Executive Secretary, along with a second, yet-to-be-named, Executive Secretary. Captain Hugh (Mike) Flanagan, U.S. Navy, will serve as the DSB Secretariat Representative.

The task force members are granted access to those Department of Defense officials and data necessary for the appropriate conduct of their study. The Under Secretary of Defense for Acquisition, Technology, and Logistics will serve as the DoD decision-maker for the matter under consideration and will coordinate decision-making as appropriate with the other stakeholders identified by the study's findings and recommendations. The nominal start date of the study period will be within 3 months of signing this Terms of Reference, and the study period will be between 9 to 12 months. The final report will be completed within 6 months from the end of the study period. Extensions for unforeseen circumstances will be handled accordingly.

The study will operate in accordance with the provisions of Public Law 92-463, the "Federal Advisory Committee Act," and DoD Directive 5105.04, the "DoD Federal Advisory Committee Management Program." It is not anticipated that this study will need to go into any "particular matters" within the meaning of title 18, United States Code, section 208, nor will it cause any member to be placed in the position of action as a procurement official.

Frank Kendall

Appendix B: Task Force Membership

Chairs

Mr. Chris Inglis
U.S. Naval Academy

Mr. James Gosler
JHU Applied Physics Laboratory

Members

Dr. James Babcock
Federal Data Systems

Mr. Robert Butler
Cyber Strategies, LLC

Dr. Donald Duncan
JHU Applied Physics Laboratory

Mr. Daniel Ennis
UMD Global Cyber Initiative

Dr. Joe Keogh
Booz Allen Hamilton

Dr. John Manferdelli
Google

Dr. Joseph Markowitz
Private Consultant

Hon. Judith Miller
Private Consultant

Mr. Robert Nesbit
Private Consultant

LtGen John Sattler, USMC (Ret.)
Private Consultant

Ms. Teresa Shea
In-Q-Tel

Dr. Thomas S. Walcott
USCYBERCOM

Ms. Leigh Warner
Private Consultant

Mr. Glenn "Rick" Wilson
Private Consultant

Maj Gen Brett Williams, USAF (Ret.)
IronNet Cybersecurity, Inc.

Government Advisors

Ms. Katherine Charlet
OUSD(P)

Mr. Mark Elliott
OUSD(I)

Mr. Robert Joyce
National Security Council

Mr. Eric Parker
OUSD(I)

Mr. Shawn Turskey
USCYBERCOM

Executive Secretaries

RADM T.J. White, USN
USCYBERCOM

Col Eduardo Monarez, USAF
USCYBERCOM

Defense Science Board Secretariat

Dr. Craig Fields
DSB Chairman

Mr. Edward Gliot
DSB Executive Director

Dr. Eric Evans
DSB Vice Chairman

CAPT Jeff Nowak
U.S. Navy

Study Support

Ms. Brenda Poole
SAIC

Ms. Juliet Fielding
SAIC

Appendix C: Briefings Received

05–06 October 2016 Meeting

OSD Policy Perspective
Ms. Katherine Charlet, OUSD Policy

Perspective on USCYBERCOM Capabilities
and Modalities
Dr. Stephen Orr IV, U.S. Naval Academy

NSA Tailored Access Operations (TAO)
Discussion
Mr. Robert Joyce, National Security Agency

USCYBERCOM Perspective and Discussion
RADM T.J. White, USN, USCYBERCOM

30 Nov–01 Dec 2016 Meeting

Operational Strategy
*Dr. Richard Harknett, USCYBERCOM and
National Security Agency*

Joint Intelligence Operations Center,
USCYBERCOM
CAPT Mike Studeman, USN, USCYBERCOM

Operation GLOWINGSYMPHONY
*Brig Gen Tim Haugh, USAF; CAPT Steve
Donald, USN, Joint Task Force Ares*

A Member's Perspective
Mr. Robert Butler, Cyber Strategies, LLC

Joint Staff
*Col Dean Clothier, USAF; CAPT Jeff
Bernhard, USN, Joint Staff J-39*

Current Policy and Legal Perspectives Panel
Discussion
*Hon. Judith Miller, Private Consultant; Ms.
Katherine Charlet, OUSD Policy; Dr. Walter
Sharp, DoD*

14–15 December 2016 Meeting

History of Special Activities
ADM William Studeman, USN (Ret.)

Discussion
Rob Schrier, Subject Matter Expert

OSD(P) Perspective on Strategic Cyber
Operations
Mr. Charles Swett, OSD(P)

FBI Perspective
*Ms. Vanessa Bopp, FBI; Mr. Colby Daughtry,
FBI*

USD(I) Perspective
Mr. Mark Elliott, OUSD(I)

17–18 January 2017 Meeting

Cyber-Enabled IO Campaign Planning
*COL David Lamm, National Defense
University*

IC Perspectives
*Dr. Tom Donahue, Cyber Threat Intelligence
Integration Center*

Best Practices in Protection
*Mr. Tony Sager, CISecurity; Mr. Curtis
Dukes, CISecurity*

State Department Perspective
Amb. Dan Fried, Department of State

OUSD(AT&L) Perspective
Mr. Adam Nucci, OUSD(AT&L)

21–22 February 2017 Meeting

Global Cyberspace Operations
Synchronization (GCOS)
COL Stephen Letcher, USA, USCYBERCOM

UK Perspectives and Insights
Ms. Sally Ward, GCHQ

USCYBERCOM Excursion – Cyber Innovation
Lab
*Col Mike Burke, USAF, Cyber National
Mission Force*

USPACOM Perspective
USPACOM J3 and J6

USSTRATCOM Perspective
Mr. Richard Bibey, USSTRATCOM

IC Perspectives on Strategic Cyber Issues
Mr. Vinh Nguyen, ODNI

Australian Perspective
Mr. Mike Williams

04–05 April 2017 Meeting

Industry Perspective
Mr. Dmitri Alperovitch, Crowdstrike

USCYBERCOM – CIO Perspective
*Mr. G. Dennis Bartko, USCYBERCOM
Capabilities Development Group*

The Future of Cyber Autonomy
*Dr. David Brumley, Carnegie Mellon
University*

IC Perspective
*Mr. Glenn Gaffney, Central Intelligence
Agency*

Current Administration's Perspectives on
Cyber
*Mr. Joshua Steinman, National Security
Council*

24–25 May 2017 Meeting

State Department Perspective
Mr. Chris Painter, Department of State

Industry Perspective
Mr. John Watters, FireEye

Industry Perspective
Mr. Matt Devost, FusionX

Industry Perspective
Mr. J. Michael Daniel, Cyber Threat Alliance

Industry Perspective
Dr. Michael Sulmeyer, Harvard University

White House Perspective
Mr. Robert Joyce, National Security Council

12–13 July 2017 Meeting

DHS Perspective
*Mr. Thomas McDermott, Deputy Assistant
Secretary for Cyber Policy*

Global Engagement Center (GEC) Discussion
Mr. Daniel Kimmage, GEC

Department of Commerce Perspective
*Mr. Adam Sedgewick, Department of
Commerce*

Appendix B

NATIONAL CYBER STRATEGY

of the United States of America

SEPTEMBER 2018

THE WHITE HOUSE
WASHINGTON, DC

My fellow Americans:

Protecting America's national security and promoting the prosperity of the American people are my top priorities. Ensuring the security of cyberspace is fundamental to both endeavors. Cyberspace is an integral component of all facets of American life, including our economy and defense. Yet, our private and public entities still struggle to secure their systems, and adversaries have increased the frequency and sophistication of their malicious cyber activities. America created the Internet and shared it with the world. Now, we must make sure to secure and preserve cyberspace for future generations.

In the last 18 months, my Administration has taken action to address cyber threats. We have sanctioned malign cyber actors. We have indicted those that committed cybercrimes. We have publicly attributed malicious activity to the adversaries responsible and released details about the tools they employed. We have required departments and agencies to remove software vulnerable to various security risks. We have taken action to hold department and agency heads accountable for managing cybersecurity risks to the systems they control, while empowering them to provide adequate security. In addition, last year, I signed Executive Order 13800, *Strengthening the Cybersecurity of Federal Networks and Critical Infrastructure*. The work performed and reports created in response to that Executive Order laid the groundwork for this National Cyber Strategy.

With the release of this National Cyber Strategy, the United States now has its first fully articulated cyber strategy in 15 years. This strategy explains how my Administration will:

- Defend the homeland by protecting networks, systems, functions, and data;

- Promote American prosperity by nurturing a secure, thriving digital economy and fostering strong domestic innovation;

- Preserve peace and security by strengthening the ability of the United States — in concert with allies and partners — to deter and, if necessary, punish those who use cyber tools for malicious purposes; and

- Expand American influence abroad to extend the key tenets of an open, interoperable, reliable, and secure Internet.

The National Cyber Strategy demonstrates my commitment to strengthening America's cybersecurity capabilities and securing America from cyber threats. It is a call to action for all Americans and our great companies to take the necessary steps to enhance our national cybersecurity. We will continue to lead the world in securing a prosperous cyber future.

Sincerely,

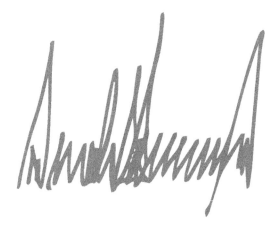

President Donald J. Trump

The White House
September 2018

Table of Contents

Introduction

America's prosperity and security depend on how we respond to the opportunities and challenges in cyberspace. Critical infrastructure, national defense, and the daily lives of Americans rely on computer-driven and interconnected information technologies. As all facets of American life have become more dependent on a secure cyberspace, new vulnerabilities have been revealed and new threats continue to emerge. Building on the National Security Strategy and the Administration's progress over its first 18 months, the National Cyber Strategy outlines how the United States will ensure the American people continue to reap the benefits of a secure cyberspace that reflects our principles, protects our security, and promotes our prosperity.

How Did We Get Here?

The rise of the Internet and the growing centrality of cyberspace to all facets of the modern world corresponded with the rise of the United States as the world's lone superpower. For the past quarter century, the ingenuity of the American people drove the evolution of cyberspace, and in turn, cyberspace has become fundamental to American wealth creation and innovation. Cyberspace is an inseparable component of America's financial, social, government, and political life. Meanwhile, Americans sometimes took for granted that the supremacy of the United States in the cyber domain would remain unchallenged, and that America's vision for an open, interoperable, reliable, and secure Internet would inevitably become a reality. Americans believed the growth of the Internet would carry the universal aspirations for free expression and individual liberty around the world. Americans assumed the opportunities to expand communication, commerce, and free exchange of ideas

would be self-evident. Large parts of the world have embraced America's vision of a shared and open cyberspace for the mutual benefit of all.

Our competitors and adversaries, however, have taken an opposite approach. They benefit from the open Internet, while constricting and controlling their own people's access to it, and actively undermine the principles of an open Internet in international forums. They hide behind notions of sovereignty while recklessly violating the laws of other states by engaging in pernicious economic espionage and malicious cyber activities, causing significant economic disruption and harm to individuals, commercial and non-commercial interests, and governments across the world. They view cyberspace as an arena where the United States' overwhelming military, economic, and political power could be neutralized and where the United States and its allies and partners are vulnerable.

Russia, Iran, and North Korea conducted reckless cyber attacks that harmed American and international businesses and our allies and partners without paying costs likely to deter future cyber aggression. China engaged in cyber-enabled economic espionage and trillions of dollars of intellectual property theft. Non-state actors — including terrorists and criminals — exploited cyberspace to profit, recruit, propagandize, and attack the United States and its allies and partners, with their actions often shielded by hostile states. Public and private entities have struggled to secure their systems as adversaries increase the frequency and sophistication of their malicious cyber activities. Entities across the United States have faced cybersecurity challenges in effectively identifying, protecting, and ensuring resilience of their networks, systems, functions, and data as well as detecting, responding to, and recovering from incidents.

"We will continue to lead the world in securing a prosperous cyber future."

DONALD J. TRUMP
SEPTEMBER 2018

The Way Forward

New threats and a new era of strategic competition demand a new cyber strategy that responds to new realities, reduces vulnerabilities, deters adversaries, and safeguards opportunities for the American people to thrive. Securing cyberspace is fundamental to our strategy and requires technical advancements and administrative efficiency across the Federal Government and the private sector. The Administration also recognizes that a purely technocratic approach to cyberspace is insufficient to address the nature of the new problems we confront. The United States must also have policy choices to impose costs if it hopes to deter malicious cyber actors and prevent further escalation.

The Administration is already taking action to aggressively address these threats and adjust to new realities. The United States has sanctioned malign cyber actors and indicted those that have committed cybercrimes. We have publicly attributed malicious activity to the responsible adversaries and released details of the tools and infrastructure they employed. We have required departments and agencies to remove software vulnerable to various security risks. We have taken action to hold department and agency heads accountable for managing the cybersecurity risks to systems they control, while empowering them to provide adequate security.

The Administration's approach to cyberspace is anchored by enduring American values, such as the belief in the power of individual liberty, free expression, free markets, and privacy. We retain our commitment to the promise of an open, interoperable, reliable, and secure Internet to strengthen and extend our values and protect and ensure economic security for American workers and companies. The future we desire will not come without a renewed American commitment to advance our interests across cyberspace.

The Administration recognizes that the United States is engaged in a continuous competition against strategic adversaries, rogue states, and terrorist and criminal networks. Russia, China, Iran, and North Korea all use cyberspace as a means to challenge the United States, its allies, and partners, often with a recklessness they would never consider in other domains. These adversaries use cyber tools to undermine our economy and democracy, steal our intellectual property,

NATIONAL CYBER STRATEGY

---

and sow discord in our democratic processes. We are vulnerable to peacetime cyber attacks against critical infrastructure, and the risk is growing that these countries will conduct cyber attacks against the United States during a crisis short of war. These adversaries are continually developing new and more effective cyber weapons.

This National Cyber Strategy outlines how we will (1) defend the homeland by protecting networks, systems, functions, and data; (2) promote American prosperity by nurturing a secure, thriving digital economy and fostering strong domestic innovation; (3) preserve peace and security by strengthening the United States' ability — in concert with allies and partners — to deter and if necessary punish those who use cyber tools for malicious purposes; and (4) expand American influence abroad to extend the key tenets of an open, interoperable, reliable, and secure Internet.

The Strategy's success will be realized when cybersecurity vulnerabilities are effectively managed through identification and protection of networks, systems, functions, and data as well as detection of, resilience against, response to, and recovery from incidents; destructive, disruptive, or otherwise destabilizing malicious cyber activities directed against United States interests are reduced or prevented; activity that is contrary to responsible behavior in cyberspace is deterred through the imposition of costs through cyber and non-cyber means; and the United States is positioned to use cyber capabilities to achieve national security objectives.

The articulation of the National Cyber Strategy is organized according to the pillars of the National Security Strategy. The National Security Council staff will coordinate with departments, agencies, and the Office of Management and Budget (OMB) on an appropriate resource plan to implement this Strategy. Departments and agencies will execute their missions informed by the following strategic guidance.

PILLAR I

Protect the American People, the Homeland, and the American Way of Life

Protecting the American people, the American way of life, and American interests is at the forefront of the National Security Strategy. Protecting American information networks, whether government or private, is vital to fulfilling this objective. It will require a series of coordinated actions focused on protecting government networks, protecting critical infrastructure, and combating cybercrime. The United States Government, private industry, and the public must each take immediate and decisive actions to strengthen cybersecurity, with each working on securing the networks under their control and supporting each other as appropriate.

OBJECTIVE: Manage cybersecurity risks to increase the security and resilience of the Nation's information and information systems.

Secure Federal Networks and Information

The responsibility to secure Federal networks — including Federal information systems and national security systems — falls squarely on the Federal Government. The Administration will clarify the relevant authorities, responsi-

bilities, and accountability within and across departments and agencies for securing Federal information systems, while setting the standard for effective cybersecurity risk management. As part of this effort, the Administration will centralize some authorities within the Federal Government, enable greater cross-agency visibility, improve management of our Federal supply chain, and strengthen the security of United States Government contractor systems.

Priority Actions

FURTHER CENTRALIZE MANAGEMENT AND OVERSIGHT OF FEDERAL CIVILIAN CYBERSECURITY: The Administration will act to further enable the Department of Homeland Security (DHS) to secure Federal department and agency networks, with the exception of national security systems and Department of Defense (DOD) and Intelligence Community (IC) systems. This includes ensuring DHS has appropriate access to agency information systems for cybersecurity purposes and can take and direct action to safeguard systems from the spectrum of risks. Under the oversight of the OMB, the Administration will expand on work begun under Executive Order (E.O.) 13800 to prioritize the transition of agencies to shared services

PILLAR I: PROTECT THE AMERICAN PEOPLE, THE HOMELAND,
AND THE AMERICAN WAY OF LIFE

and infrastructure. DHS will have appropriate visibility into those services and infrastructure to improve United States cybersecurity posture. We will continue to deploy centralized capabilities, tools, and services through DHS where appropriate, and improve oversight and compliance with applicable laws, policies, standards, and directives. This will likely require new policies and architectures that enable the government to better leverage innovation. DOD and the IC will consider these activities as they work to better secure national security systems, DOD systems, and IC systems, as appropriate.

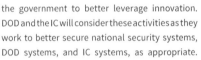

ALIGN RISK MANAGEMENT AND INFORMATION TECHNOLOGY ACTIVITIES: E.O. 13833, *Enhancing the Effectiveness of Agency Chief Information Officers*, empowers Chief Information Officers (CIOs) to more effectively leverage technology to accomplish agency missions, cut down on duplication, and make information technology (IT) investment more efficient. Department and agency leaders will empower and hold their CIOs accountable to align cybersecurity risk management decisions and IT budgeting and procurement decisions. The Administration, through OMB and DHS, will continue to guide and direct risk management actions across Federal civilian departments and agencies, and CIOs will be empowered to take a proactive leadership role in assuring IT procurement decisions assign the proper priority to securing networks and data.

IMPROVE FEDERAL SUPPLY CHAIN RISK MANAGEMENT: The Administration will integrate supply chain risk management into agency procurement and risk management processes in accordance with federal requirements that are consistent with industry best practices to better ensure the technology that the Federal Government deploys is secure and reliable. This includes ensuring better information sharing among departments and agencies to improve awareness of supply chain threats and reduce duplicative supply chain activities within the United States Government, including by creating a supply chain risk assessment shared service. It also includes addressing deficiencies in the Federal acquisition system, such as providing more streamlined authorities to exclude risky vendors, products, and services when justified. This effort will be synchronized with efforts to manage supply chain risk in the Nation's infrastructure.

STRENGTHEN FEDERAL CONTRACTOR CYBER-SECURITY: The United States cannot afford to have sensitive government information or systems inadequately secured by contractors. Federal contractors provide important services to the United States Government and must properly secure the systems through which they provide those services. Going forward, the Federal Government will be able to assess the security of its data by reviewing contractor risk management practices and adequately testing, hunting, sensoring, and responding to incidents on contractor systems. Contracts with Federal departments and agencies will be drafted to authorize such activities for the purpose of improving cybersecurity. Among the acute concerns in this area are those contractors within the defense industrial base responsible for researching and developing key systems fielded by the DOD. Further, as recommended in the E.O. 13800 *Report to the President on Federal IT Modernization*, the Administration will support adoption of consolidated acquisition strategies to improve cybersecurity and reduce overhead costs associated with using inconsistent contract provisions across the Federal Government. It will also act to ensure, where appropriate, that Federal contractors receive and use all relevant and shareable threat and vulnerability information to improve their security posture.

ENSURE THE GOVERNMENT LEADS IN BEST AND INNOVATIVE PRACTICES: The Federal Government will ensure the systems it owns and operates meet the standards and cybersecurity best practices it recommends to industry. Projects that receive Federal funding must meet these standards as well. The Federal Government will use its purchasing power to drive sector-wide improvement in products and services. The Federal Government will also be a leader in developing and implementing standards and best practices in new and emerging areas. For example, public key cryptography is foundational to the secure operation of our infrastructure. To protect against the potential threat of quantum computers being able to break modern public key cryptography, the Department of Commerce, through the National Institute of Standards and Technology (NIST), will continue to solicit, evaluate, and standardize quantum-resistant, public key cryptographic algorithms. The United States must be at the forefront of protecting communications by supporting rapid adoption of these forthcoming NIST standards across government infrastructure and by encouraging the Nation to do the same.

Secure Critical Infrastructure

The responsibility to secure the Nation's critical infrastructure and manage its cybersecurity risk is shared by the private sector and the Federal Government. In partnership with the private sector, we will collectively use a risk-management approach to mitigating vulnerabilities to raise the base level of cybersecurity across critical infrastructure. We will simultaneously use a consequence-driven approach to prioritize actions that reduce the potential that the most advanced adversaries could cause large-scale or long-duration disruptions to critical infrastructure. We will also deter malicious cyber actors by imposing costs on them and their sponsors by leveraging a range of tools, including but not limited to prosecutions and economic sanctions, as part of a broader deterrence strategy.

Priority Actions

REFINE ROLES AND RESPONSIBILITIES: The Administration will clarify the roles and responsibilities of Federal agencies and the expectations on the private sector related to cybersecurity risk management and incident response. Clarity will enable proactive risk management that comprehensively addresses threats, vulnerabilities, and consequences. It will also identify and bridge existing gaps in responsibilities and coordination among Federal and non-Federal incident response efforts and promote more routine training, exercises, and coordination.

PRIORITIZE ACTIONS ACCORDING TO IDENTIFIED NATIONAL RISKS: The Federal Government will work with the private sector to manage risks to critical infrastructure at the greatest risk. The Administration will develop a comprehensive understanding of national risk by identifying national critical functions and will mature our cybersecurity offerings and engagements to better manage those national risks. The Administration will prioritize risk-reduction activities across seven key areas: national security, energy and power, banking and

PILLAR I: PROTECT THE AMERICAN PEOPLE, THE HOMELAND,
AND THE AMERICAN WAY OF LIFE

---

finance, health and safety, communications, information technology, and transportation.

LEVERAGE INFORMATION AND COMMUNICATIONS TECHNOLOGY PROVIDERS AS CYBERSECURITY ENABLERS: Information and communications technology (ICT) underlies every sector in America. ICT providers are in a unique position to detect, prevent, and mitigate risk before it impacts their customers, and the Federal Government must work with these providers to improve ICT security and resilience in a targeted and efficient manner while protecting privacy and civil liberties. The United States Government will strengthen efforts to share information with ICT providers to enable them to respond to and remediate known malicious cyber activity at the network level. This will include sharing classified threat and vulnerability information with cleared ICT operators and downgrading information to the unclassified level as much as possible. We will promote an adaptable, sustainable, and secure technology supply chain that supports security based on best practices and standards. The United States Government will convene stakeholders to devise cross-sector solutions to challenges at the network, device, and gateway layers, and we will encourage industry-driven certification regimes that ensure solutions can adapt in a rapidly evolving market and threat landscape.

PROTECT OUR DEMOCRACY: Securing our democratic processes is of paramount importance to the United States and our democratic allies. State and local government officials own and operate diverse election infrastructure within the United States. Therefore, when requested we will provide technical and risk management services, support training and exercising, maintain situational awareness of threats to this sector, and improve the sharing of threat intelligence with those officials to better prepare and protect the election infrastructure. The Federal Government will continue to coordinate the development of cybersecurity standards and guidance to safeguard the electoral process and the tools that deliver a secure system. In the event of a significant cyber incident, the Federal Government is poised to provide threat and asset response to recover election infrastructure.

INCENTIVIZE CYBERSECURITY INVESTMENTS: Most cybersecurity risks to critical infrastructure stem from the exploitation of known vulnerabilities. The United States Government will work with private and public sector entities to promote understanding of cybersecurity risk so they make more informed risk-management decisions, invest in appropriate security measures, and realize benefits from those investments.

PRIORITIZE NATIONAL RESEARCH AND DEVELOPMENT INVESTMENTS: The Federal Government will update the National Critical Infrastructure Security and Resilience Research and Development Plan to set priorities for addressing cybersecurity risks to critical infrastructure. Departments and agencies will align their investments to the priorities, which will focus on building new cybersecurity approaches that use emerging technologies, improving information-sharing and risk management related to cross-sector interdependencies, and building resilience to large-scale or long-duration disruptions.

IMPROVE TRANSPORTATION AND MARITIME CYBERSECURITY: America's economic and national security is built on global trade and transportation. Our ability to guarantee free and timely movement of goods, open sea and air lines of communications, access to oil and natural gas, and availability of associated critical infrastructures is vital to our economic and national security. As these sectors have modernized, they have also become more vulnerable to cyber exploitation or attack. Maritime cybersecurity is of particular concern because lost or delayed shipments can result in strategic economic disruptions and potential spillover effects on downstream industries. Given the criticality of maritime transportation to the United States and global economy and the minimal risk-reduction investments to protect against cyber exploitation made thus far, the United States will move quickly to clarify maritime cybersecurity roles and responsibilities; promote enhanced mechanisms for international coordination and information sharing; and accelerate the development of next-generation cyber-resilient maritime infrastructure. The United States will assure the uninterrupted transport of goods in the face of all threats that can hold this inherently international infrastructure at risk through cyber means.

IMPROVE SPACE CYBERSECURITY: The United States considers unfettered access to and freedom to operate in space vital to advancing the security, economic prosperity, and scientific knowledge of the Nation. The Administration is concerned about the growing cyber-related threats to space assets and supporting infrastructure because these assets are critical to functions such as positioning, navigation, and timing (PNT); intelligence, surveillance, and reconnaissance (ISR); satellite communications; and weather monitoring. The Administration will enhance efforts to protect our space assets and support infrastructure from evolving cyber threats, and we will work with industry and international partners to strengthen the cyber resilience of existing and future space systems.

Combat Cybercrime and Improve Incident Reporting

Federal departments and agencies, in cooper-ation with state, local, tribal, and territorial government entities, play a critical role in detecting, preventing, disrupting, and investigating cyber threats to our Nation. The United States is regularly the victim of malicious cyber activity perpetrated by criminal actors, including state and non-state actors and their proxies and terrorists using network infrastructure in the United States and abroad. Federal law enforcement works to apprehend and prosecute offenders, disable criminal infrastructure, limit the spread and use of nefarious cyber capabilities, prevent cyber criminals and their state sponsors from profiting from their illicit activity, and seize their assets. The Administration will push to ensure that our Federal departments and agencies have the necessary legal authorities and resources to combat transnational cybercriminal activity, including identifying and dismantling botnets, dark markets, and other infrastructure used to enable cybercrime, and combatting economic espionage. To effectively deter, disrupt, and prevent cyber threats, law enforcement will work with private industry to confront challenges presented by technological barriers, such as anonymization and encryption technologies, to obtain time-sensitive evidence pursuant to appropriate legal process. Law enforcement actions to combat criminal cyber activity serve as an instrument of national power by, among other things, deterring those activities.

Priority Actions

IMPROVE INCIDENT REPORTING AND RESPONSE: The United States Government will continue to encourage reporting of intrusions and theft of data by all victims, especially critical infrastructure partners. The prompt reporting of cyber incidents to the Federal Government is essential to an effective response, linking of

PILLAR I: PROTECT THE AMERICAN PEOPLE, THE HOMELAND,
AND THE AMERICAN WAY OF LIFE

related incidents, identification of the perpetrators, and prevention of future incidents.

MODERNIZE ELECTRONIC SURVEILLANCE AND COMPUTER CRIME LAWS: The Administration will work with the Congress to update electronic surveillance and computer crime statutes to enhance law enforcement's capabilities to lawfully gather necessary evidence of criminal activity, disrupt criminal infrastructure through civil injunctions, and impose appropriate consequences upon malicious cyber actors.

REDUCE THREATS FROM TRANSNATIONAL CRIMINAL ORGANIZATIONS IN CYBERSPACE: Computer hacking conducted by transnational criminal groups poses a significant threat to our national security. Equipped with sizeable funds, organized criminal groups operating abroad employ sophisticated malicious software, spearphishing campaigns, and other hacking tools — some of which rival those of nation states in sophistication — to hack into sensitive financial systems, conduct massive data breaches, spread ransomware, attack critical infrastructure, and steal intellectual property. The Administration will advocate for law enforcement to have effective legal tools to investigate and prosecute such groups and modernized organized crime statutes for use against this threat.

IMPROVE APPREHENSION OF CRIMINALS LOCATED ABROAD: Deterring cybercrime requires a credible threat that perpetrators will be identified, apprehended, and brought to justice. However, some foreign nations choose not to cooperate with extradition requests, impose unreasonable limitations, or actively interfere in these efforts. The United States will continue to identify gaps and potential mechanisms for bringing foreign-based cyber criminals to justice. The United States Government will also increase diplomatic

and other efforts with countries to promote cooperation with legitimate extradition requests. We will push other nations to expedite their assistance in investigations and to comply with any bilateral or multilateral agreements or obligations.

STRENGTHEN PARTNER NATIONS' LAW ENFORCEMENT CAPACITY TO COMBAT CRIMINAL CYBER ACTIVITY: The United States should also aid willing partner nations to build their capacity to address criminal cyber activity. The borderless nature of cybercrime, including state-sponsored and terrorist activities, requires strong international law enforcement partnerships. This cooperation requires foreign law enforcement agencies to have the technical capability to assist United States law enforcement effectively when requested. It is therefore in the interest of United States national security to continue building cybercrime-fighting capacity that facilitates stronger international law enforcement cooperation.

The United States will strive to improve international cooperation in investigating malicious cyber activity, including developing solutions to potential barriers to gathering and sharing evidence. The United States will also lead in developing interoperable and mutually beneficial systems to encourage efficient cross-border information exchange for law enforcement purposes and reduce barriers to coordination. The Administration will urge effective use of existing international tools like the United Nations Convention Against Transnational Organized Crime and the G7 24/7 Network Points of Contact. Finally, we will work to expand the international consensus favoring the Convention on Cybercrime of the Council of Europe (Budapest Convention), including by supporting greater adoption of the convention.

PILLAR II

Promote American Prosperity

The Internet has generated tremendous benefits domestically and abroad, and it helps to advance American values of freedom, security, and prosperity. Along with its expansion have come challenges that threaten our national security. The United States will demonstrate a coherent and comprehensive approach to address these and other challenges to defend American national interests in this increasingly digitized world.

OBJECTIVE: Preserve United States influence in the technological ecosystem and the development of cyberspace as an open engine of economic growth, innovation, and efficiency.

Foster a Vibrant and Resilient Digital Economy

Economic security is inherently tied to our national security. As the foundations of our economy are becoming increasingly rooted in digital technologies, the United States Government will model and promote standards that protect our economic security and reinforce the vitality of the American marketplace and American innovation.

Priority Actions

INCENTIVIZE AN ADAPTABLE AND SECURE TECHNOLOGY MARKETPLACE: To enhance the resilience of cyberspace, the Administration expects the technology marketplace to support and reward the continuous development, adoption, and evolution of innovative security technologies and processes. The Administration will work across stakeholder groups, including the private sector and civil society, to promote best practices and develop strategies to overcome market barriers to the adoption of secure technologies. The Administration will improve awareness and transparency of cybersecurity practices to build market demand for more secure products and services. Finally, the Administration will collaborate with international partners to promote open, industry-driven standards with government support, as appropriate, and risk-based approaches to address cybersecurity challenges to include platform and managed service approaches that lower barriers to secure practice adoption across the breadth of the ecosystem.

PRIORITIZE INNOVATION: The United States Government will promote implementation and

PILLAR II: PROMOTE AMERICAN PROSPERITY

continuous updating of standards and best practices that deter and prevent current and evolving threats and hazards in all domains of the cyber ecosystem. These standards and practices should be outcome-oriented and based on sound technological principles rather than point-in-time company specifications. The Administration will eliminate policy barriers that inhibit a robust cybersecurity industry from developing, sharing, and building innovative capabilities to reduce cyber threats.

INVEST IN NEXT GENERATION INFRASTRUCTURE: The Administration will facilitate the accelerated development and rollout of next-generation telecommunications and information communications infrastructure here in the United States, while using the buying power of the Federal Government to incentivize the move towards more secure supply chains. The United States Government will work with the private sector to facilitate the evolution and security of 5G, examine technological and spectrum-based solutions, and lay the groundwork for innovation beyond next-generation advancements. The United States Government will examine the use of emerging technologies, such as artificial intelligence and quantum computing, while addressing risks inherent in their use and application. We will collaborate with the private sector and civil society to understand trends in technology advancement to maintain the United States technological edge in connected technologies and to ensure secure practices are adopted from the outset.

PROMOTE THE FREE FLOW OF DATA ACROSS BORDERS: Countries are increasingly looking towards restrictive data localization and regulations as pretexts for digital protectionism under the rubric of national security. Those actions negatively impact the competitiveness of United States companies. The United States will continue to lead by example and push back against unjustifiable barriers to the free flow of data and digital trade. The Administration will continue to work with international counterparts to promote open, industry driven standards, innovative products, and risk-based approaches that permit global innovation and the free flow of data while meeting the legitimate security needs of the United States.

MAINTAIN UNITED STATES LEADERSHIP IN EMERGING TECHNOLOGIES: The United States' influence in cyberspace is linked to our technological leadership. Accordingly, the United States Government will make a concerted effort to protect cutting edge technologies, including from theft by our adversaries, support those technologies' maturation, and, where possible, reduce United States companies' barriers to market entry. The United States will promote United States cybersecurity innovation worldwide through trade-related engagement, raising awareness of innovative American cybersecurity tools and services, exposing and countering repressive regimes use of such tools and services to undermine human rights, and reducing barriers to a robust global cybersecurity market.

PROMOTE FULL-LIFECYCLE CYBERSECURITY: The United States Government will promote full-lifecycle cybersecurity, pressing for strong, default security settings, adaptable, upgradeable products, and other best practices built in at the time of product delivery. We will identify a clear pathway toward an adaptable, sustainable, and secure technology marketplace, encour-

"The National Cyber Strategy is a call to action for all Americans and our great companies to take the necessary steps to enhance our national cybersecurity."

DONALD J. TRUMP
SEPTEMBER 2018

NATIONAL CYBER STRATEGY

aging manufacturers to differentiate products based on the quality of their security features. The United States Government will promote foundational engineering practices to reduce systemic fragility and develop designs that degrade and recover effectively when successfully attacked. The United States Government will also promote regular testing and exercising of the cybersecurity and resilience of products and systems during development using best practices from forward-leaning industries. This includes promotion and use of coordinated vulnerability disclosure, crowd-sourced testing, and other innovative assessments that improve resiliency ahead of exploitation or attack. The United States Government will also evaluate how to improve the end-to-end lifecycle for digital identity management, including over-reliance on Social Security numbers.

Foster and Protect United States Ingenuity

Fostering and protecting American invention and innovation is critical to maintaining the United States' strategic advantage in cyberspace. The United States Government will nurture innovation by promoting institutions and programs that drive United States competitiveness. The United States Government will counter predatory mergers and acquisitions and counter intellectual property theft. We will also catalyze United States leadership in emerging technologies and promote government identification and support to these technologies, which include artificial intelligence, quantum information science, and next-generation telecommunication infrastructure.

Priority Actions

UPDATE MECHANISMS TO REVIEW FOREIGN INVESTMENT AND OPERATION IN THE UNITED STATES: The confidentiality, integrity, and availability of United States telecommunications networks are essential to our economy and national security. We must be vigilant to safeguard the telecommunications networks we depend on in our everyday lives so they cannot be used or compromised by a foreign adversary to harm the United States. The United States Government will balance these objectives by formalizing and streamlining the review of Federal Communications Commission referrals for telecommunications licenses. The United States Government will facilitate a transparent process to increase the efficiency of this review.

MAINTAIN A STRONG AND BALANCED INTELLECTUAL PROPERTY PROTECTION SYSTEM: Strong intellectual property protections ensure continued economic growth and innovation in the digital age. The United States Government has fostered and will continue to help foster a global intellectual property rights system that provides incentives for innovation through the protection and enforcement of intellectual property rights such as patents, trademarks, and copyrights. The United States Government will also promote protection of sensitive emerging technologies and trade secrets, and we will work to prevent adversarial nation states from gaining unfair advantage at the expense of American research and development.

PROTECT THE CONFIDENTIALITY AND INTEGRITY OF AMERICAN IDEAS: For more than a decade, malicious actors have conducted cyber intrusions into United States commercial networks, targeting confidential business information held by American firms. Malicious cyber actors from other nations have stolen troves of trade secrets, technical data, and sensitive proprietary internal communications. The United States Government will work against the illicit appropriation of public and private sector technology and technical knowledge by foreign competitors, while maintaining an investor-friendly climate.

Develop a Superior Cybersecurity Workforce

A highly skilled cybersecurity workforce is a strategic national security advantage. The United States will fully develop the vast American talent pool, while at the same time attracting the best and brightest among those abroad who share our values.

Priority Actions

BUILD AND SUSTAIN THE TALENT PIPELINE: Our peer competitors are implementing workforce development programs that have the potential to harm long-term United States cybersecurity competitiveness. The United States Government will continue to invest in and enhance programs that build the domestic talent pipeline, from primary through postsecondary education. The Administration will leverage the President's proposed merit-based immigration reforms to ensure that the United States has the most competitive technology sector. This effort may require additional legislation to achieve the sought after goals.

EXPAND RE-SKILLING AND EDUCATIONAL OPPOR-TUNITIES FOR AMERICA'S WORKERS: The Administration will work with the Congress to promote and reinvigorate educational and training opportunities to develop a robust cybersecurity workforce. This includes expanding Federal recruitment, training, re-skilling people from a broad range of backgrounds, and giving them opportunities to re-train into cybersecurity careers.

ENHANCE THE FEDERAL CYBERSECURITY WORKFORCE: To improve recruitment and retention of highly qualified cybersecurity professionals to the Federal Government, the Administration will continue to use the National Initiative for Cybersecurity Education (NICE) Framework to support policies allowing for a standardized approach for identifying, hiring, developing, and retaining a talented cybersecurity workforce. Additionally, the Administration will explore appropriate options to establish distributed cybersecurity personnel under the management of DHS to oversee the development, management, and deployment of cybersecurity personnel across Federal departments and agencies with the exception of DOD and the IC. The Administration will promote appropriate financial compensation for the United States Government workforce, as well as unique training and operational opportunities to effectively recruit and retain critical cybersecurity talent in light of the competitive private sector environment.

USE EXECUTIVE AUTHORITY TO HIGHLIGHT AND REWARD TALENT: The United States Government will promote and magnify excellence by highlighting cybersecurity educators and cybersecurity professionals. The United States Government will also leverage public-private collaboration to develop and circulate the NICE Framework, which provides a standardized approach for identifying cybersecurity workforce gaps, while also implementing actions to prepare, grow, and sustain a workforce that can defend and bolster America's critical infrastructure and innovation base.

Preserve Peace through Strength

PILLAR III

Challenges to United States security and economic interests, from nation states and other groups, which have long existed in the offline world are now increasingly occurring in cyberspace. This now-persistent engagement in cyberspace is already altering the strategic balance of power. This Administration will issue transformative policies that reflect today's new reality and guide the United States Government towards strategic outcomes that protect the American people and our way of life. Cyberspace will no longer be treated as a separate category of policy or activity disjointed from other elements of national power. The United States will integrate the employment of cyber options across every element of national power.

OBJECTIVE: Identify, counter, disrupt, degrade, and deter behavior in cyberspace that is destabilizing and contrary to national interests, while preserving United States overmatch in and through cyberspace.

Enhance Cyber Stability through Norms of Responsible State Behavior

The United States will promote a framework of responsible state behavior in cyberspace built upon international law, adherence to voluntary non-binding norms of responsible state behavior that apply during peacetime, and the consideration of practical confidence building measures to reduce the risk of conflict stemming from malicious cyber activity. These principles should form a basis for cooperative responses to counter irresponsible state actions inconsistent with this framework.

Priority Action

ENCOURAGE UNIVERSAL ADHERENCE TO CYBER NORMS: International law and voluntary non-binding norms of responsible state behavior in cyberspace provide stabilizing, security-enhancing standards that define acceptable behavior to all states and promote greater predictability and stability in cyberspace. The United States will encourage other nations to publicly affirm these principles and views through enhanced outreach and engagement in multilateral fora. Increased public affirmation by the United States and other governments will lead to accepted expectations of state behavior and thus contribute to greater predictability and stability in cyberspace.

Attribute and Deter Unacceptable Behavior in Cyberspace

As the United States continues to promote consensus on what constitutes responsible state behavior in cyberspace, we must also work to ensure that there are consequences for irresponsible behavior that harms the United States and our partners. All instruments of national power are available to prevent, respond to, and deter malicious cyber activity against the United States. This includes diplomatic, information, military (both kinetic and cyber), financial, intelligence, public attribution, and law enforcement capabilities. The United States will formalize and make routine how we work with like-minded partners to attribute and deter malicious cyber activities with integrated strategies that impose swift, costly, and transparent consequences when malicious actors harm the United States or our partners.

Priority Actions

LEAD WITH OBJECTIVE, COLLABORATIVE INTELLI-GENCE: The IC will continue to lead the world in the use of all-source cyber intelligence to drive the identification and attribution of malicious cyber activity that threatens United States national interests. Objective and actionable intelligence will be shared across the United States Government and with key partners to identify hostile foreign nation states, and non-nation state cyber programs, intentions, capabilities, research and development efforts, tactics, and operational activities that will inform whole-of-government responses to protect American interests at home and abroad.

IMPOSE CONSEQUENCES: The United States will develop swift and transparent consequences, which we will impose consistent with our obligations and commitments to deter future bad behavior. The Administration will conduct interagency policy planning for the time periods leading up to, during, and after the imposition of consequences to ensure a timely and consistent process for responding to and deterring malicious cyber activities. The United States will work with partners when appropriate to impose consequences against malicious cyber actors in response to their activities against our nation and interests.

BUILD A CYBER DETERRENCE INITIATIVE: The imposition of consequences will be more impactful and send a stronger message if it is carried out in concert with a broader coalition of like-minded states. The United States will launch an international Cyber Deterrence Initiative to build such a coalition and develop tailored strategies to ensure adversaries understand the consequences of their malicious cyber behavior. The United States will work with like-minded states to coordinate and support each other's responses to significant malicious cyber incidents, including through intelligence sharing, buttressing of attribution claims, public statements of support for responsive actions taken, and joint imposition of consequences against malign actors.

COUNTER MALIGN CYBER INFLUENCE AND INFORMATION OPERATIONS: The United States will use all appropriate tools of national power to expose and counter the flood of online malign influence and information campaigns and non-state propaganda and disinformation. This includes working with foreign government partners as well as the private sector, academia, and civil society to identify, counter, and prevent the use of digital platforms for malign foreign influence operations while respecting civil rights and liberties.

PILLAR IV

Advance American Influence

The world looks to the United States, where much of the innovation for today's Internet originated, for leadership on a vast range of transnational cyber issues. The United States will maintain an active international leadership posture to advance American influence and to address an expanding array of threats and challenges to its interests in cyberspace. Collaboration with allies and partners is also essential to ensure we can continue to benefit from the cross-border communications, content creation, and commerce generated by the open, interoperable architecture of the Internet.

OBJECTIVE: Preserve the long-term openness, interoperability, security, and reliability of the Internet, which supports and is reinforced by United States interests.

Promote an Open, Interoperable, Reliable, and Secure Internet

The global Internet has prompted some of the greatest advancements since the industrial revolution, enabling great advances in commerce, health, communications, and other national infrastructure. At the same time, centu-

ries-old battles over human rights and fundamental freedoms are now playing out online. Freedoms of expression, peaceful assembly, and association, as well as privacy rights, are under threat. Despite unprecedented growth, the Internet's economic and social potential continues to be undermined by online censorship and repression. The United States stands firm on its principles to protect and promote an open, interoperable, reliable, and secure Internet. We will work to ensure that our approach to an open Internet is the international standard. We will also work to prevent authoritarian states that view the open Internet as a political threat from transforming the free and open Internet into an authoritarian web under their control, under the guise of security or countering terrorism.

Priority Actions

PROTECT AND PROMOTE INTERNET FREEDOM: The United States Government conceptualizes Internet freedom as the online exercise of human rights and fundamental freedoms — such as the freedoms of expression, association, peaceful assembly, religion or belief, and privacy rights online — regardless of frontiers or medium. By extension, Internet freedom also supports the free

PILLAR IV: ADVANCE AMERICAN INFLUENCE

flow of information online that enhances international trade and commerce, fosters innovation, and strengthens both national and international security. As such, United States Internet freedom principles are inextricably linked to our national security. Internet freedom is also a key guiding principle with respect to other United States foreign policy issues, such as cybercrime and counterterrorism efforts. Given its importance, the United States will encourage other countries to advance Internet freedom through venues such as the Freedom Online Coalition, of which the United States is a founding member.

WORK WITH LIKE-MINDED COUNTRIES, INDUSTRY, ACADEMIA, AND CIVIL SOCIETY: The United States will continue to work with like-minded countries, industry, civil society, and other stakeholders to advance human rights and Internet freedom globally and to counter authoritarian efforts to censor and influence Internet development. The United States Government will continue to support civil society through integrated support for technology development, digital safety training, policy advocacy, and research. These programs aim to enhance the ability of individual citizens, activists, human rights defenders, independent journalists, civil society organizations, and marginalized populations to safely access the uncensored Internet and promote Internet freedom at the local, regional, national, and international levels.

PROMOTE A MULTI-STAKEHOLDER MODEL OF INTERNET GOVERNANCE: The United States will continue to actively participate in global efforts to ensure that the multi-stakeholder model of Internet governance prevails against attempts to create state-centric frameworks that would undermine openness and freedom, hinder innovation, and jeopardize the functionality of the Internet. The multi-stakeholder model of

Internet governance is characterized by transparent, bottom-up, consensus-driven processes and enables governments, the private sector, civil society, academia, and the technical community to participate on equal footing. The United States Government will defend the open, interoperable nature of the Internet in multilateral and international fora through active engagement in key organizations, such as the Internet Corporation for Assigned Names and Numbers, the Internet Governance Forum, the United Nations, and the International Telecommunication Union.

PROMOTE INTEROPERABLE AND RELIABLE COMMUNICATIONS INFRASTRUCTURE AND INTERNET CONNECTIVITY: The United States will promote communications infrastructure and Internet connectivity that is open, interoperable, reliable, and secure. Such investment will provide greater opportunities for American firms to compete while countering the influence of statist, top-down government interventions in areas of strategic competition. It will also protect America's security and commercial interests by strengthening United States industry's competitive position in the global digital economy. The Administration will also support and promote open, industry-led standards activities based on sound technological principles.

PROMOTE AND MAINTAIN MARKETS FOR UNITED STATES INGENUITY WORLDWIDE: American innovators and security professionals have contributed significantly in designing products and services that improve our ability to communicate and interact globally and that protect communications infrastructure, data, and devices worldwide. The United States will continue to promote markets for American ingenuity overseas, including for emerging technologies that can lower the cost of security. The United States will also advise on infrastructure deploy-

NATIONAL CYBER STRATEGY

ments, innovation, risk management, policy, and standards to further the global Internet's reach and to ensure interoperability, security, and stability. Finally, the United States will work with international partners, government, industry, civil society, technologists, and academics to improve the adoption and awareness of cybersecurity best practices worldwide.

Build International Cyber Capacity

Capacity building equips partners to protect themselves and assist the United States in addressing threats that target mutual interests, while serving broader diplomatic, economic, and security goals. Through cyber capacity building initiatives, the United States builds strategic partnerships that promote cybersecurity best practices through a common vision of an open, interoperable, reliable, and secure Internet that encourages investment and opens new economic markets. In addition, capacity building allows for additional opportunities to share cyber threat information, enabling the United States Government and our partners to better defend domestic critical infrastructure and global supply chains, as well as focus whole-of-government cyber engagements. Our leadership in building partner cybersecurity capacity is critical to maintaining American influence against global competitors. Building partner cyber capacity will empower international partners to implement policies and practices which allow them to be effective partners in the United States-led Cyber Deterrence Initiative.

Priority Action

ENHANCE CYBER CAPACITY BUILDING EFFORTS: Many United States allies and partners possess unique cyber capabilities that can complement our own. The United States will work to strengthen the capacity and interoperability of those allies and partners to improve our ability to optimize our combined skills, resources, capabilities, and perspectives against shared threats. Partners can also help detect, deter, and defeat those shared threats in cyberspace. In order for international partners to effectively protect their digital infrastructure and combat shared threats, while realizing the economic and social gains derived from the Internet and ICTs, the United States will continue to address the building blocks for organizing national efforts on cybersecurity. We will also aggressively expand efforts to share automated and actionable cyber threat information, enhance cybersecurity coordination, and promote analytical and technical exchanges. In addition, the United States will work to reduce the impact and influence of transnational cybercrime and terrorist activities by partnering with and strengthening the security and law enforcement capabilities of our partners to build their cyber capacity.

Notes

NATIONAL CYBER STRATEGY

Notes

Appendix C

PRIME MINISTER'S OFFICE
NATIONAL CYBER DIRECTORATE
NATIONAL CYBER SECURITY AUTHORITY

CYBER DEFENSE METHODOLOGY FOR AN ORGANIZATION

VER. 1.0

PRIME MINISTER'S OFFICE
NATIONAL CYBER DIRECTORATE
NATIONAL CYBER SECURITY AUTHORITY

CYBER DEFENSE METHODOLOGY FOR AN ORGANIZATION

VER. 1.0

JUNE 2017

\\ CONTENTS

This document has been developed by The National Cyber Security Authority (NCSA) for the protection of Cyberspace in the public interest.

This document constitutes a recommendation for all organizations in Israel.

It can be used freely for enhancing the cyber resilience of the economy.

This document was written for boards of directors and managements of companies, Cyber Defense managers, contractors and IT providers.

The document presents the minimum requirements for protection in accordance with the potential for damage. The protection plan derived from this document should be adapted to the degree of the organization's dependence on cyber.

Organizations are required to perform a risk assessment process and can build a stringent protection program from the requirements of this document.

The document appeals to the entire economy and is written in the masculine form for convenience only.

References to the document can be sent via email to: tora@pmo.gov.il

\\ INTRODUCTION

Dear managers, information security and Cyber-Defense specialists,

Cyberspace is the outcome of technological progress, connectivity and a global connection to the Internet.

The increasing dependency on Cyberspace brings tidings of technological innovation and tremendous development for man and his environment.

But alongside these, a threatening space is developing, affecting the business organizations, the integrity of production processes and the confidentiality of corporate information.

Cyber-attacks could harm the organizations and halt the production processes, causing economic damage and harming the reputation of the business.

The State of Israel conducts a national effort for the defense of civil cyber space.

The Corporate Defense Methodology is a component of the National Defense Concept, consisting of various levels of protection on the Israeli economy and its functional continuity.

The Corporate Defense Methodology considers the organization as a whole, and enables raising the level of organizational resilience through continuous integration of processes, practices and protection products.

The application of a Corporate Defense Methodology will enhance the organizational resilience and robustness in face of cyber-attacks.

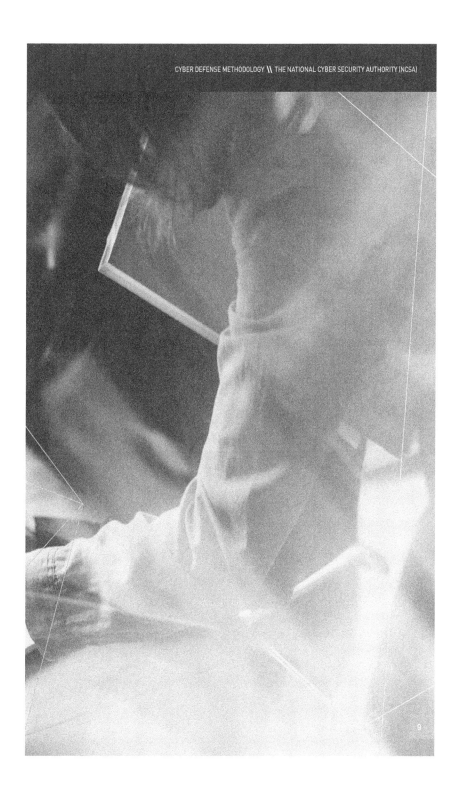

CYBER DEFENSE METHODOLOGY \\ THE NATIONAL CYBER SECURITY AUTHORITY (NCSA)

9

███████████████████████████████████████

\\ EXECUTIVE SUMMARY

The purpose of the Defense Methodology is to minimize cyber risks for organizations in Israel.

This document defines a coherent method which guides the corporate responsibility for the construction of a multi-year work plan for the protection of the organization.

Using the method presented in this document, the organization will recognize the relevant risks, formulate a defense response and realize a program to reduce the risks accordingly.

Stage A - the organization will understand to which category is belongs:

- **Category A** - organizations whose resulting damage potential from cyber-incidents is not great.
- **Category B** - organizations whose resulting damage potential from cyber-incidents is great.

The categorization questionnaire appears on page 19.

Stage B - construction of a work plan for the organization

As for the construction of the work plan, the organization will define first what it is required to protect, the required protection level, and the protection gaps in view of the desired situation and will, eventually, construct a work plan to reduce the gaps.

An explanation as regards how to configure the protection objectives of the organization and the level of protection required is presented in this document on page 20 for Category A organizations, and on pages 25-26 for Category B organizations.

At this point, the organization must understand the controls required of the organization for its various assets. These controls are presented on pages 21-22 for category A organizations, and in pages 33-130 for category B organizations.

The final product in light of the work with this document is:

The organization will understand what are the controls necessary to implement in order to reduce cyber risks to which the organization is exposed.

These controls will constitute the work plan for reducing risks for the organization.

CYBER DEFENSE METHODOLOGY \\ THE NATIONAL CYBER SECURITY AUTHORITY (NCSA)

The work plan for organizations that are professionally guided by a dedicated facilitator on behalf of the National Cyber Security Authority (NCSA), will be built according to the direct guidance of the sector facilitator.

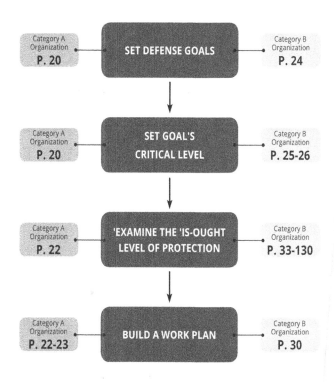

Category A Organization P. 20	SET DEFENSE GOALS	Category B Organization P. 24
Category A Organization P. 20	SET GOAL'S CRITICAL LEVEL	Category B Organization P. 25-26
Category A Organization P. 22	'EXAMINE THE 'IS-OUGHT LEVEL OF PROTECTION	Category B Organization P. 33-130
Category A Organization P. 22-23	BUILD A WORK PLAN	Category B Organization P. 30

1 \\ INTRODUCTION

Cyberspace is an integral part of our lives. On a personal level, we are looking for information on the Internet, navigate our way through road navigation software, talk on a cell phone, and some of us have a pacemaker or an insulin pump connected to the Internet - all part of Cyberspace . On the business level, we use credit cards, manage a customer data base, manage a global organization by computer networks; we market, buy and sell - all based on Cyberspace.

For many of us in everyday life in general and in business in particular, an available, accessible and reliable and constitutes a necessary condition. It is easy to understand this when the above are temporarily withdrawn from us. How will you manage the business without a mobile phone? Without the information stored on the corporate network? Without the ability to execute a credit card clearing?

Cyberspace is a space of possibilities and opportunities on one hand and a space of threats and risks on the other.

An extensive range of state spying, espionage, organized crime and the occasional crime, hacking of personal information and so on is being carried out in this space. These may affect national security (for example, by damaging through Cyberspace a critical national infrastructure, like the power grid or the water system), the conduct of business (e.g., commercial espionage, economic blackmail) and privacy (for example, by posting personal information and images).

Today, various organizations protect themselves from these threats in various forms. The information available online about ways to protect yourself from cyber risks is vast and is composed of methodologies, best practices, 'do's and don'ts', and more.

Protecting the organization against cyber threats requires a lot of knowledge. This knowledge includes a large number of specialties - technological, organizational and procedural.

Many organizations here and abroad are grappling with questions such as - 'Are we investing enough in Cyber-Defense ?', 'Do we invest correctly in Cyber-Defense ?', 'Do we invest in Cyber-Defense as is common in our industry / sector?' Organizations want to protect themselves and reduce their principal risks in Cyberspace , allowing business activity without fear.

The Defense Methodology helps organizations to map their cyber risks to which they are exposed, to understand the business significance of the realization of the risks and to define proportionate safeguards for the reduction of major risks. The Defense Methodology also defines adequate protection of corporate assets which have an impact on a sector or which belong to the state level.

The National Cyber Security Authority (NCSA) was established, among other things, in order to design, implement and integrate a national cyber protection Methodology (Government Decision No. 2444). The NCSA has decided, in this framework, to publish the Defense Methodology for organizations in the Israeli economy, starting with government ministries.

The NCSA has developed this Methodology by combining the world's leading Methodologies, with Israeli civil and security experience, adaptation to Israel's environment and adjusting it to the Israeli business culture.

2 \\ THE DEFENSE METHODOLOGY TENETS

The principal protection concept underlying the present Defense Methodology, is the "Organization as a Whole," namely, Recognizing that what is required is a defense of the organization's functional continuity and business objectives.

This concept is expressed in this document in the following manner:

A. **Management's Responsibility** – responsibility for defending information rests primarily with the organization's management.

B. **Defense according to potential Damage** – investment in protecting each asset will be proportional to its criticality to the organization's functioning.

C. **A defense based on Israeli knowledge and experience** – the Defense Methodology enables focusing on risks specific to each organization. The National Cyber Security Authority (NCSA) conducts periodical intelligence reviews and assessments, allowing the focusing of organizations on specific aspects of the various defense circles.

D. **Proactive Defense** – defense controls were defined, based on the understanding that the organization is required to invest efforts beyond traditional passive defense. This concept finds expression in defining prevention, detection, response, and recovery controls.

E. **A Multilayer Defense** – defense is a process combining three main components: People & Products & processes (3P's). The Defense Methodology defines a defensive response to each layer.

3 \\ THE DEFENSE METHODOLOGY 'S STRUCTURE

Since organizations function in dynamic environments, changes in technology, in companies' character and activity fields influence the manner in which organizations are required to defend themselves in Cyberspace .

The following methodology is based on the fact that the organization is required to assess risks periodically. This risk assessment is the basis of a multi-annual work plan to decrease gaps (implementing required controls).

3.1 THE CYCLICAL DEFENSE PROCESS

The defense process implied by this Methodology is a cyclical process, comprised of three main stages:

- **Planning and assessment** – mapping the organizational defense objectives, risk assessment, inspecting the existing defense means (controls), and devising a work plan to close defensive gaps.

- **Executing** the work plan by developing organizational processes, tools integration as well as an organizational integration of Cyber-Defense .

- **Maintaining up-to-date defenses** in light of the Cyberspace dynamism in the organization. Processes and technologies integrated in the organization are constantly changing – new computers and networks are installed, advanced software packages are acquired, new elements are linked to Cyberspace, (the Internet of Things, for example), new services are offered (such as cloud computing), etc. On the other hand, threats and attack methods are changing, thus requiring the defense tools - to change as well.

3.2 PROTECTION CONTROLS COMPILED UNDER NIST CYBER SECURITY FRAMEWORK

For many years defense standards emphasized the issue of "defending the organization", namely, **preventing** a penetration of the organization and its cyber assets. **The current reality is different** – organizations of all sizes are attacked, but these attacked only are detected, if at all, after a long time. Therefore, the American National Institute of Standards and Technology (NIST) devised a Framework for Improving Critical Infrastructure Cyber Security, investing both in the traditional preparation and protection phases as well as in the detection, containment, and recovery from cyber-attacks. The present Defense Methodology adopts the NIST Cyber Security Framework, binding together clusters of defense controls. **Within this framework the organization is defended from attack, while its capabilities to detect a successful attack, contain it, and recover with minimum impact are augmented**. These controls are based on international knowledge, adjusted for the Israeli economy, including emphases and examples to assist organizations in focusing their efforts more effectively.

Robert S. Mueller, III,
Director FBI:

"There are only two
types of companies -
those that have
been hacked and
those that will be."

IDENTIFY

Control Cluster:
- Board and Management responsibility
- Risk assessment and management
- Control, review, compatibility

PROTECT

Control Cluster:
- Access control
- Data defense
- Defending servers and workstations
- Preventing malicious code
- Encryption
- Network security
- Environment separation
- Cloud security
- Industrial controls defense
- Cellular security
- Change management
- Media security
- Supply chain and outsourcing security
- Purchase and development security
- Human resources and employee awareness
- Seminar

DETECT

Control Cluster:
- Documentation and monitoring
- Security controls reviews
- Proactive Cyber-Defense

RESPOND

Control Cluster:
- Event exercising
- Event management

RECOVER

Control Cluster:
- Business Continuity

17

4 \\ ORGANIZATIONAL PLANNING PROCESS

The planning process is comprised of the following intuitive phases:

Stage 1: "What is there to defend?" – mapping business assets / processes sensitive to cyber-attacks.

Stage 2: "Impact on the organization's objectives" - understanding cyber-attacks' impact on business assets / processes, by filling a business value questionnaire.

Stage 3: "How to protect correctly" - required controls are derived from the values defined in Stage 3.

Stage 4: Ideal versus real – detecting defensive gaps in relation to required controls.

Stage 5: "Designing a project plan" – improving the defense level in order to reach the desired risk level (including the understanding the essence of the exposure to risk, in case of neglecting to install the required controls).

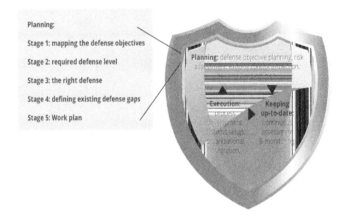

Planning:

Stage 1: mapping the defense objectives

Stage 2: required defense level

Stage 3: the right defense

Stage 4: defining existing defense gaps

Stage 5: Work plan

5 \\ THE DEFENSE METHODOLOGY IN THE EYES OF THE ORGANIZATION

This Methodology presents two different levels of recommendations, which are derived from damage potential to an organization due to a Cyber-incident:

- **Category A Organization** - Low damage potential. The organization will carry out a simple process of mapping protection goals in order to quickly understand the necessary protection method required.

- **Category B Organization** - significant damage potential. An organization that relies heavily on Cyberspace and is required to perform a more detailed process.

The division is done after answering the following question:

IF A CYBER-INCIDENT SHOULD OCCUR IN YOUR ORGANIZATION, WILL THE COST OF HANDLING THE INCIDENT BE HIGHER THAN NIS 500,000?

Tip: the cost of damage resulting from a cyber-incident includes direct and indirect damage to the business. These costs include: temporary service shutdown, damage to reputation, cost of sanctions imposed in light of the breach of law and regulatory requirements, and more.

When answering the following question, it is necessary to take into account the total cost. Organizations that responded negatively to the question above belong to category A. Organizations that responded in the affirmative belong to category B.

Additional requirements: in case where additional obligations, by virtue of being subject to the existing regulations, apply to the organization, it may be transferred from Category A to category B. In addition, an organization may require its various suppliers to meet requirements of category B organizations.

5.1 IMPLEMENTATION OF THE DEFENSE METHODOLOGY FOR A CATEGORY A ORGANIZATION

The Defense Methodology for a category A organization is confined to pages 20-23 of this document.

Stage 1: Asset Mapping

It is necessary to perform a mapping of major assets. Check with technical support the types of equipment and computing assets used in the organization.

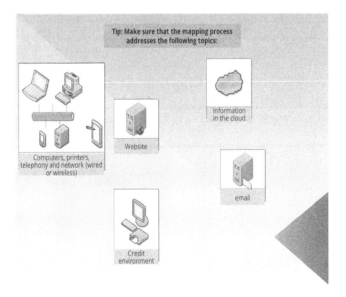

Tip: Make sure that the mapping process addresses the following topics:

Computers, printers, telephony and network (wired or wireless)

Website

Information in the cloud

email

Credit environment

Steps 2 and 3: The Required Level of Protection and how to Correctly Protect - The Ten Commandments for a Category A Organization

A category A organization requires for protection consistent with the damage potential. Therefore the organization is required to implement extremely cost effective controls.

A breakdown of protection requirements is found in Appendix C of this document.

These controls are divided into the following ten categories of protection:

1. Management responsibility		
Understand existing cyber threats, and devise a work plan to close defense cyber gaps.		
2. Avoid malicious Code: Use technologies to cope with malware, and update the organization system defenses.	**3. Encryption:** Encrypt remote access of employees and suppliers, using commercial encryption means. Encrypt access to sensitive data, use an encrypted communication medium (both from domestic surfing through wireless networks to the organization and vice versa to customers and suppliers).	**4. Cloud computing and software purchase:** require (contractually) the supplier to comply with common software and data protection standards.
5. Data protection: define protection mechanisms to protect data existing in the organization.	**6. Computer protection:** define a required computer defense level. Including changing equipment default passwords, removal of unnecessary software programs, redundant connection blocking, removing unnecessary admin accounts.	**7. Human resources:** instruct new employees and remove former employees' authorizations.
8. Documentation and monitoring: document and monitor exceptional activities, which may attest to cyber threats.	**9. Network security:** ensure that network access is under the organization's control (suppliers and employees cannot connect remotely at will) and that the network is prepared to withstand denial of service attacks	**10. Business Continuity:** recover capabilities from site failures, deletion of data, file locking.

Stage 4: Protection Gaps Definitions

A review of the implementation of the controls is set out in Appendix C.

Getting a recommendation from the IT service provider regarding a prioritized work plan for handling gaps.

Stage 5: Work Plan

Every control in the controls chapters protects against cyber risk arising from cyber damage. The control reduces the cyber risk which could harm the objectives of the organization.

The program will take the following into account when preparing a work plan for closing controls gaps:

- **The effectiveness of the control** (its contribution to the reduction of risk to the organization)
- **The cost of implementing the solution** - represented below through a 'solution cost' axis (duration of implementation, complexity of realization, required personnel and equipment)
- **Implementation speed** - represented below by the circle size

An example of the weighting of the parameters mentioned above in an organization might look like this:

CYBER DEFENSE METHODOLOGY \\ THE NATIONAL CYBER SECURITY AUTHORITY (NCSA)

A lookout table:

Control Cluster	Exists / does not exist	Control effectiveness	Implementation Cost	Data / prioritizing weighting
Management responsibility				
Malware prevention				
Encryption				
Cloud computing and software purchase				
Data protection				
Computer protection				
Human resources				
Documentation & monitoring				
Network security				
Business continuation				

The proposed work plan will be endorsed/approved by the CEO

A CATEGORY A ORGANIZATION HAS HEREWITH FINISHED READING THE PRESENT DOCUMENT

23

5.2 IMPLEMENTING THE DEFENSE METHODOLOGY IN "B" CATEGORY ORGANIZATIONS

Stage 1: Asset Mapping

The organization will map its assets, their functions and interfaces (Web services, API, etc.). Include assets stored in the cloud (XaaS).

The asset mapping Stage should link OT/IT assets to main business processes. Following this phases the organization will be able to distinguish between critical and secondary assets.

This definition will assist in protecting assets in relation to impact.

The asset mapping will include the following list as a minimum:

Type of Asset	Name and manufacturer	Purpose	Local / cloud	Interfaces	Remarks
Organizational application					e.g. DWH, CRM, ERP, WMS, Payroll system, organizational portal, etc.
Infrastructure					e.g. Communication equipment, telephony, Email, storage
Network					e.g. LAN / WAN, wireless, optical, satellite
OT					e.g. Closed circuit television, HMI systems, controllers, etc.

Tip: Assume that whatever you are not aware of is not properly secured. In order to conduct a full IT asset mapping, get a full assets list from the IT department, and work with the purchase department which maintains a full list of products and services.

In mapping OT assets – It is recommended to meet with the operations and security managers (especially in industrial organizations).

An organization that prepared a business continuity plan, may be assisted by the damage assessment and in assessing the dependency of organizational processes on data assets (BIA usage).

Attention: object mapping resolution

Defense object mapping is a time and resource consuming process. In order to carry it out effectively, **attention should be paid to the required mapping resolution.**

For example: on the one hand, one should not specify all servers and terminals, but on the other hand a rough generalization of all servers as one asset may result in disproportionate defense costs.

Stage 2: required defense level

The defense level required for each asset is derived from the latter's organizational value level. Within the defense Methodology, assets are rated at four value levels: 1 notes a low value level, 4 notes the highest value level.

Tip: **common biases in asset value assessment**
Asset value assessment should be conducted in cooperation with business units. An owner may "over value" his asset from the business aspect. But sticking to the value questionnaire's criteria should help assessing assets correctly upon a united, unbiased scale.

At the end of step 2, the organization will be able to define the most important assets to its business activities.

A close cooperation of the business entities within the organization - understanding the business significance of assets and their influence on the business functioning - is required in filling the questionnaire.

C
I
A

Attention:

In cyber and data security it is common to assess potential impact by three categories:

- **Impacting data confidentiality –** for example, a cyber-attack intended to leak customers' details to the Internet.

- **Impacting data integrity –** for example a cyber-attack intended to falsify a company's financial reports.

- **Impacting data availability –** for example, a cyber-attack denying information from the company or its customers (shutting down a web site, locking files or planting ransomware).

Define the value level of each asset by filling the following questionnaire:

Question	1	2	3	4
1. What is the level of damage caused to the organization following leakage from the asset? **C**	The damage is estimated at: A) Cost of up to NIS 500,000 to the organization. and/or B) An investment of up to two man-months for handling the incident.	The damage is estimated at: A) Cost of more than NIS 500,000, but less than NIS 5,000,000 to the organization. and/or B) An investment of more than six man-months, but less than five man-years, for handling the incident. and/or C) The asset is defined as a database to whom apply the medium security level in accordance with data protection regulations of the Law, Information and Technology Authority. and/or D) There is a clear danger to public health.	The damage is estimated at: A) Cost of more than NIS 5,000,000 to the organization. and/or B) An investment of more than five man-years for handling the incident. C) The asset is defined as a database to whom apply the medium security level in accordance with data protection regulations of the Law, Information and Technology Authority. D) There is a clear danger to human life.	A significant damage will occur, which will include one of the two scenarios below: A) There is a clear and present danger to the lives of many people. B) The estimated economic damage is over NIS 20,000,000.
2. What is the level of damage caused to the organization following the disruption of information existing in the system? **I**				
3. What is the level of damage caused to the organization following a long-term system shutdown? **A**				

Each asset value score is the highest score received for the three questions (Impact = MAX 1-3). This score is also called **Risk Intensity**. This score defines the maximum damage expected to affect the organization with regards to each asset.

Stage 3: How to protect correctly

In stage 2 we defined for each asset the value extent (intensity) on a scale of 1-4. The degree of protection of any asset is derived directly from the degree of its value (the resulting value raises the intensity level).

Next to each protection control in chapter 6 there is a definition whether it is required for an asset whose intensity score is 1, 2, 3 or 4

For each asset it is necessary to implement the total of all controls whose value is less than or equal to the intensity score of the asset. Thus for example, for an asset whose intensity score is 3 it is necessary to implement all controls whose value is 1, 2 and 3.

This definition helps to adjust the controls required for the application of the defense goal against the damage potential.

Stage 4: Protection Gaps Definitions

Check what is currently implemented in the organization and what is necessary to perform opposite the protection controls listed in Chapter 6.2. At the end of this process, the organization will receive a list of gaps (gap analysis).

Since not all of the controls are implemented in the same way in an organization, it is important to ensure that the essential protection goals of the organization are examined individually. The reason lies in the fact that a control is not always embedded in every objective of the organization. Experience shows that even though most controls are implemented laterally in organizations, there are not a few cases where a control has not been implemented in a specific system.

Since not all controls are necessary for implementation in every asset, use the value level set for each asset in stage 3 for the benefit of the gap list focus.

This gaps list will be the basis for building the organization's work plan (Stage 5).

Calculating an asset's risk level - weighting the data

Weigh the potential impact (I) with the probability for such a cyber-event to happen.

Probability (P) – calculated by defining an asset exposure level (an asset linked to the Internet, yet having no defense mechanisms, is highly exposed to cyber-attacks, while an asset isolated in a secured room is less exposed).

In order to define an asset exposure level, fill the following questionnaire:

Question	1	2	3	4
1. How many users exist in the system?	Up to 50	50-500.	500-5,000.	More than 5,000
2. Who are the system users?	Internal employees only	Regular external suppliers.	Casual external suppliers.	The general public.
3. How many interfaces exist in the system?	None	1-5.	5-10.	More than 10
4. What is the nature of the system interfaces?	None	Intra-organizational interfaces.	External interfaces with suppliers.	Interfaces to the general public.
5. What kind of information exists in the system?	No business sensitivity.	A company's internal information.	Medical information or customers information.	Sensitive business information.
6. Is there a remote access to the system?	No	Via 2FA	Via an encrypted channel.	Via a commercial takeover software
7. What is the level of compartmentalization permissions in the system?	Full compartmentalization (permissions by groups / roles)	Individual compartmentalization (individual permissions per employee)	Basic compartmentalization (manager and user)	No compartmentalization (identical permissions to everyone).
8. What is the current update level of the system?	The most recent version.	Up to 3 versions back.	More than 3 versions back.	Versions that are no longer supported by the manufacturer.
9. What is the policy for updates and security patches?	Installing full updates at least once a quarter.	Installing security updates only at least once a quarter.	Critical security updates only at least once a quarter.	No orderly updating process.
10. What is the physical security level of the system?	Accessible to unauthorized individuals only.	Accessible to all employees of the organization.	Accessible to external contractors.	Accessible to all visitors to the organization.

The exposure score of each asset is the average score of the 10 questions (P = Average 1-10), also called the risk **probability** (P).

Weighting an asset's risk level, response costs and implementation complexity

In order to calculate the required protection level, multiply by three the impact rating, and add the probability rating: an asset's risk level = (I) * 3 + (p).

1	2	3	4	(P)Probability (I) Impact
7	10	13	16	4
6	9	12	15	3
5	8	11	14	2
4	7	10	13	1

An example calculation of an asset's risk is presented in Annex A.

After this Stage, the organization will possess a list that could look like this:

control	The entire organization:	CRM System	Suppliers payment system
4.30 Implement Multifactor Authentication for login of accounts with excessive privileges across the network.	Exists partially	Exists	Required to implement
6.4 Set up and implement security measures to detect and alert on unauthorized changes to configuration settings.	There is an orderly process in the organization	The system is in the cloud and we have no direct control over this requirement	Exists
16.2: Use contractual and legal tools when purchasing an information system or a service from providers.	There is no organized process of signing suppliers in the organization.	The supplier signed a declaration.	This is a supplier from abroad which we are unable to sign. We will consider the requirements in the generic agreement with him.

Stage 5: Work Plan

Every control in the controls chapters protects against cyber risk arising from cyber damage.

The priority of application of the controls lacking in an organization in the framework of the work plan will be determined by the weighting of **asset risk level, the cost of the solution and the complexity of the implementation**.

The priority of application of the controls lacking in an organization in the framework of the work plan will be determined by the weighting of:

- **The asset risk level** - Y-axis in the example below.

- **The cost of the implementation of the solution** - X-axis in the example below.

- **The speed of the implementation of the solution** - expressed through the size of the circle in the example below.

A possible example for weighting the cost of the realization, the asset's cruciality and the speed of execution

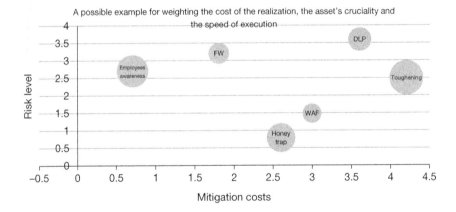

CYBER DEFENSE METHODOLOGY \\ THE NATIONAL CYBER SECURITY AUTHORITY (NCSA)

31

6 \\ CONTROLS CHAPTERS - IMPLEMENTATION AND CONTROL STAGES

6.1 INTRODUCTION

The protection requirements from an organization are called professionally: controls. In order to protect the organization in the cyber field, the organization is required to implement controls in various fields. These controls include the processes, procedures, defense systems and technologies, which the organization has implemented to reduce the risk of the realization of a Cyberspace incident.

These controls are incorporated on the basis of different topics, such as controls for the protection of servers and end stations, user management controls, monitoring controls, and more.

 For the sake of focusing, critical protection controls (those with the highest 'cost-benefit' value) have been marked in this document by a Key icon.

For the benefit of construction of a is proportional Defense Methodology the controls in this document are classified in levels ranging on an axis of 1-4, when controls of level 1 are the most basic controls, required from every organization and every asset, while controls of Level 4 are those which are required for a protection target whose potential for harm is 4.

6.2 HOW TO PROTECT

Family	ID	Monitoring	Complementary Explanation	Monitoring application example	Control level
Identify					
1. Board of Directors' Responsibility. Management Responsibility					
Cyber assets constitute currently critical assets that support organizational objectives. Protecting them can be as important as the protection of physical assets, finances, and employees. Cyber defense is the responsibility of the organization's management. This responsibility expressly requires to be reflected through the perception of Cyber-Defense by the organization's Board of Directors, the Cyber-Defense policy of Management and organizational procedures for Cyber-Defense. Like any defense program, Cyber-Defense is not hermetically sealed, and the Management is required to decide on the level of risk it is willing to take, considering the costs of controls versus the price of the risk materializing within the organization and its impact on customers, suppliers and national targets. Furthermore, the organization's Management must implement mechanisms for handling cyber-events which may occur, in order to reduce the damage to the organization.					
Directorate Responsibility	1.1	The organization's Board of Directors will approve the corporate information security and the Cyber-Defense policy once. year and allocate resources needed for its implementation.	Once. year the Board will be presented with the corporate information security and Cyber-Defense policy, as derived from the organization's cyber risk map. The Board of Directors will approve the risk map and the policies derived from it.	It is recommended to appoint one representative from among the Board members who will be. knowledge focal center (at the managerial level) on the subject. For the benefit of this requirement, it is important to ensure that the risk map is presented to the Board of Directors in. business language alongside the current existing response of the organization and the disparities required in order to reduce the gap and reach an acceptable level of risk. It is important that the Board of Directors will define the risk level that the organization would such as to take ('risk appetite'. for example, as. function of an attribution threat or. cost. benefit) test.	2

Family	ID	Monitoring	Complementary Explanation	Monitoring application example	Control level
Management Responsibility	1.2	The current risk map as it emerges from the organizational cyber risk survey, should be approved annually.	The organization will map out the risks it is exposed to in the cyber field. The risk will be ranked and presented to Management alongside the definition of the planned response.	Organizations with level. assets can carry out an independent survey by mapping assets and sensitive business processes and work on the basis of the risk assessment method of the Defense Methodology . As regards organizations with protection goals on level. or higher, it is recommended to use an external factor for carrying out the survey period	2
Management Responsibility	1.3	Identify legislation and regulations pursuant to the law, applicable to the organization.	All relevant requirements under the law,. standard,. contract with the organization, and all measures undertaken by the organization in order to comply with the requirement, will be clearly defined, documented, and updated for every information systems and Cyber-Defense activities of the organization as. whole.	1. Prepare. list of all the legal requirements, regulations, and contractual obligations that have been identified. An example of statutory and regulatory requirements can be the compliance with the Ministry of Justice (database registration and privacy protection), the protection of credit cards in accordance with the PCI standard requirements, requirements of suppliers and customers for compliance with Cyber-Defense procedures signed by the organization, maintaining copyrights and working with licensed software rather than with. pirated one, and more. 2. Perform and document compliance audits, indicating that the above requirements are carried out in the organization.	2

2. Risks Management and Assessment:
An organization's cyber Defense Methodology is based on the process of managing and assessing cyber risks. This is. cyclical process that must be performed when the organization's cyber environment is changing, both within the organization (absorption of new systems, technological changes, changes in business processes, etc.) and outside the organization (constant change of Cyberspace threats to the organization). According to this Defense Methodology, risk management in an organization requires to identify the goals of the defense, define which controls are necessary to protect them and build. suitable work plan.

Family	ID	Monitoring	Complementary Explanation	Monitoring application example	Control level
Risks Management and Assessment	2.1	Design, process for setting organizational boundaries, mapping the organization's defense goals and assessing the value level of the defense goals. 	The mapping of the defense goals can be accomplished by mapping the organization's work processes, systems, databases and technological infrastructure. The value level of the defense goals is determined in accordance with the effects of the breach on security, availability and integrity of information.	Defining the goals will include all the aspects where the organization must consider the current risk level against the desired level. These targets may include, among other things,. list of systems, infrastructure, business processes, key people and everything that the organization has defined for itself as. Cyber-Defense goal. Please note that there are defense goals which were added in recent years and by mistake have not been mapped. Good mapping will include, for example, the IOT world, including security cameras, elevators and electrical stairs, assembly and other 'software integrated' components, which often are not managed by the organization's IT professionals (do not constitute classic IT assets). These assets are often at the heart of the action of the organization's operation and are no less vulnerable to cyber-attacks (such as an amusement park Ferris wheel, fuel pump, central air-conditioning system, command and control system for turbines, etc.)	2

Family	ID	Monitoring	Complementary Explanation	Monitoring application example	Control level
Risks Management and Assessment	2.2	Define and implement periodic cyber risk assessment process in accordance with the organization's threats outline, the level of exposure to threats of the defense goals, and the protection controls implemented in the organization.	The purpose of the risk assessment process is to provide an updated map of the actual cyber risks (residual risks) in order to define, plan to address the risks. The survey must be carried out periodically and must be updated following changes in processes and systems in the organization.	It is possible to base the risk assessment process on the Cyber-Defense Methodology.	2

3. Monitoring, Reviewing and Compliance:

Every organization is required to protect its cyber assets in order to comply with basic legal aspects of copyright protection (for example, not using unauthorized software), to protect corporate records and protect private information which is located in the company's database. Coded information, if there is any, is kept in accordance with the relevant rules of the legislature. Some organizations are required to meet additional legislative requirements. The organization must build control mechanisms to verify on an ongoing basis that it meets the requirements of the law, the relevant regulation, according to the sector (health, insurance, capital markets, etc.), this Defense Methodology, the Board policy and Management decisions regarding aspects of Cyber-Defense.

Family	ID	Monitoring	Complementary Explanation	Monitoring application example	Control level
Control, Review and Compliance	3.1	Review periodically the various information processes for the purpose of ensuring compliance with security standards, policy and any information security requirement.	A 'Management survey' of the various processes must be carried out, to confirm compliance with the standards and Information Security requirements. This survey will examine the various parameters in the field of Cyber-Defense and provide Management with snapshot regarding the organization's strengths and weaknesses.	A Management survey provides lateral vision on the state of the organization in terms of its current level of protection. These surveys will present to the organization the areas in which it is required to focus, vs. areas in which the organization is more mature (such as the CMMI maturity model). The areas that the survey can refer to might be, for example, secure development, level of awareness, monitoring capabilities, maturity level of response teams, organization procedures, etc. It is important to ensure that the processes defined as critical in the framework of the organization's business continuity program are given proper protective response.	2

Family	ID	Monitoring	Complementary Explanation	Monitoring application example	Control level
Control, Review and Compliance	3.2	The organization will ensure the writing of. protection policy, which will address all aspects detailed herein.	The purpose of the monitoring is to ensure that the organization's Management has defined its guidelines regarding protection aspects of various topics, such as human resource protection policies, supply chain protection policies, monitoring and control policy etc.		
Control, Review and Compliance	3.3	Make sure that the various information systems comply with corporate information security. Cyber-Defense standards, and that they are implemented securely on. regular basis. in accordance with the corporate information security and Cyber-Defense policy.	Periodic reviews should be carried out in order to ensure that the various information systems comply with the information security and Cyber-Defense requirements that the organization has set and that they are immune against attacks.	The proper implementation of this monitoring will be carried out by writing an annual or multi-year corporate plan for performing periodic cyber surveys on corporate assets. The surveys can be in the form of. white. gray or black box, while prioritizing the review of systems that received. high score in the values questionnaire. As regards level. systems, it is recommended that the review be carried out by an independent body outside the organization.	2
Monitoring, Auditing and Compliance	3.4	Automatic check of the organization's level of protection.	Use automated tools, which simulate the attacker activity automatically.	Since performing penetration tests is an action that requires for the most part human involvement, the ability to cover many systems in real time is limited. For the benefit of addressing time and knowledge limitations, there are some products that enable the Director of Defense to receive notification using tools that simulate. 'war game'. attacking the organization using various methods in order to detect attack vectors and weaknesses to address.	4

Family	ID	Monitoring	Complementary Explanation	Monitoring application example	Control level
Protect					

4. Access Control:
Many factors require access to the organizational information for proper functioning, both human elements (the organization's employees, customers and suppliers) and technological factors (applications). These require access to different systems and information types. In order to prevent abuse of this access, the organization must implement monitoring and protection which will ensure that anyone can access only the information they need, and that it is not being used by an unauthorized party. It is also required to ensure that the accessing parties are identified and verified unequivocally. For this purpose, it is required to manage the various users (human and applications) on an ongoing basis, add, abolish or change their privileges as appropriate and record their activities. Extra caution is needed in providing elevated privileges to people and applications (many attacks make use of impersonating parties with elevated privileges) and to detect the corporate network remotely. Access control is one of the basic areas of Cyber-Defense of the organization and requires care for detail.

Family	ID	Monitoring	Complementary Explanation	Monitoring application example	Control level
Access Control	4.1	Develop, document and implement an access control policy.	The access control policy is designed to ensure that only authorized parties can access the organization's information and systems to view and make changes, all in accordance with the definitions of their roles and subject to supervision.	The organization's access control policy may be included as. chapter of its information security policy.	2
Access Control	4.2	Set up user accounts that support the business functions of the organization. 	At the very least, separate the 'Administrator' account from. 'user' account. It is also necessary to set up users who manage the system security functions (such as creating users, managing access and system privileges, managing the information security systems, etc.).	Creating corporate users as standard users, assigning 'administrator' users per defined function only (administrators).	1

Family	ID	Monitoring	Complementary Explanation	Monitoring application example	Control level
Access Control	4.3	Examine the list of users periodically and update it accordingly.	The organization will examine every pre-defined period the list of users and remove irrelevant users as needed.	The periodic users review process and its documentation using access control procedure organizing, ongoing monitoring through an automated or manual array, will be performed by systems administrators. This review is conducted in order to identify both inactive users, users who have left the organization and to ratify the privileges of existing users. For example, if an employee has moved to another position in the organization, in many cases he is 'dragged' with the previous privileges.. review of the business side by the system administrator may float such cases.	2
Access Control	4.4	Disable, remove temporary accounts automatically after specified time.	The organization will set fixed time period, after which temporary account will be blocked automatically.	If possible, set up temporary accounts with time allocation for any system that interfaces with an Active Directory or management system or an Identity Management system (IDM). Accounts that must be extended require special approval.	3
Access Control	4.5	Disable, remove inactive accounts automatically after specified time.	The organization will disable, remove inactive accounts after fixed period of time, defined in the policy.	Periodic reports must be issued regarding users' login activity in system that interface with an Active Directory as well as accounts that were closed long time ago (as defined in the access control procedure.) Delete such accounts.	3
Access Control	4.6	Document in an automatic log record any creation, modification, enabling, disabling, and removal of accounts.	The organization will document any change to user accounts and will conduct an automatic or manual follow-up of the execution of the documentation.	This can be implemented through monitoring (SIEM), which will interface with per task management systems in the organization. Active Directory, IDM, servers, applicative systems as well as communication and information security equipment.	3

Family	ID	Monitoring	Complementary Explanation	Monitoring application example	Control level
Access Control	4.7	Monitor account activity in order to detect anomalous usage and report unusual use to the appropriate officials.	Examples of anomalous use: Logging into the system on certain days and at certain times, login from addresses incompatible with normal use pattern.	Can be applied using. SIEM system for monitoring users in sensitive groups. The information collection will be made from sources such as Active Directory, communications and information security equipment (firewalls, etc.).	3
Access Control	4.8	Define and enforce conditions for blocking accounts.	Examples of entry blocking conditions: Weekend, night hours.	It is possible to define in the user setting an entry restriction on the Active Directory account, so that the restriction will not allow connection during non-working hours.	4
Access Control	4.9	Define and enforce logical access privileges to the system and the information in accordance with the access control policy.	The access control can be done on. personal level (identity-based), or the role level (role-based), and aims to control the access of entities (users or computer processes) to objects (files, records, devices etc.).	Users will be managed centrally through an organizational Enterprise Directory, e.g. an Active Directory, Open LDAP and more. The per task system will be mapped to the user profile.	1
Access Control	4.10	Limit user privileges to the essential minimum to perform their duties.	The organization will define. minimum level of privileges for each role as well as. minimal privilege level for. basic user (without. defined role) required for access to the organization's systems.	User privileges will be in accordance with their role.. basic profile will be defined and given to the user, and additional privileges will be granted according to need and with the approval of. direct supervisor; if there is an IDM system. basic profile and applicative profiles can be mapped. After improvement of the process privileges will be given depending on the role.	2

Family	ID	Monitoring	Complementary Explanation	Monitoring application example	Control level
Access Control	4.11	Define officials, carry out. separation of duties and give it expression through granting system privileges.	The purpose of the separation of duties is to reduce the potential for abuse of privileges. The separation includes, for example, separation of business functions between employees or officials, as well as ensuring that the information security team that manages the access control does manage the access control Review functions at the same time.	A per task mapping which supports. separation of powers must be carried out and implemented within user privilege profiles, e.g.. developer vis-à-vis. software tester (each of them will have access to. different environment:. developer will work in. development environment. a low environment;. tester will work in. higher environment. pre-production), etc.	3
Access Control	4.12	Access to sensitive systems and applications will be made only through. designated mediation hardened component (Terminal).	For the benefit of applying. uniform 'hardened' policy to sensitive resources, ensure that access to them will be made only after going through the mediation component (such as. proxy server or terminal).	It is possible to exercise this control by defining access in the firewall component so that connection to sensitive assets is permitted only through the link component, including testing and the stringent corporate policy (such as preventing the ability to perform 'copy. paste', preventing download files capability, CLI locking, etc.) .	4
Access Control	4.13	Define employees who are authorized to publish information in. system accessible to the public (such as. Web site), and implement this authorization as part of the privileges granting process.	The organization will define users whose job require the ability to publish information on public sources and will document the above-mentioned functions as part of the organization's procedure.	In Content Management Systems (CMS), it is necessary to grant editing rights and publication privileges only to content managers.	3

Family	ID	Monitoring	Complementary Explanation	Monitoring application example	Control level
Access Control	4.14	Restrict user login to the system after several unsuccessful login attempts using the lock option to log in for. specified time, or until. release by. system administrator.	The purpose of this monitoring is to deal with the risk of Denial of Service attacks. This control must be implemented at both levels of connecting to the operating system and of connecting to specific applications.	It is possible to limit the number of failed login attempts within the Group Policy and the Domain Policy.	2
Access Control	4.15	Limit the number of simultaneously-allowed connections of. single user.	The purpose of this monitoring is to detect the connection from two different places using the same identification. Such. scenario might be an indication of unauthorized use of. user account.	It is possible to limit the number of simultaneous connections in the Remote Logon policy in the Group Policy.	3
Access Control	4.16	Lock connections resulting from temporary inactivity and disable the continued connection until the identification and re-authentication of the user. As part of the connection locking hide information that has appeared on screen prior to the locking.	This control is usually applied at the level of the operating system, but it can also be implemented at the application level. It should be noted that. connection locking is not. regular substitute for log-out.	This can be achieved by setting. screen saver. If possible, make sure that self-development systems and shelf products systems include. Session Time Out mechanism.	3
Access Control	4.17	Write down and implement usage restrictions and configuration requirements for remote connection.	A policy for handling remote connections is required, which defines the limits of the use of remote connection to the organization's resources. The use of systems that provide secure remote access to the organization's resources is required as well.	It is possible to implement secure access to the organization through systems such as VPN or SSH, which are consistent with corporate policies for remote connection to enterprise resources.	2

Family	ID	Monitoring	Complementary Explanation	Monitoring application example	Control level
Access Control	4.18	Remote connections should be monitored.	Automatic monitoring of remote connections allows organizations to detect cyber-attacks, as well as allowing to ensure compliance with remote access procedures by controlling the activities carried out during the remote connection.	It is possible to interface the remote access systems with monitoring systems such as SIEM, and verify that login events are indeed recorded. Special emphasis should be placed on remote login by external suppliers to the organization for maintenance and support, and on monitoring their activities effectively (e.g. Through monitoring and screen-recording tools).	3
Access Control	4.19	Route all remote connections through, set number managed network access control points.	Reducing the number of access control points reduces the attack surface.	Review the organization's attack surface mapping and transfer sensitive corporate services to the network area located behind the firewall. Redirect traffic to it from the VPN network through access from the VPN server. Eliminated direct extra-organizational to access these services.	3
Access Control	4.20	Implement additional safeguards when executing sensitive commands via remote connection.	Sensitive commands are, for example, booting, server or cancellation of. transaction. Make sure that it is impossible to execute such commands in the framework of. normal login system.	Access to sensitive servers as well as to the systems management will be carried out by an Out-of-Band management network, which can be accessed through. dedicated management server (requiring identification and authentication).	3
Access Control	4.21	Prohibit remote login in order to manage the system, and limit access to the system from networks that are not managed by the organization.	The organization will not allow direct remote access to management interfaces, unless securely, and only after verification and connecting to. management network.	Administrator Login must be avoided when remotely connecting to systems (can be done in Linux also by eliminating PermitRootLogin).	4

Family	ID	Monitoring	Complementary Explanation	Monitoring application example	Control level
Access Control	4.22	Protect the connection to. system from. wireless network using user. devices authentication, encryption and setting usage limits.	The organization will allow connection to. wireless network only for devices managed. authenticated by it, and only for identified users. The purpose of this monitoring is to prevent illegitimate and unidentified use of the wireless network.	Access to the wireless network will be allowed only after identification opposite the Access Point.	2
Access Control	4.23	Calibrate the signal strength of the wireless signal in order to reduce the chances of signals will be received outside the organization's facility.	The organization will review the broadcast signals of the wireless networks and will ensure that the signal does not exceed. predefined range.	Mapping of the reception range can be carried out using spatial overview and special equipment (Radio) in coordination with the wireless system provider. it is also possible to conduct independently via Radio Analyzer and scanning around the area of the building.	4
Access Control	4.24	Prohibit connecting to organizational systems from. wireless network.	Access to enterprise systems will be allowed only for computer equipment through. wired connection to the organization's network.	Do not connect the wireless networks to the organization's network, but only on. dedicated Internet router for surfing only. It is also possible to implement. proxy server of the wireless network.	2
Access Control	4.25	Write down and implement usage restrictions and configuration requirements for connection through mobile devices.	The organization will write down and implement. policy for monitoring information security for mobile devices that access the organization's systems. The policy should address both the devices provided and managed by the organization as well as personal devices of the organization's employees or guests.	Write down. mobile devices policy, which defines the limits of the use of mobile devices (such as cell phones and tablets): what can be saved and accessed in the organization via. mobile device.	2

Family	ID	Monitoring	Complementary Explanation	Monitoring application example	Control level
Access Control	4.26	It is imperative to implement full encryption of the information stored on mobile devices in order to protect the confidentiality and integrity of the information.	The organization will encrypt the disk space of mobile devices that connect to conduct its systems.	This can be applied through. policy which will be distributed to mobile devices using Mobile Device Management and supported by the majority of Android and Apple devices.	3
Access Control	4.27	Ban logging into. sensitive system through mobile devices.	The organization will block and enforce through technological controls access to sensitive organizational systems via mobile devices.	This can be applied by identifying the mobile device's browser, or, alternatively, do not allow the exposure of sensitive systems to networks accessed by mobile devices (neither behind the VPN segment, or, alternatively, to connect mobile devices to. VPN segment that is different from the other computers).	4
Access Control	4.28	It is necessary to identify and validate uniquely the users of the system.	The organization will verify in an unequivocal manner. user connecting to the organization's systems.	Each system user will have. unique username (which is mapped to. particular person). As for generic user, it will be indicated who has the generic username and applicative users will be owned by the system administrator.	2
Access Control	4.29	Implement Multifactor Authentication for login to accounts with excessive privileges across the network.	The organization will implement local identification by several identification means (two or more) in sensitive accounts.	Can be realized, for example by using magnetic cards, fingerprints or other mechanisms supported by Active Directory.	2
Access Control	4.30	Implement Multifactor Authentication for local login of accounts with excessive privileges.	The organization will implement identification by several identification means (two or more) in sensitive accounts in local login.	Can be realized, for example by using magnetic cards, fingerprints or other mechanisms supported by Active Directory.	3

Family	ID	Monitoring	Complementary Explanation	Monitoring application example	Control level
Access Control;	4.31	Implement an authentication mechanism which is replay-resistant for connecting each account (with an emphasis on. verification mechanism by encryption means).	The organization will implement an eavesdropping-proof identify mechanism (such as an identity mechanism which issues. one-time identification) for all accounts.	Can be realized through mechanisms such as smart cards or one-time password.	4
Access Control;	4.32	Implement Multifactor authentication to connect remotely to the system.	The organization will implement remote identification by several identification means (two or more) for the organization's systems.	Can be realized through mechanisms such as smart cards or one-time password in remote access to systems such as VPN.	2
Access Control,	4.33	Identify and validate uniquely devices which are in the progress of connecting.	The organization will recognize unequivocally devices connecting to the corporate network.	Can be realized by using digital certificates issued to end point and portable computers.	3
Access Control	4.34	Manage means of identification to the system, including: selecting means of identification of an employee or office holder and their placement and blocking after. period of disuse.	Manage. pool of identification methods and their issuance. Also, It is possible to cancel the means of identification through. central system.	Can be realized through OTP management system if it. stronger identification means than the existing system is required.	2
Access Control	4.35	The organization must enforce. password policy through technology.	The policy enforcement must include at. minimum: setting. minimum complexity, variance from previous passwords, set expiration time,. requirement to define. new password after an initial login.	Can be realized by using Group Policy and Domain Policy.	2

Family	ID	Monitoring	Complementary Explanation	Monitoring application example	Control level
Access Control	4.36	Ensure that the feedback from the information system throughout the verification process does not provide information that could cause harm if discovered or if it will be used by unauthorized parties.	Disguise the authentication fields by hiding the password.	Can be realized through built-in mechanisms in the operating systems. It is also possible to implement in Web pages by defining the field as, Password.	2
Access Control	4.37	Implement encrypted authentication mechanism.	The goal is that the identifying information will not be exposed (Clear text). Exposed identification information can be stolen if transferred through an unencrypted communications medium, for example, in case of an MIDM attack.	Can be realized through mechanisms such as smart cards or one-time password.	2

5. Protecting the information:
In the digital age we live in, information is one of the most significant assets for most organizations, whether it is business information, customer data or any data collected and maintained by the organization for the purpose of its business operations. Accordingly, the organization must act to protect its information from theft, tampering, or deletion, and sometimes it is even obligated to do so under the provisions of the law. These controls apply to protecting the information itself, its classification, storage, portability and so on.

Family	ID	Monitoring	Complementary Explanation	Monitoring application example	Control level
Protecting the information	5.1	Prevent unauthorized or unintentional data transfer via shared system resources.	The organization must prevent the transfer of information in an unauthorized manner, e.g. by using shared folders, email, removable media etc.	Restrict the use of shared folders for transferring information, especially when there are also per task to unauthorized parties. It is possible to use. DLP system in order to prevent the transfer of information stored in shared folders.	1

Family	ID	Monitoring	Complementary Explanation	Monitoring application example	Control level
Protecting the information.	5.2	The organization must write down and implement relevant policy and procedures to protect the information and update it periodically.	The policy must include at least. reference to various types of information in the organization. system. The policy must include clear definitions about taking out information beyond the boundaries of the organization, and the method of releasing that information. In addition, it is necessary to refer to all the channels and terminal equipment in the organization: workstations, servers, mobile equipment, including computers, tablets, mobile phones and wearable computing equipment (smart watches, etc.).	This control can be implemented by writing. policy document regarding the protection of information in the organization. The document must include definitions for the various types of information in the organization, what types of information can be sent outside the organization. Furthermore, it is also necessary to write complimentary procedures on how information is sent securely.	2
Protecting the information.	5.3	The organization must write down and implement an organizational information classification policy and implementation procedures for the organization's employees for the purpose of labeling the information.	The classification policy must include clear definitions of how and in what way to classify each type of characterized information.. procedure for guiding how to handle each classification of information should also be added.	1. Characterize the types of information available in the organization according to their importance. based on business needs, or rules and regulations applicable to the organization. 2. Produce. matrix that includes all of the classification categories. what is included in every classification (i.e. What types of information, for example: private, business, health, public security, etc.) and the different types of information handling (storage, transfer, destruction, physical and logical protection, etc.).	3

Family	ID	Monitoring	Complementary Explanation	Monitoring application example	Control level
Protecting the information.	5.4	Implement safeguards to prevent information leakage when transferring information to internal or external parties.	The organization must implement mechanisms for the protection of information when moving between enterprise systems and when sending it to parties outside the organization in accordance with corporate information protection policy.	Can be realized using several technologies, each of which may prevent certain scenario: 1. An information leak prevention system; 2. secure system for transferring information such as secure. encrypted email, an electronic safe etc.	2
Protecting the information.	5.5	Implement protection mechanisms for monitoring and preventing access, use or removal of information, defined as sensitive by the organization, to unauthorized entities within and outside the organization.	The organization must implement mechanisms for the protection of information while saving it in the organizational storage arrays, which may be physical, virtual and cloud servers, as well as when safeguarding the organizational workstations; ensure that the protection mechanisms do not allow replication, printing, sending, deleting, etc. of information defined as sensitive information contrary to the policy established regarding that information.	Can be realized using technologies to prevent information leakage in order to monitor, warn and prevent these actions. Can also be implemented using document protection solutions (Document Security) as well as through monitoring and restricting access to sensitive files (expanded on in the chapters on access control and monitoring).	3

Family	ID	Monitoring	Complementary Explanation	Monitoring application example	Control level
Protecting the information.	5.6	Prevent remote operation of computer accessories (webcams, microphones, speakers, headphones, or any accessory that may be connected to PC) and provide an explicit indication regarding the fact that computer accessories are physically active with the user.	Prevent blocking, disabling remote operation of cameras, microphones and so on.	It is preferable to permanently block computer accessories which are not used in order to reduce this risk.	3

6. Protection of workstations and servers:
Workstations and servers are the basic computing equipment in any organization; protecting this equipment is fundamental to prevent attacks on the organization and protecting corporate information. Workstations and server protection controls have several layers of protection, Toughening Services (White, Black List), preventing the creation of security breaches by using both maliciously and accidentally, and more.

Family	ID	Monitoring	Complementary Explanation	Monitoring application example	Control level
Protection of workstations and servers.	6.1	Define, document and implement, toughening policy for workstations and servers, which meets the requirements of the organization's information security.	The organization will define toughening requirements for systems within the organization with an emphasis on what are the basic requirements, the frequency of updates and the level of classification and then document the requirements in an overall framework which will serve as basis for toughening procedures.	It is possible to use baseline documents of the official manufacturers and standards organizations, such as DISA, SANS, etc.. Also, define in the organization's procedures who is responsible for the implementation of the actual toughening and how the ongoing test of the controls is carried out. The toughening documents shall include, inter alia,. reference to the usage of unauthorized, safe services, approved ports, removal of inactive accounts and so on. It is important to make sure that the toughening will be carried out in accordance with the relevant functionality of the application (such as toughening IIS servers opposite TOMCAT, WEB server toughening opposite. DB server toughening etc.).	1

Family	ID	Monitoring	Complementary Explanation	Monitoring application example	Control level
Protection of workstations and servers.	6.2	Implement mechanisms for centralized management, implementation and validation of the system configuration.		On Windows systems It is possible to use Group Policy tools such as Active Directory; in Linux systems It is possible to use, for example, Red Hat's tools, or, alternately, management and auto configuration distribution tool like Chef.	3
Protection of workstations and servers.	6.3	Set up. policy to control, enforce and monitor the installation of software on the organization's PCs.	The purpose of the control is to make sure that the software is installed on endpoints and servers only with approval and after examination of the need and risk involved in using the software.	This control can be realized by restricting user accounts for installation. modification of the software endpoints as well as by using an Application Control tool.	2
Protection of workstations and servers.	6.4	Set up and implement security measures to detect and alert on unauthorized changes to configuration settings.	System configuration changes may reduce the level of protection of the asset. Thus, for example,. change of password length setting, or per task to install software that is not in accordance with the organization's policy exposes it to risk.	Can be achieved by defining relevant laws in the SIEM system by comparing periodic reports (current versus previous configuration), by means of dedicated monitoring and control. command and control tools that provide an indication of the configuration changes, etc.. It Is recommended to adopt CCM (Continuity Control Monitoring) tools in order to receive notification in real time.	3

Family	ID	Monitoring	Complementary Explanation	Monitoring application example	Control level
Protection of workstations and servers	6.7	Set up and use. Whitelist of permitted-to-use software and block any other software.	The organization will define. list of permitted-to-use software and will block installation and use of any other software using the organizational configuration management system, or by using. third party tool and will block the installation of these software programs.	It is possible to set up. list of permitted-to-use software using the Active Directory, or using configuration management tools. Some of the servers and endpoints protection tools support the above capabilities.	3
Protection of workstations and servers	6.8	The organization will conduct monitoring of servers and systems which have been excluded (and whose exclusion was approved) from the implementation of. hardened configuration.	Sometimes, for business and. or operational reasons it is impossible to apply the level of protection for all assets in the same way. In such cases, the organization is required to implement. process which will require special per task to exclude. particular server or system from information security requirements following. certain need, and in doing so the organization will be responsible for providing compensating controls instead of exclusion.	It is possible to set up. sector head or an official who will constitute an 'Approving Authority' for exclusion from the policy for the benefit of the exclusion needs, will examine the operational and business need for exclusion and recommend compensating controls.	3

7. Preventing Malicious Code:
Malicious code is being used by hostile elements to the organization and is designed to penetrate it without the approval of the organization in order to harm it through Cyberspace (data theft, data tampering, damage to computer systems, etc.). Malicious code is. broad term, which includes many types of abusive software: viruses, worms, Trojans, Rootkits, Adware and more. System protection against malicious code is of paramount importance in the Cyber-Defense of an organization. The defense array includes prevention of malicious code intrusion on one hand (at entry and exit points of corporate communications, servers and endpoints), detection and the process of handling malicious code that has infiltrated the organization, on the other hand.

Family	ID	Monitoring	Complementary Explanation	Monitoring application example	Control level
Preventing Malicious Code.	7.1	The organization will activate tools and systems in its external communication points. These tools will scan and detect malicious code. These tools will operate on communication with external parties, email and browsing services.	The purpose of this monitoring is to detect malicious code prior to its entering the organization, still at the GW level.	Can be realized by using proxy servers, NGFW systems and tools dedicated to different communication protocols, such as email.	2
Preventing Malicious Code.	7.2	The organization will define procedures for handling stations, servers or networks infected by malicious code.	The purpose of this monitoring is to ensure that the organization is prepared to cope with malicious code infiltration events.	Examples of procedures: procedure for detection and removal of malware, operating system re-installation procedure, identification of trends and reaching conclusions in the case of. massive propagation and infection in the organization.	2
Preventing Malicious Code.	7.3	Implement tools to detect and prevent malicious code on endpoints and servers in the organization. These tools will be run in an active protection mode and periodic scans will be performed as well.	Since some abusive software may penetrate the security mechanisms, ensure that controls for handling malicious code will also be applied at the workstation level.	It is possible to use any tool to detect and prevent malicious code (such as antivirus) from. recognized manufacturer.	1
Preventing Malicious. Code.	7.4	The organization will implement and manage these capabilities as part of the endpoints protection tools, or will integrate tools with these capabilities in addition to existing antivirus tools.	The purpose of this monitoring is to raise the level of detection and handling of endpoints 'beyond' the basic capabilities of an existing antivirus system.	HIPS products can be used independently or as additional capabilities of software protection of anti-virus products.	3

Family	ID	Monitoring	Complementary Explanation	Monitoring application example	Control level
Preventing Malicious Code:	7.5	Advanced controls must be activated to prevent malicious code in the operating systems of servers and endpoints.	The organization will activate in the operating system mechanisms that make it difficult for malicious code to access memory or operating system functions.	Can be achieved with solutions for identifying anomalies in the operating system level.	4
Preventing Malicious Code:	7.6	Implement. tool for identifying malware at the network level.	The organization will activate tools that will be implemented at the organization's network with the aim of identifying and alerting of online malware propagation.	Examples of these tools: Honeypots, Anti-Bot technology, IDS components etc..	3
Preventing Malicious Code:	7.7	The organization will manage the malicious code prevention tool in the organization through. central system. The main management tools will enable. major reporting of suspicious incidents and system events identification (problems updating, protection inactive, component removal, etc.).	The purpose of this monitoring is to manage effectively the protection system from malicious code. Working through locally installed configuration makes it difficult to distribute updates, to ensure full coverage and to control the overall defense situation.	Most malicious code prevention systems allow the use of management tools with. centralized management interface.	2
Preventing Malicious Code:	7.8	The organization will activate detection and prevention measures, based on the detection of behavior which deviated from reasonable and acceptable behavior, in addition to the use of electronic signatures based tools.	The purpose of this monitoring is to detect activities that deviate from the norm. The encryption of multiple files, documents that attempt to access the registry files etc.. are for example events which are supposed to raise. 'red flag' in the organization.	It is possible to use tools that analyze heuristics,. user or. system's behavior.	3

Family	ID	Monitoring	Complementary Explanation	Monitoring application example	Control level
Preventing Malicious Code:	7.9	Run an automatic updating of all systems for identifying and preventing malicious code within the organization.	The organization will activate automatic updates from central server, managed by the organization or by recognized service provider. These updates will keep the protection tools constantly updated.	It is possible to use update servers, embedded within the organization's management servers as part of these systems, or, alternatively, use the manufacturer's servers If there is no central update server in the organization's network (also applies to cloud services).	1

8. Encryption;
Intelligent use of encryption is of great help in protecting the information and preventing its exposure, even when it had leaked, thus reducing much of the business significance of information leakage. It is therefore important to define applications that require encryption and the encryption type required, in accordance with laws, guidelines, procedures, regulation, business commitments and the economic feasibility in the framework of risk management. It is imperative to configure encryption on different media information may leak from (memories, communication middleware, etc.) and to define mechanisms for the managing and monitoring encryption (such as management of cryptographic keys and digital certificates in various stages). Of particular importance is the media encryption on mobile devices (laptops, mobile phones, tablets, etc.).

Family	ID	Monitoring	Complementary Explanation	Monitoring application example	Control level
Encryption	8.1	Define uses that require encryption and the encryption type required, in accordance with laws, guidelines, procedures, regulations and business commitments.	The organization will define what information and systems should be encrypted and record the configuration of the information encryption. The requirements will be derived from the requirements applicable to the organization or from information retention requirements.	Examples of such requirements are laws protecting privacy, PCI-DSS, and other security requirements.	1
Encryption	8.2	Manage and protect encryption keys during production, distribution, storage, access and destruction.	The organization will define procedures and processes for the issuance of encryption keys, protecting the private encryption keys and servers for issuing keys and certificates, toughening procedures and procedures for rekeying.	Toughening and preserving the Root Ca Servers, protection using HSM, cryptographic key distribution to systems and employees, operating the PKI array.	1

Family	ID	Monitoring	Complementary Explanation	Monitoring application example	Control level
Encryption	8.3	Ensure the availability of information even in the event of loss of encryption keys.	The organization will implement an encrypted data recovery system through the implementation of managed processes and appropriate tools.	For example,. laptops disk encryption recovery array by using the manufacturer's disk encryption tools and managed recovery processes.	3
Encryption	8.4	Implement encryption of sensitive information transmitted between the organization's systems and end-user interfaces on public communication middleware.	The organization will implement data encryption arrays for sensitive information displayed to the user through. browser,. mobile app or other systems that provide access to information through public networks such as the internet.	Using approved and updated SSL certificates in the browser.	TBD
Encryption	8.5	Implement encryption of sensitive information transmitted between systems within the organization.	The organization will implement encrypted traffic in interfaces between servers and services that transmit sensitive information and will prefer to use protocols which encode traffic.	Can be realized using protocols such as SSL, SSH, HTTPS, and more.	TBD
Encryption	8.6	Implement encryption of sensitive information transmitted between the organization and external interfaces, vendors, external systems.	The organization will implement encrypted communication with suppliers and systems outside the organization.	Can be realized using protocols such as SSL, SSH, HTTPS, SFTP and more.	2
Encryption	8.7	Implement encryption mechanisms on portable devices' media (laptops, mobile phones, tablets, etc.).	The organization will implement hard disk encryption of mobile devices and portable media devices.	Mobile devices and tablets can use the manufacturers' disk encryption system. Other operating systems can use the vendors' tools which enable disk encryption.	2

Family	ID	Monitoring	Complementary Explanation	Monitoring application example	Control level
Encryption	8.8	Use encryption mechanisms based on recognized encryption algorithms and key sizes corresponding to the outline of the threat.	The organization will not use encryption mechanisms with known weaknesses and vulnerabilities, and will match the encryption strength, including the encryption key sizes, to the outline of the threat.	For example: do not use outdated encryption methods, such as SHA1, SSLv1, SSLv2, or encryption keys smaller than 128 Bit, etc.	2
Encryption	8.9	Manage. digital certificates array for the issuance and revocation of digital certificates and use digital certificates from trusted sources only.	The organization will manage an array for the issuance of digital certificates and an array for the revocation of certificates (CRL). In addition, it will also use external certificates issued by trusted sources only (Trusted CA).	Can be realized through an orderly and up-to-date CRL server array. and the use of external certificates from approved services (Trusted CA).	2
Encryption	8.10	Define. process for the renewal of digital certificates prior to expiration.	The organization will ensure that the digital certificates in regular use are renewed prior to their expiration. If the certificates are replaced. older certificates are distributed to certificate revocation servers (CRL).		2
Encryption	8.11	Carry out periodically. proactive replacement of sensitive encryption keys.	The organization will define the life of sensitive cryptographic keys and take care to replace them in time. It is also necessary to implement. replacement process of encryption keys in sensitive applications.		2

Family	ID	Monitoring	Complementary Explanation	Monitoring application example	Control level
9. Network security: The communications infrastructure of the organization is key factor connecting all computing resources at its disposal, both among themselves and to the internet and to other organizations. The communications infrastructure is critical to everyday activities in many organizations, and its shutdown or damaging it have significant meaning for the organization. Therefore the organization's network is starting point for many types of attacks on the organization, and consequently it is imperative to protect it against internal and external threats. Network Protection includes functional, technological, processing and procedural separations, control and monitoring of networks, filtering and blocking suspicious information, and more. Extensive network controls, because many attacks are carried out through the corporate network. Great importance is given to controls designed to protect corporate networks connection among themselves, corporate communications nodes and of course with the internet.					
Network security	9.1	Write down and implement, communication network protection policy, Review and update it periodically.	The organization must write down and implement, network security policy. The policy should include, reference to topics such as access channels to the public Internet network and configuring their protection, in addition, it should address core aspects of internal communications and external communication.	Writing, policy document or its integration as, chapter in the organization's information security policy.	2
Network security	9.2	Separate user functionality from network management services.	Management interfaces are to be separated from other user interfaces in order to reduce their exposure to unauthorized access to management interfaces.	Can be realized through, separate login page for users and for administrators. A separate communication network used to connect to the equipment management interfaces. Restricting IP address authorized to access the management interface and so on.	3
Network security	9.3	The organization will operate technological devices in order to protect services against Denial of Service attacks.	Defend against Denial of Service attacks (DOS) of various types, such as loading the computing resources to collapse, loading the communication bandwidth, loading the website to crash and more.	Control can be implemented using tools such as firewall systems (using an IPS module), intrusion prevention systems (IPS), applicative firewalls (WAF), as well as restrictions on the amount of volume of traffic towards certain systems, or limiting the number of queries performed on the system.	1

Family	ID	Monitoring	Complementary Explanation	Monitoring application example	Control level
Network security;	9.4	Disconnect network connection linked to the session at its conclusion, or after. specified time of inactivity.	The organization will apply limits on the lifetime of the connection, and will monitor and break communication without trans task.	Control can be implemented using. firewall and setting it so that network connections receive. Timeout after. set period of inactivity.	2
Network security;	9.5	Set guidelines for the use of IP telephony technology (VOIP) and also monitor its use.	The organization will define when and how it is permitted. prohibited to use VOIP services (embedded in the organization's systems or as an external service) and will operate information security measures in order to enforce those settings.	Can be applied by Separating the VoIP network from the standard network, limiting non-telephony connectivity equipment to the network using measures such as NAC, identification of the equipment opposite VOIP servers as well as the use of encryption and identification using SSL.	2
Network security;	9.6	Make sure that the Address Translation Service (DNS) is provided by. trusted server (intra-enterprise and extra-enterprise.)	The organization will allow the obtaining of Address Translation Service (DNS) only from. secure internal server, in order to prevent erroneous communication rouing (intentionally or unintentionally) to hostile targets.	Internal DNS servers will be configured and will provide. response to the organization's servers. It is also possible to configure dedicated DNS servers for more secure areas of the network.. Enterprise servers will be configured so that any request to. DNS service will be performed solely through those servers	1
Network security;	9.7	Make sure that the answers received from the address translation server are reliable and were not altered during the transtask..	The organization will ensure that answers returned from the address translation server cannot be modified through mechanisms such as underwriting answers that are sent by. digital certificate.	Can be applied using DNSSEC extensions of the DNS service.	2

Family	ID	Monitoring	Complementary Explanation	Monitoring application example	Control level
Network security	9.8	Protect the communications credibility at the session level, so that both ends of the session will be sure of the correctness of the identity of the second party (MITM protection, session hijacking, etc.).	The organization will activate reliability monitoring through technology such as digital certificates while establishing communication between various system services.	It is possible to use SSL certificates for identifying the service and. secure internal CA server which issues certificates for the various services in the organization. The service is supported in an Active Directory infrastructure and Microsoft's Kerberos services. The session management monitoring can be applied using session monitoring at the server level (such as IIS or Apache), or at the network level using Load Balancer.	2
Network security	9.9	Monitor the organization's outbound. inbound network traffic.	The purpose of this monitoring is to ensure that traffic into and out of the organization will be permitted only in accordance with the defined policy (access through authorized protocols, approved service, from. to approved destinations, etc.).	Can be realized through the application of firewalls which distinguishing between the enterprise's network and external networks.	2
Network security	9.10	Monitor and control major communication junctions within the organization's network.	The organization will divide its network into sub-networks, according to risk level. data classification in the systems.	The networks can be separated through. corporate firewall between environments, setting up environments such as. buffer zone (DMZ) for services outbound to the internet, management networks which will be connected behind. secure connection, networks that contain sensitive services and sensitive systems.	3
Network security	9.11	It is necessary to limit the number of communication channels outside the system.	The organization will reduce and unite communication channels to ensure better control over the connections to the system.	Using. terminal server to connect to the system.	2

Family	ID	Monitoring	Complementary Explanation	Monitoring application example	Control level
Network security	9.12	Block by default all network traffic and allow manually any desirable traffic by means of exception rules.	The organization will define the filtering rules of network traffic so as to block by default all traffic not explicitly defined as allowed.	Configuring, 'Zero rule' in the firewall, blocking all traffic not explicitly enabled. Make sure that routes are set up so that all traffic will be routed through firewalls.	1
Network security	9.13	Prevent devices from creating local communication over the system in parallel to communication via an external connection..	The purpose of this monitoring is to prevent. situation where the computer acts as. bridge that connects the external world to the internal network of the organization.	It is possible to configure the workstation by. policy that determines that only one network card is active at any time on the server, connections will be configured only to the hub of the organization, behind. firewall, while eliminating other network cards (which are not connected to. required network by definition, such as storage network), such as wired. wireless network cards.	2
Network security	9.14	Communication should be routed within the organization to external networks through authenticated and managed proxy servers.	The organization will determine that all communications to external networks will be made only through proxy servers. In order to create. medium which will prevent direct communication that exposes the organization's resources to the internet, and also in order to facilitate implementation of concentrated controls and protections of communication channels versus the Internet.	Can be applied via. proxy server connected to the world, while surfing is performed only through it. The proxy server will be configured with the option to restrict connections to unauthorized sites and categories. Also, servers will be configured so that Internet access is enabled only for updates through the proxy server (if it is impossible to use. dedicated updates server of the system manufacturer).	3

Family	ID	Monitoring	Complementary Explanation	Monitoring application example	Control level
Network security	9.15	Implement mechanisms to prevent unauthorized physical connection to the corporate network.	Connecting unauthorized equipment to the enterprise network exposes enterprise resources to damage of confidentiality and integrity of information and computing resources and their availability.	Can be implemented through using NAC systems.	2
Network security	9.16	It is necessary to apply mechanisms that filter communication that does not match the structure of the expected protocol. information.	These mechanisms must be implemented in order to defend against malicious use of insecure, unlicensed protocols. Also, ensure that communications packages arrive in the correct configuration and have not been altered before reaching the destination.	For example, traffic filtering that does not meet firewalls standards, XML Firewalls Application.	3
Network security	9.17	Make sure that in the event of operational failure of one of the border protection devices (firewalls, etc.), the system security level is not compromised.	Information security equipment must be configured to block communication in case of failure.	Most of the information security equipment can be configured so as to give redundancy toward the secondary equipment (secondary firewall for the benefit of redundancy, another secure communication route, etc.), and if there is no redundancy, the failure will move the system into, Fail-Close status.	2
Network security	9.18	Border protection mechanisms must be used to separate system components that support business tasks or services, defined by the organization as requiring separation.	The organization will determine that the separation of networks into secure areas will be carried out through dedicated information security equipment.	It is possible to use tools such as firewall, VPN tool allowing to connect securely to management networks, access control at the router level, proxy servers.	2

Family	ID	Monitoring	Complementary Explanation	Monitoring application example	Control level
Network security:	9.19	Use separate network addresses (different sub-network) to connect to different security zones.	The organization will determine that each sub-network will have. separate address range, which will be published to the firewall and routers.	Can be realized through centralized addresses management on the central firewall management interface, or through manual registration (managed and controlled) of the different network addresses.	1
Network security:	9.20	Implement mechanisms for maintaining the integrity and confidentiality of the network traffic on. public medium.		For example, encrypting outbound traffic outside of the organization, communication lines encryption on. public medium.	2
Network security:	9.21	Define, document and implement. toughening policy for communications equipment, which meets the requirements of the organization's information security.	The organization will define toughening requirements for the communication systems within the organization with an emphasis on what are the basic requirements, the frequency of updates and the level of classification and then document the requirements in an overall framework which will serve as. basis for toughening procedures.	Baseline documents and references to the requirements of toughening in the policy documents. Also, define who is responsible for the implementation of the actual toughening and how the ongoing test of the controls is carried out. The toughening documents shall include, inter alia,. reference to the usage of unauthorized. safe services, approved ports, removal of inactive accounts and so on. It is important to make sure that the toughening will be conducted in accordance with the manufacturer's recommendations. Toughening recommendations can be found in accepted industry standards, such as DISA, SANS and the official website of the manufacturer.	3

Family	ID	Monitoring	Complementary Explanation	Monitoring application example	Control level
Network security	9.22	Implement mechanisms for centralized management, implementation and validation of the communications equipment.		Can be applied by type of telecommunications equipment and according to the central management mechanism of any manufacturer. Also, it is possible to apply the various media components toughening manually by using the management interface of each component separately.	3
Network security	9.23	A mechanism (central or local) for managing firewall policy.	The organization will define the firewall systems management policy, which will include reference to the process of adding, removing illegal routing rules in the system, including an approval process to add, remove rules. It is also necessary to set up the manner of documenting and detailing as regards any rule that opened in the firewall for its proper management.	Can be implemented directly in the system management interface. It is possible to apply. process of approval for opening, removal of rules, as well as the creation and actual removal of rules in the system by using automated change management systems.	2
Network security	9.24	Improvement of the firewall rules.	The organization will carry out. process of reviewing the rules of the firewall system and improving them, in order to maintain system integrity and for confirming that there are no rules which could expose the organization to unnecessary risks.	Can be applied mechanically using automated systems to manage the changes, or, alternatively, perform. manual process of examining rules and definitions.	3
Network security	9.25	Periodic network scans.		Can be performed using free scanning tools, such as NMAP, Superscan others.	2

Family	ID	Monitoring	Complementary Explanation	Monitoring application example	Control level
10. Separation of Environments: An enterprise network can include several environments, such as:, production environment, development environment, testing environment, management environment and more. These environments are often linked together, while also differing in the type of information that exists in them, the required level of availability, in their management and in the level of defenses and information security controls embedded in them. As such, attackers exploiting weaknesses in the less protected environment in order to obtain. foothold in the corporate network and use it to attack the more secure environments. In order to protect workspaces, the organization must create, separation and. barrier between different environments through physical separation (at the level of communication, storage, virtualization, keys management, etc.), control over information transfer between environments, separation of users and their privileges, information and software transfer processes between environments, integration of security tools, filters and monitoring tools.					
Separation of Environments:	10.1	Write down and implement. Separation of Environments policy, Review and update it periodically.	The organization will write and implement. policy of separation of environments, such as production, development, testing, support, Internet, guest network environments, etc. The purpose of the separation is to prevent the ability to move between environments by utilizing the access pertasks or shared infrastructure.	The policy should contain. definition of the environmental types of separation, the separation level required (e.g. Logical or physical separation) and referral to appropriate procedures.	2
Separation of Environments:	10.2	Configure separate environments for development, testing and production. 	The organization will define and delineate the environments that need to be separated in order to prevent leakage of cyber-incidents between the environments in case of damage to one of them.	Definition of different environments, mapping systems and technological demarcation (networks, servers and databases) of each environment.	2

Family	ID	Monitoring	Complementary Explanation	Monitoring application example	Control level
Separation of Environments	10.3	Restrict the use of sensitive production data (customer data or data defined by the organization as sensitive) in non-production environments if they are not protected at the same level as in. production environment.	Since the lower environments are accessed by developers and quality assurance personnel in. less controlled manner, there is concern that sensitive data will leak out. In addition, the level of security in these environments usually based on. lower security level than in the production environment. In order to reduce exposure due to the access of developers and others to the test and integration environments, it is necessary to prevent sensitive data transfer in these environments.	It is possible to use anonymization processes (task or data scrambling identifiers), or. synthetic test data for development and testing environments.	2
Separation of Environments	10.4	Separate user privileges for various environments and define the privileges for each environment separately.	It is necessary to manage users and privileges in. single user management system, however, it is necessary to set up. separate privileges registry for each environment separately, so that environments containing sensitive information would not be exposed to unauthorized access in case of hacking. user account or abusing privileges.	Setting up. separate user account for the employee for any environment in which he is required to operate. Access privileges will also be defined separately for each account, depending on the business need of the employee.	2

Family	ID	Monitoring	Complementary Explanation	Monitoring application example	Control level
Separation of Environments.	10.5	Set up an approval process for data transfer from the production environment to other environments and set up. process for secure data transfer.	The transfer of sensitive data from the production environment to other environments is sometimes required as part of the development and testing processes. In order to prevent abuse of these processes, it is necessary to implement. controlled data transfer process, which requires appropriate approvals prior to execution.	Can be applied using. mechanized process, including approval by information security factors.	2
Separation of Environments	10.6	Set up. controlled process of software component transfer from the development and testing environments to the production environment.	Implement software components transfer process to the production environment, designed to ensure the completion of testing procedures and obtaining appropriate approvals before executing the transfer.	Can be applied in the framework of 'Going-to-Production Committee' which concentrates changes in the production environment and their approval before executing the transfer.	3

Family	ID	Monitoring	Complementary Explanation	Monitoring application example	Control level
Separation of Environments	10.7	Separate environments that implement different security level in. manner that takes into account the level of threat posed to the 'more secure' environment than the 'less secure' one.	Production environments tend to be carefully managed and have wide controls and safeguards, while development and testing environments tend to have looser management and contain fewer controls and safeguards. To avoid damage to the production environment due to the utilization of weaknesses in low environments, set the different systems and environment security levels and separate environments that implement different security levels.		2
Separation of Environments	10.8	Apply the separation between environments in the telecommunications network, storage systems, virtualization, identification processes and management of encryption keys.	A complete separation between environments requires the application of separate physical networks and separate infrastructures. Using shared infrastructures requires the implementation of mechanisms of separation from suppliers, adapted to the level of threat and the nature of the risks posed to the technology environment		3

Family	ID	Monitoring	Complementary Explanation	Monitoring application example	Control level
Separation of Environments:	10.9	Implement bidirectional filtering mechanisms in communications and data transfer interfaces between environments, to prevent passage of malicious code, attacking weaknesses, applicative interfaces exploitation and uncontrolled release of information.	A complete separation between environments requires the application of separate physical networks and separate infrastructures. Using shared infrastructures requires the implementation of mechanisms of separation from suppliers, adapted to the level of threat and the nature of the risks posed to the technology environment	Can be realized via advanced filtering technologies that enable content filtering and advanced filtering rules.	3

11. Public cloud computing:
Many organizations rely increasingly on cloud services for processing and storing information. Alongside the advantages of the move, the organization is required to manage the resulting risk of valuable information for the organization being transferred to, third party (the cloud service provider). Therefore, it is the duty of the organization to ensure that the cloud services do not affect the level of its Cyber-Defense, by setting appropriate requirements to the cloud service provider. The organization has to understand the security services division of responsibilities between the service provider and the organization, and implement protection monitoring accordingly, at both the enterprise and provider level. The organization is required to ensure that the cloud service provider undertakes to comply with standards and regulations required from the organization, conduct the appropriate Cyber-Defense controls for information value and to define appropriate control processes. The business continuity plan of the organization is required to take into account situations of revocation of the ability to access cloud services. Ensure that the cloud service provider implements mechanisms for information security monitoring and reports to the organization regarding exceptional events.

Family	ID	Monitoring	Complementary Explanation	Monitoring application example	Control level
Public cloud computing	11.1	It is necessary to understand the division of responsibilities between the service provider and the organization, and implement protection monitoring accordingly.	When using public cloud services there is. division of responsibility of cyber protection between issues under the responsibility of the supplier and issues remaining under the responsibility of the customer. This division of responsibility depends on the nature of the service and the implementation model. The organization has to understand what are the issues that are within its responsibility and implement the consequences of this responsibility.	In the case of services such as PaaS or IaaS infrastructure, the client responsibility is to manage the users, to monitor usage by users, manage the data and ensure its security, secure applications and interfaces and often secure operating systems and infrastructures. all depending on the nature of the service, as defined in the agreement with the provider. These controls can be implemented using monitoring and control tools provided as part of the service, using the tools available in the organization or by external suppliers, which provide cloud security services.	1
Public cloud computing	11.2	Write down and implement. policy for usage and protection of public cloud services. Review and update it periodically.	The organization's management must define. policy and guidelines as regards the conditions and rules for the use of public cloud services and the manner by which the organization implements Cyber-Defense in the event of use of public cloud services.	A policy on the use of cloud services deals, generally, with the following issues: What are the services that may be used in the organization, what are the specific requirements of the organization, topics that include contracting with suppliers, privacy risk management, supervision and control. When writing this policy take into account the legal requirements regarding outsourcing, published by The Israel Law, Information and Technology Authority (ILITA).	2

Family	ID	Monitoring	Complementary Explanation	Monitoring application example	Control level
Public cloud computing:	11.3	Make sure the cloud service provider undertakes to comply with the required standards and regulations, depending on the organization's obligations and standards agreed with the provider.	Various organizations are subject to regulatory guidelines relating to the use of cloud services, such as privacy protection, sectorial regulation or contractual liability to third parties. These obligations often dictate strict rules for the use of cloud services.	For example: the implementation of the Bank of Israel directives, Capital Market Supervision, ILITA guidelines, Government ICT Authority directives and others. When making this comparison, it is necessary to examine all active applications in the cloud in the organization. This mapping can be done, inter alia, by examining the users' browsing history and comparing it with the software providers list by examining existing rules in the relevant communication components (such as firewall, filtering, etc.). In many cases software for payroll management, document sharing, forms building and surveys and more are in the cloud, and the organization is 'unaware' of that (Shadow IT).	2

Family	ID	Monitoring	Complementary Explanation	Monitoring application example	Control level
Public cloud computing	11.4	Define and implement processes for periodic supervision and control of the provider's compliance with its obligations.	Cyber protection application in cloud services based on the service provider' strict fulfillment of its obligations. It is necessary to take supervision measures in order to ensure that the provider fulfills these, either by direct supervision or by an independent third party which reviews periodically the provider's compliance with its obligations.	For example: sending questionnaires to the provider, auditing the provider, using external and objective Review services, indicating the provider's compliance with its obligations. The service. software provider will send to the client. detailed record of its compliance with the requirements defined in the agreement, and their implementation.. provider's deviations from the agreement have to be approved by the director of Cyber-Defense in the organization. For example, in case of. fundamental requirement by the organization for compliance with specific SLA policies, or. password policy that the provider cannot perform,. formal procedure is required, whereby the provider explains why it cannot meet that requirement and whether it expects to close this gap. These data will be transferred to the director of Cyber-Defense in the organization for approval and for defining compensating controls to reduce the risk.	2
Public cloud computing	11.5	It is necessary to carry out independent information security checks of interfaces to cloud services that are exposed to the Internet.	Testing of cloud services by the organization. by. third party hired for this purpose, or by some other objective party. makes it possible to identify information security exposures and handle them without having to rely exclusively on the provider.	The relevant tests can include: testing of penetration of user interfaces, management interfaces and applicative interfaces, audits in accordance with generally accepted standards, or audits covering specific topics defined in the contract with the provider.	3

Family	ID	Monitoring	Complementary Explanation	Monitoring application example	Control level
Public cloud computing	11.6	Make sure that no data, which under the regulation and responsibilities of the organization must not be transferred, is transferred to the cloud services.	There is data that the organization is prevented from transferring for storage or processing in public cloud services due to regulatory considerations or Commitment to third parties. Prior to transferring data to the cloud make sure that such data are not kept or transferred to the cloud services.	For example, an examination of the data fields that the organization plans to transfer to the cloud services before making. decision on the matter. Can also perform by deletion or substitution of such data in the records transferred to the cloud services. Consultation with. qualified legal entity when performing an examination and evaluation of the sensitivity of the data and the possibility of transferring it for storage in the cloud.	1
Public cloud computing	11.7	The business continuity plan of the organization is required to take into account situations of revocation of the ability to access cloud services.	Cloud services are external to the organization, and connection to them is usually through public infrastructure, such as the Internet. It is necessary to consider, as part of the business continuity plan, situations where there is no access to the cloud. whether due to. malfunction at the provider, or because of. failure in the infrastructure of accessing the provider.	For example, alternative methods for providing services to customers in the event of disconnection of cloud services, updated data files in the organization, containing information that exists in the cloud services.	2

Family	ID	Monitoring	Complementary Explanation	Monitoring application example	Control level
Public cloud computing	11.8	Set up and implement mechanisms for access control, suitable for access interfaces to cloud services, in accordance with the threats and exposures relevant to each interface.	Cloud services typically have several types of interfaces: user interfaces, management interfaces and maintenance and applicative interfaces. Generally, these interfaces are exposed to the Internet and public networks, and therefore it is imperative to set strong access control mechanisms, appropriate to the nature of the threats relevant to the interface, to the technological exposure level of and the outline of the threats.	For example, strong authentication management interface, limiting access to sensitive interfaces to certain Internet addresses.	2
Public cloud computing	11.9	Ensure that the cloud service provider implements secure development processes and integrates information security testing in the development and maintenance stages.	The main exposure areas of 'software as. Service' (SaaS) in the cloud are user and application interfaces. In order to reduce such exposures, the cloud service provider must implement secure development processes and integrate appropriate security checks during development and maintenance stages. The organization must ensure that the provider properly implementing these processes.	For example, the provider's declaration that it is implementing secure development processes, presentation of results of periodic information security tests performed on the provider's systems.	3

Family	ID	Monitoring	Complementary Explanation	Monitoring application example	Control level
Public cloud computing	11.10	Ensure that the cloud service provider implements mechanisms for information security monitoring and reports to the organization regarding exceptional events.	There are areas in the field of Cyber-Defense, which are under the responsibility of the cloud service provider. The organization should ensure that the provider performs monitoring of these areas and reports to the organization (the service's client) regarding suspected cyber-incidents, in order that the organization could take protective actions at his side: containment and recovery.	Can be applied through the inclusion of the issue in the contract with the provider and periodic reporting by the provider on the number of events that have occurred and their analysis.	2
Public cloud computing	11.11	There must be. mechanism for monitoring security events in order to detect cyber-events in the cloud services.	In order to get. complete picture of cyber-incidents and suspicious events, the organization must monitor cloud service activities. This monitoring can be carried out using the cloud service provider's systems or by connecting the organization's monitoring systems to the log records produced by the cloud service provider's systems.	Can be realized by receiving events feed from the provider's system to the monitoring systems of the organization, or by accessing the provider's monitoring interfaces.	3

Family	ID	Monitoring	Complementary Explanation	Monitoring application example	Control level
Public cloud computing	11.12	Define and implement mechanism that allows full functional continuity and deletion of data stored by the cloud service provider in case of termination of the service agreement with the provider.	Upon termination of the contract with the cloud service provider, the organization must enable functional continuity and retention of the records belonging to it, which have been preserved or processed using cloud services. In addition, ensure deletion of data that has remained at the provider and is owned by or under the responsibility of the organization.	Can be realized through the inclusion of this issue in the contract with the provider.	2

12. Industrial Controls:
Industrial control Systems (ICS) are responsible for controlling assembly lines, healthcare systems, electrical systems, building management systems (elevators, escalators, etc.), water infrastructure, etc. Due to the simplicity of these components, it was customary in the past to exclude them from the systems that the organization protects from cyber threats. However, these components are, favorite target for attackers, because damaging them could lead to serious damage to the organization and its customers. Accordingly, the organization is required to attribute high importance to the protection of these components and take special care to separate and isolate then from communication networks as much as possible. For this purpose, it is required to set corporate policy regarding the controls, to protect their communications, manage physical access, the authorized personnel and the operations that may be performed (software updates, connect removable media, etc.) and implement mechanisms that monitor interference in their activities through. cyber attack. These controls are also suitable for embedded systems (OT) in general.

Family	ID	Monitoring	Complementary Explanation	Monitoring application example	Control level
Industrial Controls	12.1	Write down, manage and monitor the corporate policy for the protection of the industrial control system environment.		Can be realized by writing policies and supporting procedures that define unique requirements for the industrial control system environment with respect to the nature of the controls' environment (Manufacturing. Logistics. environmental control. power production, etc.). Reference should be made to regulatory aspects available for these environments (e.g. FDA, GXP, cyber Authority).	2

Family	ID	Monitoring	Complementary Explanation	Monitoring application example	Control level
Industrial Controls	12.2	Defined rules for proper use of equipment in the production environment and place signage explaining these rules.	The organization will define, signage explaining the data security practices at the work stations governing and monitoring the production environment.	The signage may include the use of shared workstations, the use of removable media devices, users log off and more.	1
Industrial Controls	12.3	Define the sensitive processes where industrial control environments exist according to their degree of sensitivity.	The organization will map the processes where control environments exist and define the main business processes involving these controls in order to understand the level of business and regulatory damage that could result from such environments.	Document mapping processes and environments according to severity.	2
Industrial Controls	12.4	Separate control networks from other systems and external networks.	The organization will set apart control networks, users' networks or servers into separate networks so as to restrict direct access between networks	The separation can be carried out using firewalls and separate VLANs for every monitoring network. Given the option, it is preferable to separate by, one-way diode and allow only the release of information out of the organization.	1
Industrial Controls	12.5	Separate the management system of industrial equipment controllers and the operative components of the system.	Implement adequate separation between the operational controls network and the management system of the controls.		2

Family	ID	Monitoring	Complementary Explanation	Monitoring application example	Control level
Industrial Controls	12.6	Do not connect devices that are not production environment controls to the production controls network.	The organization will not install equipment that is not part of the Industrial Control System in the controls network. Equipment which is required to be connected will be connected to. separate network, and communication will be enabled individually.	If necessary to connect different equipment for interfaces with production systems, it must be connected by. separate network segment behind the firewall.	1
Industrial Controls	12.7	Support providers access to the production network will be possible with prior authorization as well as by using secure and identified communication, which allows recording the provider's actions.	The organization will implement. secure communications network for suppliers' access and will review the supplier's access to the organization by providing pre-authorization for any provider connection to the control network.	Can be applied using. VPN server management system for dedicated users for each will provider (user priority for every employee of the provider). which will be usually locked and open only when necessary.	2
Industrial Controls	12.8	No direct access from the industrial controls environment to the internet is allowed, neither from the human-machine interfaces environment.		It is possible to limit the control networks in the firewall and disable direct communication access from these networks to the internet. Updates will be allowed from. buffer network individually, only after passing through equipment such as. proxy.	2
Industrial Controls	12.9	Unnecessary services will be limited in the production environment and support systems, such as human-machine interfaces and smart sensors.	The organization will cancel and. or limit unnecessary services for all systems in the control environment, whether at the level of operating system, communications level and application level.	It is possible to be based on the manufacturers toughening documents of the operating system and applications, and shut down services, block ports, limit applicative access to certain functions and more.	2

Family	ID	Monitoring	Complementary Explanation	Monitoring application example	Control level
Industrial Controls	12.10	Use reliable communication between industrial controls and terminal equipment if possible.	Use protocols that allow the source and destination authentication and encryption of the medium supporting the equipment.	In the event that it is possible to use secure versions of these protocols. use these versions (SFTP, HTTPS, SNMPv3 and others).	2
Industrial Controls	12.11	Set. unidirectional communication equipment from manufacturing to the sensory systems.		Set up tools for unidirectional communication transfer between sensors and systems in sensitive environments.	4
Industrial Controls	12.12	Wireless networks in the production environment will be separate from enterprise wireless networks.	The organization will implement. dedicated wireless network separate from the enterprise wireless network, to be used solely for control network communications. This network will not redirect to the enterprise network and vice versa.	It is preferable to avoid using. wireless network in the control networks, but if necessary for business. this network will be set up separately, and its management will be also separate and it will not be linked to any VLAN's internal network.	1
Industrial Controls	12.13	Wireless communication in the production environment will be limited by using secure protocols.		Use WPA-2 PSK, and if possible, it is recommended to use. digitally certified version for these wireless networks.	1
Industrial Controls	12.14	A separate user will be defined for each end client using. wireless network in the production environment.	The organization will set up. separate user for everyone and every wireless network equipment.	It is recommended to connect the wireless network to. dedicated Radius server, which will authenticate users of this network and enable their management.	2
Industrial Controls	12.15	Access to human-machine interfaces will be allowed through personal users for each operator.	The organization will define. personal user to anyone who works with the human-machine interface. If the position is shared, it is possible to use smart card identification.		2

Family	ID	Monitoring	Complementary Explanation	Monitoring application example	Control level
Industrial Controls	12.16	Access to human-machine interfaces will be allowed by using strong authentication.	The organization will define strong authentication in accessing human-machine interface.	It is possible to use, variety of means, such as biometrics, smart cards, OTP and more.	4
Industrial Controls	12.17	Monitoring systems will be installed and activity recording will be carried out on the management servers.	The organization will set up, system for the recording, registration of activity logs on the management servers of the control environment.	It is possible to use, variety of means, such as tools for recording user screens and activities, recording of application logs, etc..	2
Industrial Controls	12.18	Install utilities such as intrusion detection tools in the management networks' environment of the production environment.		Can be realized by using Network IPS, HIPS tool and similar tools, such as Honeypots.	3
Industrial Controls	12.19	Install tools for file signature verification (Integrity Checking) to scan files being transferred to the management environment or installed in the management environment.		Can be realized using, variety of File Integrity Checking tools.	3
Industrial Controls	12.20	Install dedicated anti-malware tools in human-machine interfaces.		Can be implemented using anti-malware dedicated tools, depending on the type of system.	1
Industrial Controls	12.21	Manufacturer's software updates will be installed on the lower environments (test environments) prior to their being installed in the production environment.	The organization will ensure the installation of updates in, test environment and will run them over time in order to test the stability of the system and the process.	Can be realized by establishing, lower environment (at least partially), diverting communication to this environment during, maintenance window in the production environment and testing the process.	2

Family	ID	Monitoring	Complementary Explanation	Monitoring application example	Control level
Industrial Controls	12.22	Install operating system updates that are supported by the provider in the production environment.	The organization will implement within. reasonable time operating system and application updates as received from the system vendor and will demand from the vendor security updates for serious flaws as they are published.		1
Industrial Controls	12.23	'Lock Configuration' tools will be installed on End Of Life systems, including obsolete operating systems.	The organization will implement tools that lock the system configuration in. 'clean' configuration if there is no option to update the equipment.		3
Industrial Controls	12.24	The ability to connect removable media to production equipment, including controllers, human-machine interfaces and sensors will be limited.		Can be realized by physically eliminating the USB devices (Fort Lock), or logically by operating system policy. GPO.	2
Industrial Controls	12.25	Removable media file transfer to the production systems will be carried out after 'laundering' the transmitted files.	The organization will implement. system of files 'laundering' and testing them thoroughly using some tools prior to transferring them to the controls environment.	Can be realized through the acquisition of. specialized laundering station, or, alternatively, by establishing. dedicated station, which includes several different scan engines.	2
Industrial Controls	12.26	There will be. redundancy system for critical components in the production environment.	The organization will implement. redundancy system of servers and critical sensors in the control environment for the purpose of process continuity.	In order to build redundancy it is recommended to consult with the control system vendor.	2

Family	ID	Monitoring	Complementary Explanation	Monitoring application example	Control level
Industrial Controls	12.27	Physical access will be limited for business needs only to the industrial controls environment as well as to communications equipment in this environment.	The organization will limit physical access to the communication racks, hubs and management stations of the controls' environment	Can be realized by converting dedicated rooms to concentrated communications and servers, and perform access control using access tags. Biometrics for this environment.	2
Industrial Controls	12.28	Logical access will be limited for business needs only to the industrial controls environment as well as to communications equipment in this environment.	The organization will limit the access of corporate users who have no business relevance to the control system and will prevent their access to these networks and equipment.		2
Industrial Controls	12.29	Logical access will be limited, to the extent possible, (functional) to the production systems, including control interfaces, sample interfaces and human-machine interfaces.	Access to the management systems will be limited according to user profiles.. system controller will not change settings and parameters of. system. Changing the parameters will be carried out by an administrative user.	It is possible to verify with the system's manufacturer whether the system can use different user profiles.	3
Industrial Controls	12.30	Carry out information security testing in the production and management environments and interface, including penetration tests.	The organization will define. comprehensive tests outline for tests including the variety of control network components, with an emphasis on comprehensive information security tests for all components, in order to maintain the continuity of the business process.	Can be realized by checking the configuration of the environment, running simulations during downtime windows and performing penetration tests in these networks if possible and. or during maintenance operations.	2

Family	ID	Monitoring	Complementary Explanation	Monitoring application example	Control level
Industrial Controls	12.31	Set up unique monitoring scenarios in the production environment and monitor them through an organizational monitoring array.	The organization will define. range of dedicated monitoring scenarios for the control environment in accordance with the threat outline and the importance of the system to the business process.	Network monitoring in control networks is different from ordinary systems monitoring since the sensitivity threshold is lower. Any deviation from the amount of normal communication between the controls and the management interfaces and sensors may indicate. potential cyber-incident, since the activity in these environments is continuous and monotonous.	2

13. Securing Mobile Phones

Cell phones have become major professional tools, they contain the contacts. email correspondence, various enterprise applications, passwords and more. in many cases they allow access to corporate networks and web browsing. Hence, correct definition of phone privileges. of their business use and their protection is critical to the organization's Cyber-Defense. It is necessary to set for them access control, configuration security, implementation of dedicated protection tools, securing communication channels with the organization, centralized management including remote control in case of loss, and more.

Family	ID	Monitoring	Complementary Explanation	Monitoring application example	Control level
Securing Mobile Phones	13.1	Set up mobile phone usage policy and update it periodically.	The organization must set up. mobile phone usage policy according to its needs, including access to enterprise applications and maintaining the organization's sensitive data on the mobile phone.		2
Securing Mobile Phones	13.2	Implement protection mechanisms for controlling access to mobile phones, such as passwords or biometric measures.	The organization must set the parameters for controlling access to mobile devices, such as. password of. certain length and automatic locking.	Can be realized using automated policy settings, applied on the device when connected to. network organization.	2

Family	ID	Monitoring	Complementary Explanation	Monitoring application example	Control level
Securing Mobile Phones	13.3	Implement security settings on phones, that restrict access to mobile phone, keep software up to date, limit risks of installing dangerous apps and so on.	The organization must set various parameters for implementation in the operating systems of mobile phones and enforce implementation of these settings on the devices. These settings include enforcement of software updates, restricting hazardous services, limiting installing unknown or risky software and so forth.	Can be realized using automated policy settings, applied on the device when connected to the enterprise network or through, centralized management system.	3
Securing Mobile Phones	13.4	Implement encryption of sensitive data stored on mobile devices.	The organization's sensitive data, stored on the mobile device, such as corporate email, sensitive files and sensitive applications, will be encrypted using the device's operating system or through dedicated applications.	Settings can be applied using applications which perform data encryption (Secure Email application, for example), or by means of encrypted partitions using the operating system.	2

Family	ID	Monitoring	Complementary Explanation	Monitoring application example	Control level
Securing Mobile Phones	13.5	Implement dedicated protection tools that detect and block unauthorized access and hostile applications on mobile devices.	Mobile devices, especially those owned by employees of the organization, are particularly exposed to the infiltration of hostile programs, whether inserted into. device without the knowledge of its owner or disguised as an innocent application. In order to prevent malicious code that could expose sensitive enterprise information, run specialized applications that detect and prevent the running of hostile code.	Can be applied using commercial systems designed for protecting mobile devices, or using commercial devices that implement this type of defense capabilities.	3
Securing Mobile Phones	13.6	Implement encryption of sensitive data in inbound and outbound communication of mobile devices.	Data communications, inbound and outbound from mobile phones, makes use of unsecured public networks. In order to protect the information from exposure, it is necessary to encrypt it.	Can be realized using conventional encryption protocols and using applications which perform encryption operations while accessing the organization's network.	2
Securing Mobile Phones	13.7	Implement access control measures on the organization's mobile network.	Mobile devices that connect to the corporate network are using remote access interfaces to the network. In order to secure this interface, access control must be implemented, such as the use of digital certificates technologies and passwords.		3

Family	ID	Monitoring	Complementary Explanation	Monitoring application example	Control level
Securing Mobile Phones	13.8	Implement. centralized management system, which manages the configuration of mobile devices and enables remote deletion of data from the device.	The enforcement of secure configuration of mobile phones and the remote control of sensitive data stored on mobile devices is made possible through. central management system and management components, which are applied to the devices.		2
Securing Mobile Phones	13.9	Implemented. central information security monitoring system, which receives alerts on unusual events on mobile devices and enables containment and response to incidents.	In order to detect attack incidents on mobile devices and enable their containment an. suitable response. it is necessary to implement. centralized monitoring system, which receives alerts from components applied to the mobile devices.		3
Securing Mobile Phones	13.10	Set. policy for the protection or restriction of calls made through mobile phones.	Mobile devices use unsecured public networks. the organization must set etiquette and caution rules when making phone sensitive calls.		4

14. Change Management:
The organization's cyber environment also needs to make changes and periodic updates, being part of the organization's development and update process. These include the acquisition of companies and integrating them within the organization's infrastructure, technological upgrades, addition or changing business processes (e.g. Supply chain), and more. These changes or updates Processes entail great risk of harm to the systems of the organization and the information in them. Accordingly, the organization must manage the changes so that they will reduce the risk. This management includes, configuration management policy for the cyber environment in the organization, its documentation and ongoing updating.

Family	ID	Monitoring	Complementary Explanation	Monitoring application example	Control level
Change Management	14.4	Write down and implement. configuration management policy. Review and update it periodically.		The chapter of Change Management is in the corporate information security policy and supporting procedures.	2

Family	ID	Monitoring	Complementary Explanation	Monitoring application example	Control level
Change Management	14.2	Set up, record and update when necessary the required basic configuration of the information system.	The organization will record the information system configuration during its establishment, including documentation of components, communication, system settings, as well as its installation procedure.	Can be applied by preparing. system portfolio.	2
Change Management	14.3	Examine the existing configuration of the information systems on. periodic basis and when events occur, which were defined by the organization and are an integral part of the process of installing and updating. version.	The organization will record the changes in the information systems during major reconfiguration, or once every period (whichever comes first).	Can be realized through. process of documenting changes.	2
Change Management	14.4	It is necessary to implement automatic mechanisms in order to keep the basic configuration of the information system up to date, including its integrity and preparedness of the settings.	The organization will implement. backup and restore set for the configuration of the information system and its components.		3
Change Management	14.5	Keep previous versions of the system configuration to support Rollback.	The organization will ensure that there are tools and methods for rollback for unsuccessful changes.	Can be applied using. full system backup before the change and through gradual upgrading of components (testing environment. DR environment, etc.).	2

Family	ID	Monitoring	Complementary Explanation	Monitoring application example	Control level
Change Management	14.6	Determine which changes to the system are defined as configuration changes, document configuration change requests and their status (approved, executed, rejected) and keep them for defined period of time.	The organization will manage, process of ratification of changes before applying them.	Can be applied through holding weekly change management meetings and ratifying changes while explaining the nature of the change.	2
Change Management	14.7	Implement an automatic mechanism for documenting requests for configuration changes, for alerting the certifying authority and to prohibition against making changes until receipt of all necessary approvals.	The organization will operate an information system which will coordinate the change management process in general and the changes ratification process in particular.		4
Change Management	14.8	Analyze changes in the information system in order to determine potential security effects before implementing the change (due to the weakness, lack of compliance, malice, etc.).	The organization will manage, risk assessment process as part of the organizational change management. Potential impacts on system availability and reliability will be documented, as part of the stages of submitting an application for changes.	Can be applied via, supplementary questionnaire for management changes request, which will list its risks when carrying out the changes.	2
Change Management	14.9	Analyze configuration changes in the information environment in, separate test environment prior to its implementation in the production environment.	The organization will examine the changes in, separate test environment before implementing changes in the production environment.	Can be realized through maintaining, test environment, in, version resembling the production environment.	2

Family	ID	Monitoring	Complementary Explanation	Monitoring application example	Control level
Change Management	1410	After carrying out configuration changes in the information system, check the security functions in order to make sure that they work properly.	The organization will check the entire system and its components with respect to the information security aspects, including: authentication, authorization, encryption, toughening and any other information security functionality in the system.	It is necessary to execute, through the required monitoring overview and, if necessary, even through tests such as controls survey and penetration tests.	3

15. Media Security

Media (magnetic, removable, optical, mechanical) are used for entering and extracting information from the organization. Media used for storage and portability of information both within the organization and outside it. This information may be sensitive for the organization, its customers or its suppliers, and therefore it is necessary to protect it from getting into the hands of any unauthorized factor. Media may also be used to insert abusive software within the organization. Therefore, it is necessary to define and implement a policy of handling and protection of media (including media scrapping).

Family	ID	Monitoring	Complementary Explanation	Monitoring application example	Control level
Media Security	15.1	Write down and implement. media protection policy (magnetic, removable, optical, mechanical). Review and update it periodically.	The organization will write and implement. usage and protection policy for media, including reference to the use of the media, the manner of its storage and the destruction of the information stored on this media and. or the destruction of the media itself at the end of use (or the end of life of the media).	The policy will consider, for example, the types of approved devices against those prohibited to make use of, whether use of the media is allowed or prohibited (such as. computer. portable memory, work phone) for private purposes, is it permitted go out with this media outside the organization, and how, what to do with the media when it is faulty. deprecated. From this policy will stem the relevant procedures for the organization, such media mapping processes and distributing media (such as purchasing magnetic discs for the servers, optical media) and providing access to the aforementioned media in accordance with the organization's procedures for the relevant officials (such as access to hard disks only to IT personnel, access to removable media for the relevant officials, etc.).	2
Media Security	15.2	Label each media according to the security level of the data stored, noting its treatment in relation to data security and distribution limitations aspects.	The organization will define labeling procedures and processes of the media, as well as label the media according the security level of the data stored.	The media can be labeled with stickers glued to backup tapes, outgoing packages of hard disks, and optical disks.	2

Family	ID	Monitoring	Complementary Explanation	Monitoring application example	Control level
Media Security	15.3	Store media securely.	The organization will define date storing security methods, according to various media types (magnetic, optical, removable).	Can be implemented by physical protection of physical media storing areas, backup encoding and storing magnetic media at. licensed storing facility; protecting communication cabinets containing servers, storing devices and hard disks; storing optical media and storing components of encoding devices (HSM), in strongboxes.	2
Media Security	15.4	Define media blackening and/ or destruction processes.	The organization will define procedures and processes for the blackening (Blackening, deleting all sensitive data from. component, prior to its exiting the organization or assignment to. different use) and destruction of media, as well as conducting. continuous surveillance of the implementation of these blackening and destruction procedures. Ensuring that sensitive data does not exit the organization without control.	Blackening of media can be performed manually (such as individual deletion of sensitive data: credit card details, details which may serve to identify clients, etc.), or technologically (systematic deletion of pre-known patterns). Media destruction can be done by shredding/magnetizing/ resetting by overwriting.	2
Media Security	15.5	While connecting removable media to the organization's network, clean it, to ensure that the media do not contain malware or other malicious components.	The organization will define. data whitening process (scanning for and cleaning malicious code threats), before incorporating the media within the organization's systems	Can be implemented by defining special whitening stations, to scan the media before its connection to the organization's systems.	2

Family	ID	Monitoring	Complementary Explanation	Monitoring application example	Control level
Media Security	15.6	Define and implement media use limitations, using security means	The organization will define and implement media use limitations technologies and methods. In order to minimize data leakage from or malicious code penetration threats to the organization's network, via removable media.	Can be implemented by toughening workstations according to the system/ station type, or the employee's authorizations, allowing only authorized employees to connect removable memory devices (such as. Disk On Key) to the computer. On may implement. definition by which any data stored from. station on. removable device will be encrypted.	2
Media Security	15.7	Implement encryption mechanism to secure digital media transferred outside the organization. 	The organization will implement encryption technologies regarding media intended to exit the organization, or is in constant use outside the organization (removable media)	Can be implemented by removable data encryption tools, encryption of backup tapes, during backup. etc.	3
Media Security	15.8	Periodically inspect the media whitening and destruction equipment, to validate its effectiveness.	The organization will define an inspection process of media whitening and destruction equipment, including checking the effectiveness of the implemented processes and technologies.	Whitening/destruction systems can be inspected periodically by samples, such as trying to insert. "dummy" file, trying to read or retrieve. sensitive file from obsolete media.	3

16. Supply chain and Outsourcing:
Many organizations are dependent on services bought from external suppliers. These may be sub-contractors producing computerized components, suppliers of computing services, various applications bought from external suppliers, etc. Such services may be linked to the organizations' systems, therefore consitute potential attacking channels. Therefore, the organization has to defend itself against being damaged by its suppliers. It does it with legal and contractual demands from its suppliers, by surveying suppliers' Cyber Defense mechanisms, by devising work procedures, etc.

Family	ID	Monitoring	Complementary Explanation	Monitoring application example	Control level
Supply chain and Outsourcing	16.1	Defend against supply chain threats on the system, as part of. Defense in Breadth	The organization will map and detect threats and risks stemming from suppliers' systems/services, technologies and processes, and map the risks as. part of the organizational risk/threat management.	The mapping process may be aided by. cyber intelligence collection about the supplier, in order to consider such information in considering and deciding on risk management. One should consider the supplier's existing mechanisms, controls and processes, and their influence on the business processes supported by the system/service. For example: automation controls and virtual servers installed by the supplier on. cloud platform, and their toughening method, may influence the organization if these environments are not toughened enough or the cloud services supplier is not secured/situated in. hostile country, etc.	2
Supply chain and Outsourcing	16.2	Use legal and contractual tools when purchasing. data system or. service from external suppliers 🔑	The organization will use contractual mechanisms, such as limited liability and other legal mechanisms, to minimize the risks emanating from the purchase.	In addition to limited liability and indemnity clauses, compliance with regulatory and legal requirements, one may stipulate clauses such as early alerts, in service or expanded support interruption beyond the system's End-Of-Life, confidentiality agreements, and secure data storage, or any other clause constituting. control factor, compensating for the risks embedded in establishing the system/purchasing the service.	2
Supply chain and Outsourcing	16.3	Perform. supplier survey prior to signing. services/ products purchase contract	The organization will survey the suppliers character and conduct, prior to signing the contract	The supplier survey may examine: the supplier's maturity, integration. customer number, stability, service capability, data security mechanism, business continuity, etc.	3

Family	ID	Monitoring	Complementary Explanation	Monitoring application example	Control level
Supply chain and Outsourcing	16.4	In cases of connection to the supplier's network, one should implement preventive controls, in order to minimize damages caused by the supplier's infrastructures.	The organization will use its own or other designated controls in order to minimize damages caused by the supplier's infrastructures.	Such controls can be environment/interface separation, sanitation of the supplier's output, separating communication by, proxy server, etc.	3
Supply chain and Outsourcing	16.5	Before installation, inspect the data security aspect of the system/service.	The organization will inspect the system/service with its own tools, as well as by trying to penetrate it before moving into production.	The system can be examined either by vulnerability management tools or by risk surveys and penetration tests, to insure the non-existence of dire findings which may damage the organization and its processes.	4
Supply chain and Outsourcing	16.6	Define the importance level of the system/service in relation to depended business processes	The organization will define. certain system as critical if any damage it suffers influences. critical business process.	Add the system/service to the critical systems list. Monitor it to verify its continuity.	3
17. Securing purchase and development					
In purchasing and development processes the organization introduces cyber components into its systems (purchasing new software system, developing specialized tool). Malware may penetrate the organization's network via purchasing and development processes. On the other hand, various defenses may be integrated during product's development, which will assist the organization in the future to cope with cyber threats. The controls are intended to minimize the risks that, purchase or, system/software developed will introduce cyber risks into the organization. Controls include: defining, policy to direct all entities within the organization (purchase, legal, project managers, developers, etc.); defense requirements from purchase/development entities; risk management in purchase/development, defenses all along the software/system life cycle.					
Securing purchase and development	17.1	Write, implement, and periodically review, purchase and development policy.	The controls are intended to verify that all systems comply with the security benchmark defined by the organization, both those developed in-house and those purchased from the shelf or as, cloud service.	This policy will include, inter alia, reference to the SLA level desired, complying with protection requirements at all levels (password policy, Logs, encryption etc.), remote access, developers access to production etc.	2

Family	ID	Monitoring	Complementary Explanation	Monitoring application example	Control level
Securing purchase and development.	17.2	For systems with. 3+ value level, ensure compliance with standards, by an external. independent. entities.	The organization will ensure that assets ranked in the value questionnaire, 3 or above, comply with all requirements of the Defense Methodology. This shall be done by. surveyor external to the developing/ purchasing organization.	In cases of in-house development, one may be assisted by. counseling/ recording firm to examine compliance of the system protection with the Defense Methodology. In cases of external purchase, ensure that the system complies with the Methodology 's level. requirements, or, alternately, require the supplier to present certificates of compliance with common standards, such as SOC1/SOC2, as well as other requirements (such as compliance with PCI, HIPAA, etc. according with the type of data stored/processed by the system) these certificates will be stored and backed up in the purchasing/ development agreement (including. commitment to notify if the certificate is voided or expires.	4
Securing purchase, and development.	17.3	**Cyber risk management.** evaluate the cyber and data security risks **involved in the development or purchase of. new system/ service.** Manage them according the existing risk management processes.	The control in intended to verify that protection aspects are considered from the initiation and planning through the development and production phases. Ensure that initiation, purchase or development follow. survey of the risks involved. and their integration within the organizational risk management.	It is recommended to carry out the initial risk management in the initiation phase, so as to be prepared to integrate controls within the development process, or ready to live with the detected risks. One may be assisted in risk management with known methods, such as SSDLC, SANS/OWASP publications. Take note to outsourcing and cloud systems, they incorporate specific risks, some of which are. described in this document. It is recommended to become familiar with the recommendations of specific standards: ISO 27017, CSA etc.	3

489

CYBER DEFENSE METHODOLOGY \\ THE NATIONAL CYBER SECURITY AUTHORITY (NCSA)

Family	ID	Monitoring	Complementary Explanation	Monitoring application example	Control level
Securing purchase and development	17.4	**Cyber protection as part of the development life cycle**. it is necessary to take into account security considerations at each stage in the life cycle of system development and define officials for security aspects at every stage. 	The organization will promote an orderly process of secure development, defining the stages of implementation of information security at every stage in the development process and make sure that the key factors responsible for various stages in the development process accept responsibility for their roles on the issue of the developed system's security and are equipped with the necessary knowledge to do so.	It is possible to define information security requirements at the initiation phase, at the design phase (the POC phase), at the implementation phase (procurement, development and implementation phase) and at the submission stage (information security testing and trials before going to production). At these stages it is necessary to define the guidelines and responsibility to make sure that the security considerations and requirements in the process are met. Security considerations in the project will also include aspects that are not technological, or that do not relate directly to the development and submission, such as storing information at the supplier at the end of development, compartmentalization at the suppliers' premises, remote access procedures, SLA, commitment to support the product for. specified period, the method of transferring files and information of the customer to the supplier, etc. Use the controls included in the Outsourcing chapter herein.	

Family	ID	Monitoring	Complementary Explanation	Monitoring application example	Control level
Securing purchase and development	17.5	Include the following requirements and criteria for closing the purchase contract of the system. component. service: functional security requirements, requirements for protection, monitoring requirements, documentation requirements, setting up. production environment, admission requirements.	The goal is. formal definition of protection requirements for each project and contracting at the contractual level.	It is possible to define. templates collection of documents of information security requirements to use when characterizing systems in development. procurement. The document will include the controls expected from the vendor to be addressed in accordance with the expected values level of the planned system according to the criteria of the Defense Methodology.	
Securing purchase and development	17.6	The system's developers should be required to supply. functional description of the security controls to be implemented, and information regarding the design and implementation of these controls.	The organization will demand full documentation of the data security controls integrated within the system, to ensure compliance with the data security requirements, and for the sake of the organizational risks and threats management process.	It is recommended to get hold of the functional. high, and low levels design documents (FD, HLD, DD/LLD), including controls documentation, as part of the system's full documentation. Such documentation will include, inter alia, the encryption type, the input tests, the Cyber-Defense scripts, etc. as. part of the documentation, the supplier will refer to its own development and to external applications (libraries, plugins, third party software, external interfaces, etc.). This control is not intended to verify the mere implementation of security requirements, but its manner (protocols, processes, supporting tools, etc.).	3

Family	ID	Monitoring	Complementary Explanation	Monitoring application example	Control level
Securing purchase and development		**Secure Architecture.** implement secure architecture principles within the characterization, design, development, implementation, and alteration of. data system.	The organization will ensure that secure architecture is implemented in system planning, whether in-house, or while controlling an external supplier processes.	Secure architecture principles can be derived from controls described in the present document, from common standards, etc.	2
Securing purchase and development	17.7	**Secure architecture.** implement secure architectural principles in. framework of specification, design, development, realization and change in the information system.	The organization will ensure that when designing systems and services. secure architecture is implemented, whether planning is carried out, coordinated or supervised by the organization, or through the control of the organization of the work of the external supplier.	Secure architecture principles can be derived from controls cited in sections of this document, and other accepted standards.	
Securing purchase and development	17.8	**Secure development.** require system developers to employ secure development tools and methods, as an integral part of the development process.	The organization will integrate secure development methodologies, and ensure their assimilation within systems and services suppliers performing developing processes.	A software supplier will deliver documentation of its actual implementation of secure development principles, detailing the tools and methods used, the controls to be supplied for the system's protection level, etc.	3

Family	ID	Monitoring	Complementary Explanation	Monitoring application example	Control level
Securing purchase and development	17.9	**Secure operation.** maintain. data system management manual, including the best security configuration method.	The installation and operation manual, will include the information necessary for. secure configuration.	Within the configuration documentation include. an installation manual. infrastructure and application toughening, recommended deployment, etc. For. and above value level systems, pre-affirm the recommended system configuration, such as open ports, network use, employing verified protocols, default password changing, etc. since configuration change management is hard to control and follow manually, assets of value level. and above will include. compensation mechanism for automatic configuration changes testing (rules within the SIEM, central configuration management system, Continuity control monitoring).	2
Securing purchase and development	17.10	**Securing the supply chain.** demand suppliers to comply with the organizational security requirements, to regulations, standards and directions.	The organization will ensure that its suppliers comply with its directives, as well as with the regulations of the states where it is active.	The organization's regulatory requirements can be defined as part of. standard data security requirements screen, designated to all external service suppliers.	1
Securing purchase and development	17.11	Data security testing and correction should be performed before integrating systems and services. Such tests will include, at least, functionality testing (compliance with requirements) and security exposure.	The organization will ensure that security tests were performed before. new system or service are operational, and following each update.	In cases of services supplied by external suppliers, one may rely of tests performed by or for the supplier.	2

CYBER DEFENSE METHODOLOGY \\ THE NATIONAL CYBER SECURITY AUTHORITY (NCSA)

Family	ID	Monitoring	Complementary Explanation	Monitoring application example	Control level
Securing purchase and development	17.12	Document the data security flaws and vulnerabilities correction process.	The documentation is intended to ensure the integrity and effectiveness of the process.	The control is intended to verify that flows are treated according to the organization's policy. This tracking will locate long standing grave flows, unsolved companywide flows, will assist the Cyber-Defense manager in devising periodic work plans, and will be presented to the management periodically.	2
Securing purchase and development	17.13	Perform. Static Code Analysis as. part of data security test of. new system/service	The organization will test level. systems with automatic tools replacing manual surveys (Code Review)	Code analysis can be performed by automatic tools, testing various code configurations (source code, compiled, URL etc.) thus identifying loopholes. Perform code analysis before purchasing. system and following any changes to its environment.	3
Securing purchase and development	17.14	Validate system risk and vulnerability evaluation following the completion of its development.	The risk evaluation validation is intended to ensure that the risk evaluation performed in the analysis Stage is matching that of the developed system.	Perform. risk survey following the completion of development and prior to production	3
Securing purchase and development	17.15	Data security tests should be performed by an external, independent, entity.	The organization will define the scope of the survey to be performed by the supplier, and its type (white/ gray/ black hat). The survey will be performed by an external, independent. entity.	Conducting. PT in-house may give rise to conflict of interests within the organization. Employing an external entity will improve product defense. In using automatic tools,. third party can validate that the tool is performing penetration tests covering the system's scope. The same party will make the outputs accessible to the organization (writing the final report). Testing will be carried in an environment similar as possible to production.	3

Family	ID	Monitoring	Complementary Explanation	Monitoring application example	Control level
Securing purchase and development	17.16	Perform penetration testing to the system/ service.	The purpose of control is to examine the effectiveness of the controls and protections in practice. This is accomplished through challenging and attempts to penetrate the system. infrastructure.	These tests can be carried out by applying automatic assault tools or through human factor. These tests may include attempts to get unauthorized access, introduce malicious code to the database and implement well-known attacks, such as SQLI, XSS, CSRF etc.	3
Securing purchase and development	17.17	Verify that the system tests include verification; that defined data security controls are implemented according to the original design.	Maintain. tagging list of defense requirements defined to the system, and verify that all requirements are actually fulfilled in-house and by the supplier.	At the delivery phase, verify that all requirements defined in the LLD, are actually implemented. Document the test nature and outcomes.	3
Securing purchase and development	17.18	Require the supplier to perform Dynamic Code Analysis of. new system/service	Require the supplier to perform Dynamic Code Analysis of. new system/service	Dynamic Code Analysis will be performed by existing, off the shelf, tools or by Fuzzing, as well as by automatic scanning tool during. system run. The organization will inspect periodically sample reports or findings, to verify correction of flows accordingly.	3
Securing purchase and development	17.19	Implement. tamper resistance mechanism within the system.	The organization will verify that the developers implemented within the system. tamper resistance capability.	Tamper resistance mechanisms can be implemented by digital signatures, encryption, creating copies, etc.	4
Securing purchase and development	17.20	Implement methods to prevent intrusion of false system components	Such mechanisms are intended to prevent the intrusion of false software of hardware components into the organization. intentionally or by misleading an element of the supply chain.	Such mechanisms may be: verifying software components, inspection and verification of incoming software files, etc. such mechanisms can consist of various security levels. from compartmentalization of physical access to computers, BIOD password, dusk encryption, limiting the operating system to BOOT from the HD only, rules within the SIEM system etc.	3

Family	ID	Monitoring	Complementary Explanation	Monitoring application example	Control level
Securing purchase and development	17.21	Verify that purchased, developed systems implement input verification mechanisms.	Developed systems will implement unexpected inputs filtering mechanisms, such as unexpected lengths or formats. These may lead to unexpected outcomes, and have negative impact on the system's immunity, integrity, or availability, according to its value level.	Can be done for level. systems with. supplier declaration regarding input verification and the use of standard software libraries filtering inputs according to their expected characteristics. For level. systems. technological solution is required (such as WAF) at the network level, or. similar mechanism at the application level. in delimiting the penetration tests, verify that input tests are fully covered (OWASP can be. good reference point), and in accord with the organization's policy.	2
Securing purchase and development	17.22	Verify that purchased/ developed systems implement error management mechanisms.	Developed system will implement mechanisms to capture errors and to present system errors without exposing sensitive data. In any case verify that the error mechanism does not expose sensitive system data, such. table or user names, software language and versions, etc.	Can be done by implementing an error management mechanism, presenting standard errors.	2
Securing purchase and development	17.23	Verify that purchased/ developed systems implement output verification mechanisms.	Developed systems will implement mechanisms to filter unexpected outputs, which may result from an attack on the system, and expose sensitive data.	Can be implemented by using standard software libraries, that filter output according to its expected formats. Or by anomalies identification systems, based of the system/user/ operating system behavior, etc.	3
Securing purchase and development	17.24	Verify that developed/ purchased systems implement session reliability mechanisms	Developed systems will implement mechanisms intended to prevent session hijacking, man-in-the-middle etc.	Can. done by proper session management, deleting connections at the end of users' activities, tokens randomness, etc.	2

Family	ID	Monitoring	Complementary Explanation	Monitoring application example	Control level
18. physical and environmental protection: Physical and environmental protection is an important Cyber-Defense layer of the organization, intended to block physical penetration of the cyber environment. Preventive activities include, inter alia: allowing physical access to the organization's installations to authorized persons only, physical protection of the cyber infrastructures: electricity, air-conditioning, water damages, etc. In addition, an effective physical protection prevents malicious damaging of equipment, as well as notifying the authorities in such attempts. This chapter covers only physical protection of cyber components.					
Physical and environmental protection	18.1	Write, implement, and periodically control and update physical and environmental protection policy.	The control aims to define the organization's policy regarding locking doors at the end of the day, security cameras, visitors, and external employees' entry into the company's sites and sensitive areas, proper protection of server and control rooms, etc.		2
Physical and environmental protection	18.2	Write and implement procedures, to integrate, physical and environmental protection policy and relevant controls	Prepare site physical access control procedures, including; 1. Physical access procedure; 2. Guests procedure;. computer/ communication room access procedure.		2
Physical and environmental protection	18.3	Define and maintain. list of all persons authorized to enter the site containing the asset. Issue identification means to authorized persons, survey the list periodically, deleting persons whose access is no longer necessary.	Maintain and update the authorized persons list.	Issue employee/visitor card for identification	2
Physical and environmental protection	18.4	Enforce physical access control at the installation's entrance/exit points.	Enforce physical access control at all sites of the organization.	A door. card reader, lock, biometric reader,. guard, combination code, etc.	2
Physical and environmental protection	18.5	Maintain logs of physical access to the installation.	Record and store logs of all entries and exits of all visitors.	Store all entries and exits manually, by. guard, or in. database.	3

Family	ID	Monitoring	Complementary Explanation	Monitoring application example	Control level
Physical and environmental protection	18.6	Control, record, secure and enforce physical access control to communication/ computing areas (server rooms/ communication cabinets.	Limit physical access of unauthorized elements into communication/ computing areas (server rooms/ communication cabinets. The organization will define, list of authorized persons and enforce access according to its procedures.	Define physical and logical access permits for authorized persons. 2. Record by logs or log books all access to computer rooms. In cases where it is not possible to record access to communication cabinets and server rooms, consider physical protection by locks, preventing access to unauthorized persons.	2
Physical and environmental protection	18.7	Have physical control of the system output devices, in order to prevent unauthorized elements from acquiring the output (printers, fax machines, etc.)	The control insures that outputs reach their original owners. It is especially important for outputs containing personal information, such as medical or insurance data, private employees' details, etc. in such cases, ensure that the information reaches only those authorized to see it.	Can be achieved in several configurations: 1. By printing control system, requiring, code, or employee card to receive output. 2. Place printers in closed rooms with limited access. 3. It is possible to use fax2mail services, or at least ensure that the proper receiver is in the vicinity, fax machine, before, message is printed. 4. At the end of the day, insure that all output devices located publicly, are "clean" thus private information is not available to unauthorized persons.	3
Physical and environmental protection	18.8	Monitor the physical access to the installation containing the asset, in order to detect and respond security events, and to periodically survey activity logs.	This control is intended to block access of unauthorized elements to sensitive areas. An access potentially allowing them to act maliciously, such as installing listening devices, connecting to the network, stealing hardware, etc. Proper control means, that only persons authorized by the organization have access to these areas.	Monitor all physical entrances to sensitive areas, such as server rooms, communication cabinets, etc., by registering all entries and exits.	3

Family	ID	Monitoring	Complementary Explanation	Monitoring application example	Control level
Physical and environmental protection	18.9	Monitor and raise alarm at any physical access to an asset out of normal working hours and days.	Use monitoring and alarm technologies in order to detect unauthorized access attempts out of normal working hours and days.	Use alarm systems/security company, to monitor and alarm from unauthorized accesses to the installation.	3
Physical and environmental protection	18.10	Define and maintain. response array to unauthorized accesses to the installation.		By an organizational security officer,. security company, etc.	3
Physical and environmental protection	18.11	install. closed circuit television system, to monitor any physical access to the asset. Store the recordings for. pre-defined period.	Install. closed circuit television system, to monitor any physical access to the asset. Monitor the CCT continually by. security person.		4
Physical and environmental protection	18.12	Record all visitors to the installation	Record all visitors to the organization's installations	Maintain. visitors' log/ record, in. designated system all visitors to. specific installation.	2
Physical and environmental protection	18.13	Prevent damage from the system's electrical equipment and cables	Be punctilious in installing and tagging all electrical cables in the server rooms, and communication cabinets.	Tag all cable endings so that employees may easily detect their association with servers/systems, thus avoiding faulty disconnections.	2
Physical and environmental protection	18.14	The organization should be able to securely supply electricity for short periods. in order to enable an ordered shutdown of. system, or its transfer to an alternative power source		Install. UPS array. to secure an ordered shutdown of systems, in cases of power shortages.	2
Physical and environmental protection	18.15	The organization should be able to securely supply electricity for longer periods, in order to achieve. continuity of business activities		An electrical generator is. good option.	3

Family	ID	Monitoring	Complementary Explanation	Monitoring application example	Control level
Physical and environmental protection	18.16	Implement and maintain an automatic emergency lighting system, including emergency exits and evacuation paths.			1
Physical and environmental protection	18.7	Implement and maintain fire extinguishing systems, specifically for data systems, supplied by an autonomous power source.			1
Physical and environmental protection	18.18	Maintain and monitor acceptable temperature and humidity level at the asset installation		Especially in server rooms.	2
Physical and environmental protection	18.19	Protect the asset from water leakage, by either. master shutoff or insulating valves			2
Physical and environmental protection	18.20	Verify and monitor system elements entering and exiting the installation		For example by. removal procedure of software/ hardware elements from the organization, especially those that may store sensitive data. Monitoring and controlling information exiting the organization can be done by following hardware which exited (Laptops delivered to suppliers, disks on key, etc.). Periodic registering and monitoring will include: who received hardware, for how long, for what purpose, estimated retrieval date.	2
Physical and environmental protection	18.21	Implement security controls in alternative work sites (such as DR), assessing their effectiveness.		The physical security level at an alternative site, such as the DR site, will be acceptable, and suitable to the data stored there. Control implementation will be anchored in the contract with the alternative site management, and reviewed periodically.	2

Family	ID	Monitoring	Complementary Explanation	Monitoring application example	Control level
Physical and environmental protection	18.22	Place system elements where damage impact potential, and unauthorized access probability are minimal,	If possible, locate systems (server/ communication rooms) in the best protected location, in the building's center, away from external walls and water sources (including piping).		3

19. Human Resources:
The organization's employees are an important organizational protection layer. On the one hand, they may detect and warn against suspicious events in real time; on the other, they may constitute vulnerabilities, which may lead to cyber-events, either by mistake or by being misled by attackers. Therefore, in recruiting, the organization should double check potential employees in relation to the sensitivities of their functions, inform its employees about cyber threats, possible defenses and reporting. The organization will define conduct rules of employees in the external cyber space (social networks, exposing internal information in Cyberspace etc), which may harm its protection level. All security authorizations of employees quitting the organization must be canceled.

Family	ID	Monitoring	Complementary Explanation	Monitoring application example	Control level
Human Resources and employees' awareness	19.1	Evaluate the sensitivity levels of various functions in the organization, and define proper sorting criteria in employee recruitment.	Define minimum requirements in recruitment, and higher requirements for sensitive functions.	Minimum requirements can include, for example, background tests, and data verification, confidentiality test or. lie detector test. It is recommended to devise. matrix defining various tests for specific functions. For example, non-existence of. criminal record, conducting security classification tests when necessary, confidentiality and lie detector tests, verification of data submitted by potential employees, credential issued by former employers, technical support employees are required to pass. computerized confidentiality test, those having higher authorizations (ADMIN) are required to undergo an external test, etc.	2
Human Resources and employees' awareness	19.2	Conduct background test in recruitment and promotion to higher sensitivity functions	Conduct background tests to candidates/ employee prior to authorizing access to data systems	Background tests may include: background data verification. questioning former employers, confidentiality/lie detector tests, economic background verification, security clearance, etc.	3

APPENDIX C 501

Family	ID	Monitoring	Complementary Explanation	Monitoring application example	Control level
Human Resources and employees' awareness	19.3	Sign up employees on their commitment to the organization's cyber requirements.	The employee will sign documents, attesting to his awareness of the fact that the organization's systems contain secret business data, which should not be disclosed without. specific authorization in accordance with the organization's rules.	Can be implemented by signing up all employees on non-disclosure agreements, kept in their files; by an IdM system controlling information about users on computers, and enabling periodical ratification of each employee.	2
Human Resources and employees' awareness	19.4	The organization will sign up all employees on non-disclosure agreements beyond their employment	Each employee will sign. non-disclosure agreement, and declare that no documents or other data storing devices containing business data are in his possession.	Can be implemented by signing up employees on NDAs, and by conducting tests on sample employees. Such reviews can be performed by monitoring users' activities on the network to locate anomalies (trying to access files unauthorized files, to copy large data amounts, etc.)	2
Human Resources and employees' awareness	19.5	Define security requirement of suppliers and third parties.	The organization will define data security requirements as. part of its supplier relations policy. Such as limitations on data sharing, NDAs, instructing in the organization's security rules, suppliers' instruction, etc.	Can be implemented by. rule booklet, and by signing up suppliers at the beginning of their employment. Conduct. periodic refresher.	2
Human Resources and employees' awareness	19.6	Define regulations on using data systems at work. These rules define responsibilities and proper use of data systems, emphasizing sensitive systems.	The organization will define conduct rules in relation to data systems, distributing them among its employees.	Can be implemented by procedures defining download policy, surfing in data sharing sites, using private/business addresses, etc. By recording users' conduct, by coursework for new employees, and by tools such as URL filtering. control Applications.	1

Family	ID	Monitoring	Complementary Explanation	Monitoring application example	Control level
Human Resources and employees' awareness	19.7	Define rules and limitation on the use of social networks.	Define rules and limitation on the use of social networks; limitations on the publication of organizational information in the social media and public sites; representation of the organization in the social media; and access to social networks from the organization's systems.	User conduct in the social networks can define guidelines on the organization's representation in these networks, on divulging information and on precautions while accessing social networks from the organization's systems.	2
Human Resources and employees' awareness	19.8	Define and implement, sanctioning procedure following disobedience of data security rules.	The organization will define disciplinary procedures to deal with breaches of security by employees or contractors, will record disciplinary measures taken.	For example: an employee who breached clear instructions will be summoned, alongside his superior, to clarify matters with security elements. This may result in disciplinary measures up to termination of employment. Pay attention to cases requiring involvement of legal entities or authorities.	3
Human Resources and employees' awareness	19.9	Examine and update employee's authorizations when changing functions	Define procedures of labor mobilization, including authorization updates in line with new functions (removing unnecessary authorizations, defining new ones as required for the new function).	Authorization updates can be performed manually, by notifying the authorization elements in the organization, or automatically where authorization interfaces are integrated in the human resources systems (a computerized identification management system). In labor mobilization, it is preferable to delete all existing authorizations and define. new set.	1

CYBER DEFENSE METHODOLOGY \\ THE NATIONAL CYBER SECURITY AUTHORITY (NCSA)

Family	ID	Monitoring	Complementary Explanation	Monitoring application example	Control level
Human Resources and employees' awareness	19.10	Delete all authorizations and block user accounts at the termination of employment.	Define an updating process for the termination of employment, including removal of authorizations and user accounts.	Authorization updates can be performed manually, by notifying the authorization elements in the organization, or automatically where authorization interfaces are integrated in the human resources systems (a computerized identification management system). In employment termination, delete all existing authorizations, freeze, and later user accounts.	2

20. Training and Instructions:
A Cyber-Defense policy is important to minimize cyber-attacks on the organization. Many current attacks are performed using social engineering, for example, penetration or Ransomware attacks, fishing via email impersonation in order to perform authorized activities (money transfers), etc. the organization's employees are significant tools in an attacker's hands, therefore seminars and awareness raising activities are important organizational tools in coping with such risks. The organization is required to periodically instruct employees at all levels in Cyber-Defense, general seminars to raise awareness, as well as specific seminars to functionaries in sensitive positions, and to practice them regularly.

Family	ID	Monitoring	Complementary Explanation	Monitoring application example	Control level
Training and instructions	20.1	Develop, record and implement, data security awareness policy	The organization will define data security awareness policy, including periodical refreshers, types of personnel to be instructed in various subjects, and follow up means.	Can be implemented by writing, seminars policy, including content, performance and follow up responsibilities. This policy will define various target audiences (new employees, key personnel, employees whose employment is terminated, suppliers, external elements, etc.), who is in charge of the seminars, control and supervision (signing, declaration, an examination, etc.), required achievement, frequency of instruction, and essential subjects.	2
Training and instructions	20.2	Conduct basic data security training to employees.	The organization will conduct basic training, relating to proper use of information, data security rules, internal and external threats, including threatening signals.	Can be implemented by internal or external coursework, suited to the organization's policy and needs.	2

Family	ID	Monitoring	Complementary Explanation	Monitoring application example	Control level
Training and instructions	20.3	Conduct specific data security training to functionaries accessing sensitive data.	The organization will conduct initial and periodical seminars, including (according to function): operating environmental security controls, operating physical security controls, practice in conduct during data and cyber security events, systems' suspicious behaviors, identifying malware.	Can be implemented by internal or external coursework, suited to job definitions, and the organization's policy and needs.	3
Training and instructions	20.4	The organization will raise employees' awareness of social engineering.	Verify that functionaries are aware of fooling and impersonation attempts of potential attackers.	Can be done in-house or by an external company. Such attempts can include "illegitimate" requests from support personnel, requesting information on behalf of somebody else, attempts to act without user verification, initiating requests in the social networks or via Emails, etc.	4

Detect

21. Recording and monitoring

The Defense Methodology assumes that regardless of all defenses, some attackers will succeed in penetrating the organization. As part of coping with cyber-event, the organization must be capable of identifying such events and treating them. The organization is required to record relevant activities in its systems, which may indicate cyber-events. In addition, the organization should monitor this documentation in manner that will allow it to detect there events as soon as possible, for quick reactions and damage minimization. The controls are intended to define events, and create effective documentation and monitoring infrastructures.

Family	ID	Monitoring	Complementary Explanation	Monitoring application example	Control level
Recording and Monitoring	21.1	Define, implement, and periodically review, recording and monitoring policy		Recording and monitoring organizational policy, and supporting rules, such, data security monitoring center, event recording rules, etc.	2

Family	ID	Monitoring	Complementary Explanation	Monitoring application example	Control level
Recording and Monitoring	21.2	Determine events to be recorded by the system (logged), and for which periods. These control records should form the basis for the debriefing of security events. Define which systems should be audited (servers, communication elements, applications, databases, etc.)	The organization will determine which events in its systems will be recorded within its data security systems, as well as monitoring rules, used in these events. It will determine. minimum length of time of keeping these records, complying with state regulations.	Can be implemented by ex post factum characterization of common events.	2
Recording and Monitoring	21.3	Examine periodically the recorded event definitions and the effectiveness of the recording system	Examine periodically the working premises vis-a-vis changes in the organization's systems, to assure completeness of recording. In addition, examine periodically the recorded events normalcy, and their accord with the organization's definitions and needs.	A periodic examination of the recording mechanisms and their accord with the organization's systems. For central control system, it is possible to use automatic mechanisms to verify the activities and normalcy of the events recording system.	2
Recording and Monitoring	21.4	Employ. mechanism producing event control records. At least record events from systems containing sensitive customer data, from systems critical to the organization's functioning, and from core systems (servers, communication elements, applications, databases, etc.)	The organization will ensure that infrastructure and applicative systems employ logs, and the records are stored for. spell defined by the organization. Control records will hold information such as event type, timing, source, user name. In any case, the organization will monitor sensitive systems, parts of its critical infrastructure, and those managing core processes.	Usually, infrastructure systems contain logging mechanisms. In cases of applications, verify the existence logging options. It is possible to operate central logging mechanisms, linked to the organization's systems, and logging events to. central database.	1

Family	ID	Monitoring	Complementary Explanation	Monitoring application example	Control level
Recording and Monitoring	21.5	The organization will define additional data required for logging its systems, including, unique identifier of each activity, command, and query.	A basic system log does not necessarily record all data required to investigate an event. Therefore, the organization should define events/ data required to be logged. Sensitive systems require. deep and detailed logging of activities, in order to create quality alerts.	Define fields to be monitored in various systems. Occasionally it is necessary to define monitoring at the development stages, or to expand monitoring databases in order to collect such detailed information.	3
Recording and Monitoring	21.6	The organization will implement. central monitoring and alert system.	Define and implement. central monitoring and alert system, to collect data from various systems and to centralize analysis, alert, and coping with suspicious events.	For example, SIEM system, combining security information management (SIM) and security event management (SEM), and providing. real-time analysis of security alerts generated by network hardware and applications.	3
Recording and Monitoring	21.7	Logging mechanism will include, at least, data about the event, timestamp, source and target of the activity, user identifier, process identifier, success/ failure, file name.		For organization of value level. an up, verify that the activity log does record all required data. In most cases it is possible to use logging mechanisms already existing in infrastructure systems. In applicable systems, verify the existence of. functioning log.	1
Recording and Monitoring	21.8	Allocate enough logging storage space.	The organization will allocate enough storage space for its long term logging and monitoring needs.	Pre-plan data storage requirements. Perform periodical capacity planning.	2
Recording and Monitoring	21.9	Create an alert mechanism in cases of logging failures.		The organization will monitor its data security monitoring system, to be alerted when no events are recorded for. period of time from an information system that is normally monitored. Such cases can be defined as rules in most logging and monitoring systems (SIEM, Log Management).	2

APPENDIX C

Family	ID	Monitoring	Complementary Explanation	Monitoring application example	Control level
Recording and Monitoring	21.10	Define sensitive activities that the organization wishes to monitor.	This control is intended to ensure that the organization defined scenarios to be monitored, and is capable of obtaining such information.	Can be done by questioning the business elements about work processes and unauthorized activities. The following events and scenarios to be monitored can be gleaned from IT personnel: irregular activities in the network, such as access to sensitive files; multiple failed identification attempts; copying multiple files to local storage spaces, illegitimate behavior of. supplier or outsourcing employee, etc. in order to monitor such events, use. SIEM system as well as local reports, output from various systems, security cameras, questioning employees, etc.	2
Recording and Monitoring	21.11	Review and analyze periodically the control records. Report the findings to specific functionaries.	The organization will extract data security and trends reports, reporting to the management or to. specific functionary.	It is possible to extract such reports from any data security monitoring system, such as SIEM	2
Recording and Monitoring	21.12	The organization will use automated mechanisms to identify suspected cyber-incidents out of monitoring records.	In order to detect suspicious events, it is necessary to generate alerts and indications from monitoring data collected from enterprise systems. Event that the organization has defined as suspects should be handled in accordance with the outline of the organizational threats.	Can be implemented using reports, queries and rules applicable to the monitoring database, or by. dedicated monitoring system such as SIEM.	2

Family	ID	Monitoring	Complementary Explanation	Monitoring application example	Control level
Recording and Monitoring	21.13	The monitoring system will collect control records from various data sources in order to get complete corporate picture.	The organization will implement 'Correlation Engine', aimed at integrating data from different information sources (different systems), enabling identification of lateral events and advanced attacks on the enterprise systems.	For example, combining data from the system and communication systems, from infrastructure and application systems, from various physical access control systems, surveying vulnerabilities and integrating inputs from cyber intelligence sources.	4
Recording and Monitoring	21.14	Protect control records from unauthorized access, change, or deletion.	The organization will secure the storing area, and toughen the monitoring array, to prevent the updating of log records.	Can be implemented by limiting access to the monitoring records storage, and servers.	2
Recording and Monitoring	21.15	Backup control records on periodical basis, store backup files away from the monitoring system.		The organization will define ongoing backup methods of the monitoring array definitions (backup monitoring rules and configurations), as well as of the collected logs.	3
Recording and Monitoring	21.16	Use cryptographic mechanisms to protect the integrity of records and control tools.	Log files will be stamped by digital stamping and hashing, to verify non-alteration.	Most SIEM systems support these functions, verify its proper functioning.	3
Recording and Monitoring	21.17	Make sure it is possible to retrieve and or search records stored as far back as possible.	Periodically, the organization will ensure that old (as possible) control records may be retrieved.	For example, it is possible to extract report from the establishment of the system, to verify that such events exist in the monitoring system.	4
Recording and Monitoring	21.18	Implement user's session mechanism in the information systems.	Define the recording mechanism and employment rules of this mechanism, including cases when it is necessary to record, privacy rules and access authorization to the recording system.	Can be implemented by operating user's session system over workstation, installation on terminal or application servers.	4

Family	ID	Monitoring	Complementary Explanation	Monitoring application example	Control level
Recording and Monitoring	21.19	Implement mechanism identifying and alerting from attack attempts in real time.	These alert mechanisms will detect and alert on an attack attempt.	Can be implemented by defining SIEM rules, alerting from attack and data security events. And by establishing, security operations center (SOC)	4
Recording and Monitoring	21.20	Monitor incoming and outgoing communication to identify irregular or unauthorized activities.		Can be implemented by analyzing organizational firewall traffic and IPS, and correlate vis-à-vis external feeds to identify communication to suspicious servers.	3
Recording and Monitoring	21.21	Implement specific monitoring devices of user activities of high risk levels (as user with high security clearances).	The organization will characterize sensitive organizational functions, ensuring that these are covered by specific monitoring rules, in relation to sensitive activities.	It is possible to compare with. group of sensitive users within the Active Directory, or to load. list of such users to the SIEM array. It is possible to alert after defining any new ADMIN user within the DC.	3

22. Security Controls Assessment:
Security Controls Assessments are meant to assess the actual controls implementation, in line with this Defense Methodology, and to assess the defense effectiveness. It is desirable to perform the assessment by an independent organizational entity or an external one. The effectiveness can be assessed by penetration and vulnerability tests, Red Teams, etc; the controls are required to assess periodically that Cyber-Defense systems are properly defined and up to date with changes in the organization and possible cyber threats.

Family	ID	Monitoring	Complementary Explanation	Monitoring application example	Control level
Security Control Assessment	22.1	**Policy.** write and implement. data security vulnerability management policy, review and update it periodically.	The organization will define. policy of vulnerability management, including: identifying and assessing vulnerabilities, correcting vulnerabilities, responsibilities, and ongoing follow-up.		2

Family	ID	Monitoring	Complementary Explanation	Monitoring application example	Control level
Security Control Assessment	22.2	**Procedure** -Write. data security vulnerability management procedure, including assessing and correcting vulnerabilities.	The organization will prepare. procedures and plan portfolio, to implement and operate. data security vulnerability management array, emphasizing identification systems, tools and surveyors employment, sub-suppliers and employees' employment to deal with the findings. In addition the data security vulnerability management array will include one or more of the following tests: Security Control Assessment, malicious user test, internal threat assessment, and other tests defined by the organization.	The Security Control Assessment program will include various procedures and processes, intended to detect vulnerabilities,. follow up of correction processes and mechanisms, parallel process interfaces (data security update management, data security system configuration management, secured development, etc.). The organization will integrate in the data security vulnerability management program, penetration test simulating internal and external users, configuration assessment systems, etc.	2
Security Control Assessment	22.3	Assess system penetrability on. periodical basis	The organization will assess penetrability of infrastructures and applications (internal and external, if managed by the organization) on. periodical basis	Financial organizations, for example, conduct annual, even multi-annual, penetrability assessments of all their systems, thus being able to perform continuous follow-up.	3
Security Control Assessment	22.4	Appoint an independent company to assess penetrability.	The organization will employ external data security experts to conduct these assessments.	Occasionally one may conduct these assessments by an internal team, not subject to the IT but to. security not in charge of correcting the faults.	4
Security Control Assessment	22.5	The organization should employ an independent team to conduct penetration assessments, and Red Team exercises, to simulate attack attempts on its assets.	The organization will employ an external data security team, to simulate attack attempts, in order to test its controls and response capabilities.	This control can test the response capabilities of the monitoring teams, and the infrastructure and data security teams' capabilities to block such attempts in real time.	4

Family	ID	Monitoring	Complementary Explanation	Monitoring application example	Control level
Security Control Assessment	22.6	Conduct continuous vulnerability assessments, according to the organizational vulnerability management process, by. designated tool for all data systems (internal and external).		Can be implemented by installing. security control assessment tool, and assessing every few weeks, months (it is possible to define specific timings to various environments).	2
Security Control Assessment	22.7	Verify that the security control assessment tool is always up to date, containing all vulnerabilities discovered and reported.	Verify that the assessment tool is updatable. licensed (thus regularly updated), and updated.	Can be assessed against update dates of the vulnerabilities list. Verify communication with the supplier's updating site, or the existence of. mirror site within the organization.	2
Security Control Assessment	22.8	The organization should validate vulnerabilities detected by the automatic system, by an internal process, including an assessment of vulnerabilities identified in other systems.	The organization will define. validation process, dealing, at least, with detected critical vulnerabilities, verifying, manually or automatically, the existence of these vulnerabilities in other systems.	For example, if. critical vulnerability is discovered in Windows, or in the system's database, it is possible to assess non-updated servers, running the same version by. tool.	4
Security Control Assessment	22.9	Conduct Credentialed Scans, with the vulnerability assessment tool	The organization will appoint. Credentialed Scanner for the system being scanned, allowing. thorough assessment of all processes and updates installed, as well as vulnerabilities in its toughening definitions.	Most security control assessment tools allow. Credentialed Scan.	4

Family	ID	Monitoring	Complementary Explanation	Monitoring application example	Control level
Security Control Assessment	22.10	Verify the existence of an automatic tool comparing past and present vulnerability scans, to allow control and trend analysis.	The organization will conduct an automatic follow-up of detected vulnerabilities, in order to detect high risk systems, or systems with unsatisfactory controls implementation.	Can be implemented with the scanning tools or by an interface to third party systems (such as SIEM).	4
Security Control Assessment	22.11	Verify harmony of outputs of different security control assessment tools implemented in the organization, in order to obtain. full present situation of various vulnerabilities.	Verify that all vulnerabilities assessment and control tools are linked to. central system, in order to obtain. unified present situation of all vulnerabilities and controls.	Can be done by establishing an interface between vulnerability scanning and Patch Management tools to. central interface, such as SIEM, or. Data Analytics/BI tools, in order to produce one encompassing vulnerability report.	4
Security Control Assessment	22.12	Integrate an automatic central fault correction mechanism	The organization will integrate. central system, to manage vulnerabilities and their correction.	Can be implemented by establishing interfaces between the vulnerabilities management array and the organizational reading system, or by using. designated system (GRC).	3
Security Control Assessment	22.13	Control the vulnerability correction process. Apply measurable objectives to correct vulnerabilities, according to their gravity.	The organization will define SLA objectives to deal with vulnerabilities, according to their gravity. In addition, define alerts in relation to deviation from time tables of vulnerabilities correction, vis-à-vis the measures and objectives defined (SLA)	For example, critical vulnerabilities will be corrected immediately, high vulnerabilities within. month, medium within three months, etc. In addition implement SLA alerts to calls opened in the vulnerability management array, and report about deviations from these objectives.	3

23, Proactive Cyber Defense:
Proactive cyber controls allow the organization flexibility in defending itself against varying attacks. The organization will collect updated data about cyber threats and coping measures, and information about its digital presence, translating the last into ad-hoc applicable controls. In addition, the organization will implement. deception array of potential attackers (honey traps and other luring and deception technologies) in order to confuse the attacker, reduce his motivation, trap him as soon as he penetrates the organization, etc. The organization will implement behavior patterns based analysis controls in sensitive environments.

Family	ID	Monitoring	Complementary Explanation	Monitoring application example	Control level
Proactive Cyber Defense	23.1	The organization will define and periodically update. proactive Cyber-Defense program.	A proactive Cyber-Defense program will detect new threats, adjust controls to detected threats, collect intelligence and other data, survey new controls.		3
Proactive Cyber Defense	23.2	The organization will collect up-to-date cyber threats and coping methods information.	The organization will learn from public information sources about new cyber threats, relevant to its business and technologies.	One can get access to information, free tools, tutorials and more at open sources such as Metasploit, security companies' sites, etc., and contact intelligence companies.	3
Proactive Cyber Defense	23.3	The organization will collect data about its digital presence (business activities, customers, internal users).	Such collection is intended to identify cases of sensitive date exposure on the Internet, including the "Dark Net."	Use the services of specialized companies.	3
Proactive Cyber Defense	23.4	The organization will use cyber threat information to devise and improve applicable controls.	The organization will map the changes necessary to its data security systems' definitions, as well as its infrastructure and application controls, to cope with new threats.	Changes may apply to networks, firewalls, applicative systems and interface definitions, etc. Update systems' rules following the updating of their definitions.	3
Proactive Cyber Defense	23.5	The organization will implement. luring and deception array of potential attackers.	The organization will integrate technologies to lure, deceive, and delay potential attackers, to improve its identification and coping capabilities.	Systems such as Honeypots, designated, monitored virtual servers, file stamping. Can be implemented in various ways, such as defining fictitious users, objects within the DC, intended to lure attackers, concealing files with "coveted" names, such as "Salaries," "Passwords," "Secret," etc.	3
Proactive Cyber Defense	23.6	The organization will integrate controls based on behavior pattern analysis (system and user) in sensitive environments.	The organization will integrate systems, identifying anomalies in the server and network levels of service and sensitive data environments.	Such systems can function at the server level (Advanced Threat Analytics) and network level (MacAfee, NTBA, STRM Sourcefire 3d, etc.)	3

Respond

Family	ID	Monitoring	Complementary Explanation	Monitoring application example	Control level
24. Events Management and Reporting					
The organization should be able to manage an ongoing cyber-event in manner reducing damage, neutralizing the threat and returning to normal. This alongside debriefing the event, drawing lessons, and adjusting the defense array accordingly. Such controls are intended for this objective. In his framework, the organization will define coping measures in cyber-event, reporting channels to employees about suspected security event, the professional entity (within or without the organization) supplying professional knowledge, support and assistance in monitoring, identifying, investigating, and reacting to cyber-events. The organization will define reports to be produced in the occurrence of cyber-events and their endings (for example to the national CERT, and regulator, etc. Inspect response capabilities periodically using tests defined by the organization.					
Events Management and Reporting	24.1	Write and implement. reactive policy to events. Review and update the policy periodically.	The organization will write and implement. reactive policy to data security events, as. part of its organizational data security policy, and will review and refresh that policy.	In writing events' treatment policy, define functionaries and response teams, gravity levels, and communication means with the authorities (the Police, ILITA. The Israel Law. Information and Technology Authority, The National Cyber Authority, the regulator, etc.). Define event managers (various functionaries may be in control during various events, such. ransomware attacks, threats to publish users' data, etc.). It is important to write this policy in cooperation with relevant third parties, such as regulators. suppliers, emphasizing cloud systems, outsourcing employees, etc. It is recommended to define situations during which. situation room should be opened. when and how to involve management, reporting frequency. appealing to the national CERT. Cyber-Defense Authority. recovery, etc.	2

Family	ID	Monitoring	Complementary Explanation	Monitoring application example	Control level
Events Management and Reporting	24.2	Develop. cyber and data security event coping plan	The organization will develop. plan to identify, cope with and respond to cyber and data events, including: an outline of realizing response capabilities to security events;. description of capabilities to cope with events, response to the organization demands, considering its tasks and size, events requiring reporting; supplying measuring means of the organization's capabilities to cope with events; resources and management support required to maintain and improve response capabilities		2
Events Management and Reporting	24.3	Develop coping capabilities with cyber and data security events, including preparations, detection and analysis, interception and recovery.	These controls aims to assure that the organization maintains the knowledge and tools needed to debrief, contain, and manage an event effectively and to cope with its consequences.	Can be implemented by the security event coping plan, emphasizing the recruitment of professionals serving as. basis for detection and response to events, training the team to cope with various events (viruses spread, ransomware, coping with DDOS, leaked information, etc.). Can be implemented by debriefing tools or ERT's)	2

Family	ID	Monitoring	Complementary Explanation	Monitoring application example	Control level
Events Management and Reporting	24.4	Integrate automatic mechanisms to support coping with events.	Managing multiple events and alerts is. complicated business. Therefore, it is required to automate as much as possible alert status follow-up, required activities, decisions, etc.	Can be implemented by linking command and control systems to events monitoring and detection systems. It is possible to define response procedures within command and control systems. Can be implemented by decision support systems, Work Flow management systems, or Ticketing systems. It is recommended that such tools will assist the organization in locating long time events, grave events not dealt with properly, and situation requiring immediate intervention	3
Events Management and Reporting	24.5	Record data security events and coping with, including data collection, activities and conclusions.	The organization will maintain. centralized reporting mechanism, in order to have unified and full situation report of the event and risks evaluation.	Can be implemented centrally by. SOC (Security Operations Center), collecting and recording data.	2
Events Management and Reporting	24.6	Define data security reporting channels for employees.	The organization will apply obligatory reporting procedures, formats, in cases of cyber-events	Can be implemented by instructing employees about data security events and their reporting procedures. It is recommended to approach the national CERT for assistance in response and recovery.	1
Events Management and Reporting	24.7	Define. functionary whose job is to supply professional knowledge, support, and escort in monitoring, detection, debriefing and responding to data security events.	The organization will appoint. professional entity to serve as. professional knowledge source, in the identification and debriefing of data security events.	It can be an internal or external entity, experienced in identifying, debriefing, and responding to events. It will guide the teams operating the events, sharing his experience in cyber-events.	3
Events Management and Reporting	24.8	Integrate. mechanism providing accessibility to information about reactions to cyber and data security events.	The organization will provide access to. file containing detection and response procedure in cyber and data security events.	Can be implemented by any data or documentation management system, or by. printed copy.	2

124

Family	ID	Monitoring	Complementary Explanation	Monitoring application example	Control level
Events Management and Reporting	24.9	Instruct relevant functionaries in reacting to security events.	The organization will train all entities involved in coping with data security events in identifying and responding to such events. These seminars will be refreshed periodically.	Such. seminar portfolio should include response procedures, best practices and tools serving to make this information accessible during such events.	2
Events Management and Reporting	24.10	Integrate event simulations within training, to improve the teams' response effectiveness in crises.	The organization will simulate data security events scenarios, in order to test its readiness and prepare accordingly.	Some exercises will simulate guided events, and the teams' reactions will be measured by the exercise's controller. Other exercises will simulate events in production environments, with real means, such as phishing exercises.	3
Events Management and Reporting	24.11	Implement automatic mechanisms to provide realistic training environments.	The organization will simulate real data security events in environments simulating the organizational environment.	Cases can be simulated in testing environments or in designated external laboratories (a professional cyber laboratory).	4
Events Management and Reporting	24.12	In order to check effectiveness. Examine response capabilities periodically, using test defined by the organization, including, simulation of. real event. Record the outcomes of each periodical test.	In order to test response capabilities to data security events, the organization will simulate real attacks, inter alia with automatic attack tools. The organization will record and derive lessons from these exercises, and produce. debriefing report.	Can be measured by an event script, counting detected events, and response quality (minimizing damages, communication among entities, concentration, and operation, recovery). Events detection can be integrated with real penetration attempts carried out in the organization. Real attack tools will be used in the test.	3

Recovery

25. Business Continuity:
The organization's objective is to maintain business continuity and minimize damages from cyber-events. This is what business continuity controls are here for. The organization should verify fast recovery of its cyber infrastructures. Prepare alternative infrastructures (including availability and redundancy), periodically test and practice its business continuity plan. Effective, available, and reliable backups are critical to business continuity, and should be exercised regularly.

Family	ID	Monitoring	Complementary Explanation	Monitoring application example	Control level
Business continuity	25.1	Write, implement, review, and update. business continuity policy, regarding Cyber-Defense .	The organization will prepare. business continuity plan. derived from its objectives and implementing controls and processes in order to achieve these objectives. The plan will take into consideration various disaster scenarios and critical processes. The organization will define those assets supporting critical business tasks and functions (physical and digital). The organization will define maximum spell of essential services closure before returning to normal (in emergencies). As. part of the continuity plan the organization will define the time spell within which essential tasks will return to normal since the plan's operation.	The organization will write, implement, and periodically update. business continuity plan. This plan will define the organization's conduct in normal and emergency periods in order to ensure business continuity (including common indices, such as RTO) in cases of cyber-events. It is possible to use aids such as ISO 22301 standard.	2
Business continuity	25.2	Prepare required capacity planning for emergencies (computing, communication, support services).	The organization will ensure that systems and infrastructure intended for business continuity in emergencies, support the desired capacity for the required scopes and time spells.	Can be implemented following. mapping of critical services, defining recovery and survivability objectives of each service. Normally, the organization measures the required capacity in the alternative site, in terms of communication infrastructures, system infrastructures, applications. and licensing.	2

Family	ID	Monitoring	Complementary Explanation	Monitoring application example	Control level
Business continuity	25.3	Instruct employees concerning business continuity.	The organization will instruct employees in business continuity procedures.	Refer to employees' functions in recovery, temporary gathering sites, logistics and operations, and recovery objectives of the team and organization levels.	2
Business continuity	25.4	Exercise the business continuity plan on. periodic basis.	The organization will prepare and conduct preparedness exercises, to test the effectiveness of the business continuity plan.	Can be implemented by exercising various scenarios. It is recommended that the exercising will include the IT aspects of the business continuity plan, such as telephone and computer communications, as well as complimentary aspects such as suppliers and (local and cloud) services, guided by the BCP plan. It is also important to raise emergency awareness, by considering the need and urgency of shifting new versions to the production environment, by being strict in escorting visitors, by trying to recover files, by exercising cyber-event management, decision making at the management level, debriefing and drawing lessons.	2
Business continuity	25.5	Exercise the business continuity plan by periodic simulations.	The organization will use simulations and involve employees expected to be involved in the recovery plan implementation.	In order to carry out simulations as close to reality, prepare disaster scenarios, operate the plan (in. reduced manner) in the DR environment, and test the validity of the plan	3
Business continuity	25.6	Test the continuity plan periodically and fill gaps discovered.	The organization will review and correct its business continuity plan periodically.	For example:. testing program, performing. partial shift to an emergency environment, or to various systems, in order to test the shifting processes.	2

Family	ID	Monitoring	Complementary Explanation	Monitoring application example	Control level
Business continuity	25.7	Test the continuity plan in the alternative site, to familiarize the continuity team with the site and its resources, and to evaluate the site's capabilities to support activities requiring continuity.	The organization will prepare processes and procedures to familiarize and exercise the backup site, as part of exercising the business continuity.	Can be done by traveling to the backup site, becoming familiarized with the system stored there, and exercising the actual shift to the alternative site.	2
Business continuity	25.8	Use automatic tools to thoroughly test the continuity plan	The organization will use automatic tools allowing control and testing of the plan's effectiveness.	Such tools can be. control of the backup array, including failure alerts, control of High Availability, between the main and secondary sites, monitoring communications between sites, etc.	8
Business continuity	25.9	Perform. full system recovery as part of continuity plan testing.	The organization will perform periodically. full recovery from backup, of systems defined as parts of the Disaster Recovery plan.	For example. full recovery into the backup environment. Following recovery, perform acceptance testing to verify full functionality. Including data comparisons, configuration testing, and working with the recovered systems.	3
Business continuity	25.10	Establish an alternative backup and computing site allowing. full recovery at the same security level as the main site.	The organization will establish and maintain. secondary site, containing systems' copies, as well as data and storing security systems, all supporting recovery and business continuity of critical processes.	Can be implemented by duplicating servers and survival environments in the alternative site. Virtualization technics etc.	2
Business continuity	25.11	In order to avoid both sites being attacked simultaneously, verify physical and logical separation.		The organization will verify. proper geographical distance between both sites, as well as among computer networks and support infrastructure.	2

Family	ID	Monitoring	Complementary Explanation	Monitoring application example	Control level
Business continuity	25.12	Define the backup site in. manner supporting the recovery plan	The organization will define systems and communication lines in. manner allowing. fast and effective recovery.	This can be implemented by High Availability systems in various configurations, allowing fast data duplication and availability post recovery in the alternative site.	2
Business continuity	25.13	Identify potential accessibility problems to the alternative site in cases of regional disasters, and take proper preventive steps.	The organization will verify site accessibility in cases of disaster.	For example verify the existence of several approaches, survivability to earthquakes, and remote accessibility.	2
Business continuity	21.14	Prepare backup site infrastructure agreements, containing priority of service clauses, according to the organization's recovery objectives.	The organization will verify that its service agreements contain clauses committing the supplier to service and response times compatible with its objectives.	It is possible to verify that the SLA agreements with the backup site supplier system programmers' response and recovery times are compatible with the organization's service RTO. It is possible to dictate first priority in critical services' recovery.	2
Business continuity	21.15	Verify the alternative site's preparedness to function as. main site, and support essential tasks and business functions.	The organization will verify that all services (including support and infrastructure) in the backup site are available and functional at any given time.	Can be verified by preparing detailed tagging lists for support and infrastructure systems, and by periodical normalcy tests (as well as during exercising).	2
Business continuity	25.16	Prepare backups to communication networks, and verify the existence alternative communication services, in order to reduce dependence on. single point of failure.	The organization will verify the existence of an alternative communication network between its main and backup sites, as well. dual communication link to the main site.	Can be verified by purchasing and operating backup communication lines, thus minimizing dependence on. single point of failure.	2
Business continuity	25.17	Require alternative, emergency service suppliers to prepare and periodically test. business continuity plan.	The organization will verify that suppliers' recovery objectives are compatible with its own.	Suppliers can provide their own emergency plans, including recovery objectives of services supplied to the organization.	2

Family	ID	Monitoring	Complementary Explanation	Monitoring application example	Control level
Business continuity	25.18	Prepare and protect backups of the user, system, and documentation levels.	The organization will back up all critical business data, and ensure their availability, integrity, and confidentiality.	Backup disks, tapes, and cloud.	1
Business continuity	25.19	Verify backup reliability and availability.	The organization will ensure reliable and available backups.	Can be done with periodical recovery tests.	2
Business continuity	25.20	Retain. backup copy of critical data away from the main site.	The organization will ensure that backup copies are retained in. remote site, protected from environmental disasters (fires, etc.).	Can be done by directly backing up to. remote site, or by regular delivery of the backup media to that site.	2
Business continuity	25.21	Implement. transaction recovery mechanism for transaction based systems.	The organization will install. mechanism to recover failed transactions due to system failure or. shift to. backup system.	Can be implemented in. variety of configurations:. double writing configuration (two parallel transactions in both main and backup systems), verifying. transaction post-sending, retaining, and tagging failed transactions. In Queue Management Systems, the queue can be backed up.	2
Business continuity	25.22	Verify. recovery capability to. known operational status.	Verify the existence of mechanisms enabling recovery of data or configuration to. known status.	Can be performed by. configuration back up at. point of time (before implementing changes), and by determining data recovery points, and rollback mechanisms.	3
Business continuity	25.23	Verify service and critical infrastructure redundancy.	The organization will verify redundancy of critical services and infrastructures, in order to minimize dependence of. single point of failure.	Can be implemented by redundancy of critical infrastructures, such as communication equipment, main network services, security and storage systems, etc.	3

CYBER DEFENSE METHODOLOGY \\ THE NATIONAL CYBER SECURITY AUTHORITY (NCSA)

131

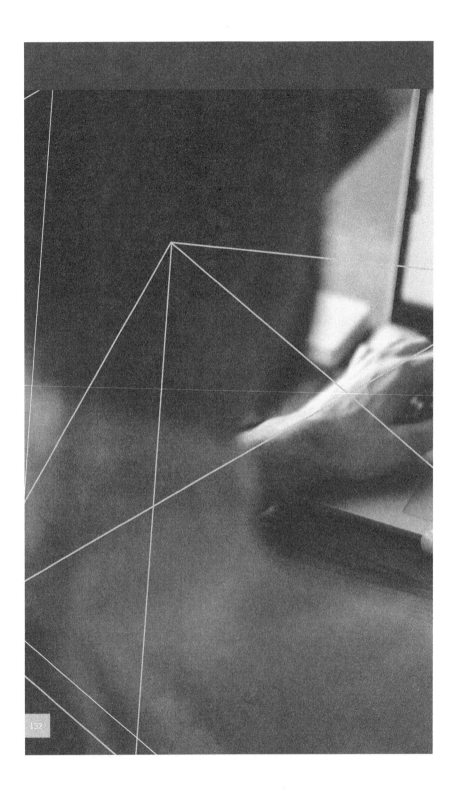

132

APPENDIX A \\
EXAMPLE OF RISK ASSESSMENT EXECUTION FOR AN INFORMATION ASSET

In the example below the calculation is: Risk = 3i + P = 3X3 + 2

	Question	Sample Answer	Weighted Score
Impact Level Questionnaire (intensity). **This questionnaire appears on page 26 in the document.**	What is the level of damage caused to the organization following **disclosure of information** from the system? C	2	
	What is the level of damage caused to the organization following the **disruption of information** existing in the system? I	1	Maximum value 3
	What is the level of damage caused to the organization following a long-term **system shutdown**? A	3	
Exposure Level Questionnaire (Probability). **This questionnaire appears on page 28 in the document.**	How many users are in the system?	2	
	Who are the system users?	4	
	How many interfaces does the system have?	1	
	What is the nature of the system interfaces?	1	
	The type of information existing in the system	3	The average value 2
	Remote access to the system.	1	
	System user permissions compartmentalization level.	2	
	Current infrastructure	3	
	Updates and security patches	4	
	Physical Security	2	
	Weighted System Risk Score		3*3+2=11

After answering the above questionnaire for all the assets of the organization, the following list is obtained:

Probability (P) / intensity (I)	4	3	2	1
4	16 System A	13	10 System C	7
3	15	12	9	6
2	14	11 System B System D	8	5 System E
1	13	10	7	4

APPENDIX B \\
TOOLKIT FOR THE IMPLEMENTATION OF THE
DEFENSE METHODOLOGY

In order to assist with the implementation of the Defense Methodology and make it accessible to various target audiences, a toolkit will be developed under the National Cyber Security Authority (NCSA). In addition, various economic entities may develop toolkits, as is customary in similar cases around the world.

The toolkit that the NCSA plans to develop consists of:

1. An automation process of the Defense Methodology through a convenient and efficient technological platform.

2. Generic forms and procedures ready for use by the organization, as for example a corporate policy document referring to Cyber-Defense aspects, Defense Methodology controls procedure, form templates, and more. The organization must **adapt** these examples and templates to its needs.

3. A risk assessment calculator, for the automation of some simple formulas of the Defense Methodology.

4. Examples of cyber assets mapping.

5. Enrichment information for controls.

6. Best Practices for selected controls.

7. Training kits for various target populations.

It is possible to view a toolkit that supports the Defense Methodology according to the following hierarchy:

• **A National Perception** - on the basis of which we write the Defense Methodology for the organization.

• A Defense Methodology - presents the various protection issues at the basic level (e.g. monitoring, awareness, networks separation, supply chain management, etc.)

• Best Practices - on the basis of this Methodology , we will write together with you specific guidelines for technology / service etc. such as Best Practice for hardening DB servers of a particular type or for working correctly with WIN 10 operating system, etc.

- **Professional Extensions** - alongside the Defense Methodology there will be extension documents that provide additional information which is not dependent on a specific technology (Best Practice), but, on the other hand, is more comprehensive and detailed than the basic requirements of the Defense Methodology ('professional extension').

The above information will be made accessible to the field in various forms (guides, online courseware, One pager for small businesses, training courses, etc.)

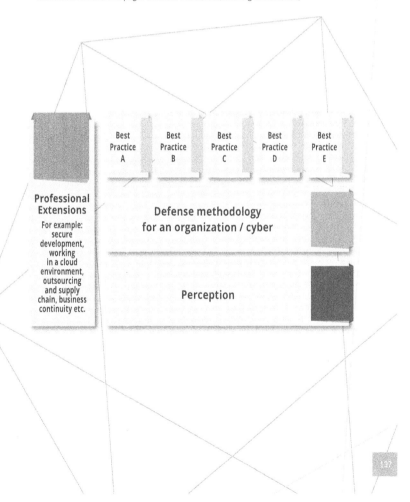

Professional Extensions

For example: secure development, working in a cloud environment, outsourcing and supply chain, business continuity etc.

Best Practice A

Best Practice B

Best Practice C

Best Practice D

Best Practice E

Defense methodology for an organization / cyber

Perception

APPENDIX C \\
CONTROLS FOR THE DEFENSE
OF A CATEGORY A ORGANIZATION -
HIGHLIGHTS FOR IT SERVICE PROVIDERS

Family	Header	Monitoring	Complementary Explanation
Management Responsibility	Corporate governance:	Examine periodically the organization's approach to information security and Cyber-Defense management and its implementation.	In the framework of this monitoring, examine the security controls implemented in the organization as well as the information security and protection policy of critical business processes of the organization.
Preventing Malicious Code:	Detecting and preventing malicious code on endpoints and servers in the organization.	Implement tools to detect and prevent malicious code on endpoints and servers in the organization. These tools will be run in active protection mode and periodic scans will be performed as well.	Since some artifacts may penetrate the security mechanisms, ensure that controls for handling malicious code will also be applied at the workstations level.
Preventing Malicious Code:	Automatic updates	Run automatic updating of all systems for identifying and preventing malicious code within the organization.	The organization will activate automatic updates from a central server, managed by the organization or by a recognized service provider. These updates will keep the protection tools constantly updated.
Encryption:	Encryption Criteria	Define uses that require encryption and the necessary encryption type, in accordance with laws, guidelines, procedures, regulations and business commitments.	The organization will define what information and systems should be encrypted and record the configuration of the information encryption. The requirements will be derived from the requirements applicable to the organization or from information retention requirements.
Protection of workstations and servers:	Hardening Policy	Define, document and implement a hardening policy for workstations and servers, which meets the requirements of the organization's information security.	The organization will define hardening requirements for systems within the organization with an emphasis on the basic requirements, the frequency of updates and the level of classification and then document the requirements in an overall framework which will serve as a basis for writing the hardening procedures.

Family	Header	Monitoring	Complementary Explanation
Protection of workstations and servers:	Hardening Implementation	It is necessary to define the system configuration to provide the minimum functionality required (while blocking unneeded functions, ports and protocols).	The organization will define hardening procedures for each system and server type, based on acceptable practices to include, at a minimum: 1. Reduction of the system's attack surface by blocking unnecessary ports; 2. Turning off unnecessary services; 3. Removing guest user accounts; 4. Preference to using secure communication protocol between servers; 5. Getting email updates in an orderly manner; 6. Blocking sensitive functions of the system; 7. Sending system events logs to a monitoring server ; 8. Blocking software installation by unauthorized users.
Public cloud computing:	Shared Responsibility	It is necessary to understand the division of responsibilities between the service provider and the organization, and implement protection monitoring accordingly.	When using public cloud services there is a division of responsibility for cyber protection between issues under the responsibility of the supplier and issues remaining under the responsibility of the customer. This division of responsibility depends on the nature of the service and the implementation model. The organization has to understand what are the issues that are within its responsibility and implement the consequences of this responsibility.
Public cloud computing:	Sharing sensitive information	Make sure that no data, which under the regulation and responsibilities of the organization must not be transferred, is transferred to the cloud services.	There is data that the organization is prevented from transferring for storage or processing in public cloud services due to regulatory considerations or Commitment to third parties. Prior to transferring data to the cloud make sure that such data are not kept or transferred to the cloud services.
Protecting the information:	Protection of information stored on shared resources	Prevent unauthorized or unintentional data transfer via shared system resources.	The organization must prevent the transfer of information in an unauthorized manner, e.g. by using shared folders, e-mail, removable media etc.
Network security:	Managing connections (Sessions) - at network level	The organization will operate technological devices in order to protect services against Denial of Service attacks.	Defend against Denial of Service attacks (DOS) of various types, such as loading the computing resources to collapse, loading the communication bandwidth, loading the website to crash and more.

Family	Header	Monitoring	Complementary Explanation
Network security:	Sessions Reliability	Make sure that the Address Translation Service (DNS) is provided by a trusted server (intra-enterprise and extra-enterprise.)	The organization will allow obtaining Address Translation Service (DNS) only from a secure internal server. In order to prevent erroneous communication routing (intentionally or unintentionally) to hostile targets.
Network security:	Network Limits	It is necessary to limit the number of communication channels outside the system.	The organization will reduce and unite communication channels to ensure better control over the connections to the system.
Network security:	Network Limits	Block by default all network traffic and allow manually any desirable traffic by means of exception rules.	The organization will define the filtering rules of network traffic so as to block by default all traffic not explicitly defined as allowed.
Network security:	Network Limits	Use separate network addresses (different sub-network) to connect to different security zones.	The organization will determine that each sub-network will have a separate address range, which will be published to the firewall and routers.
Access Control:	Users Management	Set up user accounts that support the business functions of the organization.	At the very least, separate the 'Administrator' account from a 'user' account. It is also necessary to set up users who manage the system security functions (such as creating users, managing access and system privileges, managing the information security systems, etc.).
Access Control:	Permissions Management	Define and enforce logical access privileges to the system and the information in accordance with the access control policy.	The access control can be done on a personal level (identity-based), or the role level (role-based), and aims to control the access of entities (users or computer processes) to objects (files, records, devices etc.).
Human resources and employee awareness	Employees Etiquette	It is necessary to set rules of conduct in work with the enterprise information systems. These rules define the responsibilities and the rules of proper use of the enterprise information systems, with an emphasis on sensitive systems.	The organization will define behavior practices with respect to information systems and will distribute then to all the employees
Human resources and employee awareness	Managing permissions during recruitment / mobility / departure.	Review and update the access rights of an employee while moving from job to job .	Define updating processes of employee mobility and updating permissions in accordance with the new role (removing unnecessary permissions and establishing the required permissions for the new job).
Security in procurement and development	Security requirements in procurement and in systems development	Supply chain security - require service providers to comply with corporate security requirements, regulations, standards and guidelines.	The organization will ensure that service providers comply with the organization's compliance requirements as well as with regulatory requirements applicable in the countries where the organization operates.

Family	Header	Monitoring	Complementary Explanation
Physical and environmental protection	Emergency Lighting	Implement and maintain automatic emergency lighting, which will be activated in the event of a break or disruption in the power supply and will include emergency exits and evacuation routes in the facility.	
Physical and environmental protection	Fire Protection	Implement and maintain resources / systems for fire detection and suppression for the information systems which have an independent energy source.	
Documentation and Monitoring	Monitoring mechanism.	Activate a documentation mechanism that produces control records on incidents in the organization. It is necessary to record, at least, events from systems containing sensitive customer information, performance-critical enterprise systems and core systems (servers, communications components, applications, databases, etc.).	The organization will ensure that infrastructure systems and applicative systems activate an events listing mechanism, and that records are kept for a period set by the organization. The control records will contain information such as the type of event, when it occurred, the event source, the user name. In any case, monitor the sensitive information processing systems, which are part of the organization's critical infrastructure, or that manage the organization's core processes.
Documentation and Monitoring	Monitoring mechanism.	The documentation and monitoring mechanisms will include, at a minimum, information on the nature of the act committed, timestamp, source and target of the operation, a user ID, process ID, failure / success, mixed file name.	
Event Management and Reporting	Handling cyber-incidents and information security	Define reporting channels of employees to the bodies in charge in order to report suspected security incidents.	The organization will apply procedures on events that require reporting as well as the manner of reporting about an event defined as a cyber-incident.
Business Continuity	Resources availability	perform backups at user and system level and a system and documentation and ensure the protection of the backups.	The organization will perform a backup of all critical information in the information systems which support the business processes and will guarantee the availability, integrity and confidentiality of the backups.

APPENDIX D \\
STANDARDS COMPLIANCE

The Defense Methodology draws its knowledge base from accepted international standards, such as NIST 800-53 and ISO 27001. In order to make it easy for organizations to adopt the controls that appear in this document, the National Cyber Security Authority (NCSA) has mapped the existing controls to equivalent controls in the aforementioned standards. In particular, an organization that complies with the Defense Methodology and requires ISO 27001 accreditation standard can use the standard compliance appendix.

Later on, in parallel with the development of the corporate Defense Methodology , the National Cyber Security Authority (NCSA) will map the controls opposite leading domestic and international standards. Among the most important standards to be mapped soon are the following:

• Proper Banking Conduct Circular 357 + 361

• Cyber Risk Management Circular of the Capital Market Department

• Guidelines of the Israel Law, Information and Technology Authority (ILITA)

• ISO 27032

COMPLIANCE WITH ISO 27001

In view of the fact that this standard was constructed through relying much on international standards and in particular on the ISO 27001 standard, the completion which is required from an organization that implements this Defense Methodology in favor of full compliance with the requirements towards a certification Review is not large.

In order to facilitate for organizations that are certified or are considering to begin an ISO 27001 certification process, attached hereby is a conversion table, which reflects the Defense Methodology controls against the Statement of Applicability of the Standard. This table is on the National Cyber Security Authority (NCSA) website.

CYBER DEFENSE METHODOLOGY \\ THE NATIONAL CYBER SECURITY AUTHORITY (NCSA)

APPENDIX E \\
CRITICAL PROTECTION CONTROLS FOR ACHIEVING A HIGH SCORE IN A SHORT TIME

The Defense Methodology defines a risk management process, and subsequently a requirement for exercising controls in the framework of a work plan. On the other hand, in some organizations there is a need to focus the first activities on performance. These activities include, in fact, the controls with the highest 'cost-benefit'.

The SANS Institute is considered one of the world's leaders in critical protection controls definitions, which are the most effective controls (CSC - Critical Security Controls). The implementation of controls, which cover 20 subjects, provides the organization with an 88% response from known assaults.[1]

An organization that wants to get a quick snapshot of its defense preparedness can go over the critical protection controls, which are marked with a key symbol in Chapter 6 as part of the various control families.

The controls in this document were based on the same logic, but they do not necessarily represent the key controls of the SANS Institute.

Family	Detection
Risk Management and Risk Assessment	2.1.
Access Control:	4.2, 4.4, 4.17
Protecting the information:	5.1.
Protection of workstations and servers:	6.5.
Preventing Malicious Code:	7.1 ,7.2 ,7.3 ,7.9
Encryption:	8.6
Network security:	9.1 , 9.9, 9.12, 9.24, 9.25
Separation of Environments:	10.2, 10.4
Public cloud computing:	11.4, 11.6
Media Security	15.7.
Supply chain and outsourcing	16.2.
Security in procurement and development	17.14
Physical and environmental protection	18.6.
Training	20.2.
Documentation and Monitoring	21.1.
Security controls assessment surveys	22.6.
Event Management and Reporting	24.12
Business Continuity	25.1, 25.19

1 https://www.sans.org/critical-security-controls/history

APPENDIX F \\
THE CONTROLS BANK

The controls bank is a significant element of the Defense Methodology . The bank, established on the basis of global common standards, contains many elements intended to enhance the understanding of the organization in implementing the controls.

For reasons of convenience and efficiency, necessary layers of information were inserted in the body of this document in order to implement the Defense Methodology. At the same time enriching layers of additional information have been set and written about every control. These layers currently are:

1. **CIA** - information security aspects which are protected by the control - availability, integrity or confidentiality.

2. **Cyber Kill Chain -** the stage in the attack chain where the control plays a role.

3. **Assets Categories** for which the control is relevant - IT, OT, services or databases.

4. **The risk levels** at which implementation is required - as the level of risk of an asset is higher, so controls providing a higher level of protection will be required, adapted to the relevant risk to the asset (levels 1-4 derived from the third stage of the risk management process described in this document).

5. **Control Type** - A control can be a guiding control (such as a procedure), preventive control (such as malware filtering systems), or detecting (such as monitoring and alarm systems).

6. **Control compliance with common standards** (in the first stage of the Defense Methodology publication the controls are mapped to standards ISO 27001 and NIST 800-53).

Extended and supplemental information on controls chapters can be found on the National Cyber Security Authority (NCSA) website.

APPENDIX G \\
COPING WITH A SIGNIFICANT CYBER-INCIDENT

The Defense Methodology assumes that it is impossible **to guarantee complete protection** from cyber-attacks. Therefore, the controls chapters are designed to prepare the organization to cope with and recover from cyber-incidents with minor damage. On the other hand, in light of past experience we know that management of significant cyber-events is a professional field that requires specialized knowledge, tools, infrastructure and specialized professional training, which do not exist in every organization. The National CERT was established under the NCSA in order to assist organizations in dealing with such events. The CERT's mission is to enhance the cyber resilience of the Israeli economy by providing initial assistance and treatment for cyber threats as well as to coordinate and obtain relevant information from the various bodies in Israel and abroad.

CERT roles and activities:

- Incident Handling – starting with reporting, assisting and coordinating cyber-incident handling, up to assistance with recovery and investigation.
- Vulnerability and Artifact Handling - receiving artifacts, carrying out research to understand them and dissemination of methods and ways to handle them.
- Coping with and prevention of cyber threats - through proactive activities to detect, identify, and investigate them.
- Developing and disseminating knowledge for protection to target audiences - including tools and technologies for information sharing.
- Information and awareness raising - the general public, specialized audiences and the professionals engaged in cyber security.
- Developing and nurturing relationships with equivalent bodies in the world - exchange of information, Defense Methodologies etc..

Application for assistance to recover is possible, inter alia, through the following means:

A) By email: team@cert.gov.il.

B) By phone: 0723990800

C) By filling the form available on the CERT website at:
https://cert.gov.il/ContactUs/Pages/ContactUs.aspx

CYBER DEFENSE METHODOLOGY \\ THE NATIONAL CYBER SECURITY AUTHORITY (NCSA)

PRIME MINISTER'S OFFICE
NATIONAL CYBER DIRECTORATE
NATIONAL CYBER SECURITY AUTHORITY